Chasing
Shadows

SPECTRAL PURSUITS

Suzanne Catherine Rossi

ISPN: 978-1-7635707-0-2

DEDICATION

This book is dedicated to the following amazing humans.
To my fellow Investigator and Co-Founder of Perth Paranormal
Investigations Agency Jack Bryant. There is no one I would like to walk
around a deserted graveyard with at night more.
To my husband Alex Rossi. Without your support I would never be able to
do what I do. I love the fact you love my little bit of crazy.
My beautiful 1 year old daughter Lillian Ann, without whom this book would
have been completed a year earlier.
To my parents Pauline and Noel who fostered my love of the unexplained
with humour.
To my sister, Louise, my fearless ally against the ghosts of our childhood.

PREFACE

The paranormal has always held a dual fascination and fear for me since childhood. I found myself drawn to tales of ghostly apparitions and unexplained phenomena, eagerly absorbing any information I could find through books, shows, and personal accounts. Yet, simultaneously, these stories filled me with a sense of fear and dread. The thought of encountering a ghostly presence at the top of our darkened staircase or under my bed sent me diving under the covers or hiding behind the couch. Even as I yearned to hear about ghost stories during family trips to castles, I couldn't shake the fear of encountering one round every corner and in every dark corridor. It was this complex mix of curiosity and apprehension that sparked my interest in paranormal investigation.

Which perspective was accurate: the captivated girl poring over stories under her covers with a torch, or the girl too frightened to explore a castle, fearing an encounter with a ghost? The reality is that both scenarios hold truth.

The allure of the unknown draws people to embark on quests for the mysterious. Often, individuals join organised ghost hunts or eerie walks, accompanied by friends, venturing into the depths of the forest to seek out the enigmatic. One such haunting tale unfolds around the ancient wych elm nestled within the woods. In the hollow of this tree, the skeletonised remains of an unidentified woman, thought to be approximately 35 years old, were discovered by four unsuspecting teenagers on April 18, 1943. This eerie discovery took place in Hagley Wood, near my childhood home, when I was just 17 years old.

Locals have dubbed her "Bella," a name bestowed upon her by mysterious graffiti that appeared six months after her remains were discovered. Legend has it that her spirit lingers near the tree where she was tragically laid to rest, haunting the very place where she met her untimely end. Yet, beyond its chilling ghostly allure, Bella's story unfolds as a captivating tale intertwining with the intrigue of possible espionage. Set against the backdrop of World War II, when the Nazis sought vital information to orchestrate the Birmingham Blitz, her mysterious demise takes on deeper layers of mystery and intrigue. For those who relish a gripping mystery, Bella's story promises a compelling read.

As you step into a location rumoured to be haunted, a sense of nervous anticipation grips you. In some places, the atmosphere feels dense with energy, almost suffocating, as if the very walls are closing in and every breath is a struggle. The palpable heaviness of the air seems almost tangible, making you feel as though you could reach out and touch it. In contrast, other locations exude a light and airy ambiance, only for the atmosphere to shift suddenly in the blink of an eye. You reassure yourself that the whispered voice you just heard cannot harm you, even as the temperature drops abruptly, sending a chill through your bones akin to stepping into a commercial freezer. Yet, despite your efforts to remain composed, you can't shake the feeling of unseen eyes watching your every move, causing the hairs on the back of your neck to stand on end.

But what about the serious exploration of the paranormal? How does one go about conducting a thorough investigation? What equipment is necessary, and what types of hauntings and entities exist? How does one go about resolving a haunting, and can ghosts pose a threat to us? If so, what measures can be taken for protection? And how do we document and explain the existence of something that is invisible to the naked eye? These were the questions that fuelled my curiosity when I embarked on my paranormal journey. As we embark on this journey together, we seek answers to these compelling questions, including how to justify and measure the figures caught or the eerie sounds that echo through an empty location? These inquiries are the cornerstone of a paranormal investigator's work, and this book aims to provide the knowledge and guidance needed to confidently undertake your own investigations.

In the realm of the paranormal, we find ourselves constantly chasing shadows—elusive, intangible, and ever-mysterious. These shadows, whether fleeting glimpses in the corner of our eye or ominous figures lurking in the darkness, beckon us to explore the unknown, to unravel the secrets that lie beyond the veil of our understanding.

As we embark on this journey together, this book serves as a guiding light, illuminating the path through the shadowy realms of the supernatural. With each turn of the page, we venture deeper into the darkness, armed with curiosity, courage, and a thirst for answers.

So let us chase these shadows, not in fear, but with a sense of wonder and determination, knowing that within their depths lies the key to unlocking the mysteries of the unseen world.

Etymology

The term "supernatural" comes from the Latin words "super" meaning "above" or "beyond" and "naturism" meaning "nature." Thus, it refers to phenomena or entities that are beyond the laws of nature.

On the other hand, "paranormal" combines the prefix "para-" meaning "beside" or "beyond" with "normal," indicating phenomena that are beyond what is considered normal or scientifically explainable.

Both terms essentially convey the idea of phenomena lying beyond the scope of natural or scientific understanding. In this book, we will utilise the terms "supernatural" and "paranormal" interchangeably to encompass a broad spectrum of phenomena that defy conventional scientific explanation or natural laws. While they may carry nuanced distinctions in certain contexts, for the purpose of this narrative, both terms serve as descriptors for phenomena lying beyond the boundaries of typical human understanding or empirical observation. By adopting this interchangeable usage, we aim to embrace the richness and diversity of experiences that challenge our understanding of the world around us, inviting readers to explore the mysteries and complexities that lie beyond the confines of traditional knowledge.

ACKNOWLEDGMENTS

I would like to thank the following, in no particular order for their help in the completion if this book.

Alexander Rossi for the endless amounts of reading and editing. For your input and guidance with the stories and topics. Without your help it would never have been possible to complete this book.

Jack Bryant for the experiences of getting out and about and who contributed by sharing his insights.

For all those I have met and investigated with over the years, for your teaching and curiosity.

I would like to especially thank Diran Yardimli, who is the cover artist for this book and BookCoverZone for making it possible.

CONTENTS

ABOUT THE AUTHOR

Suzanne Catherine Rossi was born in 1980 and raised in Birmingham England. She showed a specific interest in all things unexplained from when she was a child and pursued that interest into adulthood. Emigrating to Australia in 2016, She co-founded the Perth Paranormal Investigation Agency (PPIA) with her friend Jack Bryant.

She resided in Perth, Western Australia with her husband Alexander and daughter Lillian.

If you would like to write to the Author, you can contact her via the website or via e mail. The Author appreciates hearing of your experiences, learning how you have enjoyed this book and how it has helped you.

Paranormalinvestigationsagencies.com

Paranormalinvestigationsperth@gmail.com

In the Still of Night

In the still of night, when shadows creep,
And whispers linger, soft and deep,
There walks a figure, pale and white,
A silent spectre in the dim moonlight.

It moves with grace, devoid of sound,
A wisp of memory, earthbound.
Through corridors of time it roams,
In search of solace, in search of home.

Its presence haunts the darkest hour,
A ghostly echo of life's power.
For in its wake, it leaves behind
The echoes of a restless mind.

It speaks of tales long left untold,
Of love and loss, of stories old.
Its ethereal form a gentle sigh,
A whispered breath, a lullaby.

So in the still of night, when all is calm,
And stars above shine bright and warm,
Remember those who've passed before
Their spirits linger evermore.

For death is but a fleeting phase,
A passage through life's tangled maze
And though they're gone, they're never far,
For in our hearts, they are the stars.

In the still of night, when shadows creep,
And whispers linger, soft and deep,
Embrace the ghosts that haunt your soul,
For they are fragments of the whole.

In crafting this book, I have made the decision to change some names to protect the privacy of individuals involved, while retaining the authenticity of the experiences shared. Though the characters may carry pseudonyms, the essence of their stories remains deeply rooted in my own genuine encounters and observations. By altering names, I aim to respect the privacy of those whose paths intersect with mine within these pages, while still offering a sincere portrayal of the events and emotions that have shaped my journey .

"Energy cannot be created or destroyed, it can only be changed from one form to another."

Albert Einstein

INTRODUCTION TO THE PARANORMAL

Perhaps your fascination with the paranormal began in childhood, or maybe you've had a personal experience that sparked your curiosity. You might be eager to delve deeper into the mysteries of the unknown, particularly by investigating locations near where you live. For many, chasing shadows has evolved into a captivating pastime, amplified by the accessibility of paranormal investigations through social media platforms. However, amid this surge in interest, how many truly grasp the nature of their interactions? How many are fully cognisant of the diverse types of hauntings and entities that may be encountered? Are they aware of the very real harm that can be done when the shadows they chase, chase back?

The realm of the paranormal is a captivating yet unnerving place for those who encounter it first hand. It is a domain where the unexpected is the norm, where uncertainty hangs in the air like a palpable presence. It is a mix of anxiety and excitement, felt intensely when unexplained responses echo through a voice recorder or when a motion detector jolts to life in a silent room. There is a chill down the spine when a disembodied voice breaks the eerie silence, leaving you searching for rational explanations. And if you're fortunate, there are moments of awe, like witnessing a full-bodied apparition glide silently through a hospital hallway during a lockdown. These are my experiences, and despite years of investigations, the thrill and occasional fear persist, leaving me with more questions than answers.

The notion of a ghost, also referred to as a spectre or spirit, originates from the ancient belief in the separation of a person's spirit or soul from their physical body, and that spirit or soul may persist after death. Consequently, numerous early civilizations developed funeral rituals aimed at preventing the deceased person's spirit from returning to "haunt" the living. Ghosts are thought to be formed at the instant of death, adopting the likeness and traits of the departed individual.

The intrigue and fascination surrounding the paranormal and the afterlife have endured throughout history. While paranormal research is a more modern development, it gained prominence in the 1920s thanks to figures like Harry Price, who responded to the spiritualist fervour of the Victorian era. Interest in the paranormal often stems from profound questions about life, spirituality, and mortality. The fear of death has historically driven a quest for understanding, giving rise to elaborate beliefs about the afterlife. Across cultures and belief systems, notions of ghosts or spirits have been nearly ubiquitous.

The fascination with the paranormal frequently originates from inquiries about existence, spirituality, and mortality. The apprehension of death often prompts a quest for comprehension, leading to the development of intricate beliefs about the afterlife. Across diverse cultures and belief systems, the concept of ghosts or spirits is nearly universal.

To the Romans, belief in ghosts was as ingrained in daily life as birth and death themselves. They perceived each individual as infused with a divine essence, and upon death, this essence—their spirit—transitioned to the afterlife. However, they also held that spirits could revisit the living, either to reunite with loved ones or to exact vengeance upon those who had wronged them.

The ancient Egyptians regarded ghosts as integral to their daily existence. They crafted tomb paintings, inscriptions, and effigies with the intention of facilitating the spirits' return for a temporary visit, albeit with the expectation that they would eventually depart to their own realm. Additionally, individuals would pen letters to the deceased, seeking their intervention in matters of business and perceived injustices.

In a recent development in 2021, the Smithsonian Magazine published an article uncovering the earliest known portrayal of a ghost. This depiction was discovered on a clay tablet that serves as a guide to exorcising ghosts. Dating back to around 3500 BCE, this artifact offers a fascinating glimpse into ancient beliefs surrounding the supernatural and efforts to confront and banish spectral entities.

While communicating with the dead could have led to persecution as a witch in certain historical periods, by the Victorian era, it evolved into an almost fashionable pursuit.

My family was no exception to this phenomenon. My father, Noel, often recounted tales of my mother's great aunt Alice, renowned for her interest in the occult and paranormal. Like many others of her era, she was caught up in the fervour of spiritualism and seances, which reached its peak during that time. Although I never had the opportunity to meet Alice, as she passed away before my time, I can't help but wonder if we shared some common interests and traits.

The 19th century was characterised by a flurry of new ideas and advancements in science, exemplified by figures like Charles Darwin, and in technology, notably with the advent of photography. This era heralded a pinnacle of rationality and scientific inquiry. Yet, surprisingly, it was also marked by a heightened interest in the supernatural. This curiosity was fuelled by widely reported famous hauntings of the time, captivating the public's imagination. Notably, some of the finest horror writers emerged during this period, including Mary Shelley and Bram Stoker. Through their works, they skilfully intertwined supernatural themes and monstrous creatures, leaving an indelible mark on literature and popular culture.

Supernatural narratives often intersected with advancements in science or technology during this era. In Mary Shelley's "Frankenstein," for instance, the creation of the supernatural being was depicted as a result of the sinister manipulation of electricity, a relatively new and widely feared invention at the time. Concurrently, the phenomenon of spirit photography gained popularity, utilising what we now recognise as double exposure techniques. However, this newfound technology was often exploited by charlatans who preyed on the public's fascination with the supernatural. These individuals would promise to capture images of deceased loved ones, capitalising on the emotional vulnerability of those longing for a tangible connection with their departed relatives. Often these photographs came at a steep financial cost.

During this period, table-tipping séances and clairvoyant shows, captivated the public imagination and offered lucrative opportunities for those skilled in the craft. These sessions were often conducted in dimly lit or completely darkened rooms, providing the perfect cover for performers to employ elaborate tricks without detection. Historical accounts from the era detail various methods used to deceive participants. Some practitioners utilised long kid evening gloves, stuffed with wool to surreptitiously touch their clients. Others employed black gloves, painted with luminous paint for a ghostly effect. Yet another tactic, involved concealing a "spirit baby" beneath their skirts—a stuffed shape attached to a stick—that could be manipulated to appear as though it was peering over the table from the otherworld. These deceptions underscored the lengths to which charlatans would go to exploit the public's fascination with the supernatural for financial gain.

Queen Victoria and Prince Albert were indeed known to engage in attempts to communicate with the deceased, through séances and table-tipping. A practice that intensified following Albert's untimely death, which left Victoria in mourning for the remainder of her life. Mediums of the time capitalised on this growing interest, offering their services for a fee and attracting large audiences to their theatrical performances. During the latter part of the 19th century, séances often featured the mysterious substance known as ectoplasm, purportedly emanating from the medium while they were in a trance-like state.

To bolster their claims, mediums would often arrange for photographers to capture images of them, conjuring spirits or ectoplasm. However, many of these photographs were later revealed to be hoaxes, employing simple tricks such as double exposure or having a tea towel hang from the mouth. Despite the deceptive practices involved, people of the era fervently believed in the ability of mediums to connect them with their departed loved ones. This belief was fuelled by the high mortality rates of the time, as well as the prevalence of deadly diseases.

Desperate to communicate with their deceased relatives, individuals were willing to pay exorbitant sums to mediums, sometimes even relinquishing their homes, valuables, or altering their wills at the medium's request. Women, in particular, were often targeted by unscrupulous mediums. The Victorian period was marked by high rates of maternal and infant mortality, leaving many grieving mothers eager to hear from their lost children.

Mary Lincoln, wife of President Abraham Lincoln, was among those who believed fervently in the supernatural. During one event, she encountered a man named Lord Colchester, who claimed to be a medium capable of connecting her with the deceased. Despite the scepticism of her husband, Mary was intrigued by Lord Colchester's claims and engaged in conversation with him regarding contacting the dead.

Mary Lincoln, deeply grieving the loss of her beloved son Willie, welcomed Lord Colchester to hold séances at the White House, where Willie had passed away in 1862. The death of Willie had left Mary shattered, and she had been known to hold séances in an attempt to communicate with him. During one of Lord Colchester's sessions, attendees reported hearing loud raps and bangs, which he purported to be communications from Willie to his mother. These sounds seemed to emanate from beneath the table and the floor, filling Mary with overwhelming joy, amidst her profound sadness. She wholeheartedly believed that these manifestations were indeed her son, reaching out to her, providing her with solace in her grief.

Abraham Lincoln, however, harboured doubts regarding the authenticity of Lord Colchester's séances. Seeking to uncover the truth, he enlisted the expertise of Dr Joseph Henry, from the Smithsonian Institution to investigate. Dr Henry attended the next session incognito, and as anticipated, the mysterious bangs and raps resurfaced. It was swiftly revealed that the sounds were produced by a device concealed beneath the fraudulent medium's coat. The entire charade unravelled, much to the dismay of Mary Lincoln, who had earnestly believed in the communication with her deceased son.

Lord Colchester, far from being a gentlemanly figure, was exposed as a cunning con artist, who preyed upon Mary's vulnerability and grief. He had masqueraded as a titled individual with the expectation that Mary would pay handsomely to reconnect with her departed child. Despite the heart breaking deception, Mary remained resolute in her belief in the supernatural for the remainder of her life. She continued her quest to communicate with her late son Willie, as well as her husband and two other deceased sons. Mary passed away in 1882 at the age of 63, one would hope for a reunion with her beloved children in the afterlife.

This incident, stands as one of the earliest recorded instances of a paranormal investigator being dispatched to debunk purported supernatural phenomena.

EARLY PARANORMAL INVESTIGATION

In the early days of paranormal investigation, scientists were primarily concerned with debunking fraudulent performances rather than proving the existence of ghosts. Their objective was to transition these performances from the stage to the laboratory, where they could apply scientific methods to investigate the phenomena. This led to the establishment of psychical laboratories across Europe, England, and the USA during the early 1900s. These facilities served as dedicated spaces for rigorous and controlled scientific inquiry into the supernatural, a commitment that some investigators pursued throughout their lifetimes.

One of the most prominent figures in early 20th-century paranormal investigation, was Dr Harry Price. He described his research as an "endeavour to determine, through precise experimental methods, the extent to which alleged phenomena in séance rooms could be explained by natural means". Price sought to understand if science could elucidate the practices of mediums and occultists. To this end, he incorporated seance rooms into his laboratory setups and invited mediums to participate in controlled experiments. Price's approach, which included paying mediums for their participation, diverged from the practices of the Society for Psychical Research (SPR). Consequently, he established his own institution, the National Laboratory for Psychical Research, in 1925.

Price employed state-of-the-art scientific equipment in his investigations, including barographs to record atmospheric pressure, thermometers to measure temperature fluctuations, cameras to capture visual evidence, and microscopes for detailed analysis. Additionally, he sometimes utilised restraints as part of his experimental setups. These sophisticated tools, enabled Price to conduct thorough and meticulous investigations into supernatural phenomena, striving to apply empirical methods.

Imagine the following scene: A dimly lit laboratory, Harry Price moved with purpose among the rows of scientific equipment and apparatus, his eyes alight with anticipation. The air was charged with an electric energy, a palpable sense of anticipation, mingling with the faint whirring of machinery. Around him, shelves lined with jars of specimens and books on occult lore, cast eerie shadows against the walls.

At the centre of the room, a large wooden table stood as the focal point of the investigation. On its surface lay an array of instruments—barographs, thermometers, and cameras—all poised to capture any spectral activity that might manifest. Nearby, a microscope awaited, ready to scrutinise any anomalous samples that might be collected.

In one corner, a series of restraints hung ominously from the wall, a reminder of the precautions necessary when dealing with the unknown. Despite the rational explanations that science might offer, there lingered an undeniable sense of unease, a recognition that not all phenomena could be easily explained.

With a steady hand, Price adjusted the settings on his equipment, his mind focused on the task at hand. In this laboratory of inquiry and exploration, he stood ready to confront the mysteries of the paranormal, armed with the tools of science and a relentless determination to uncover the truth.

In 1923, during an investigation involving a purported medium named Mrs. Marjory Crandon, Harry Price documented the first recorded, notable drop in temperature. The mercury in the thermometer plummeted from 15.5 to 9.4 degrees Celsius, a dramatic and unexplained shift that caught Price's attention. Despite his meticulous scrutiny and exhaustive analysis, Price was unable to find a rational explanation for this phenomenon. This temperature drop stood as a compelling piece of evidence, challenging conventional scientific understanding, and prompting further inquiry into the mysteries of the paranormal.

Mrs. Crandon, also known as Mina, benefited from her husband's prestigious background as a graduate of Harvard Medical School and as a respected surgeon. This fact afforded her credibility, in the eyes of many observers. During séances, her purported ectoplasm would often manifest in the form of a hand-like shape, emerging from her skirts. A phenomenon her husband attributed to otherworldly origins, rather than human anatomy. This manifestation was attributed to a spirit named Walter, though little else was known about him, besides his affinity for materialising his hand from Minas skirt.

Given her elevated social status as the wife of a surgeon, Mrs. Crandon was treated with more respect, compared to mediums from lower social strata. Despite thorough searches, before and after investigations, the manifested hand was never discovered. Some investigators at the time, speculated that she concealed the hand in her vagina. This theory was never substantiated. Searches during this era were limited to cursory checks, as more intimate examinations would have been deemed inappropriate, particularly for a woman of Mrs. Crandon's stature.

Interestingly, Mrs. Crandon was known for her unconventional behaviour, often conducting séances in the nude outside of the laboratory. While she garnered criticism from notable figures like Harry Houdini, who debunked many of her claims, she also found support from prominent individuals. People such as Arthur Conan Doyle, renowned for his Sherlock Holmes novels believed her entirely. This dichotomy of criticism and support, underscores the complex and controversial nature of her paranormal endeavours.

Mina permitted Harry Price and his colleagues to take fingerprints of the manifested hand, during a séance. A wax mould was created, capturing the unique patterns of the hand and fingerprints. There is a captivating photo documenting the process, as the hand protruded from the top of her skirts. These fingerprints were meticulously compared to those of previous séance attendees. Upon examination, there was a compelling suspicion that the fingerprints matched those of her dentist and personal family friend. However, given the early stage of fingerprint analysis at the time, this conclusion was never definitively established.

The investigation sparked heated debates among the investigators of that era, with some endorsing the analysis and its implications, while others contested the validity of the experiment. Disagreements ensued regarding the integrity of the wax mould and the potential for evidential compromise. This echo contemporary debates in paranormal research, where the validity of video, audio, or photographic evidence is often scrutinised and questioned. Such debates are essential in maintaining scientific rigor and ensuring that evidence meets rigorous standards. Embracing scrutiny and accountability from peers, elevates the credibility of research findings, fostering a culture of transparency and intellectual integrity, in paranormal inquiry.

As a field, paranormal investigation has evolved considerably since its early days, offering us greater insights into the nature of paranormal activity and the entities that may be involved. Yet, despite our progress, much remains unknown about the spirit world and its inhabitants. This fact necessitating continual adaptation of our theories and methodologies, as new information emerges. The ongoing debate surrounding proof and the legitimacy of evidence persists, mirroring the controversies of the past.

Mina, whose performances captivated audiences well into the late 1930s, became a subject of contention among investigators. While some discredited her claims, others, including Sherlock Holmes author Sir Arthur Conan Doyle, endorsed her abilities. However, prominent figures like magician Harry Houdini and paranormal investigator Harry Price remained sceptical, attributing her feats to fraudulent practices, aimed at financial gain. Today, such displays would likely be met with scepticism and scrutiny, given our understanding of the physical limitations of paranormal manifestations.

Despite scepticism surrounding Mina's alleged abilities, the phenomenon of supernatural materialisation remains a subject of interest. However, it is unlikely that spirits manifest physically, as suggested by Mina's purported encounters with the spirit named Walter, in the form of limbs.

Harry Price, renowned for his investigations into psychical phenomena and exposure of fraudulent spiritualists, left a lasting legacy in the field. His notable inquiry into Borley Rectory, regarded as England's most haunted house, showcased his dedication to unravelling mysteries of the paranormal. Though the rectory has since been demolished, its legacy endures, inviting curiosity and intrigue from modern investigators.

Sadly, it seems that Harry Price hasn't dropped us a line from the other side, since his earthly departure in 1948. However, I will keep an ear out and report back if this should be reported.

Harry Price is widely regarded as the pioneer of paranormal investigation, and his influence on the field remains significant to this day. While the motives and methodologies of paranormal investigation have evolved over time, the fundamental approach remains unchanged. It is crucial for paranormal investigators to strike a balance: They should not approach every phenomenon assuming it is of supernatural origin, nor should they close themselves off entirely to the possibility of spirit activity. In today's paranormal community, there exists a spectrum of beliefs.

Nowhere is this more evident than in the case of the renowned Mr. James Randi. Born in 1928 and passing away at the age of 92, on October 20th, 2020, he was a celebrated magician known as the Amazing Randi. Beyond his magical performances, Randi was also an author and a staunch sceptic, utilising his knowledge of magic to debunk claims of the paranormal.

The James Randi Educational Foundation (JREF) made headlines for over two decades with its $1,000,000 US prize money, famously known as the million-dollar challenge. The challenge was straightforward, employing a scientific method, aimed at controlling the environment in which individuals demonstrated their alleged paranormal abilities. For instance, if someone claimed to bend spoons with their mind, they couldn't use their own spoons; the foundation would provide them. Similarly, those claiming remote viewing or clairvoyant abilities, had to provide highly specific results, not vague approximations. Even claims of stigmata were subject to scrutiny, under the watchful eye of cameras.

Unlike Harry Price, who primarily sought to investigate and understand paranormal phenomena, Randi's mission was to disprove any such claims. He targeted high-profile individuals, insisting that those being tested must have a media presence. Well-known figures like Uri Geller, James Van Praagh, Sylvia Browne, and John Edward, among others, were challenged to participate, though most declined. The JREF aimed to use this public challenge as a means to educate the public, about what they believed, to be false and often fraudulent paranormal claims.

While the JREF no longer offers the prize money, they remain open to testing established psychics, preferably with an independent TV crew present. Similar challenges exist worldwide, with groups like the Australian Sceptics, Belgian and European Sceptics, and the Independent Investigations Group offering monetary prizes, for evidence of paranormal phenomena under controlled conditions.

Modern-day paranormal investigators often strive to find a balance between scepticism and open-mindedness, much like the societies and scientists of previous generations. However, the field remains diverse, with individuals ranging from staunch believers in every paranormal occurrence to adamant sceptics who debunk everything.

For example, I once worked with a woman who, despite seeing her deceased father in the back of her car, through the rear-view mirror, adamantly claimed she didn't believe in ghosts. This paradox left me puzzled because, to me, such a vivid encounter, seemed like compelling evidence of an afterlife. It is instances like these that highlight the complexity of human interpretation in paranormal investigations.

The question that begs to be asked is: What kind of paranormal investigator do you aspire to be? In our group, the Perth Paranormal Investigations Agency (PPIA), we aim to strike a balance between the scepticism of Harry Price and the curiosity of Mary Lincoln. When analysing evidence, we advocate for a healthy dose of scepticism while maintaining an open mind to the possibility of something beyond the ordinary.

Unlike figures like James Randi and Harry Price, we don't focus on testing individuals and their alleged abilities. Instead, our attention is directed towards investigating locations, whether they're homes, businesses, or public buildings. Our goal is to observe and measure phenomena, occurring in natural environments, rather than testing people's claims.

While we welcome the input of psychics and sensitives on our investigations, their observations are just one piece of the puzzle. We understand that their perceptions must be corroborated with other evidence and considered within the broader context of the investigation.

When looking at the kind of paranormal investigator you want to be let us take a scenario that actually happened to me.

During one investigation at an old gaol, I experienced a chilling encounter that left me rattled. In a dimly lit corridor surrounded by cells, I heard the unmistakable sound of shuffling, then rapid footsteps approaching from behind me. The rush of cold air sent shivers down my spine, and before I could comprehend what was happening, a nearby cell door slammed shut with tremendous force, echoing throughout the prison. The suddenness and intensity of the experience left me, and my fellow investigators, startled and on edge, reminding us of the unpredictable nature of our work.

In this scenario, what would be your first steps be when investigating what just happened? What were the immediate thoughts that came to mind when reading the account of this series of events?

When investigating such an incident, my first steps, would involve gathering as much information as possible from both eyewitness accounts and any available physical evidence. I would interview my fellow investigators to get their perspectives on what they heard and felt, noting any discrepancies or additional details that may provide insight.

Next, I would conduct a thorough examination of the surroundings, paying close attention to the cell door that slammed shut. I would look for any signs of tampering or malfunction that could explain the sudden closure. Additionally, I would check for drafts or other environmental factors that may have contributed to the rush of cold air.

Based on the description of the events, my immediate thoughts would indeed gravitate towards the possibility of something or someone, rushing up behind and causing the cell door to slam shut. The sequence of footsteps, rush of air, and sudden door closure aligns with this hypothesis. However, I would remain open to alternative explanations and conduct a comprehensive investigation, to rule out any other potential causes.

It is fascinating, to see how a thorough investigation can unravel the mystery behind seemingly paranormal occurrences. In this case, examining the door closely revealed crucial details about its construction and weight, compared to the other doors in the area. Discovering that it was a replica, shed light on its unique properties.

Testing the door's response to vibrations and patiently waiting for a replication of the event, provided valuable insights. The rush of cold air was debunked as a natural occurrence of the corridor acting as a wind tunnel. The door closing, was attributed to the wind hitting the lighter, door causing it to slam shut.

It is a reminder, of the importance of methodical investigation and keeping an open mind while searching for explanations. While some occurrences may seem inexplicable at first, a careful examination often reveals logical, natural causes behind them.

The footsteps and the shuffle, are not something that could be explained and to this day, I believe, that this was paranormal.

I have a particular dislike of this, as it tends to happen at haunted locations for me. It has happened so frequently, after years of going out on location, that it rarely bothers me anymore.

It is intriguing how certain experiences can become almost familiar, even in the realm of the paranormal. Despite the logical explanations, for some phenomena, there are still occurrences that defy easy explanation. My encounters with the sudden footsteps and shuffle, both at the old gaol and other locations, highlight the enduring mystery of the paranormal.

The distinctness of the footsteps and the sensation of being charged at, evoke a visceral response, prompting you to expect a physical presence. Yet, the absence of any visible entity, leaves you grappling with the unexplained. Your intuition leads you to connect this encounter with the history of the locations, suggesting a possible link to its past.

These encounters serve as reminders of the enigmatic nature of the paranormal and the ongoing quest for understanding. Despite years of investigation, some phenomena, continue to defy rational explanation, adding layers to the intricate tapestry of the unexplained.

I have developed a keen sensitivity to these unexplained occurrences, especially in haunted locations. While the footsteps and shuffling may defy conventional explanation, repeated encounters have instilled a sense of familiarity, even if unsettling at times. This kind of exposure over the years can desensitise one to the initial fear, yet it doesn't diminish the mystery behind these experiences.

During our recent investigation of the Sunset Hospital in Perth, Australia, my fellow investigator Jack and I, encountered this peculiar incident, as we made our way back to the parking lot, at the end of the night. Without warning, we heard a distinct shuffle followed by rapid footsteps approaching from behind us, on the path. Instinctively, we halted and turned, fully expecting to confront someone charging towards us. To our bewilderment, there was no one in sight. The path lay empty, with no signs of another presence nearby. Despite our thorough search, we found no explanation for the unsettling encounter. Reflecting on our earlier interactions at the hospital, I couldn't shake the feeling that this mysterious presence, might have been a lingering spirit, perhaps a former soldier from the hospital's past.

That evening, we had joined another team called Paranormal Perth, who were walking ahead of us. Later, we discovered that they too had experienced a similar occurrence along the same path. Something or someone, running up behind them with loud footsteps, only for them to turn around and find nothing there. It is intriguing to note, that spirits may tailor their actions to provoke specific fears, in each investigator. For instance, I know of a sensitive individual who frequently encounters spirits appearing as clowns, reflecting his personal fear of them. How these entities discern and exploit individual fears, remains a mystery.

It appears that both in confined spaces, like a prison and in expansive settings, like at sunset, there are intelligent spirits that manifest in various ways. Some may exhibit phantom footsteps, possibly indicative of residual hauntings, while others may boldly approach, sending a chill through those they encounter. Those inclined to startle might sneak up from behind, while others may run directly at you. Despite these behaviours, I've never experienced harm from such spirits; it seems their intent is more to startle than to cause harm. Although there are anecdotes of spirits pushing people down from behind, I've not encountered this myself. When spirits do approach from behind, I've found that acknowledging their presence and expressing discomfort can help. Nowadays, I simply acknowledge their existence and continue on my way.

In conclusion, it is essential not to approach investigations with preconceived notions or predetermined outcomes. We must remain open-minded and diligent in testing and analysing the phenomena we encounter. Striving to determine whether it can be explained through rational means or if it resides within the realm of the unknown. However, this can be challenging. Many of us in the field hold strong beliefs in the afterlife and have personally experienced spirit activity. Consequently, there is a tendency to interpret occurrences in a manner that aligns with our beliefs, potentially clouding our judgment. For sceptics, spending time at locations and witnessing phenomena first hand, can lead to a shift in perspective. It is difficult to dismiss the numerous voices captured through audio or video recordings, or the shadow figures glimpsed in photographs, especially in places marked by tragedy and suffering. Likewise, it is hard to ignore the unsettling sounds, like growls or breaths, experienced while exploring a location alone. The accumulation of such experiences challenges us to re-evaluate our understanding of the world around us.

Evidence that withstands debunking, should indeed be subject to rigorous evaluation and corroboration. It is this kind of information that holds significant value, for those interested in understanding death and the afterlife. For some, it provides the confirmation they've been seeking, validating their beliefs and experiences. However, for others, it raises further questions, adding layers of complexity to an already enigmatic topic. This ongoing quest for understanding is why individuals fascinated by the paranormal, often maintain a lifelong interest, in exploring the mysteries of existence. Each piece of evidence, each experience, contributes to a deeper comprehension of the unknown, fuelling curiosity and prompting continual exploration.

Approaching investigations with an open mind, a well-defined methodology, and positive intentions is crucial, especially in the realm of the paranormal. This sets the stage for a positive and respectful exploration of hauntings and other supernatural phenomena. By maintaining an open mind, researchers can remain receptive to unexpected discoveries and avoid biases that may skew their findings. A clear and tested methodology ensures that investigations are conducted systematically, allowing for accurate data collection and analysis. Furthermore, conducting investigations with the best of intentions, fosters a respectful attitude towards the spirits or entities being studied and promotes ethical research practices. Indeed, this approach lays the foundation for a meaningful and enriching journey, into the mysteries of the paranormal world.

YOUR JOURNEY BEGINS

Now that you have a clear understanding of how you want to approach paranormal investigations and the principles guiding your methodology, what's the next step? When I first delved into the paranormal field in my younger years, I began with thorough research. I delved into the various types of hauntings, studying case after case both locally and beyond. Eventually, I took the step to join a local paranormal group, participating in their investigations and learning from seasoned members.

A crucial aspect of my early journey, involved meticulous planning and learning from experienced investigators. I crafted a detailed game plan, outlining what to watch for during investigations, who to contact in case of emergencies, and the potential options for resolving hauntings. I observed and absorbed knowledge from those with more experienced than myself.

Planning also involved preparing for negative encounters and potential attachments, understanding the risks involved in exploring realms beyond our comprehension. It is essential to have a support system in place, including a list of trusted individuals, to call upon if situations become overwhelming. I strongly advise readers to take similar precautions.

Research remains a cornerstone of paranormal investigation. It is the foundation upon which we build our beliefs and understanding. Continual learning is key, as opinions, technologies, and understanding evolve over time. Fortunately, access to information has never been easier, thanks to the internet and social media. Connecting with other like-minded individuals and forming or joining groups, can provide invaluable support and resources.

Building a network within the paranormal community is also vital. Establishing relationships with well-established groups and individuals can offer guidance, assistance, and a sense of camaraderie. Should you ever require help or advice in the future, having a network of trusted contacts can prove invaluable.

In summary, the next steps for those entering the paranormal field, involve thorough research, meticulous planning, learning from experienced investigators, and building a supportive network within the community. By following these steps, you can embark on your journey into the unknown, with confidence and preparedness.

I have encountered situations where I've been scratched, feeling an intense burning sensation, and have heard growls so loud that they echoed throughout the location, leaving both the living and the spirits present, aware of their anger. (Visit Woodman Point Quarantine Station here in Perth). There have been instances where I have felt genuinely threatened, prompting me to vacate certain areas. Fortunately, I've been relatively fortunate compared to others who have endured lasting effects, from their paranormal encounters. Every investigator must exercise caution when dealing with the unknown and approach their work with the seriousness it warrants. Negative encounters can have profound and lasting effects, impacting one's mental, emotional, and even physical well-being. It is essential to prioritise safety and well-being, in all paranormal investigations, recognising the potential risks involved and taking appropriate precautions.

It is common for different groups or individual investigators, to be drawn to specific types of paranormal phenomena. It is equally common, for some to have clear boundaries regarding what they are, or are not, willing to investigate. For instance, some investigators may refuse to engage with hauntings caused by darker entities. There is no shame in setting personal boundaries, and it is essential to consider where those boundaries lie. This should be before, finding yourself in a situation that makes you uncomfortable or faced with something clearly non-human.

For example, I have established strict rules for my own safety and comfort. I refuse to allow any paranormal contact to occur within my home, and I steer clear of participating in summoning rituals or occult practices when dealing with darker entities. It is crucial to have a clear understanding of where your personal limits lie, especially when working within a group of investigators, where comfort levels may vary. By respecting your boundaries and those of others, you can ensure a safer and more productive investigative environment.

It is quite common for investigators to enter an investigation with certain expectations, only to encounter something entirely unexpected. This has certainly been the case for me, on numerous occasions. Additionally, it is often the case that a location harbours a mixture of paranormal entities, including both human and non-human entities. For example, there are locations where trapped human spirits coexist with shadow people or even more malevolent, demonic energies.

It is essential to remain vigilant and open-minded during investigations, as you never know what you might encounter. You can be talking to a spirit, who says they are your long lost, great aunt Alice, but it turns out to be something entirely different. Eventually, most, if not all investigators, will face

14

situations where their expectations are challenged, and they come face-to-face with entities or energies they were not prepared for. This only strengthens the importance of thorough preparation, clear boundaries, and a cautious approach, when delving into the world of the paranormal.

An example that highlights this involves the renowned RMS Queen Mary. I have had the opportunity to explore this historic ship, on multiple occasions. The first visit took place during a family holiday when I was a teenager, accompanied by my parents, Pauline and Noel, and my sister Louise. It was a memorable stop on our vacation itinerary. Years later, in 2016, I returned to the Queen Mary, for my honeymoon, with my husband, Alexander. Despite its reputation for housing around 150 spirits, our overnight stay yielded no paranormal encounters. Disappointingly, the following year, the "ghosts and legends haunt experience" was unveiled, touted as the world's largest interactive haunted attraction. Needless to say, my expectations were not met.

The RMS Queen Mary is a magnificent vessel, earning its place among Time Magazine's list of the 10 most haunted places on earth. While there are numerous reported spirits on board, none are as infamous or contentious in the paranormal community, as the spirit, said to haunt the first and second-class swimming pool areas.

Entering the first-class swimming pool room is a breath-taking experience. The room boasts a striking design, with stairs descending on both sides upon entry. Its sandstone-coloured tiled walls and raised balcony are accented by a captivating aqua hue. The tiled floor surrounding the pool is a deep, dark colour, adding to the room's allure. Four imposing square pillars and an arched roof lend an air of grandeur, evoking the opulence of the ship's glory days.

Although the pool itself is no longer in use, the room has become a sought-after location for numerous TV shows and movies over the years, thanks to its stunning visual appeal.

Indeed, it is not the grandeur of the room that makes it compelling, but rather the haunting associated with it and its surroundings. Upon entering, the atmosphere is far from pleasant. Perhaps it is the vastness and emptiness of the space, or maybe it is the unsettling sensation of being watched that permeates the air. Whatever the cause, the feeling of being observed, is anything but welcoming.

The haunting of the pool rooms revolves around the tragic tale of a young girl, who met her demise by drowning in one of the ship's pools, during the 1940s. She is one of the most frequently encountered spirits on board, reportedly seen by visitors, staff, and even captains throughout the years. Despite the absence of water for decades, her wet footprints have been documented in the area. Descriptions of her sightings vary, but she is typically described as a girl around 5 or 6 years old.

Nicknamed "Jackie" by the ship's crew, she is often sought out by curious individuals each year, both in the pool areas and the corridors surrounding them. Her presence adds an eerie layer to the ship's already mysterious ambiance, leaving many pondering the circumstances of her untimely demise and the lingering imprint she has left behind.

One of the most compelling pieces of evidence regarding Jackie's presence, is the multitude of EVPs (Electronic Voice Phenomena) that have been captured over the years. These recordings often feature Jackie's voice singing, saying hello, laughing, and even calling for her mother. In some instances, her voice has been heard as a disembodied sound, audible to those present without the need for a recording device. Witnesses who encounter her, describe her as playful, yet imbued with a sense of sadness, and often report detecting cold spots in her vicinity.

Jackie's haunting is believed to be highly intelligent, as she interacts and responds to individuals who engage with her. It is a tragic narrative that appears to have bound her sweet spirit, to the place where she tragically lost her life. Touched by her story, many in the paranormal community have ventured into the area, in hopes of contacting her, and they are seldom disappointed. Her presence adds a poignant layer to the ship's history, reminding visitors of the enduring impact of past tragedies on the present.

This case garnered significant attention, notably featuring on the popular show Ghost Adventures, and becoming a passion project, for the renowned psychic Peter James. According to James, The Queen Mary housed hundreds of spirits, solidifying its reputation as one of the most haunted places in the world. Leading ghost tours starting in 1991, James personally visited the ship around 1,000 times before his passing in 2007.

James's interactions with Jackie, in particular, were well-documented, with numerous film and voice recordings, capturing her presence more than any other spirit. His fondness for Jackie was evident, a sentiment shared by many drawn to the stories of child spirits. She was even given a name: Jacqueline "Jackie" Torin, a young girl who reportedly met her demise in the 1940s after a diving incident, in the second-class pool. This narrative, has been perpetuated by The Queen Mary Liner to this day, adding a layer of depth to the ship's storied history.

The prevailing narrative surrounding Jackie, while compelling, is unfortunately, not supported by historical records. Despite the abundance of evidence suggesting the presence of a young girl spirit named Jackie, aboard the Queen Mary, the reality is, no such individual fitting the description of Jackie, appears in the ship's documented history.

Remarkably, there are no records indicating any drowning incidents, in the ship's pools during its operational years. Cunard, the liner's owner, maintained meticulous records of all occurrences aboard their vessels, and Jackie's supposed demise, does not appear in any of these records.

In total, there are 49 recorded deaths onboard the Queen Mary, comprising 16 crew members, 31 passengers, and 2 General Infantry during its service as a Troop ship, in World War II. However, there is no record of a child matching Jackie's description, among these casualties, at any point in the ship's history.

This revelation challenges the popular narrative surrounding Jackie and highlights the importance of corroborating paranormal claims with historical evidence. It prompts a re-evaluation of the stories and legends associated with the Queen Mary, highlighting the need for critical inquiry and scepticism in the field of paranormal investigation.

It is a widely held belief, among many in the paranormal community, that Jackie may not be a human spirit at all, but rather a nonhuman entity, assuming the guise of a child. This phenomenon is not uncommon, as darker entities, often, adopt less intimidating forms, to conceal their true nature. Several psychics who have encountered Jackie, have independently reached the same conclusion—that she is not a human child at all but a non-human entity.

One particularly intriguing piece of evidence of this, comes from an episode of Ghost Adventures, filmed after Peter James's passing. Despite his physical absence, Peter's highly distinctive voice, came through via EVP (Electronic Voice Phenomenon), during the episode. In response to a direct question posed to him, regarding Jackie's true nature, Peter's EVP response, seemed to confirm that Jackie, was indeed not a human spirit.

And yet, there are those who still flock to the ship today, in the hopes of interacting with the sweet little girl who drowned in the pool.

We simply do not know who or what, 'Jackie' is or where this being came from. what we do know, is people come from all over, to get the opportunity to talk to her. Regardless of having no idea what the true nature of her existence is or what intentions she may have toward the living.

This field of research is inherently unpredictable, and investigators must be prepared to handle unexpected developments with confidence and clarity. Establishing clear boundaries is essential, as interactions with spirits and entities can be complex and potentially hazardous. Like people, spirits may attempt to push these boundaries, particularly with those who allow them to do so. Thus, maintaining a firm stance and exercising caution are paramount, for investigators navigating the complexities of the paranormal realm.

1 TYPES OF HAUNTING

HAUNTINGS: AN INTRODUCTION

Amidst the shroud of twilight, where shadows dance with whispers and the air hangs heavy with anticipation, lies a place forgotten by time. In the heart of this forgotten realm, where the trees stand as silent sentinels and the moon casts its pale gaze upon the land, there exists a presence that lingers, a spectre of bygone days. It is a place where the boundary between the living and the dead blurs, where echoes of the past reverberate through the hollows, and where every step forward feels like a descent into the unknown. Welcome to the threshold of the eerie, where the line between reality and nightmare fades, and the chill of the unknown seeps into the very marrow of your bones.

Before embarking on a paranormal investigation, understanding the various types of hauntings should be a minimum. In this chapter, we will delve into these diverse phenomena and explore the theories surrounding them. As the old adage goes, "forewarned is forearmed," and this should be the motto of every paranormal investigator.

Recorded hauntings, have permeated history across cultures, dating back thousands of years, to the beginnings of written and oral traditions. They are as prevalent in ancient civilisations as they are in contemporary times. Many historical ghost tales, feature well-known figures and landmarks, intricately woven into local mythology, legend, and folklore. Written accounts of ghosts and methods for exorcising them, date back as far as 3500 years ago, with some cultures, passing down such knowledge orally, for even longer periods.

Historically, the supernatural and the natural world were deeply intertwined. It shaped everyday life and influenced cultural practices. These cultures developed mythologies, religions, and rituals to navigate encounters with supernatural beings, which were perceived as genuine and often terrifying threats. Some societies sought to control these entities through various practices, a tradition that continues to this day. Such measures were often the only means of coping with the perceived dangers posed, by the supernatural entities that inhabited their world.

During the first century AD, Pliny the Younger, a prominent figure in Ancient Rome, served as a respected Lawyer, Author, and Magistrate. Renowned for his detailed and insightful portrayals of Roman society, his works remain subjects of academic scrutiny to this day. Among his writings, he provided a vivid account of a haunting experience in Athens that captured widespread attention at the time.

Pliny recounted, encountering the spectre of a long-bearded man who rattled chains within his home. Disturbed by this apparition, he sought the assistance of scholars and religious authorities, to alleviate the haunting presence. This account stands as one of the earliest recorded ghost stories within Roman culture, illustrating the enduring fascination with the supernatural throughout history.

In the year A.D. 856, the first recorded case of a poltergeist, occurred at a farmhouse in Germany. The family residing there, endured torment as the poltergeist engaged in various disturbing activities, including throwing stones, pulling covers, and even starting fires. In attempting to describe this inexplicable phenomenon, the inhabitants coined the term "poltergeist," encapsulating the unsettling and disruptive nature of the entity's presence.

Among the earliest and most widely reported ghosts in England, is that of Anne Boleyn, who met her tragic fate at the hands of her husband, King Henry VIII, in May 1536. Shortly after her execution, sightings of her ghost were reported at both the Tower of London and her family residence, Hever Castle. While Anne Boleyn's apparition is notable for its historical significance and widespread documentation, ghost stories had pervaded English folklore, long before the 16th century.

In more contemporary times, the White House in the United States has become known for its plethora of spirit activity. Abraham Lincoln, the 16th president, has been reportedly sighted by various dignitaries, including Queens, Prime Ministers, and First Ladies, following his assassination on April 15th, 1865. These sightings most often occur, during times of significant upheaval, with Lincoln most frequently observed, during the administration of Franklin D. Roosevelt, amid World War II and the Great Depression. One notable sighting occurred in the early 1980s when Tony Savoy, White House operations foreman, encountered Lincoln, sitting in a chair at the top of a staircase.

Interestingly, Lincoln's wife, Mary, who held seances in the White House, claimed to have encounters with the spirits of numerous former residents. These included Thomas Jefferson, Andrew Jackson, and President John Tyler. Mary's interest in spiritualism was fuelled by the tragic death of her son Willie in the White House in February 1862.

Similarly, Winston Churchill has been reportedly seen in the Prime Minister's old stateroom aboard the RMS Queen Mary. Visitors to the room, have reported smelling his distinctive cigar smoke, despite smoking being banned on the ship. Churchill's apparition has also been witnessed in various wartime locations, significant to him during his lifetime. One I may have encountered in the War Rooms in the 2000s.

Moreover, battlefields, such as The Somme, Gallipoli, Gettysburg, and Hastings, continue to be sites of active paranormal phenomena. Sightings of soldiers and sounds of battle are still reported to this day. These locations are believed to host a mixture of residual and intelligent hauntings, preserving the memory of their tumultuous and tragic histories.

It is not uncommon, for locations with significant emotional resonance, to report sightings of ghosts, particularly in cases of traumatic or sudden deaths. Hauntings extend beyond old buildings and famous individuals, as new homes can also experience paranormal activity. Spirits may be tethered to the land upon which they once resided, a phenomenon especially prevalent in countries with long-established histories and settled populations. The United Kingdom serves as a prime example, with settlers spanning centuries and numerous structures, long since vanished, yet their former inhabitants linger in the shadows and corners of the land.

The prevalence of hauntings is staggering, and those who encounter them are often profoundly affected. For some, hauntings present a genuine problem, causing distress and harm, while for others, they offer solace and healing in times of deep grief. Additionally, encounters with non-human entities can be particularly disturbing and require specialised management and understanding.

My inaugural encounter with the paranormal, occurred unexpectedly, while I was assisting at Saint Martin's Church, in the Bullring, Birmingham, England. A place where I went, helped with Sunday school and often lent a hand. This centuries-old church, situated in a bustling central location, exuded a serene beauty. Among the church staff were two individuals, whom we will refer to in this book as David and Stephen. Both served as vergers or caretakers of the stunning church. Frequently, I would linger behind to aid them with their tasks and assist in final checks of the building before we finally departed.

One evening, while walking through the church, where I anticipated being alone, I was startled by what I can only describe as the sound of whispering voices. Despite the late hour and the prevailing stillness, it felt as though a group of people were gathered nearby, engaged in hushed conversation. Although I couldn't discern the words, the proximity of the sound made it apparent that it was not originating from outside the church. While old churches are known to echo, this was different—it felt palpable, as if I could almost reach out and touch it. As the whispering grew louder, I found myself overcome with unease, prompting me to hastily retreat to the office, where David and I departed hastily.

It was not until my next encounter with David, that I disclosed what I had experienced in the church. To my surprise, he revealed that I was not alone in hearing the phantom whispers—he and Stephen had also encountered the unsettling phenomenon of whispering on many occasions. Typically occurring around closing time, they found it deeply unnerving and would swiftly depart from the church, as soon as possible. Strangely, I never experienced the whispers again in the years I was there.

Saint Martin's Church harbours yet another spectral presence. On one occasion, while the two were alone in the church, David witnessed a figure traversing from one side of the altar to the other, before disappearing towards the vestry room. Assuming it was Stephen, he called out, only to find Stephen appearing behind him moments later. It became apparent that the figure David had seen, was not Stephen, and upon investigation, no other individuals were found within the locked down church. Personally, I never encountered this mysterious figure, whose origin and purpose remain shrouded in mystery. Reports suggest he is often sighted near the front of the church, during the early evening hours.

For those new to paranormal investigation, it is essential to grasp the potential risks involved. By discussing real-life hauntings, like those experienced in Saint Martin's Church, I hope to promote awareness and preparedness, ensuring safety when encountering paranormal phenomena.

On another occasion, I found myself alone in the kitchen of my house, washing dishes with my headphones on and listening to music. Suddenly, I distinctly heard my name being called from right beside me. The voice was so loud and clear that it pierced through the music playing in my headphones. I was so startled by the experience that I immediately called my mother to share what had happened. She suggested that my recent focus on our family tree, and thus the deceased, might have influenced my perception. While her explanation aimed to reassure me, I remained convinced that someone had indeed called my name. Even to this day, I cannot shake the certainty of belief that moment I had a paranormal encounter with someone. Who it was, is completely unknown.

These encounters, coupled with the common signs of ghostly presence, have left me with an enduring fascination and a heightened awareness of the paranormal. Let us begin with the basics: what are the typical indicators of a ghostly presence? While this list is not comprehensive, it encompasses some of the more prevalent encounters individuals may experience.

Common signs of ghosts:

- Apparitions: Visible appearances of spirits or entities, which can range from transparent, misty, and incomplete all the way up to solid forms. There are wonderful case examples of places where people interact with who they believe are reenactors, only to find out later, there is none. There are some places where the spirit attached to property joins and offers tours to unsuspecting individuals, before vanishing at the end.

- Unexplained Sounds: Strange noises such as footsteps, voices, whispers, knocks, or banging that have no apparent source. These are usually the common signs that begin a haunting.

- Temperature Changes: Sudden drops or rises in temperature in specific areas without any natural explanation.

- Electromagnetic Field (EMF) Disturbances: Fluctuations in electromagnetic fields, that occur unexpectedly, often associated with paranormal activity. Feeling a wave of cold air come over you or through you and your body reacting to a change in the atmosphere, sending shivers up your spine or hair standing on end, are common example.

- Physical Interactions: Objects moving or being thrown without any apparent physical cause. Feeling your clothes being pulled, being pushed, touched, or feeling breath on your neck are all common experiences. The range from the friendly to the aggressive with burns, bruises, and scratches.

- Feelings of Presence: Sensations of being watched, touched, or experiencing a presence when no one else is around. We are going to elaborate on this a little more in this chapter.

- Unusual Odours: Unexplained smells such as perfume, sulphur, or rotting flesh that can accompany paranormal activity. This is often a good indicator if we are dealing with darker entities or human spirits.

- Electronic Disturbances: Malfunctioning of electronic devices or appliances without any identifiable reason. This could be batteries being drained, TVs turning themselves on and off, Radio or children's toys repeated going off and on without explanation. Lights flickering are a common one. I knew of a case where the resident ghost would make the phone ring, the alarm would be tripped all the time and she even used to turn the microwave on.

- Animals Reacting: Pets or animals behaving strangely, such as growling, barking, or seeming to react to unseen entities. They may refuse to enter an area of the house, or you may see a complete change in an animal's behaviour. It is believed across many cultures and belief systems that animals can see what we cannot. Animals can also react to an area that has been the site of extreme tragedy, like birds refusing to sing and animals falling silent or simply not entering the area.

- Psychological Effects: Feelings of fear, anxiety, or unease experienced by individuals in specific locations or environments. Now this is not surprising. Fear is a normal reaction to something that we cannot understand, that suddenly pops up at the end of your bed at night to say hello. Some spirits can make the living experience the emotions or illness they did when they were alive. Some deliberately cause fear and anxiety if they are more negative than positive.

These are the fundamental indicators that something out of the ordinary might be happening at a location, possibly indicating paranormal activity. Sometimes, the signs are glaringly obvious, such as witnessing a full-bodied apparition climbing stairs at 2 AM. Other times, they may be subtle, like peripheral movements or unexplained sensations. Hauntings can include the presence of one or more of these phenomena—or none at all—depends on the circumstances.

Before delving into the various types of hauntings, it is critical to pause and consider alternative explanations. There are numerous reasons why someone might perceive a home as haunted, that have nothing to do with the paranormal. High electromagnetic field (EMF) readings, for instance, can evoke feelings of a presence and being watched. Psychological and environmental factors also influence our perceptions of a location.

Unfamiliar and unsettling environments can heighten our sensitivity to subtle sounds and sensations. Environmental elements like creaking floorboards, drafts, and sudden noises contribute to feelings of unease. While it has been suggested that very old buildings emit low frequencies that induce these sensations—similar to high EMF readings—scientific evidence does not support this assertion, about older structures.

Infrasound is another factor often cited as a potential explanation for the perception of paranormal activity at a location or home. It pertains to low-frequency sounds that fall below the threshold of human hearing. Infrasound encompasses a broad frequency range, spanning from below 20 Hertz (Hz)—referred to as infrasound—to 200 Hz, classified as low-frequency sound. This phenomenon is utilised by whales and elephants for long-distance communication and is naturally generated by phenomena such as storms and weather patterns. Additionally, human activities and technologies contribute to the production of infrasound.

In 1980, coincidentally the year of my birth, engineer Victor Tandy made a pivotal discovery while working in a lab with a haunted reputation. Workers would only operate in pairs due to reported occurrences, ranging from objects moving to full-blown apparitions. Tandy himself claimed to have seen an apparition in this very laboratory.

One day, while engrossed in his work, Tandy heard a tool fall and witnessed a fencing foil, clamped in a vise begin to vibrate. Despite identifying a nearby fan as the source of the vibrations—which had knocked the tool to the floor—he could not shake a growing sense of unease and the feeling of being watched. His subsequent investigation revealed that the fan emitted a frequency of 19Hz. Turning off the fan alleviated the feelings of unease, only for them to return upon its activation. Tandy conducted an experiment, removing the fan for some workers but not others. Those without the fan reported no unease or anxiety, while some with the fan left or refused to work alone.

This discovery, was further validated in other cases where low frequencies were recorded at locations known for hauntings. For instance, in a 14th-century pub in Coventry, England, reports of a Grey Lady in the cellar led to the discovery of an item vibrating at 19Hz. However, it remains unclear whether the Grey Lady vanished after the frequency was removed or the identity of the apparition Tandy claimed to have witnessed. Nonetheless, these cases suggest a possible role for infrasound, in certain paranormal encounters.

While high EMF readings or low-frequency sounds may explain some phenomena, they fail to account for others, such as objects being thrown or moved, disembodied voices, or Class A electronic Voice phenomena. Moreover, they do not address hauntings occurring in locations devoid of EMF or infrasound.

Understanding the type of haunting occurring at a location, is crucial for addressing disturbances effectively. Even in cases where resolution may not be necessary—such as public locations known to be haunted—determining the nature of the haunting remains essential for safety and well-being. Despite common beliefs that ghosts cannot harm, and it is true that physical harm is rare, but emotional and mental distress are not. It is a stark reality, that there are entities out there, and sometimes, they pose a threat.

As we venture into the realm of paranormal investigation; it becomes evident that not all encounters fit neatly into a single category. While some phenomena may be attributed to environmental factors like high EMF readings or infrasound, others defy conventional explanations. This diversity underscores the complexity of the paranormal landscape and the need for a comprehensive framework to understand and address these encounters. Hence, before categorising hauntings into distinct types, it is imperative to acknowledge the multifaceted nature of paranormal activity and the myriad factors that may influence our perceptions and experiences. By approaching our investigation with an open mind and a willingness to explore various possibilities, we can gain deeper insights into the mysteries that lie beyond.

RESIDUAL HAUNTING

Residual hauntings are like echoes frozen in time; remnants of past events imprinted on the very fabric of a place. Unlike interactive spirits that engage with the living, residual hauntings play out like spectral recordings, trapped in a perpetual loop of emotion and action. Imagine entering a room and feeling an inexplicable chill, hearing whispers of conversations long gone, or witnessing ghostly figures re-enacting scenes from another era. These phenomena evoke a profound sense of eeriness, as if you've stumbled upon a ghostly stage where the actors are forever stuck in their roles, unaware of the passage of time. Residual hauntings blur the lines between past and present, leaving observers with a spine-tingling reminder of the mysteries that linger beyond our understanding

In my view, a residual haunting stands out as one of the most prevalent phenomena, encountered in paranormal investigations. Many instances of paranormal activity can be categorised as such. Unlike intelligent hauntings, which involve interactive spirits, a residual haunting appears more akin to a playback of past events or emotions. It is parallel to watching a recorded scene unfold, where the events have already transpired.

This type of haunting is often associated with intense emotions that linger in the environment. Consider a scenario where tension fills the air after an argument, even after the voices have quieted. Similarly, for individuals sensitive to emotions, being in the presence of heightened feelings can be draining. This phenomenon stems from the transfer of energy from one person to another, a concept recognised for some time. Expressions like; "you could cut the tension with a knife", hint at the palpable energy present in such situations. Have you ever sensed someone's distress, before they uttered a word, relying solely on intuition and subtle cues? This is a manifestation of picking up on another's energy and nonverbal communication cues.

What if the emotional energy, emitted by individuals, could be absorbed by the environment, and later replayed? This is the underlying concept behind

25

the theory of a residual haunting. How and why, this occurs, remains a mystery. Analogous to the transfer of thermal energy into water in a kettle, could emotional energy be transferred and stored, later manifesting as a playback of past events?

Numerous theories attempt to explain this phenomenon, though debate persists. One widely discussed theory is the Stone Tape Theory, which posits that ghosts and hauntings resemble recorded tape impressions. According to this theory, during moments of intense emotion or trauma, energy impressions are projected and imprinted onto objects, akin to recordings. The term "Stone Tape", originates from the observation that residual hauntings often occur in environments rich in stone.

The notion of residual hauntings, predates modern paranormal investigation and originates from scientific inquiry into the nature of sound and memory. Charles Babbage, a prominent 19th-century scientist, credited as a forefather of the programmable computer, explored how spoken words lingered in the air, long after being uttered. He proposed that these words, though inaudible to most, remained suspended in the atmosphere indefinitely, capable of unlocking memories, for those attuned to them. This concept, termed "place memory" laid the groundwork for what would later evolve into the Stone Tape theory.

During the Victorian spiritualist movement, the idea gained traction, particularly among mediums whose purported communication with spirits, often involving extended dialogues. Place memory was invoked to explain how audiences could hear spirits conversing for hours on end—a phenomenon attributed to the residual impressions left in the environment.

Residual hauntings, characterised by the repetitive playback of past events, align with this concept of place memory. Unlike intelligent hauntings, which involve interactive spirits, residual hauntings lack consciousness or awareness. They are like ghostly echoes, devoid of substance or threat, as they merely replay events, like scenes from a long forgotten play. Here is what we have gleaned, from our years of investigation and hands-on experience:

- Residual Hauntings usually occur in places of high emotion. This could be where someone has died, it could be the replay of a person in great distress or angst. It could be an emotion or feeling. Often in places of high residual energy people feel sick or have headaches. It could be extreme anxiety or fear.
- They are more prevalent in stone buildings.
- Residual energy can be attached to clothes, furniture, objects, and places.
- It can take the form of apparitions, sounds, smells and can be dramatic or subtle.

- Residual energy is static and non-interactive.

The ability to discern between a residual haunting and an active intelligent haunting, is often one of the initial skills, developed by paranormal investigators. Here are some key indicators that suggest you may be encountering a residual haunting rather than an active intelligent one:

- Apparitions reported will be like moving pictures and typically will be seen in the same places, walking down the same hallway, appearing in the same window, or sitting in the same chair. They will be doing the same motion over and over again. They will be unaware of the living people around them and there is never interaction between the ghost and the witnesses.
- Strange sounds, such as footsteps, voices, knocking, and rapping's, are common. As are the sounds of doors opening and closing. The tend to occur at the same place and same time.
- There may be elevated levels of humidity. It has been suggested that water embedded in a location may hold a sort of recording of the haunting that is taking place. Water is believed to be a conduit for energy.

When I lived in the England, one the renowned residual hauntings, involved Catherine Howard, the fifth wife of Henry VIII. Catherine, charged with adultery, faced her arrest in her chambers. Desperate to reach Henry, who was praying in the chapel, she broke free from her guards and fled down the long gallery. However, her escape was short-lived as she was swiftly apprehended and dragged back, screaming, and kicking. This traumatic event has been witnessed and heard, echoing through the haunted gallery of Hampton Court Palace, for centuries since.

It is intriguing that the only haunting, officially recognised in England's Public Records Office, is deemed a dramatic, residual haunting. This haunting unfolded in a field south of Birmingham, my hometown, which now appears like any other field in the area. Yet, during the English Civil War, it was the scene of a fierce battle. I have had the privilege of visiting this quaint spot, where all that remains today, is a weathered plaque honouring the fallen soldiers. However, the significance of bringing the reader to this location, extends beyond its historical significance.

The English Civil War, which erupted on 22 August 1642, pitted Royalists against Parliamentarians, after King Charles I's tumultuous attempt, to arrest some of Parliament's members, during an active session. By October of that year, King Charles I advanced on Edghill, setting the stage, for one of the war's bloodiest battles. With approximately 14,000 soldiers on each side, the clash was fierce and devastating. However, the Battle of Edgehill ultimately yielded no decisive outcome for the war itself, rendering the sacrifices of thousands of troops, tragically futile. An estimated 3,000 soldiers were left wounded, and many more perished due to the lack of medical care and rampant disease, in the aftermath. What adds to the tragedy, is the disregard for the fallen soldiers as their bodies were left unburied, in the open field, vulnerable to looting for valuables like money and clothing. Such treatment of the deceased, would understandably incite anger among both the living and the dead.

Amidst this desolation, a strange series of events unfolded around two months later, during the Christmas season of that year.

Shepherds traversing the battlefield at night, reported a chilling spectacle: the echoes of clashing swords, men's agonised screams, and the haunting cries of horses, all intertwined with the desperate calls of dying soldiers. Looking skyward, the shepherds beheld a surreal sight—the apparitions of fallen warriors re-enacting the Battle of Edgehill, as if the conflict had never ceased. Stricken with terror, the shepherds fled their posts, their fears compelling them to awaken the local priest.

Upon arrival, the priest bore witness to the spectral re-enactment of the battle, confirming the shepherds' accounts. So profound was the phenomenon that a pamphlet documenting the event circulated among the villages by January 1643, drawing crowds eager to witness the eerie spectacle. Even King Charles I himself learned of the ongoing spectral battle and dispatched a Royal Commission to investigate.

Members of the commission not only corroborated the sightings but also identified familiar faces among the spectral combatants, including Sir Edmund Verney, the king's standard-bearer, who had perished during the battle. As months passed, the relentless cries and phantom clashes wore heavily on the local populace, prompting concerns about the fate of the restless souls. Seeking resolution, villagers proposed that the haunting stemmed from the improper treatment and lack of proper burial, for the fallen soldiers.

Responding to these concerns, the community came together to provide the fallen troops with a dignified Christian burial and solemn service. With the completion of this act of reverence, the spectral re-enactments ceased, and the Battle of Edgehill was finally laid to rest. From that moment onward, the soldiers were believed to have found peace at last.

However, even after the proper burial and acknowledgment by the Royal Commission, reports persist of spectral phenomena at Edgehill. Witnesses still recount hearing the echoes of swords and cannon fire in the dead of night, while sightings and photographs of ghostly soldiers in and around the battlefield, continue to surface.

The witnessing of these apparitions by the Royal Commission, led to their acknowledgment in the Public Record Office, making them the only ghosts documented in the public record to this day. Both of these instances are categorised as residual hauntings—a haunting phenomenon, characterised by the repetitive playback of a past traumatic event, within our physical realm. This certainly appears to be the case for the events at Edgehill, where the echoes of a brutal battle linger on, haunting the land and those who dare to tread upon it.

The Battle of Edgehill presents a more nuanced case, challenging easy categorisation. The cessation of visions after the soldiers received proper burials, suggests a level of awareness on their part, possibly indicating an intelligent haunting. Yet, the persistence of spectral sounds and sightings implies a lingering energy, characteristic of a residual haunting.

It is plausible that some of these spirits may have been unaware of their demise, trapped in an eternal struggle until their earthly remains were laid to rest. The act of burial may have served as a catalyst for them to put down their spectral weapons and accept their fate.

In essence, the phenomenon at Edgehill appears to blend elements of both residual and intelligent hauntings, reflecting the complex nature of paranormal manifestations. Battlefields, in particular, often harbour a mix of residual echoes and intelligent spirits, each contributing to the eerie atmosphere that persists, long after the conflict has ended.

An eerie incident at Penn Hall, Gettysburg College, unfolds like a chilling scene from a wartime horror film. Two women, accustomed to routine elevator rides, on their way home, found themselves thrust into a harrowing tableau of Civil War-era suffering. Despite their frantic attempts to control the lift, it descended inexorably into the basement, revealing a hauntingly vivid scene.

Before them lay makeshift beds, wounded soldiers, and bustling medical personnel, all frozen in a spectral re-enactments of wartime triage. The air hung heavy with the stench of blood, and the women could hear the agonised cries of the injured echoing through the chamber. In the heart of this macabre theatre stood a doctor, poised to perform a grisly amputation, oblivious to the modern-day witnesses.

For the women, it was a surreal journey across temporal boundaries, a disconcerting collision of past and present. The encounter, marked by its visceral realism and palpable terror, defied rational explanation. Was it a residual haunting, a haunting echo of Penn Hall's wartime past replaying before their eyes? Or could it be an intelligent haunting, a spectral entity revisiting a traumatic moment from its mortal existence?

In either case, the chilling episode serves as a haunting reminder of the enduring legacy of war, etched into the very fabric of the building of location itself.

Residual hauntings can manifest in a myriad of ways, often with subtlety rather than spectacle. In the United Kingdom, where history and folklore intertwine, these echoes of the past can be found in the most unexpected places. From the creak of floorboards in centuries-old manor houses, to the whisper of voices in abandoned castles, the spectral remnants of bygone eras linger on.

Consider the chilling tale of a phantom carriage that traverses the lonely roads of Dartmoor, its spectral horses galloping through the mist-shrouded night. Or the ghostly apparition of a Victorian lady, forever pacing the parapets of a windswept cliffside castle, her mournful gaze fixed on the turbulent sea below.

In the shadowy depths of ancient forests, spectral huntsmen pursue phantom prey with spectral hounds at their heels, their ghostly cries echoing through the trees. Meanwhile, in the quiet corners of rural villages, the ethereal strains of long-forgotten music drift on the evening breeze, conjuring visions of long-lost celebrations and festivities.

Yet not all residual hauntings are rooted in the distant past. In bustling city streets, the ghostly echoes of wartime air raids reverberate through the night, a haunting reminder of the city's darkest hours. And in modern homes, the faint echoes of laughter and conversation linger in the air, faint traces of the lives once lived within those walls.

Across the United Kingdom, these spectral echoes serve as poignant reminders of the rich tapestry of history that weaves through the fabric of the land. From the grandeur of stately homes to the humblest of country lanes, the echoes of the past are everywhere, waiting to be heard by those with the courage to listen.

Before delving into specific cases, it is worth noting that residual hauntings are as diverse as the places they inhabit. From ancient castles steeped in legend to nondescript suburban homes, these echoes of the past can manifest anywhere that significant events have left their mark. Some notable cases offer intriguing glimpses into the varied nature of residual hauntings. Let us explore a few examples that stand out among the countless tales across the United Kingdom.

The Burning Manor House
Located in the West Midlands in County Warwickshire, England, Baginton Manor House once stood proudly, just 150 meters north of the Baginton Church. This country estate, erected during the post medieval period, bore witness to a tragic fate, when it succumbed to flames in 1889. Reduced to ashes, its grandeur was lost to history. Yet, its spectral presence endured.

Around a decade after its fiery demise, a startling apparition manifested. A witness, passing by the site of the former manor, was stunned to see flames engulfing the air where the house once stood. Alarmed, they called for aid, fearing a rekindled inferno. However, upon arrival, responders found no trace of fire or dwelling. Perplexingly, no reconstruction had taken place on the grounds since the 1889 conflagration.

Years passed, but the spectral vision persisted. Subsequent witnesses attested to seeing the eerie sight of the burning manor house, its spectral flames dancing against the night sky. Despite the passage of time, the ghostly echoes of Baginton Manor House continued to haunt the landscape, a poignant reminder of its fiery fate.

Ghostly Battle

In Alvaston, Derby, near the site of the castle, a recurring residual haunting has captivated witnesses for decades. The eerie phenomenon traces back to the early 20th century when three young girls were startled by the sounds of a phantom battle, unfolding in the vicinity of the castle. Their chilling accounts included the haunting cries of women, the sharp crackle of gunfire, the thunderous gallop of unseen horses, and the clamour of men engaged in combat.

Decades later, in the mid 1980s, four individuals ventured out late at night only to encounter the same auditory spectacle. The echoes of battle resounded once more, echoing through the stillness of the night.

The most recent encounter with the ghostly battle occurred in 2009, when two brothers passing through the area were engulfed by the sounds of conflict. Despite their efforts, they could not pinpoint the origin of the cacophony, which reverberated ominously close and loud.

Given the rich history of the locale, spanning numerous conflicts across different epochs, it remains a mystery which battle echoes through time, in this spectral re-enactment. Yet, the haunting echoes of Alvaston's past continue to linger, etching their presence into the fabric of the present.

Roman Centurion
Roman Troops

Nestled at 140 Mansfield Road in Derby, England, Little Chester, also known as Chester Green, stands as a picturesque park. Adorned with verdant trees, inviting visitors to indulge in moments of recreation and tranquillity, amidst its lush surroundings, it is a favourite place to sit and relax. However, beneath its serene facade, this locale harbours tales of spectral encounters, blending both intelligent and residual hauntings, into its storied landscape.

The Intelligent haunting that frequents this park, is said to manifest in the spectral form of a lone Roman Centurion, glimpsed by startled onlookers on multiple occasions. Yet, it is the Residual haunting that garners widespread attention, painting the park with echoes of ancient history. Witnesses attest to the unmistakable sound of marching footsteps, echoing through the night in rhythmic cadence. Though the legion of Roman soldiers remains unseen, their spectral presence reverberates through the park, with haunting regularity.

Such occurrences have not gone unnoticed, drawing the attention of local media outlets, which have documented numerous reports detailing the phantom footsteps that pervade the night air. For those who venture into Little Chester after dusk, a moment of hushed stillness may grant them an eerie glimpse into the spectral realm, where the echoes of Roman troops persist, in their eternal march through time.

Former Howard Hotel
Prison

In Derby, a city steeped in history and intrigue, echoes of its judicial past linger within the walls of the Old County Gaol, now transformed into the Howard Hotel. Once a site of sombre significance, the gaol bore witness to the final moments of those condemned to the gallows, with public hangings marking the end of life's journey for many.

The spectre of the past still lingers in the present, as staff and guests of the Howard Hotel, recount eerie encounters with the echoes of bygone days. Reports emerge of phantom sounds reverberating through the corridors, reminiscent of cell doors slamming shut with ghostly finality. Yet, perplexingly, these spectral echoes persist, despite the absence of physical doors, removed from their hinges long ago.

The phenomenon perplexes and disturbs, disrupting the tranquillity of the night and prompting complaints from sleepless guests, who find themselves unsettled by the ghostly echoes that haunt the hotel's halls. From the depths of the basement, where prisoners once languished in captivity, to the uppermost floors, where travellers seek respite from the world outside, the echoes of Derby's judicial history, refuse to fade into obscurity.

Soldiers

As recently as 2010, the proprietor of a quaint salon in the heart of the city, recounted peculiar occurrences that stirred whispers of the paranormal. Amidst the hustle and bustle of daily life, the unmistakable sound of marching soldiers, reverberated through the shop, persisting through both daylight and the quiet of night. Yet, despite diligent scrutiny, no tangible presence could be discerned.

Speculation swirled around the source of these spectral echoes, painting a picture of local lore and legend. Whispers hinted at the existence of secret tunnels, clandestine passageways that once snaked beneath the streets, linking the salon to the grandeur of the cathedral above. These whispers, born from the depths of history, lent credence to the notion that the phantom footsteps may be a haunting echo of times long past, etched into the fabric of the city's collective memory.

Young Woman

In the quiet lanes of Derby's Spondon district, whispers linger of a spectral presence that traverses the streets. Witnesses recount the apparition of a young woman, her form shrouded in a faint, ghostly blur. With plaintive calls that echo through the night, she searches relentlessly for her lost brother, a tragic casualty of war.

Screaming

In the hushed embrace of Derby's St Mary's Bridge, where Well Street winds its ancient path, whispers of the past linger like spectres in the night. Once a grim stage for the public display of executed criminals and fallen priests, the bridge now echoes with their desperate and sorrowful cries. In the stillness of the evening, long after the world has retreated into slumber, their spectral voices rise, haunting the tranquil air with tales of bygone torment.

Derby and Bath hold a special place in my heart, as two of England's most haunted cities. During a tour of Derby Gaol, owned by the passionate paranormal enthusiast, Richard Felix, I encountered an intriguing experience. Arriving early one day after a drive down from Birmingham, we spotted what appeared to be a raised scaffold outside the Gaol, accompanied by a figure clad in a long black robe. Excitedly, I remarked to my companion, about the possibility of live actors enhancing the tour experience later that evening. However, Mr. Felix assured us there were no such individuals present, and our tour proceeded without any actors. Whether this was a jest, or an unexplained phenomenon, remains a mystery, but it sparked lively discussion on our journey home.

Curiously, Derby Gaol has its share of peculiar occurrences, including an odd sensation of tripping upon entry—a sensation shared by many visitors, including myself. Despite there no longer being a step present, guests often report feeling as though one should be there, leading to frequent stumbles. Among the reported phenomena are sightings of a towering figure cloaked in black robes, captured both in photographs and witnessed by guests. Additionally, the eerie sound of a woman's inconsolable sobbing, emanates from a particular cell, said to have once housed a female prisoner. Footsteps echoing down empty corridors, the faint jingle of keys, disembodied voices, sudden cold drafts, and the unnerving sound of doors slamming shut all contribute to the Gaol's reputation as a site steeped in spectral activity.

Derby's Eagle Centre, particularly around the market area, was the epicentre of intense and unsettling hauntings during the late 1970s and early

1980s, prompting decisive action, from local authorities. The surge in reports and the subsequent resignations of long-standing workers, spurred the council to intervene. Matters escalated when a cleaner, overcome with shock, collapsed, and required hospitalisation after hearing a chilling woman's voice—an anguished wail reminiscent of a distressed animal.

Paranormal experts were summoned, and a security firm dispatched to meticulously document the occurrences. Religious leaders were then enlisted to conduct blessings in the affected shops. The council even went so far as to distribute leaflets to shop owners, outlining protocols for dealing with poltergeist activity. Despite these efforts, the disturbances persisted, prompting the drastic measure of an exorcism for the entire centre.

In December 1983, with permission from the Vatican, the then Bishop of Derby, along with clerics from Sheffield, conducted the first exorcism in one of the haunted shops. Another exorcism followed in March 1984, proving more effective than the initial attempt. While reports of spectral sightings linger to this day, the poltergeist activity gradually dwindled and ceased entirely, by the end of 1984.

Distinguishing between intelligent hauntings and residual energy can be challenging, but there are key differences to consider. One of the primary factors is the nature of the energy itself—is it dynamic and interactive, or static and unchanging?

For instance, if you experience a cold spot that moves from one room to another unpredictably, it suggests a dynamic presence, possibly an intelligent spirit. Conversely, if the cold spot remains fixed in a specific location, such as a particular chair, it is more indicative of residual energy.

Intelligent spirits possess the ability to alter their form, size, and movement, often responding to stimuli or interacting with individuals present. They may cause objects to apport (manifest), disappear, and reappear in unexpected places, respond to questions during investigations, or manipulate electronic devices.

Residual energy, on the other hand, lacks responsiveness and interaction. It behaves like a playback of past events, repeating the same actions or sounds without deviation. It is as if the energy is imprinted on the environment, playing out like a recording with no awareness of its surroundings.

By considering these factors and observing the behaviour of the energy in question, investigators can better determine, whether they are dealing with an intelligent haunting or residual energy.

A lovely story of the museum curator in upstate New York, serves as a powerful reminder of the need for vigilance and awareness in paranormal investigations. Despite becoming accustomed to the presence of a residual apparition, the curator was shocked to encounter a distinctly different entity, within the same space.

In the museum curator's routine, the spectral apparition was almost a comforting presence—a silent observer following a repetitive path through the corridors of the old Victorian home. Gliding through doorways, ascending the stairs with an ethereal grace, and disappearing into thin air without so much as a glance in the curator's direction. She seemed like a ghostly echo from a bygone era—a residual haunting etched into the fabric of the building.

Over time, the curator had grown accustomed to her spectral visits, almost looking forward to the familiar sight of her ghostly figure, tracing the same well-trodden path. It became a part of his daily routine, an eerie but predictable aspect of his work in the museum.

One day, while chatting with a colleague, the curator's attention was drawn once again to the sound of footsteps echoing up the staircase. Expecting to see the familiar apparition glide past as usual, he hurried to the foot of the stairs with his colleague in tow, eager to share the experience.

But as they reached the landing, what they encountered was far from expected. Instead of the usual spectral figure, they were met with the unmistakable presence of a young woman in her twenties, dressed in the finery of the Victorian era. Her gaze met theirs with startling clarity, her smile acknowledging their presence, before vanishing into thin air before their astonished eyes.

In that moment, the curator's world was turned upside down. What he had believed to be a simple residual haunting—a ghostly replay of past events—was revealed to be something far more complex. The sudden appearance of this intelligent spirit, identified as one of the daughters of the original owner, shattered his preconceptions and left him reeling with the realisation that there was more to the house's haunted history, than he had ever imagined.

It serves as a cautionary tale against complacency, reminding investigators to remain alert and responsive to the potential presence of intelligent hauntings, even in familiar environments. By maintaining a sense of readiness and adaptability, investigators can more effectively navigate the complexities of paranormal encounters.

Even if the first set of footsteps sounds like a replay from the past, don't assume the second set, creeping up behind you, is just an encore!

TYPES OF INTELLIGENT HAUNTING

In the twilight's embrace there exists a realm where spirits roam, enigmatic and profound. Welcome to the realm of the intelligent haunting, where the echoes of the past weave a tapestry of mystery and intrigue. In this theatre, spectres of intellect and purpose linger, their presence a symphony of enigmatic whispers and spectral bodies. They

are not mere apparitions, but guardians of forgotten truths, seekers of solace, and bearers of wisdom lost to time's relentless march.
With each flicker of torchlight and every creak of the floorboards, they beckon us to unravel the secrets they hold, to peer beyond the veil of the mundane and glimpse the profound mysteries of existence. Here, the boundaries between the seen and unseen are connected, and the language of the soul speaks in riddles and dreams.

An "intelligent haunting", is a term frequently used by paranormal investigators to characterise a haunting, in which there appears to be some level of awareness or consciousness from the spirit or entity involved. In contrast to residual hauntings, discussed previously, intelligent hauntings involve spirits or entities that exhibit awareness of the living and may engage in interactions with them.

In an intelligent haunting, the spirit or entity may respond to inquiries, deliberately move objects, or demonstrate awareness of its surroundings by interacting with various equipment. These hauntings are often associated with trapped human spirits, who may have unresolved issues or strong emotional connections to the location. Various types of intelligent hauntings are reported, each with its own specific reasons and often requiring different resolutions. These are the kind of haunting that most paranormal investigators are chasing.

Intelligent hauntings manifest in various forms and exhibit diverse characteristics. From non-human hauntings to trapped spirits, there are numerous ways in which these phenomena may present themselves. Let's explore these different forms in more detail, beginning with non-earthbound spirits.

NON EARTHBOUND HUMAN SPIRITS

This spirit, neither bound by flesh nor constrained by mortal desires, roams the veiled corridors between worlds with a purpose as enigmatic as the depths of the cosmos. Its presence is felt in the icy tendrils of a chilling breeze, in the flicker of a candle's flame dancing with unseen hands, in the haunting echoes of distant whispers that send shivers down the spine of the living.

A non-earthbound human spirit, exists beyond the confines of the earthly plane, suggesting that upon physical death, they transition to another realm. The nature of this realm varies, depending on cultural and religious beliefs.

These spirits frequently visit their loved ones or places of significance. Their visits may serve to offer comfort or communicate through dreams,

36

indicating their wellbeing or participating in special occasions. Numerous accounts document deceased loved ones, appearing in photographs or videos during family events, such as weddings, birthdays or anniversaries.

It is comforting to imagine, that during significant life moments, our departed loved ones are present, celebrating with us or welcoming new additions to the family. The apparent awareness of many spirits, regarding events since their passing, suggests that such visitations are not uncommon occurrences for deceased loved ones.

I have encountered numerous instances, where departed loved ones return and linger, because they sense danger in the home. There have been several haunting cases over the years, where investigation reveals a deceased family member is present, acting as a protective presence for the living. Additionally, I have heard numerous references, through EVP (Electronic Voice Phenomena) to deceased loved ones expressing care and interest in children, born after their passing.

These benevolent spirits are the ones we prefer to connect with—the protective grandmother checking in on her family. People often sense their presence through feelings, dreams, familiar scents, or simply wishful thinking. In such cases, it is reassuring to inform the client that all is well and that their deceased loved one, like Grandma Mary, is watching over them.

My own experience occurred last year when I believe my mother in Law visited at the time of her death. We had been informed she was close to death and as my husband raced to the airport to fly to her location, I was left alone in the home with my toddler. As my toddler danced in front of a full sized mirror in our hallway, I felt a freezing cold breeze go straight through me and down the corridor. I knew at that moment, that she had passed. I told my daughter, who was too young to understand, her beloved Nonna had gone to Heaven. My husband never made it in time and moments later called me to tell me the news of her passing. I never told my husband I already knew. I believe that at her moment of death, she had come to see her beloved granddaughter, one last time, before moving on and finding peace.

A few years ago, in Perth, Western Australia, a peculiar case unfolded that left a family deeply unsettled. It all began when they started noticing strange occurrences on their baby monitor. Their 13-month-old daughter peacefully slept in her room across the hall, but something mysterious seemed to be afoot.

The parents were alarmed when they heard the distinct sound of shushing coming through the baby monitor. Even more unsettling, they witnessed a misty figure hovering over their baby's cot. This was not just a figment of their imagination; others in the household also bore witness to these eerie events.

Each time the parents rushed to the room, the figure vanished into thin air, leaving behind an inexplicable drop in temperature. The family, especially the mother, was understandably disturbed by these incidents. Fearful for their child's safety and well-being, they decided to have the baby sleep in their room instead.

With their nerves frayed and their sense of security shattered, the family sought answers. They could not bear the thought of being alone in their own home, gripped by the fear of the unknown. Thus, they reached out to paranormal investigators, in search of clarity and reassurance.

During their week long investigation at the property, the paranormal investigators had the baby placed back in her room and initially encountered silence. Just as they were on the verge of wrapping up, the atmosphere suddenly crackled with static electricity, and a misty figure appeared on the baby monitor camera. However, by the time they reached the room, the figure had vanished without a trace.

Deciding to extend their stay for another week, the investigators left a voice recorder in the baby's room, during their absence. Upon reviewing the recordings, they were stunned to hear a woman humming an unfamiliar tune and speaking in a language foreign to them. To their amazement, the mother identified the voice as that of her grandmother, Mira, who had passed away, nearly two decades earlier.

Mira, a Polish refugee, resettled in Mexico after World War II, had never set foot in Australia, where her granddaughter now lived. Yet, the language spoken on the recording was Polish, and the melody was a Polish lullaby—a song Mira had sung to her daughter and granddaughter, in their youth. It seemed that even in the afterlife, Mira was continuing the tradition with her great-granddaughter.

Moved by this touching revelation, the family felt a sense of peace and reassurance. They lovingly returned their baby to her room permanently, comforted by the knowledge that she was under the watchful eye of her great-grandmother. It was a perfect resolution—an example of how the return of non-earthbound spirits can bring solace and connection across generations.

In a chilling account shared on the "Otherworld" podcast in July 2023, Elish Poe, a 25-year-old elementary school teacher from Colorado, recounted a traumatic ordeal that defied explanation.

Elish found herself the target of a horrific attack in her own home, by a man whose advances she had repeatedly rebuffed. The perpetrator, whose name remains unworthy of mention, had lurked in her home for over a day, waiting for her return, fuelled by rejection. When she finally arrived, he unleashed a vicious assault, throwing her down the stairs, slamming her head against the wall, and stabbing her multiple times.

Despite the severity of her injuries, Elish miraculously survived the ordeal by playing dead, eventually prompting her assailant to flee. However, it was what happened in the aftermath of the attack, that defied rational explanation.

As Elish lay wounded and vulnerable, she claimed to have witnessed the apparitions of three individuals, who had passed away during her lifetime. Standing in the bathroom doorway, mere feet from where the assault had taken place, were her paternal grandmother, Jeanie, who had passed in 2014, and a high school friend, who had tragically taken their own life, earlier that year. Strikingly, the third spirit was unfamiliar to Elish—Alyssa Burkett, a victim of a similarly brutal attack, stabbed and shot by her ex-partner who left behind a one-year-old daughter, before she tragically succumbed to her injuries.

In Elish's account, it was Alyssa who appeared to offer tangible aid, assisting her to sit upright and reach her phone to summon help. Despite the gravity of the situation, the spirits emanated a sense of calm and comfort, smiling at Elish before dissipating upon the arrival of emergency services.

Following the incident, Elish reported encountering "shadowy figures" on numerous occasions during her recovery and beyond, an eerie reminder of the trauma she had endured. Shortly thereafter, her assailant took his own life, leaving behind a legacy of darkness and despair.

It is fascinating to delve into the myriad ways in which the departed can intersect with the living, especially in moments of crisis or danger. These encounters, though varied, often bring a profound sense of comfort to those involved. Stories abound of individuals who, in the midst of assault or impending danger, have experienced the intervention of loved ones or strangers, from beyond.

In one remarkable case, a woman found herself transported to another realm by her grandmother's apparition, offering a sanctuary from the horrors unfolding around her. Such experiences, though extraordinary, provide solace amidst chaos and terror.

It is in these moments, when the dead come back to help, we are reminded the importance of honouring the dead, like Alyssa, whose essence still stand as a beacon of hope, to those who need it.

Similarly, there are numerous accounts of individuals receiving warnings or guidance from deceased loved ones, particularly in moments of peril such as near accidents. These premonitions serve as a poignant reminder of the enduring connection between the living and the departed, transcending the boundaries of life and death.

These phenomena, distinct from crisis apparitions witnessed by loved ones at the moment of passing, offer a glimpse into the intricate workings of existence beyond the physical realm. While science may attribute such occurrences to shock or neurological processes, they defy simple explanation, often leaving us in awe of the mysteries that abound.

Moreover, spirits are not confined to interactions with those they knew in life. Instances of unknown spirits helping or appearing in familiar locations are not uncommon. Perhaps drawn by resonance with past experiences or shared circumstances, these spirits manifest their presence in unexpected ways. I believe this was the case for Alyssa.

Take, for instance, the lingering spirits at places like the RMS Queen Mary or old theatres, where former occupants continue to visit, out of fondness for the environments they once cherished. These visitations serve as reminders of the enduring ties that bind us to the places and people, we hold dear, transcending the veil between the worlds of the living and the dead.

TRAPPED EARTHBOUND SPIRITS

In stillness of the unseen realm, where the departed echo through eternity, we stand at the threshold of a profound journey. In this spectral domain, the lingering souls of the departed wander, tethered to the earth by the weight of unresolved grievances, unspoken words, and unfinished tales.
Trapped earthbound spirits, often referred to as ghosts, are believed to be the souls or energy remnants of deceased individuals who have not moved on to the afterlife for various reasons. These spirits are said to linger in the physical realm, unable to complete their transition due to unresolved issues, strong attachments, or traumatic experiences from their past lives.

According to paranormal beliefs, earthbound spirits may haunt specific locations such as houses, graveyards, or historical sites where they have a connection. They might manifest in different forms, ranging from apparitions and sounds to physical sensations and disruptions in electrical devices.

Various spiritual practices, including rituals, prayers, and energy work, are often employed to help these spirits find peace and move on. Additionally, some individuals claim to communicate with earthbound spirits through methods like mediumship or electronic voice phenomena (EVP) recordings.

Beliefs about trapped earthbound spirits vary across cultures and belief systems, but they have been a common theme in folklore, religion, and paranormal investigations, throughout history.

The notion of place-memory suggests that individuals can become intertwined with specific locations for a multitude of reasons. It could be that the place held significant personal meaning during their lifetime, or perhaps it became the site of their untimely demise, forever tethering their spirit to its surroundings. Alternatively, a strong emotional connection or attachment to a particular individual, might anchor them to a specific place.

This concept of spirits becoming bound to certain locales likely resonates with many, as it forms the basis of numerous contemporary theories surrounding the paranormal. The notion that the same ghosts often linger in the same places, finds its roots in the idea of place-memory,

By using an example like Woodman Point Quarantine Station, Perth, we can explore a spectrum of experiences regarding bound spirits. These range from benevolent and peaceful spirits to malevolent and aggressive entities, with some, even defying human classification. My encounters at Woodman Point have provided first hand insight into these diverse manifestations. Let us delve deeper into the reasons behind such hauntings, illustrated with specific examples to contextualize this phenomenon.

- Benevolent Spirits: These spirits often retain a sense of peace and goodwill, possibly due to their positive experiences at the location during their lifetime. For instance, spirits of former caretakers or patients who found solace and comfort at places like Woodman Point, may linger on, offering subtle signs of their presence, such as gentle breezes or comforting sensations.
- Unhappy Bound Spirits: Some entities remain tethered to the location due to unresolved trauma or distress suffered during their lives. These spirits may exhibit signs of unrest or sadness, seeking resolution or release. For instance, the lingering spirits of individuals who perished tragically at Woodman Point, such as those afflicted by contagious diseases during the quarantine period, may still grapple with their untimely demise, manifesting as sorrowful apparitions or unsettling disturbances.
- Aggressive Entities: On the opposite end of the spectrum are entities characterised by hostility or aggression. These spirits may harbour resentment or anger, projecting their negative emotions onto the living. For example, spirits of former patients who endured suffering or mistreatment at Woodman Point may manifest as aggressive entities, instigating feelings of fear or unease among visitors.
- Non-Human Entities: Beyond the realm of human spirits lies the enigmatic presence of non-human entities, whose origins and intentions remain elusive. These entities may defy conventional understanding, manifesting in eerie phenomena or unsettling encounters. At Woodman Point, encounters with such entities may evoke a sense of otherworldly dread or unease, challenging our perceptions of the paranormal.

It is important to note, that spirits, at say a place like Woodman Point, may exhibit traits that span multiple categories simultaneously, reflecting the complexity of their experiences and emotions. By understanding these nuanced dynamics, we can better navigate and appreciate the diversity of hauntings that characterize locations like Woodman Point Quarantine Station.

There is lots of speculation as to why a spirit maybe trapped and unable to move from this realm of existence to the other. Some of the common ones are listed as follows:

- The person died as a result of a traumatic event such as murder or their death was untimely and they cannot accept their death.

- Due to unfinished business. This could be any number of things, wishes were not met, words were not spoken, or actions were not taken.

- The spirit may have died suddenly and does not realise that he or she has died. This can often be a case in traumatic very sudden deaths or with child spirits.

- The spirit has a very strong attachment to their living loved ones who are so emotionally distraught, they can't let go. I have seen this happen with child spirits, whose parent's grief is so overwhelming, they stay to try to help them through it.

- The spirit is being kept there by someone or something. This is a book unto itself.

- They cannot rest due to an injustice done to them, that has never been rectified.

- Fear of the other side or judgment

Denial of Death: This often occurs in cases of sudden or traumatic death, such as car accidents or homicides. Spirits may remain tethered to the location where they perished, unable to accept their untimely demise. Instances of spirits haunting crime scenes or places of tragic death, are not uncommon. For example, crime scene cleaning crews, have reported encountering distressed and angry spirits of murder victims, lingering at the site of their demise. These souls are trapped by their refusal to acknowledge the circumstances of their passing, seeking resolution, before they can move on.

Some spirits linger due to unresolved matters or emotional attachments. Take, for instance, this case of a mother who passed away shortly after being diagnosed with cancer, leaving behind two young children. Her ghost remained, unable to accept her death and the separation from her daughters. It took years of intervention from psychics and paranormal experts, to facilitate closure. Eventually, she came to terms with her passing and found peace, yet her enduring love for her family keeps her spirit connected, as she is known to occasionally check in, on her loved ones. She even had a seat at her husband's re marriage.

Sixty-four years ago, on Saturday, April 16th, 1955, the tranquil atmosphere of Midland Town Hall was shattered by a tragic event, that would etch its mark on the town's history. It was around 9:30 am when Daria Mulawa from Bellevue, stepped into the Town Hall, her purpose, to visit the solicitor's office nestled within its walls.

However, fate had a cruel twist in store. Finding the solicitor's office closed, Mrs. Mulawa began her descent down the stairs, only to find herself embroiled in a heated argument with a man. Minutes later, screams pierced the air, drawing horrified onlookers to the scene. They found Mrs. Mulawa collapsed on the staircase landing, a knife lying nearby. Despite efforts to save her, she was pronounced dead shortly after.

The aftermath of this tragedy unfolded swiftly. Mrs. Mulawa's husband was apprehended the same afternoon and charged with the wilful murder of his wife. The details of the crime were chilling—she had been stabbed eleven times in a frenzied and savage assault. The couple was estranged at the time, and Mr. Mulawa would later face imprisonment, for his senseless act of brutality.

Nearly seven decades have passed since that fateful day, yet the echoes of Daria Mulawa's anguish still reverberate within the walls of Midland Town Hall. Witnesses claim to have encountered her spirit; a benevolent but profoundly sorrowful presence, trapped by the tragic circumstances of her death.

During a ghost tour at the Town Hall, I myself captured what I believe, to be an Electronic Voice Phenomenon (EVP) of Daria's screams, and later, her mournful cries. Her spectral presence serves as a poignant reminder that, at times, the victim's spirit lingers long after the crime has been committed—a haunting testament to the enduring impact of tragedy, on the human soul.

Unfinished business: This manifest uniquely in each haunting, dictated by the complexities of the individual's life and death. It can range from relatively simple matters to intricately tangled webs of emotion and circumstance, imbuing the spirit with a myriad of feelings—sadness, anger, contempt, and stubbornness among them. Despite efforts to facilitate resolution, some hauntings persist, their elusive nature defying conventional methods of crossing over.

Commonly, these hauntings centre around unresolved tasks, fractured relationships, or the pursuit of justice or vengeance. Among the most prevalent are those seeking justice that remains elusive—a poignant reminder of the human thirst for closure, even beyond death's threshold. In particular, unsolved murder cases often leave behind spirits yearning to expose the truth, to shine a light on the injustice that robbed them of their lives.

These restless spirits may resort to various means to draw attention to their plight—witnessing events, leaving cryptic messages, or causing disturbances in the physical realm. Their presence serves as a haunting testament to the enduring quest for truth and justice, a reminder that some mysteries may never find resolution, even in death.

There are unending amounts of cases that could be told here of unfinished business hauntings. However, one I find most interesting, is the cases of the Ghosts of Flight 401.

Eastern Airlines Flight 401

The tragic events of Eastern Airlines Flight 401 is one of aviation's most haunting mysteries. Eastern Air Lines Flight 40 was on a scheduled flight from New York JFK to Miami. Shortly before midnight, on December 29th, 1972, the Lockheed L-1011-1 TriStar crashed into the Florida Everglades. Among the deceased were Captain Robert "Bob" Loft, First Officer Albert "Bert" Stockstill, and Flight Engineer Donald "Don" Repo, seasoned aviators whose expertise could not avert the disaster. 99 of the 176 aboard died on impact with two dying later, from their injuries.

During the crash investigation, it was revealed that the flight crew had encountered a landing gear light problem and were preoccupied trying to fix it, when the crash occurred. The Pilots had placed the aircraft into a holding pattern (Auto pilot) while they investigated. Meanwhile, the Flight Engineer, Donald Repo had gone into the electronics bay, beneath the flight deck, to try to ascertain visually the status of the landing gear. The First Officer was trying to replace the bulb on the panel while the captain was flying the aircraft. At some point, Captain Robert Loft, got up to assist his First Officer, where he accidentally pushed on the controls disengaging the autopilot. Neither pilot noticed and with no ground reference and under night-time conditions, the aircraft continued into a gradual descent until it crashed. It was the first Jumbo Jet that ever crashed.

In the aftermath of the crash, rumours began to circulate among airline staff of spectral apparitions haunting the skies aboard other L-1011 aircraft. Witnesses, including survivors of Flight 401, reported chilling encounters with the spirits of Repo and Loft, whose ghostly presences manifested mid-flight, only to vanish inexplicably. These sightings, initially dismissed as mere hearsay, soon became an unsettling reality for those who bore witness.

A flight attendant on a New York to Miami flight (coincidentally, the same route of Flight 401) reportedly opened an overhead locker, to find Captain Lofts face peering out at her. On another flight, a flight attendant is said to have seen flight engineer Don Repos face on the oven door, He was witnessed by two fellow crew members. The face reportedly then said, "Watch out for fire in this plane." On the aircraft's return flight to New York's John

F. Kennedy International Airport, an engine failed and had to be shut down before it caught fire. On returning to the galley, another flight attendant saw an engineer fixing the oven. She later asked the flight engineer later about the oven, and he said that he hadn't fixed it, as it didn't need to be fixed. On later inspection there was a problem detected, that could have caused the oven to malfunction.

On yet another flight Don Repo appeared again sitting in the cockpit, He warned the operating flight crew of a faulty electrical circuit, which was then found and replaced. There were also reports of Bob having been seen doing his pre-flight checks of an aircraft and telling ground staff he'd already completed them. The real pilot was supposedly so unnerved about this, that he cancelled the flight.

Another pilot reportedly heard loud knocks from under the floor beneath him. He opened the trap door to see a vision of Don looking up at him, which then promptly disappeared. He heeded the warning and decided to look further. He purportedly found a problem that could have caused a serious accident, if it had gone undetected.

Loft appeared seated next to passengers, only to have them disappear mid-way through the hapless passenger talking. These sightings continued for years with the airline banning staff from discussing the hauntings or they would lose their job. The sightings were only reported aboard other L-1011s (including, in particular N318EA). These stories speculated that parts of the crashed aircraft were salvaged after the investigation and refitted into other L-1011 aircraft. The hauntings were said to be seen only on the planes that used the spare parts.

On one flight, a captain was asked to check on a passenger traveling in first class who was wearing a pilot's uniform. The senior flight attendant said he seemed dazed and unresponsive when spoken to and was not on the passenger list. The captain recognised him as being none other, than Captain Loft.

Such sightings, while undeniably unsettling, sparked speculation as to the motives behind the apparitions. Some believed Repo's appearances were a desperate attempt to avert tragedy, while Loft's continued presence hinted at a lingering attachment to the aircraft—or perhaps a refusal to accept his own demise.

The airline, however, vehemently denied the existence of such phenomena, attributing the reports to overactive imaginations or stress-induced hallucinations. Yet, the persistence of these sightings, corroborated by multiple witnesses, cast doubt on the official narrative.

In a bid to quell the rumours, the airline purportedly removed all salvaged parts from Flight 401, hoping to exorcise the lingering spirits once and for all. And indeed, with the passage of time and the purported removal of the aircraft's remnants, sightings of Loft, Repo, and their spectral counterparts ceased altogether.

In a documentary series called, "Mysteries at the Museum", a segment was made of the hauntings. A number of now retired airline staff, gave their first-hand accounts. This included an air hostess who was a survivor of the crash and knew the men. Pieces of Flight 401's wreckage can be found in Ed and Lorraine Warren's Occult Museum in Monroe, Connecticut.

But the legacy of Flight 401 lives on—a cautionary tale of the thin veil between the worlds of the living and the dead, where the echoes of tragedy linger long after the wreckage has been cleared. And while sceptics may dismiss the accounts as mere superstition, those who witnessed the ghostly apparitions first hand know that some mysteries defy rational explanation, forever shrouded in the eerie whispers of the unknown.

The Red Barn Murder

In the year 1827, the idyllic English countryside was shattered by a tale of forbidden love turned tragic. Maria Marten and William Corder, a young couple enraptured by the promise of elopement, made plans to rendezvous at the iconic Red Barn near Ipswich. Little did they know that their clandestine affair would end in infamy.

After their fateful meeting, Maria's family received correspondence from Corder, asserting their blissful union and plans for a shared future. However, the tranquillity of these missives was soon shattered by the haunting visions of Maria's stepmother. Troubled by recurring dreams of her stepdaughter's demise at the hands of Corder, she implored her husband to investigate.

Driven by a father's love and mounting suspicion, Maria's father ventured to the Red Barn, where he made a chilling discovery in the grain storage bins—a grim testament to the truth of his wife's nightmares. Beneath the earth, he uncovered the lifeless body of his beloved daughter, a victim of Corder's treachery and deceit.

Public outcry demanded justice, and Corder faced the consequences of his heinous crime in a swift and public execution. The Red Barn, once a symbol of romantic trysts and clandestine meetings, now stood as a grim reminder of the fragility of love and the depths of human depravity. And as the echoes of Maria Marten's tragic fate reverberated through the annals of history, the Red Barn became forever enshrined in infamy—a haunting testament to the enduring power of love, betrayal, and the relentless pursuit of justice.

Ann Walker

The pages of Arthur L. Hayward's "Lives of the Most Remarkable Criminals" bore witness to a chilling tale of spectral justice. the year is 1735, in the dead of night, miller James Graham found himself visited by the ghostly apparition of housekeeper Ann Walker, her ethereal form dripping with the stains of blood and the weight of unresolved injustice.

With a voice laden with sorrow and longing, Ann Walker's spirit revealed the dark truth that had sealed her tragic fate. She confessed to Graham that she had fallen victim to her own kin, a man known only as Mr. Walker, with whom she had become pregnant. In a desperate bid to conceal the scandalous pregnancy, Mr. Walker had conspired with an accomplice, named Mark Sharp, to snuff out Ann's life and bury her remains in the cold earth.

Haunted by the spectre's tormented plea for justice, Graham heeded the call to action. Venturing forth to seek the aid of a Justice of the Peace, he implored the authorities to investigate the truth behind Ann Walker's spectral revelation. True to the ghostly prophecy, the investigators uncovered Ann's lifeless body precisely, where her apparition had indicated, alongside the damning evidence that incriminated both Mr. Walker and Mark Sharp.

Trials ensued, and justice was swift and merciless. In a court of law, both Sharp and Walker were found guilty of the heinous crime that had robbed Ann Walker of her life and her voice. As the gavel fell and the verdict was pronounced, they were sentenced to face the ultimate retribution—their lives forfeit for the blood they had spilled.

Teresita Basa

In the heart of Chicago, the tragic tale of 48 year old Teresita Basa unfolded on the fateful night of February 21ˢᵗ, 1977. Her lifeless body was discovered, amidst the chaos of a raging fire that consumed her apartment. A sinister attempt to conceal the heinous crime that had been committed. She had been stabbed in the chest, the knife still protruding from her naked body when she was found. There was only one clue: a note that read; "Get theatre tickets for A.S." It was unclear whether the initials stood for a name or a company.

Basa, an Immigrant from the Philippines, moved to the United States to pursue a career in music. However, she found her calling in the helping of others, ending up working as a respiratory therapist at Edgewater Hospital. It was here she met Remy Chua, and the ladies became firm friends. Her colleagues described her as intelligent, kind, and unassuming—who lived a quiet life.

Months passed, and the case went cold. That is, until an unexpected turn of events, breathed new life into the investigation.

Four months after her death, Remy Chua, a colleague of Basa's, experienced a phenomenon that defied rational explanation. Awakening from a nap in a trance-like state, Remy spoke with a voice not her own—a voice claiming to be that of Teresita Basa herself. Remy's husband, a doctor at the hospital where the two women worked, was a witness to this, and wrote all of

47

the details down.

The Chua's decided, for fear of looking ridiculous, to keep this strange encounter to themselves. However, the spirit of Teresita Basa was not content to stay silent. With the strange occurrences continuing with more frequency, the Chua's decided they had no alternative, than to go to police with what they knew. This was Especially after Basa spirit, revealed the name of her killer. It was then that Jose Chua decided to contact the lead detective for the case, Joseph Stachula.

We can only imagine what was running through the mind of Detective Stachula when he received the call from Jose that cold August morning. Jose explained the strange events and claimed the "Teresita" spirit, had named Allan Showery, another co-worker, as her assailant.

Jose went onto explain that Showery was an orderly, who also worked at the same hospital. During one of Basa's possessions of Remy's body, she told that Showery came over the night of her murder, to fix her broken TV. But an initially friendly visit, took a turn for the worse, when Showery decided to steal an expensive pearl ring, passed down from the victim's mother. Basa even gave them the phone numbers of those who can help identify the ring and other jewellery, that was still in Showerys possession.

This eerie encounter sparked a renewed sense of urgency in the quest for justice. Homicide investigators delved deeper into the depths of Basa's murder, guided by the otherworldly testimony, provided through Remy's inexplicable trance. Their efforts were well rewarded, when they followed up at Showerys home and came face to face with his girlfriend, Yanka Kamluk. Yanka was caught in possession of the stolen jewellery. The detectives were able to identify the jewellery by calling the number that the spirit of Basa had provided. It was her cousins telephone number back in the Philippines, a detail the Chau's were not aware of. As evidence against Showery mounted, painting a damning portrait of guilt, Showery confessed to Teresita Basas murder.

Ultimately, the truth could no longer be denied. Allan Showery stood exposed as the perpetrator of Basa's senseless murder, his deeds laid bare before the eyes of justice. In a court of law, he faced the consequences of his actions, sentenced to serve 14 years behind bars for the crime. He was, however, paroled after 5 years and was granted parole in 1983. It is unknown what Teresita thought of this, though I would imagine she would not be very pleased, given the lengths she had gone, to have him convicted.

Through the extraordinary conduit of Remy Chua, Basa's voice found its echo in the halls of justice, ensuring that her memory would not be silenced by the flames that sought to consume it.

Elva Zona Heaster Shue the Greenbrier Ghost

On January 23rd, 1897, in Greenbrier County, West Virginia, the tragic tale of Elva Zona Heaster Shue began, when she was found dead in her home. She had met and married her husband, Erasmus Stribbling Trout Shue in October the previous year. Initially presumed a victim of childbirth, like so many women of her time, the truth behind her untimely demise remained shrouded in secrecy. That was until the chilling spectre of her ghost emerged to reveal the horrors of her fate, to her beloved mother. Elvas mother, Mary Jane Heaster, was suspicious of the claim that her daughter had died in childbirth, a claim Erasmus perpetuated. Mary had no way of proving otherwise, so continued on with her life and grief. Then Mary started having visions and claimed that her daughter's ghost, visited her in the night and told her that her husband had murdered her. Mary Heaster approached a local prosecutor, John Alfred Preston, and spent several hours in his office, refusing to leave until he agreed to reopen the matter of her daughter's death. John Preston agreed and had Elvas body exhumed. This decision was based more on the fact the medical examiner had told him that there had been no autopsy performed, and John believed the matter would be resolved if an autopsy was to take place.

Zona's body was examined on February 22nd, 1897, in the local one-room schoolhouse. The autopsy lasted three hours and found that Zona's neck had been broken in two places and that there was bruising, consistent with hand marks, visible around her neck.

Following an autopsy, Erasmus Shue was arrested and charged with the murder of his wife. While awaiting trial, more information about his past came to light. He had been married twice before: his first marriage had ended in divorce, with his wife accusing him of great cruelty; his second wife had died under mysterious circumstances less than a year after they were married.

Although the prosecution tried to avoid the ghost story, Shue's lawyer questioned Mary Heaster extensively about her daughter's visits. The tactic backfired when Mrs. Heaster would not waver in her account, despite intense questioning. As the defence had introduced the issue, the judge found it difficult to instruct the jury to disregard the story of the ghost, and many people in the community believed it.

He was later found guilty of her murder and sentenced to life in prison. Erasmus avoided lynching after the trial, when the sheriff, managed to break up the crowed who had come for him.

Victims of Injustice: This is a type of haunting where, ghosts are believed to be trapped and bound to the very places and people associated with the wrong, committed against them. These could be victims of a miscarriage of justice by authorities desperate to clear their names. Possibly those involved in unresolved murders, wrongful executions, or tragic deaths, where the true perpetrator was never caught. Here are a few notable examples.

Anne Boleyn

The most famous ghost of England's prior Queens, is that of Anne Boleyn. Accused of Incest and Adultery and executed, of which she was most certainly innocent, there are many sightings of her, often headless. Some 340 years after her execution, a soldier reported seeing a light burning in the closed chapel where she is buried. After climbing to a window to look within, the soldier is said to have seen a procession of knights and ladies, led by a headless Anne Boleyn herself.

The Ghost of Roger Casement:

Roger Casement was an Irish diplomat and nationalist who was executed for treason against the British Crown in 1916. This was notably for his role in the Easter Rising. The Easter Rising in a nutshell, was an armed uprising, organised by a seven-man Military Council of the Irish Republican Brotherhood. (IRB) The Rising began Easter Monday on 24 April 1916, and lasted for six days. The IRB was dedicated to the establishment of an "independent democratic republic" between 1858 and 1924. Casement was a humanitarian, he was and is, honoured as the father of human rights investigations. This was after he did an investigation into abuses of the rubber industry in Peru, among other notable achievements. However, in 1916 he set sail for Germany, to broker a deal that would have Germany provide Irish nationalists, with guns. and the agreement was the nationalists would in turn, rise up against the English. He was also known during this time, to have been involved with German plans for India to gain independence from British rule. In April 1916, Germany offered the Irish 20,000 rifles, ten machine guns and accompanying ammunition, but no German officers; it was a fraction of the quantity Casement had requested. The Royal Navey intercepted the arms before they ever reached the shores of Ireland. The weapons were not meant to land on Irish shores before the planned easter rising occurred. The shipment was intercepted by the British before landing. The IRB men that were to unload the arms, drove off a pier and drowned, rather than be arrested.

Casement, who believed the Germans were toying with him, had sent a man by the name of John McGoey to reach Ireland, to stop the Easter Rising, which he believed, would fail without the appropriate amount of arms. His instruction was to let the IRB know he wanted the arms to be distributed, but not used, until a later date. John McGoey, however, did not fulfil this promise, abandoning the Nationalist cause. In the early hours of April 21st, 1916, three days before the rising began, a German submarine, put Casement and two companions ashore in County Kerry –Casement Suffering from a recurrence of the malaria he had picked up previously, was too weak to keep up with his friends, and was discovered by The Royal Irish Constabulary. When three pistols were discovered hidden nearby, the RIC arrested Casement on a charge of illegally bringing weapons into the country. He was not rescued by the IRB, as would have been expected, because there was an order that no shots were to be fired on Irish soil, before the uprising began. His trial started on 26 June 1916. Casement's trial was controversial, with allegations of forgery and tampering with evidence. The British Government were accused of tactics aimed at influencing public opinion against him, so no one would campaign for his reprieve. This involved releasing diary's they claimed were his, explicitly talking about his homosexual relationships, something considered highly deviant at the time. He was hanged August 3rd, 1916 aged 51. Poignantly, his last 'words' were one; "Ireland".

Controversy continued, as he was buried, against his wishes, near to where he was hanged at Pentonville prison. Casement wanted to be buried in Country Antrim, Northern Ireland. Subsequent to this, Prime Ministers had all rejected requests to have his remains returned to Ireland. In 1965 that request was finally granted, but the then prime minister, only agreed on condition that they would not be buried in Northern Ireland, for fear of Catholic celebrations and Protestant reactions. Some believe his ghost lingers, seeking vindication for his actions and a recognition of his efforts for Irish independence. His placement of his remains and his legacy were all tarnished after his death, and this may be the reason he has been seen. The poet Yates, a long-time friend, who could not forgive what he considered treason, wrote a poem called, "The Ghost of Roger Casement', which may have contributed to the many reported ghost sightings, at Pentonville and beyond.

The Ghost of Ethel Rosenberg:
Ethel Rosenberg was executed in 1953 along with her husband Julius Rosenberg, after being convicted of espionage, for passing atomic secrets to the Soviet Union, during the Cold War. They died by electric chair at Sing Sing two years later. They became the first civilians in U.S. history, to be executed for wartime spying. They left behind two young sons. Many believe Ethel was wrongly convicted, and her ghost is said to haunt various locations, including Sing Sing Correctional Facility, where she was executed. Ethel's execution was botched. She was removed from the electric chair after three charges, only for it to be discovered her heart was still beating, so, gruesomely, she had to be strapped back into it. There was international outrage at her death.

The Ghost of James Hanratty:

James Hanratty was executed in 1962 for the A6 murder, he was one of the final 8 to be executed before the abolishment of capital punishment. He was hanged on 4 April 1962 at Bedford Jail. A notorious case in British criminal history, Hanratty was accused of the murder of scientist Michael Gregsten, who was shot to death in his car on the A6 roadway. Gregsten's girlfriend, Valarie Storie, was raped, shot 5 times but survived, all be it, paralysed from the waist down. The initial prime suspects were Hanratty, a petty criminal, and Peter Louis Alphon, an eccentric drifter. In police line-ups, Storie did not recognise Alphon, but eventually identified Hanratty. However, doubts about his guilt have persisted over the years, with claims of police corruption, mishandling of evidence, and potential alibis that were not properly considered. Some believe Hanratty's ghost seeks justice for being wrongfully convicted. As a side note to this story, in 2002, a DNA test conclusively proved his guilt. Hanratty was considered a psychopath and a pathological liar. Although there are those who still believe his innocence, his ghost has been seen at the place he was hanged and at the site of, what we now know, were his crimes.

The Ghost of Cameron Todd Willingham:

Cameron Todd Willingham was executed in Texas on February 17th, 2004, for the arson murders of his three daughters. However, serious questions have been raised about the evidence used to convict him, with forensic experts disputing the arson investigation, that led to his conviction. An August 2009 Chicago Tribune investigative article concluded, "Over the past five years, the Willingham case has been reviewed by nine of the nation's top fire scientists — first for the Tribune, then for the Innocence Project, and now for the commission. All concluded that the original investigators relied on outdated theories and folklore, to justify the determination of arson. Many believe Willingham was innocent, and his ghost is said to haunt seeking exoneration. In this case, he was likely innocent of this crime. He has been seen at the site of the arson, at the site of his execution and at the prison he was held at. Cameron (Todd) Willingham's rant was so obscene towards his ex-wife, and a known victim of his abuse, that the warden started the execution earlier to make him stop. Michelle Lyons, who wrote a book called Death Row: The Final Minutes, told the Mirror: "His last statement was the worst that I had ever seen. It was vulgar, it was hateful. His ex-wife was watching from the witness room, and I was told later by the chaplaincy that she had come to witness, not on his behalf but as one of the victims. He directed so much vitriol towards her, that the warden actually started the execution as he was talking, to make him stop."

The Ghost of Lady Jane Grey:

Lady Jane Grey, also known as the "Nine Days' Queen," was briefly proclaimed Queen of England in 1553, following the death of King Edward VI. However, she was overthrown by forces loyal to Mary I, and ultimately executed for treason. Many believe Lady Jane Grey was an innocent pawn in the power struggles of her time and that her execution was unjust. Reports of her ghost haunting the battlements of The Tower of London, where she was imprisoned and executed, suggest a lingering desire for justice. She was, incidentally, executed 428 years prior to the very day, I was born, at a private execution, on 12 February 1554.

The Ghost of Arbella Stuart:

Arabella Stuart was a cousin of King James I of England and a claimant to the English throne. She became embroiled in various plots and intrigues against the crown. Arbella was imprisoned by James I for marrying William Seymour, nephew of Lady Jane Grey, without Royal consent. Seeing this match as a possible threat to his throne, James placed Arbella under arrest at the Tower, where she either refused to eat or was purposefully starved. Arbella's ghost is thought to stalk the Queen's House. Her death was widely believed to be the result of foul play, orchestrated by the authorities. Reports of her ghost haunting the Tower and other locations associated with her life and death, suggest a quest for justice.

The Tower of London boasts about 13 ghosts, many of whom would fit under this category. Other notable ghosts are that of Henry VI, imprisoned in the Wakefield Tower of the Tower of London. Henry VI was murdered at the altar in the King's Private Chapel in 1471. Henry's ghost is believed to haunt the Wakefield Tower, appearing at the stroke of midnight, the time he died. The ghost of a bear, believed to be from the time of Henry III, who housed his menagerie of wild animals at the Tower of London, has been seen. The ghost of a bear is said to appear from behind the door of The Jewel Room, perhaps a spectral guard to The Crown Jewels? The ghost of a black bear is also reported to have appeared near the Martin Tower in 1816. Sir Walter Raleigh ghost has been seen often, by visitors and workers alike. Sent to the Tower no less than three times and eventually executed. Explorer Sir Walter Raleigh was imprisoned by both Elizabeth I and James I. He spent over 13 years in the Bloody Tower, during one confinement, and attempted suicide. Sir Walter Raleigh's last imprisonment, in the Beauchamp Tower, took place in 1603, before he was beheaded outside the Palace of Westminster. The faceless young woman, origins unknown, last appeared in 1957. The Spectre appeared to Welsh Guardsman Johns, while he was on sentry duty at the Salt Tower. He encountered a shapeless form with the face of a young woman, perhaps one of the many women, who suffered a terrible fate at the Tower of London. The botched execution of Margaret Pole, Countess of Salisbury, took place on Tower Green, which lies to the west of the White Tower. Margaret Pole was 67 at the time of her death. She was brought to the scaffold by Henry VIII for the crime of being the mother of Cardinal Pole. Cardinal Pole's crime was opposing Henry's self-created position, as Supreme Head of the Church of England. Eyewitnesses say the executioner on that fateful day, on May 27th, 1541, was a "wretched and blundering youth" who, unable to perform a clean execution with his axe, instead hacked at Margaret Pole's head and shoulders, as she ran to get away from him. her eternal scream echoes through the towers today.

In 1864, Captain J.D. Dundas observed a Yeoman attempting to charge a 'whitish, female figure' with his bayonet. Chillingly, this apparition appeared in the courtyard where Anne Boleyn was beheaded. If you visit the Tower of London, listen out for the sound of sandals slapping against the stone floors, reported to be from the steps of a ghostly monk.

The most poignant of all the spirits at the tower, are children. On the death of Edward IV, Edward's young son, 12-year-old Edward became King Edward V, under the protection of his uncle, the Duke of Gloucester. Wanting to take the crown himself, the Duke of Gloucester imprisoned Edward, and his young brother Richard, in the Tower of London. Their mother, Elizabeth Woodville took sanctuary at Westminster Abbey. After declaring young Edward illegitimate, the Duke of Gloucester became King Richard III. Edward and Richard were never seen again, believed to be murdered at the order of their uncle. There are reports of the sight of two boys playing and crying that occur at the Tower.

Vengeful spirits are the next on my list, of those who have unfinished business. They may seek vengeance against those who have wronged them or disturbed them. They often haunt and torment their victims inflicting as much harm as possible. This kind of haunting is a favourite in literature. In Shakespeare, Lady Macbeth and Hamlet were not immune to the vengeful ghosts of those they had wronged. In Edger Allen Poe's poem "The Tell Tale Heart", and unnamed narrator is haunted by the sounds of a beating heart, belonging to the man he has killed. One of my personal favourites is Ambrosios "The Monk", a virtuous monk, is seduced by the devil, and commits a series of heinous crimes, including murder. As the monks' sins escalate, he becomes haunted by the spectre of the victims he has wronged. Their vengeful spirits torment him, until his eventual damnation.

The Spanish Tragedy, is a tragedy written by the Elizabethan writer Thomas Kyd, between 1582 and 1592. In it, the protagonist, who has his death orchestrated by a jealous love rival, enlists the assistance of Revenge personified. He enlists this God of the underworld, to bring vengeance on all those who are guilty. Funny story, this was a play I studied in high school, that I went to see at the Shakespearian theatre in England, when it was based in Stratford. Watching from the second floor I forgot that this God, Revenge, observes the happenings from above. Suddenly from the dark, a loud bellowing voice cried out, and looking up, a large man in a black, death like Robe appeared. I received such a fright, I nearly toppled over the balcony. The actor actually grabbed me while still reciting his lines. He apologised profusely after the show, but its thanks to him, I am not in this book, haunting the Shakespearean theatre and those that attend!

As in Literature, in life, there are many cases where vengeful spirits either attack the innocent or target the guilty.

We cannot go through this section and not delve into one of the most famous cases in modern history, of a spirit seeking vengeance. It is also a case that some believe, is the only known case, of a spirit/entity deliberately killing its victim.

Though interestingly, between 1814 and 1897 in England, there were 12 deaths the coroner attributed to Ghosts. These people were literally scared to death by various apparitions, they saw at the time of the death or death occurred shortly after their encounters!

The case of this murderous spirit/entity, is known by most who are familiar with the paranormal. A replica of the house, the haunting allegedly occurred in, can still be viewed and visited today. A plaque marks the location where the long gone home stood, however, the entity is still purported to live in a cave on the property. It is known as the Bell Witch Haunting of Adams, in Tennessee. It is a case that has been subject of many tv programmes and books. If we take the story at face value, what type of haunting this was, is highly debated today.

The Bell Witch Haunting (1817-1821):

The haunting took place in Adams, Tennessee, USA, and is one of the most famous ghost stories told today. It is so famous, that it has now become local folklore.

John Bell Sr was born in 1750 and married Lucy Williams in 1782. Lucy was only 12 when they married, while John Bell senior was 32. Not unusual for the time. They had a successful farm when they lived in North Carolina and went on to have six children: Jessie, Elizabeth, known as Betsie, Richard, John Jr, Drewry Zadok, Esther and Benjamin. Little Benjamin died as a young child so was not part of this story. It is around this time that John Sr decided to move his family to Tennessee. They settled on a farm next to that of an eccentric woman named Katie Batts. Kate was the main breadwinner for her family since her husband was paralysed in a farm accident. Kate tended to cause a lot of trouble in the area. She was described as confronting, argumentative, belligerent, and difficult. Many residents of the area believed Kate to be a witch, as she had a habit of begging every woman she met for a pin. At this time there was a very real fear of witches, and many believed that giving a witch a pin, would give her magical control over you. Kate and John Bell were known to argue and had once become violent during a row over a land dispute. Kate believed the land had been stolen from her. This will become significant later on.

Around 1817, John and Elizabeth 'Betsey' Bell, became the main target of an entity that tormented the family. The entity is referred to as the Bell Witch or Kate Batts witch. The family referred to the entity as Kate, after the entity claimed at one point, to be, "Old Kate Batts' witch." The Entity continued to respond favourably and even answered to the name Katie during the haunting. There was a suspicion, which Kate Batt denied, that this entity had been summoned by her, to get back at John Bell Sr, over the land dispute. The haunting involved physical attacks on Betsey, voices, poltergeist phenomena and anything you could associate with a hunting. It culminated in the apparent Murder of John Bell Sr. Interestingly the voice of the witch could be heard with normal hearing, by anyone present at the bells homestead and even the local church.

It all started when John Bell Sr was tending his farm and saw what he believed, to be a creature that resembled a large black dog. This dog was much larger than a normal domestic dog and disappeared when he started shooting at it. Not long afterwards, his son, Drewry noticed a bird, of 'extraordinary' size, observing him before flying off. Next his daughter Betsey was said to have started seeing the form a young girl, in a green dress, watching her ominously. when approached the girl would then disappear. Household staff and slaves of the family, started reporting being followed by a large black dog like creature, when they ventured out from the home. One slave, named Dean, after encountering the witch, began carrying around a "witch ball", made by his wife, to protect him from harm.

This soon progressed to activity within and around the home. Knockings, scratching, sounds of chains being pulled along their floor, sounds of dogs fighting and stones being thrown at the property was next, followed by sheets being pulled off the children while they were sleeping.

Next came an increase in physical assaults, aimed at the children, however, Betsey became the main target of the witch. Scratches and burn like marks appeared and the children's hair would be pulled. Betsey was slapped, pinched, and would wake to pins protruding out of her body. John Bell Sr started to lose the ability to talk, with his jaw becoming paralysed and swollen, with no known cause.

In desperation they turned to a family friend and soon word of the haunting spread. People flocked to the home wanting to experience the spirit themselves. It is now that the story takes an unusual turn and one that is a rarity today. 'it', began to speak to the people who were there. The disembodied voice was heard by clergymen, family, friends, and neighbours.

The entity, when asked who it was, gave multiple accounts of why it was there. This was an intelligent haunting, that would often debate religion and other issues of the day. At one point, the witch, was able to recite word for word, two sermons that had occurred at the same time, 13 miles apart from each other. It also started telling anyone who would listen, things that had occurred in other households. When asked what it was, by a priest, the witch replied, "I am a Spirit; I once was very happy, but I have been disturbed and made unhappy."

The Bell Witch's harassment continued for years, even causing Betsey to call off her engagement to a family friend, as the Bell Witch took a disliking to her chosen fiancé. Most of the witch's abuse was aimed at John Sr, who seemed to be the main target of the Witch's rage.

Lucy Bell and John Jr, were the only members of the family left relatively unharmed. Lucy was proclaimed by the witch to be "the most perfect woman living," and if John would raise his voice to Lucy, he would get the full wrath of the entity for his troubles. The witch showed an affection and level of compassion toward Lucy, even singing to her while she was ill. John Jr. had long intense conversations, usually around religion, with the witch, and she mainly left him alone.

Neighbours and visitors were not immune from the anger of the witch either and anyone who tried to banish it, was sent away frightened and humiliated.

Central to the goals of the Bell Witch was the death of John Bell Sr. The Witch referred to him as "Old Jack Bell" and was relentless in her torment of him. He was blasted with curses, threats, and promises of serious physical harm.

After years of abuse, John Bell Sr became ill and bedridden. Even as the patriarch of the family lay dying, the entity would torment and mock him, right until he took his last breath.

John Jr had been taking care of his ill father and one day came to give him his medicine as was usual. There were two bottles of medicine that has been prescribed by a doctor. Instead, John Jr found a bottle of medicine that was not there previously, and the medicine that was there, gone. The unknown bottle was one third full of a dark, smoky liquid, of unknown origin. The voice of Witch suddenly spoke. "It's useless for you to try to relieve Old Jack – I have got him this time; he will never get up from that bed again!" When asked about the bottle of medicine, she claimed she had "gave old Jack a big dose of it last night, while he was fast asleep, which fixed him." Jack Jr immediately threw the contents of the bottle into the fire, which erupted into a large bright blue blaze. John Bell Sr, surrounded by his family, died shortly thereafter. When John Bell died on December 20th, 1820, the family blamed the Bell Witch for his death. This is mainly because the entity was vocally very pleased with John's demise and took full credit for his death.

The Bell Witch was not heard of for a while, until the funeral, disrupting the service with singing of old drinking songs. After the death of John Bell Sr, the haunting abated and the torment of the family eventually ceased.

The spirit of the Bell witch claimed to be seeking justice for the wrongs done to her and remains a prominent example of a vengeful spirit seeking retribution. However, there is a lot of debate as to the nature of this haunting. Was it a spirit? Or was it something much darker in nature? My thoughts on the matter are this. If this is indeed an accurate account, we are not dealing with a human spirit. It is much more likely; it is something that has a much darker origin. The interaction suggests something intelligent, but the manifestations are more commonly found in non-human hauntings.

Kate Batts would outlive John, dying 22 years late in 1842. The Bell Witch, still commonly referred to as 'Kate', is said to remain on the Bell property today. It is said the entity resides in a cave, on the northern side of the property. Paranormal investigators and visitors go to the site of the original house, each year, trying to contact the Bell Witch. Why? is anybody's guess!

St Valentines Day Massacre Victims

The famous gangster Al Capone, claimed that the victims of the Saint Valentine's Massacre, (widely believed to have been orchestrated by Capone), would haunt him in his cells at night. He would be heard to screaming out for them to leave him alone. Even asking the warden to make them leave or call a priest. Interestingly Al Capone is also said to haunt a number of places including Alcatraz.

Ed Gein:

Ed Gein, often cited as one of America's most infamous killers, confessed to the murders of two women in Wisconsin during the 1950s. Gein, however, was also known for his macabre behaviour of grave robbing then crafting items from his victims. Following his arrest, Gein reportedly claimed to hear the voices of his victims and expressed remorse for his actions, in the hope they would stop tormenting him. His case inspired numerous horror films, including "Psycho" and "The Texas Chain Saw Massacre."

John Wayne Gacy:

John Wayne Gacy, also known as the "Killer Clown," was convicted of the murder of at least 33 teenage boys and young men in the 1970s. Gacy, a respected member of his community and a successful businessman, often lured his victims to his home under the guise of offering them work or money. Following his arrest and imprisonment, Gacy claimed to be haunted by his victims, experiencing vivid nightmares and hallucinations of them surrounding him. He expressed a fear of death due to his victims waiting for him.

David Berkowitz, "Son of Sam":

David Berkowitz, terrorized New York City in the mid-1970s with a series of shootings that left six people dead, and several others wounded. Berkowitz, who claimed to be following the orders of a demon named "Sam," later expressed remorse for his crimes and claimed to have found religion while in prison. He reportedly spoke of being haunted by the spirits of his victims, who would come to him at night. He allegedly sought forgiveness through his newfound faith.

Jeffrey Dahmer:

Jeffrey Dahmer, also known as the "Milwaukee Cannibal," was responsible for the murder, and dismemberment of at least 17 men and boys between 1978 and 1991. Dahmer's crimes shocked the world with their brutality and depravity. Following his arrest, Dahmer expressed remorse for his actions and claimed to be haunted by his victims' faces, often experiencing nightmares and hallucinations of them in his cell at night.

It remains uncertain whether these instances represent primarily psychological responses to horror, rather than actual spirits haunting their perpetrators. These individuals typically lack genuine remorse. While they claim to be haunted by their victims, an investigation into such claims would likely reveal psychological issues, rather than paranormal occurrences. For instance, Al Capone, afflicted with syphilis, experienced deterioration in brain tissue, leading him to genuinely believe he encountered his victims, a fact he communicated to several wardens. The interpretation of similar experiences by others, as literal hauntings versus figurative interpretations, is subject to debate.

War victims are another one to add to this list. They may seek justice for the atrocities that were perpetrated against them. They can haunt battlefields, locations, and monuments. There are even stories of slaves haunting the decedents of their oppressors. One can only assume it is to make sure that the sins of the past are not repeated.

Gettysburg Battlefield in Pennsylvania, USA

Gettysburg was the site of one of the bloodiest battles of the American Civil War, resulting in tens of thousands of casualties. Visitors to the battlefield have reported numerous paranormal encounters, including sightings of ghostly soldiers in uniform, visions of injured soldiers calling to them for help, apparently aware of their presence. In the nearby adjacent area, known as the Triangular Field, there have been dozens of anecdotal reports, from reliable witnesses, who claimed unexplained malfunction of cameras, recorders, and electronic equipment specific to that area. A especially high concentration of ghostly sightings and strange experiences, seems to centre on the battlefield site known as the Devil's Den and its surrounding. The ghosts of Gettysburg seem drawn to this place, and it is speculated this is an area where a portal exists. Devils den is a famous rock formation, an elevated outcropping of haphazard boulders It served as a Confederate sniper's nest for much of the battle and was the site of particularly vicious fighting.

Initial ghost sightings began in the area shortly after the battle and have been a regular occurrence ever since. Spectral soldiers have been spotted among the rocks by many visitors at varying times of the day, and witnesses have reported hearing unexplained battle sounds echoing, in otherwise quiet moments.

Several photographers, at different times, have captured the fleeting image of one ghost soldier. He appears as an unkempt, long-haired figure, shoeless, in ripped clothing, wearing a wide brimmed hat. In some cases, it has been reported that the spirit actually spoke aloud to the witness, before suddenly vanishing without a trace. He is believed to be an intelligent spirit, bound to the area where he was killed.

There are also reports of a ghostly cavalryman on horseback who appears in the area, only to vanish soon after; as well as numerous reports of phantom sounds; gunfire, shouting voices of anguish. Dozens of photographs exist today, in public and private collections, that are alleged to be evidence of supernatural activity in the area.

There are multiple other spirits that linger from the time of the battle. The "Lady in White", is another famous Gettysburg spirit, known for her ethereal presence and sorrowful demeanour. She roams the battlefield in a flowing white dress. Witnesses describe her as appearing lost and forlorn, her face etched with sadness. Some believe she is the ghost of a woman who lost her beloved, others a mother who lost her son. Forever searching for him among the dead, that littered the battlefield.

The Jennie Wade House, has been featured on television programs such as "Civil War Ghosts," and is widely reputed to be an extremely haunted. It is the location where Mary Virginia "Jennie" Wade, the only civilian casualty of the Battle of Gettysburg, was shot and killed. Jennie was 20 years of age when she died during the battle. Her life came to a sudden and tragic end, when a stray bullet from the battle outside, pierced a wooden door, and shooting through the kitchen where she stood. The bullet struck Jennie in the heart, and she died shortly afterwards.

In the years since the battle, visitors to the house have reported hearing strange unexplained movements, unanswered voices, and the fearful cries of the spirits at various places in the house.

The Sachs Covered Bridge on Water Works Road, is reputed to be one of the most haunted places in all of Gettysburg. It is a place paranormal investigator have investigated many times. The wandering spirits of three hanged Confederate deserters are believed to haunt the picturesque bridge. reported paranormal experiences on the bridge include the smell of cigar smoke, the sound of ghostly cannons fired in the distance, or the sensation of suddenly feeling a tap on the shoulder or a hand on the back, only to turn around, to find no one is there.

Perhaps one of the saddest of these war era victims, is the amount of spirits that have been reported from the atomic attacks in Japan, on the 6th and 9th of August, 1945.

The Ghosts of Hiroshima and Nagasaki:

The atomic bombings of Hiroshima and Nagasaki during World War II resulted in the deaths of hundreds of thousands of people, most of whom were innocent civilians. The precise number of total casualties as a result of the bomb is impossible to reckon, but estimates range from 90,000 to 166,000, with about half the deaths—45,000 to 83,000—occurring on the first day. In both cities, there are reports of ghostly apparitions and paranormal phenomena associated with the sites of the bombings. Some survivors and visitors to these cities have reported encountering the spirits of those who died in the bombings, their presence a haunting reminder of the devastation people can inflict on one another. These sightings continue today. A physical therapist at a hospital in Hiroshima said herself, and one of her nurse co-workers at the hospital, always take August 6th (the day of the bomb) off and never takes a step out of the house. They claim to see all the disfigured ghosts wandering by the river and surrounding areas. Many died of their burns before they reached safety, and many died of radiation poisoning in the days and weeks that followed. By any measure, this is a hellish quantity of sudden and horrific deaths. In the Japanese context, this also means a vast number are restless ghosts, because they were denied the Buddhist funerary rites. The rites are required for a smooth passage to the next world.

Victims of Abuse or Exploitation: People who suffered abuse, exploitation, or discrimination during their lives may haunt the institutions they belonged to. The other kind of haunting is where they haunt the people specifically responsible for their suffering. They may aim to expose systemic injustices, protect others from similar harm, or simply find closure for the pain they endured. We find these kinds of spirits in asylums, foster homes and

61

other institutions that usually had a hidden history of abuse. There are many of these spirits at

These ghosts seek justice in various forms, from exposing the truth to exacting revenge on those that did them harm. They are often driven by a profound sense of injustice that binds them here in the earthly real.

The Ghosts of Sweatshop Workers:

In some cases, reports of ghostly activity are associated with locations where workers faced exploitation and abuse, such as sweatshops and factories. For example, in cities like New York City, where sweatshops were once prevalent, there are tales of ghostly apparitions and eerie occurrences in abandoned factories and tenement buildings. These stories serve as reminders of the hardships faced by workers, particularly immigrants and marginalized groups, who toiled under harsh conditions, in pursuit of meagre wages.

The Old Slave House:

Located in Gallatin County, Illinois, the Old Slave House, also known as the Crenshaw House, is a historic site that was once used as a station, on the Underground Railroad. However, the house also has a dark history of exploitation and abuse, as it was allegedly used by its owner, John Crenshaw, to kidnap and imprison free Black individuals, whom he would then sell into slavery. Visitors to the house have reported experiencing paranormal activity, including sightings of ghostly figures and strange noises, believed to be the spirits of those who suffered within its walls.

The spirit is kept here by something or someone else – Usually this occurs in places of torment like asylums, prisons and institutions. Occasionally there is a strong negative human spirit that refuses to allow others to leave, but mostly they are non-human spirits that can trap a human spirit at a location.

Fear of Judgement

One common obstacle preventing human spirits from crossing over is the fear of judgment awaiting them on the other side. This fear can be deeply rooted in their consciousness, particularly if they feel guilt or remorse for actions they committed during their lifetime. Such concerns are often intertwined with strong religious beliefs that emphasise the concept of retribution for one's wrongdoings. These spirits may dread facing judgment for specific acts or behaviours they consider morally questionable, even if others perceive them as mundane or insignificant.

For instance, I once encountered a ghost who expressed a profound fear of judgment, and this was the reason she was bound. She had died in the

1960s and when questioned about her reluctance to move on, fear of punishment was her response. Through a spirit box and voice recording, she conveyed a single word over five times, in the evening. That word was "abortion." In another experience that we had at a location in Tamworth, near Birmingham, the male spirit was reluctant to move on because of the way he had treated his family in life. This highlights how individual perceptions of morality can vary greatly, influenced by personal experiences, cultural norms, and societal values.

In addition to fear of judgment, some spirits may hesitate to transition to the afterlife, due to a general apprehension about what lies beyond. The unknown nature of the next life can evoke uncertainty and a reluctance to take the leap into the unknown.

Fortunately, many hauntings stemming from these fears can be resolved with time, reassurance and assistance. Through communication and understanding, spirits can often find peace and transition to the next phase of existence, free from the burdens that once held them back.

EARTHBOUND SPIRITS THAT CHOOSE THE STAY

While certain spirits may find themselves bound by unresolved issues or the traumatic circumstances of their demise, others make a conscious decision to linger on our earthly plain. Below are a few scenarios illustrating why spirits might opt to remain tethered to the earthly realm, by choice.

Some spirits harbour an enduring affection for the homes they once inhabited, clinging to cherished memories and reluctant to depart. The Christmas Shop in Toodyay, a place we are due to do a private investigation of soon, has a female resident spirit that fits this category.

Among the most compelling reasons encountered is the desire to remain close to their living family members. Spirits may feel a profound sense of duty towards their loved ones, seeking to provide solace, guidance, or protection, even beyond the apparent limitation of death.

Certain spirits form strong bonds with particular places, objects, or belongings, imbued with sentimental significance. Preferring the comfort of familiar surroundings, they opt to linger, rather than relinquish these ties and venture into the unknown.

An illustrative case hails from my hometown of Birmingham, where a beloved theatre serves as a poignant example. Having frequented this venue with my family on numerous occasions, I've witnessed first-hand how the allure of such places, can captivate both the living and the departed.

Birmingham Alexandra Theatre

There are a number of spirits that inhabit the lovely Alexandra Theatre in Birmingham, England. This is the theatre of my childhood, where my parents would take my sister and I, to the traditional Christmas pantomime or some other equally captivating show. A tradition my sister and I now do with our daughters. It is a warm and inviting place and one filled with good memories for those that know it. The most well known and happiest of the spirits there, is that of Leon Salberg. Leon, known as the pantomime king of England, during his day, managed the theatre for over twenty five years. After having a conversation of an upcoming pantomime Leon went up to his office and collapsed and died, of a suspected heart attack, in September 1937. He was found shortly afterwards. Very well loved by staff, performers, and patrons alike, he was buried in Witton Cemetery. Not long after his death, people who knew him, continued to see and interact with him. He is described in death as warm, friendly, and helpful. In an investigation many years ago, he was asked if he needed help to move on. his response was, "No!" as he was "happy," where he was.

I will resist the temptation to write down the many jokes and puns that are presently going through my mind, regarding theatre ghosts and final curtain calls. I will, however, just leave you with one of the most notable quotes, by renowned theatre director Peter Brook, which I find particularly apt. He famously said, "The show must go on. But why? – Sometimes there is no 'why' for a haunting, sometimes it is just simply because they want to. And that is as good a way to end a show as any.

RENOVATION HAUNTINGS

Both commercial and residential properties are susceptible to a particular type of haunting, They are intelligent hauntings, often triggered by renovations initiated by the property owners. The intensity of such occurrences can be profound, driving workers away in fear and halting construction altogether. Suddenly emerging paranormal activity, previously absent, becomes a significant obstacle.

When investigating such phenomena, thorough research into the property's history is crucial to understanding the root cause of the haunting. Typically, these are instances of intelligent hauntings, where the spirits, usually dormant, become agitated by alterations to their former domain. Just as living occupants would feel disconcerted by strangers rearranging their home, deceased owners may react with indignation to changes, like the removal of a fireplace they once crafted.

In cases where the unrest stems from the deceased owners' dissatisfaction, investigators may attempt negotiation. It is imperative to communicate to the spirits that the property now belongs to the living and that they must either accept this reality or be guided onwards. While some occupants choose to coexist peacefully with the spirits, others assert their ownership unequivocally.

For those moving into a property previously inhabited by a deceased owner, understanding, and addressing these dynamics becomes essential.

Such hauntings, can also be triggered by disturbances to a resting place or the inadvertent discovery of long-forgotten human remains. Disturbing these remains can often upset the spirits attached to them.

Here are some cases of hauntings caused by renovations to consider.

George
Green Man public house, Derby
After renovations where several Saxon bodies were discovered and disturbed beneath the pub, there was a brief intense paranormal outbreak. The landlord encountered a full-bodied figure he believed to be Saxon based on the clothes, standing by the pub's piano. This piano was also moved by unseen hands on several occasions. Other activity included a pan containing food flew off the bench and across the floor, which was witnessed by around 30 patrons, who quickly fled. He is affectionately known as George, a very un-Saxon name which might be why he gets irritated. Lights would switch on and off by themselves and banging and thumps at night ensured the landlord got very little sleep. The activity stopped when there was a service for the remains and an apology from the landlord for disturbing them. George, however, remains at the pub to this day.

The Sultan Hotel Incident:
In 1997, a major renovation project was underway at the Sultan Hotel in Jakarta, Indonesia. During the renovation, workers discovered the remains of a Dutch woman buried under the hotel's foundation. Legend has it that the woman had been involved in a romantic affair and committed suicide when her lover abandoned her. A story I find a little difficult to believe, because, even the most physical of spirits, are unlikely to bury themselves in the foundations of a building! Following the discovery, workers and hotel staff reported experiencing paranormal activity, including sightings of the woman's ghost and unexplained disturbances. Some attributed the disturbances to the restless spirit of the woman seeking justice or vengeance for her tragic fate.

POSITIVE EARTHBOUND SPIRITS

In 2008, I found myself standing in a circle among a group of people, embarking on my inaugural ghost tour of Woodman Point Quarantine

Station, Perth Western Australia. Engaged in a protection ritual, we delved into exercises aimed at heightening our collective vibrations and intentions—an entirely novel experience for me at the time.

We formed a tight circle, hands clasped, eyes shut, within a square room serving as a hub with corridors branching off in every direction. Despite its modest size, the room held a palpable atmosphere, intensified by the open doorways positioned diagonally across from each other. Beyond these portals lay elongated corridors, each lined with numerous chambers waiting to be explored.

In 2008, amidst the solemnity of our protection circle, I found myself struggling to stifle a laugh—a reaction borne from the unfamiliarity of raising vibrations. As I opened my eyes, my gaze fell upon the doorway to my right, and there, in a fleeting moment, I encountered my first paranormal phenomenon at Woodman Point.

Before me stood a figure, its form outlined in a vivid, glowing blue—a head and shoulders, devoid of features or discernible detail. It vanished as swiftly as it appeared, leaving me bewildered yet intrigued. Though hesitant to share my experience with the group, I knew deep down that I had glimpsed "the doctor," as I've come to affectionately call him—a spirit I believe I have encountered on subsequent visits.

My initial awareness of him came through the sound of moving footsteps, marking his interactive presence. Often felt and heard but rarely seen, he is known to manifest as a drop in temperature when near. Yet, despite his spectral nature, encountering him fills me with a sense of calm.

The second time I encountered this particular spirit was during my second visit, during an EVP session, I received a message—clear, direct: "I know you." It was his way of acknowledging our previous interaction, leaving me eager to reconnect in the future.

Later that day, during a spirit box session in a different area of the station, multiple spirits made their presence known, their voices resonating with clarity and coherence. One exchange, however, stood out among the rest—a nervous woman, clearly uncomfortable being there, asked a question during a spirit box session. "What are you doing here?" she asked quietly. Her inquiry was met with a rather hilarious, light hearted response: "Haunting you," came the answer, followed by a mischievous chuckle. It was a moment of levity, a reminder that even in death, spirits retain their humour and individuality—a notion that elicited laughter from us all, save for the understandably unsettled woman, who had posed the question.

It served as a poignant example of the enduring essence of the human soul, their personalities shining through in unexpected ways, even in the afterlife. Unfortunately, not all stories are as light and cheerful as these. When dealing with the paranormal, your experience can be as varied as the varied souls you encounter.

NEGATIVE HUMAN EARTHBOUND HAUNTINGS

Imagine, if you will, a figure shrouded in mist, its features obscured by the mists of time yet its presence unmistakably human. It drifts through the darkness, a silent observer of the world it once knew, forever bound to the places and people it once held dear. Yet, despite its spectral form, there is an undeniable air of sorrow that clings to it like a shroud, a poignant reminder of the tragedies that led to its earthly demise.

Negative human spirits, often referred to as malevolent or maleficent spirits, represent the darker spectrum of the spiritual realm, embodying traits such as anger, resentment, and malice. These spirits are believed to be the lingering essences of individuals who have passed away with unresolved issues or traumatic experiences, leading them to harbour negative emotions and intentions. In paranormal investigations, encounters with negative human spirits can be particularly challenging and potentially dangerous, as they may seek to cause harm, instil fear, or disrupt the lives of the living. Investigators must approach such encounters with caution, employing protective measures and discernment, to mitigate potential risks and ensure their own safety and well-being. Additionally, ethical considerations remain paramount, as investigators must respect the autonomy and spiritual journey of these spirits, while striving to understand and address the root causes of their negativity.

It is commonly assumed, that if a person displayed negative traits in life, their spirit would likely carry those traits in death. This stems from the belief that the essence of a person endures beyond the grave, with their character intact. Similar to the living, earthbound spirits retain the capacity to harbour emotions and attitudes, which can evolve over time. This includes the potential for resentment or hostility towards the living, reflecting their continued free will in the afterlife.

When such a spirit chooses to haunt a specific location or residence, it can evoke feelings of disturbance or even fear among those who encounter them. Distinct from malevolent entities, negative earthbound spirits are the lingering souls of individuals who either harboured negative traits in life or have become embittered and disoriented over time, in death.

Their intention to intimidate and unsettle the living, often leads to them being erroneously perceived as "demons" or similar negative entities.

Paranormal groups with a focus on religious aspects, sometimes misidentify these troubled spirits. Individuals with strong adherence to fundamental belief systems often categorise unhappy or enraged spirits, as demons or devils. This tendency can also stem from cultural influences, where the term "demon" has become excessively used and interchangeable.

Attempts by paranormal groups and religious leaders to expel these spirits from a location, might fail because they employ religious rituals designed to banish negative entities, such as exorcisms. Complicating matters further, I have observed numerous occasions, where human spirits themselves, via voice boxes, deliberately use the term "demon", to provoke fear from the people listening.

While confronting the unsettling presence of these malevolent spirits may seem daunting, it is crucial to remind those affected by such hauntings, that these spirits are ultimately the manifestations of angry individuals. Dealing with an angry spirit, often parallels dealing with an angry living person— establishing boundaries and understanding the root cause of their anger, can be effective strategies to encourage them to move on.

Encounters with such spirits are relatively common. However, in cases involving particularly hostile human spirits, more assertive measures may be necessary to rid them from the premises. Regardless of one's status—living or deceased—no individual should be permitted to inflict misery upon others. Anger does not grant immunity, even in death.

In another section of the Woodman Point Quarantine Station, I encountered an experience that left me disturbed, with what I believe, was the presence of one such a spirit. As we traversed from one area to another, a sudden, aggressive, audible growl, erupted right in my left ear. It was so fierce and jarring, that everyone in our group instinctively jumped and turned around, startled. However, I remained still, knowing that the sound had emanated right beside me, with no living person capable of producing such a menacing growl.

Our tour guide informed us, that this particular area is inhabited by a male spirit, who is fiercely territorial and aggressively vocal. He often growls and commands, "Get Out," making his presence unmistakably known and audible by normal hearing. This spirit does not manifest subtly; rather, he asserts his dominance with intensity and his intention is to cause fear.

Though I do not know the full extent of his story, it is evident that something has left him with a lingering hostility. Whenever I find myself in his vicinity now, I offer a quick apology for intruding on his space and hasten to leave as swiftly as possible. Since then, he has not troubled me directly, but his palpable anger and watchful gaze linger, as a reminder of his presence, urging me to move through his domain, quickly and with caution.

In another eerie encounter, this time at a Town Hall in Perth, Western Australia, during a ghost tour, I came face to face with an unfriendly earthbound spirit. While the hall is known for its playful ghost children who enjoy tugging on clothes and rolling balls around, there are also darker human spirits lurking within its walls.

Among the ghostly children who typically interact joyfully with the living, there is one little girl who stands out for her sombre demeanour. According to the story relayed by tour guides, she was allegedly brutally murdered within the Town Hall, her spirit bound there alongside that of her perpetrator. Despite attempts to move her on, she always returns, tethered by the trauma she endured and the malevolent presence of her attacker. Any efforts to intervene or guide her spirit away, unleashes the wrath of this perpetrator, who is reportedly bound by fear of retribution on the other side. I had an encounter with both the child and the adult negative spirit, about eight years ago.

During an encounter with this sweet child spirit, the atmosphere shifted dramatically, thick with anger and tension. I believe this to be the work of a deeply negative male spirit, who fiercely guards her, unwilling to let anyone interfere with her presence. The child spirit ran to hide in one of the recesses – notable by the sudden EMF spike and temperature drop in that area. It was low to the ground in a corner, as if a small child were sitting there, hiding from the malevolence that just entered the area.

I stood in the doorway of this recess, between the child and the male spirit. His energy was very strong and almost felt like electricity in front of me, where as hers was a gentle energy, crouched down in the corner of the recess. It felt like a standoff between the two of us with the guide, who was a medium, telling the male to get out of the space. I had a picture in my mind of this male looming over us, and just began to imagine the room filled with bright positive light and a protective bubble encasing myself and the child spirit. After about 3 minutes the atmosphere cleared and felt light again, the male had left the area. The little girls spirit remained in the corner for another few minutes before our EMF and temperature equipment returned to normal. The little girl left, but not before she tugged my shirt, as a way of saying thank you! There were going to be more attempts to move her on, and I hope they were successful.

Similarly, there is a menacing male spirit lurking behind the stage, known for his territorial aggression and penchant for frightening those that wander behind there. Though I personally didn't encounter him, I've spoken to others who have had first hand experiences with his growl, pushes and deep breathing in your ear.

In these instances, we are in locations steeped in tragedy and trauma, where hauntings are not merely residual but intelligent, with spirits bound by complex relationships and emotions. This dynamic is especially prevalent in places that have deaths or human anguish attached to them.

In some cases, the spirits inhabiting a location may harbour deep resentment or animosity towards the living occupants. Though I have not directly experienced such situations, I've come across accounts from fellow investigators, such as a British colleague who encountered a particularly unsettling haunting, when he moved to the US state of Mississippi.

The residents of the house were subjected to relentless attacks, plagued by nightmares, unsettling visions, and mysterious rapping's, leaving them in a state of perpetual fear. Strangely, the previous owners had not reported any such disturbances, and no haunted objects were found on the property. To uncover the source of the haunting, the investigators delved into the history of both the house and the current owners.

What they discovered was a chilling revelation: one of the former owners had been a high ranking member of the Ku Klux Klan, while the new occupants were active participants in the Civil Rights movement, nearly half a century earlier. They continued to work in this area of civil rights which was a passion for the entire family. They were an African American family. It became evident that the malevolent spirit haunting the house, harboured a deep-seated dislike for the current occupants, rooted in the stark contrast of their beliefs and more importantly the difference in the colour of their skin.

Regrettably, the resolution for this haunting proved to be the relocation of the new owners, as the animosity between the spirits and the living proved insurmountable. This serves as a stark reminder of the complexities and lingering repercussions of historical injustices, even in the realm of the paranormal, being played out in today's world.

When dealing with such intelligent yet negative hauntings, it is paramount to approach with caution and empathy, considering the intricate interplay of spirits and their lingering attachments. Here are some things to think about when dealing with more negative spirits.

- Spirits like people are complex and at one location you can find yourself dealing with all kinds of spirits in different stages of emotion. This means you should never take your guard down when dealing with the paranormal. It also means resolving the haunting for a client could be complex and take time. These usually do not have quick fixes.

- Be respectful when investigating. Just as you would react unkindly if a stranger walked into your house and started being obnoxious and provocative, so will they. You do not know their story. Often this is when people can and do get hurt. We always make a habit of saying please and thank you. An already negative and angry spirit will not take much provocation before reacting.

- Use your equipment to verify that this is intelligent haunting and try to get as much information as you can. This can be verified later if you receive names and dates for example. Maybe there Is a way to move this negative spirit on, if we can find out the reason why they may be bound.

Here are some case examples that show the complexity of situations that can lead to a human spirit becoming negative and effecting the living.

Joseph Moss
Derby Fish Market
PC Moss became the first police officer to be shot and murdered in Derby. He was shot by criminal Gerald Mainwaring in the Lock Up Yard he was working at, in 1879. His ghost was known to haunt the police station, and when it was demolished and then replaced by the fish market. Josephs's spirit remained. He tends to be an angry ghost who knocks things down and throws things. However, in 2002 a proper headstone was erected on his grave, after it was noted, his resting place was only represented by a small cross. The marking of his grave and life was made even more poignant when young people in the town, decided to take it upon themselves to look after and take care of the gravesite. Joseph seems happy with this and his anger, although sometimes present, has since subsided.

Derby's Friar Gate Hotel
One of the corridors in this building, built on the site of a friary, is haunted by a monk dressed in black robes that has been seen on and off since the 1800s. Other witnesses claim to have seen more than one monk here, sometimes headless. Although friendly another spirit that inhabits the hotel is not. It is that of a Victorian gentleman, whose name has been lost to history, they believe he may have killed himself on site. He has a habit of pushing people down stairs and rushing at people who encounter him growling.

Wilfred Barwick
In Birmingham along Coleshill Road the ghost of Barwick, a local butcher murdered in 1780, is said to haunt the road where he was killed. In February 1975 was the last reported sighting of him as he stepped out in front of a Securicor van angrily waving his fists and vanishing as the driver tried to talk to him.

Positive and negative earthbound spirits represent two different types of spiritual energies that paranormal investigators encounter during their investigations. Here is a comparison of the two, and what they mean for paranormal investigation:

Positive Earthbound Spirits:

- Light Energy: Positive earthbound spirits are often associated with light and positive energy. They may be spirits of loved ones or individuals who have passed away peacefully and are at peace with their transition.
- Comforting Presence: These spirits may offer comfort, guidance, or messages of love to the living. They are often perceived as gentle and benevolent beings.
- Helpful Interaction: Positive earthbound spirits may interact with paranormal investigators in constructive ways, providing information or insights that can be helpful in understanding the spiritual realm.
- Less Disruptive: They are generally less disruptive or harmful to the living and may even contribute positively to the energy of a space.

Negative Earthbound Spirits:

- Dark Energy: Negative earthbound spirits are associated with darker, negative energies. They may be spirits of individuals who passed away tragically, violently, or with unresolved issues.
- Malevolent Intentions: These spirits may harbour anger, resentment, or other negative emotions, and they may seek to cause harm or disturbance to the living.
- Manipulative Behaviour: Negative earthbound spirits may engage in manipulative behaviour, such as pretending to be benevolent or deceiving investigators to gain attention or energy.
- Greater Disruption: They can cause greater disruption and distress in the environment they inhabit, leading to feelings of fear, unease, or even physical manifestations.

Implications for Paranormal Investigators:

- Approach with Caution: Paranormal investigators need to approach encounters with spirits, especially negative ones, with caution and respect. It is essential to protect oneself spiritually and emotionally during investigations.
- Discernment: Investigators must develop discernment skills to differentiate between positive and negative energies. This may

involve assessing the emotional resonance of the energy, the nature of any communication or interaction, and the overall atmosphere of the environment.

- Protection Measures: Implementing protection measures, such as prayer, visualization, or spiritual tools like sage or crystals, can help shield investigators from negative energies and ensure their safety during investigations.
- Ethical Considerations: Ethical considerations are crucial when dealing with earthbound spirits. Investigators should prioritize respecting the autonomy and spiritual journey of the spirits they encounter, avoiding exploitation or manipulation for personal gain.

In summary, understanding the differences between positive and negative earthbound spirits, is essential for paranormal investigators to conduct ethical and safe investigations, while navigating the complexities of the spiritual realm.

2 NON HUMAN HAUNTINGS

In the shadowed corners of the forsaken, where the echoes of silence
reverberate with a chilling cadence, there lurk entities of ominous
presence. whispers carry the weight of forgotten nightmares, stirring
the depths of mortal fears. In the hollows of abandoned places, where
time stands frozen in a dance of decay, they linger like spectres of
forgotten warnings. Their gaze pierces through the veil of reality,
drawing forth the primal instinct of survival from the depths of the soul.
Beware the unseen hands that shape the shadows, for in their darkness
lies the ominous embrace of the unknown.

A non-human haunting, alternatively termed as an entity haunting or, in
certain cases, a demonic haunting, denotes a phenomenon wherein a location
or residence is believed to be inhabited or influenced, by a non-human entity
or spirit. Unlike human hauntings, which involve spirits believed to have once
been human, non-human hauntings entail entities speculated to have never
possessed human form. These occurrences can manifest in various locales but
are often linked with places bearing a history of violence, trauma, or occult
activities. Occasionally, they occur without apparent cause. Such entities may
be summoned to a site by individuals dabbling in practices or paranormal
communication. Those encountering non-human hauntings may report
diverse symptoms, including sensations of dread, physical discomfort like
nausea or headaches, unexplained marks, and psychological disturbances such
as anxiety, depression, nightmares, or irrational fears.

Non-human hauntings encompass a spectrum of entities, including
demons, elemental beings, shadow figures, or other supernatural entities
defying easy categorisation. Frequently depicted with malevolent or disruptive

74

intentions, not all non-human hauntings are necessarily negative, some display indifference or even benevolence. Analogous to human spirits, non-human entities may manifest through various means, such as apparitions, inexplicable noises, objects in motion, electrical anomalies, or fluctuations in temperature. Communication may occur through EVP, possession, or the manipulation of thoughts and emotions. Resolving non-human hauntings typically entails spiritual or religious interventions, like exorcisms conducted by trained clergy or shamans, house blessings, smudging rituals, or other forms of spiritual cleansing, aimed at expelling or banishing the entity. It is imperative to address any attachments these entities may have to individuals, along with their connection to a location.

Beliefs concerning non-human hauntings diverge widely across cultures and religions. Some cultures boast intricate mythologies and legends surrounding their supernatural beings, while others interpret non-human hauntings through the lens of their religious doctrines. Let's explore some of the most renowned types of non-human hauntings.

SHADOW PEOPLE

Describing entities outside the realm of human experience is indeed a challenging endeavour, given the contentious nature of paranormal discourse. Yet, certain characteristics about shadow entities garner widespread agreement, among enthusiasts and researchers alike. Primarily, they are universally recognised as non-human entities, devoid of any human origin, believed to possess an ancient lineage, with reported sightings spanning centuries and continents. Their presence tends to coincide with sites marked by human suffering and violence, suggesting an affinity for environments steeped in turmoil.

Distinguishing these entities from human spirits, particularly those presenting as shadow figures, is crucial. Genuine shadow people, distinct from their non-human counterparts, typically manifest as towering silhouettes, often towering between seven to eight feet in height, or occasionally, as diminutive forms akin to children. They traverse spaces with an eerie swiftness, darting through walls or lingering in room corners, occasionally fixing their gaze upon unsuspecting witnesses. Their appearances vary from solid forms to ethereal wisps, though they are most commonly observed at the periphery of one's vision, with unfortunate encounters sometimes bringing them face-to-face with their startled observers.

Accounts of encounters with these entities often evoke a profound sense of dread, as witnesses recount their experiences with beings darker than the abyss itself. These entities emerge as stark silhouettes amidst the darkness, their forms pitch black. Draped often in cloaks or hoods, they move with an otherworldly grace, their elongated limbs stretching beyond natural bounds, casting eerie shadows upon the walls of perception. Within the murky depths of the unknown, they linger, their presence a haunting enigma that eludes comprehension, forever dwelling on the fringes of human understanding.

Encounters with these entities often evoke an immediate and intense sensation of dread and fear, unlike the calming presence of individuals like my doctor friend, at the quarantine station. They manifest as ominous shadows, casting a watchful gaze from the corners of bedrooms or darting swiftly past doorways. Drawn to dark recesses and hidden spaces, they exhibit a keen awareness of their surroundings, displaying traits of an intelligent haunting.

Prisons, old hospitals, and asylums, sites steeped in profound human suffering and trauma, serve as favoured haunts for these entities. In some instances, they are reputed to hold human spirits in bondage, adding to the palpable atmosphere of unease that permeates these locations. Their presence, marked by an unsettling sentience, serves as a reminder of the lingering echoes of past anguish, forever etched into the fabric of these haunted spaces.

Pentridge Prison,

A notorious institution located in Victoria Australia, this prison has a history of confinement and despair and has long captured the imagination of those fascinated by the paranormal. Established in 1851 and shut in 1997, its shadowed corridors bear witness to tales of spectres that linger beyond the confines of time.

Among the most renowned of these spectral inhabitants is the enigmatic figure known as the Shadow Person. Frequently photographed and sighted in the vicinity of the scaffold, this elusive entity, despite the passage of years, remains shrouded in mystery

Captured in countless images, this shadow person serves as a reminder of Pentridge's tumultuous past. You can go on ghost tours of Pentridge, and I would encourage those that do, to take as many photos as you can, especially in the vicinity of the scaffold. For it is here that this entity most often appears in photographs, often unseen in the moment the photo is taken.

The nature of shadow entities, often shrouded in ambiguity, lends itself to a myriad of theories and interpretations. While they may occasionally present a facade of friendliness or impartiality, their underlying motives remain murky and dubious, with countless accounts detailing their attempts to inflict harm upon those they encounter.

Various theories attempt to explain the origins and intentions of these shadowy beings. Some posit that they are simply ghosts assuming a darker form, while others lean towards more sinister explanations, likening them to

76

demons or lower-level entities. Yet, the true nature of these entities remains elusive, their motives veiled in mystery.

Another explanation for shadow people come from a known phenomenon that occurs during some sleep disorders. Sleep paralysis is a phenomenon that occurs when a person is temporarily unable to move or speak, while transitioning between sleep and wakefulness. People often report feeling pressure on their chest like they are being smothered, a heaviness in the air and a deep sense of fear or danger. Often, this is accompanied by sightings of a shadow person sitting on their chest or lurking in the corners of the room. This is the most widely accepted scientific explanation for this phenomenon, that it is a visual hallucination. As terrifying for the person experiencing this, it is nothing more than the mind playing tricks on the body and should be ruled out in any conversation, regarding the presence of a shadow person.

Another example of a particular shadow person is the "Hat Man", named for a fedora or other brimmed hat on his head. The Hat Man is commonly associated with sleep disorders. And the abuse of the antihistamine diphenhydramine, commonly sold under the recognisable brand name of Benadryl. Often witnesses have claimed they can 'feel him' staring at them. In both these cases it is not paranormal it is medical Issue and being able to distinguish between two, is the job of the paranormal investigator. Good information gathering is the backbone of any good paranormal Investigation.

Nevertheless, instances of shadow entities being captured on camera or observed in waking moments, challenge purely psychological explanations. Their ability to manifest physically, even in the absence of sleep-related contexts, raises intriguing questions about their existence and nature.

Shadow entities also exhibit distinct behavioural patterns, often observed in solitary manifestations and completely devoid of the orb activity, commonly associated with other hauntings. The absence of corroborating evidence further underscores the enigmatic nature of these entities.

Despite divergent beliefs regarding their benevolence or malevolence, one consensus remains: caution is paramount when dealing with shadow entities. Their intelligence and ability to communicate, albeit often through silent observation, necessitate a vigilant approach from paranormal investigators and individuals alike.

The association of dark, intrusive, and malevolent thoughts with these shadow beings is a recurring theme in paranormal encounters, suggesting a deep-seated connection between these entities and primal fears. However, it is conceivable that in many instances, the fear experienced stems more from the disorientation and surprise of encountering the unknown, rather than from the shadow entity itself.

What we do know about shadow entities is both intriguing and disconcerting. They exhibit a level of intelligence that transcends mere apparitions, with the ability to move freely and communicate in various ways. Despite their potential for interaction, they often assume the role of silent observers, lurking in the shadows of closets, doorways, or room corners, casting an eerie presence upon their surroundings.

Opinions on the nature of shadow people are divided, with some viewing them as benevolent entities offering guidance and protection, while others perceive them as malevolent forces capable of inflicting harm upon those they encounter. Yet, it is also plausible that their intentions are multifaceted, encompassing elements of both light and darkness.

As an investigator navigating the realm of the paranormal, caution should be exercised when dealing with shadow entities. Their enigmatic nature and ambiguous motives demand a respectful and cautious approach. Whether they offer help or pose a threat, engaging with these entities requires a delicate balance of curiosity and vigilance, acknowledging the potential dangers inherent in probing things, we do not fully understand.

From the elusive spectres of shadow people to the elemental guardians of nature's essence, the journey of paranormal exploration unveils a tapestry of spiritual phenomena. We are going to delve into the presence of elemental entities which adds another layer of intrigue and more reason than ever, to be cautious when dealing with the paranormal

ELEMENTALS

Elemental spirits, are beings believed to be associated with the classical elements of nature: earth, air, fire, and water, as well as sometimes including additional elements like spirit or ether. These spirits are often depicted as guardians or manifestations of the natural world, embodying the qualities and energies of their respective elements.

Elementals originate in mythology and actually have their beginnings in supposed living creatures in various cultures such as gnomes, elves, leprechauns, Imps, and fairies. But according to many mythological systems, these creatures would often shape shift and appear as anything they desired. In some indigenous cultures they have the ability to manifest in either human or animal form. They are occasionally considered benevolent and, in some cases, indifferent or quite sinister.

Elemental spirits, believed by many to be as ancient as the Earth itself, have long been the focus of ancient magical practices, exemplified by cultures like the Druids. These entities are often depicted as conscious, intelligent beings or essence,s tied to specific elements of nature, with various interpretations and names across cultures. Rooted in folklore, mythology, and occult traditions, they serve as intermediaries between humanity and the natural world. While some view them as independent entities with their own will, others see them as forces to be controlled by those with the knowledge or authority. Regardless, their power, dealing with elementals demands utmost respect, as they can be exceedingly dangerous when provoked.

NATURE ELEMENTALS

Nature elementals are those entities that embody the four elements. Elementals are integral to the natural world, acting as guardians or manifestations. They have their own distinct purposes and behaviours. Places where elemental energies reside are revered as sanctuaries of nature, where earth, air, fire, and water come together, and where elemental spirits are believed to dwell or be especially active.

There are many cultures that leave offerings at these sites in order to appease the elementals that reside there. Crossroads and boundaries are thought to be places where the veil between the physical and spiritual realms is thin. These areas are often associated with the presence of spirits, including elemental beings, who may gather or travel between worlds.

Air spirits are associated with the element of air and are often linked to the wind, breezes, and storms or other weather events. Air elementals are also known as Sylphs are sometimes portrayed as winged creatures or as invisible forces of nature.

Fire spirits are associated with the transformative and purifying power of fire. Salamanders are a common depiction of fire elementals, believed to dwell within flames or volcanic regions. They are often depicted as lizard-like creatures or as fiery beings.

Earth spirits are often associated with the more stable aspects of nature, such as rocks, soil, grass, plants, and trees. They are believed to dwell in forests, mountains, and in underground caverns. In folklore, Gnomes and dwarves are examples of earth spirits.

Water spirits are associated with rivers, lakes, and oceans. In Folklore water nymphs or water sprites, are considered water elementals. They are often depicted as graceful, fluid beings with a deep connection to the waters they inhabit.

In some traditions, a fifth element, often referred to as spirit is included. Spirits associated with this element are believed to embody the essence of the divine, the universe, or the interconnectedness of all things. They are often depicted as transcendent beings or as representations of spiritual energy. Spirit guides would come under this category.

Exploring theories surrounding nature elementals and their habitats is indeed intriguing, though our investigations typically focus on phenomena that transcend the realm of playful gnomes and mischievous spirits. However, there are instances where elemental entities, such as banshees, emerge as significant subjects of inquiry, drawing our attention to locations steeped in legend and lore, such as Leap Castle, which we will delve into, in the following section.

The Banshee – Air Elemental

The Banshee, also known as the Ban-Sith, occupies a unique place in folklore as an air elemental associated with the portentous role of the fairy of death. While never seen, the Banshee's haunting cries instil fear in all who hear them, serving as harbingers of impending doom. Legend holds that these ethereal wails echo around the homes of families soon to experience a loss, signalling the imminent departure of a loved one's spirit to the world beyond.

In regions like Ireland and Scotland, the Banshee's cry is met with dread, for it foretells the imminent passing of a family member. These spirit beings are said to forge bonds with specific families and their descendants, serving as custodians across generations. Despite their association with death, the Banshee is not regarded as malevolent; rather, it is seen as a protective spirit, caring for the welfare of the family it accompanies both in this world and the next.

While elemental hauntings typically occur in natural settings like mountains, deserts, or forests, they are seldom encountered within built-up areas. However, exceptions arise when rituals are performed, deliberately summoning elementals to haunt specific locales, as evidenced by the case of Leap Castle in the next section.

Encounters with elementals can provoke mental and emotional distress in sensitive individuals, with indigenous cultures often offering ritual tributes to maintain harmony between people and the environment. Such encounters may manifest as poltergeist-like phenomena, including objects moving or aggressive interactions when provoked, blurring the line between playful mischief and malevolence.

DARK ELEMENTALS

Indeed, while the notion of being haunted by gnomes and leprechauns might be farfetched other elemental type hauntings are not. Among such cases, Leap Castle in Ireland stands out as a prominent example, notorious for its association with a malevolent elemental presence.

Leap Castle's eerie reputation is deeply rooted in its tumultuous history, marked by tales of violence, betrayal, and tragedy. Within its ancient walls, stories abound of spectral encounters and inexplicable phenomena attributed to the presence of an elemental entity. According to local lore, this elemental is believed to be a malevolent force, its presence evoking feelings of dread and unease among those who dare to enter its domain.

Investigations at Leap Castle have yielded reports of chilling experiences, including sightings of shadowy figures, sudden drops in temperature, and unsettling noises, emanating from empty rooms. Despite sceptics dismissing such claims as mere superstition, the pervasive atmosphere of apprehension surrounding Leap Castle persists, leaving many intrigued by the possibility of an otherworldly presence, lurking within its walls.

Leap Castle was built in around 1250 by the O'Bannon clan. It has a very long and interesting history but is most famous for the elemental that resides there.

A former resident of this castle, Mildred Darby, is believed to have been the reason this elemental appeared at the castle in the first place. She was born into the height of the spiritualist craze and when old enough, would perform occult ceremonies and seances, in order to connect with the supernatural. It was shortly after these ceremonies, that the elemental first made itself known. Mildred told the Occult Review journal in 1909, about an encounter with this elemental spirit. She said,

"I was standing in the gallery looking down at the main floor when I felt somebody put a hand on my shoulder. The thing was about the size of a sheep." She described the figure as being "thin, gaunt, shadowy." She goes on, though, saying, "Its face was human, to be more accurate, inhuman. Its lust in its eyes, which seemed half decomposed in black cavities, stared into mine. The horrible smell one hundred times intensified, came up into my face, giving me a deadly nausea. It was the smell of a decomposing corpse."

The presence of the entity at Leap Castle raises intriguing questions about its origin and nature, with two distinct possibilities emerging from the shadows. One theory suggests that the entity may be an angered nature elemental, perturbed by the meddling of individuals delving into forces they should not have been and upsetting the natural balance. Alternatively, darker forces may have been summoned by Mildred's dabbling, which now lingers within the castle's ancient walls. This entity has been seen on numerous occasions and is known to change shape and form.

In the present day, Sean Ryan, the current owner of Leap Castle, maintains a cautious approach to paranormal investigations on the premises. While he welcomes investigators, he emphasises the importance of respecting the elemental associated with the castle, urging restraint in dealings or interactions with it. Sean is keenly aware of the potential dangers posed by provoking such entities and remains vigilant in safeguarding both the integrity of the investigations and the well-being of those involved.

Despite the entity's continued presence, it has remained elusive to human observers for some time, a fact that does not go unnoticed by psychics who sense its lingering energy and see its changing form. Their reluctance to provoke or disturb the entity, reflects a shared desire to maintain peace within the castle's walls, ensuring the safety of those who live there.

As the custodian of Leap Castle's legacy, Sean Ryan navigates a delicate balance between curiosity and caution, honouring the spirits that dwell within, while preserving the sanctity of the ancient site. In doing so, he upholds a legacy of respect and reverence for the unknown, acknowledging the inherent complexities of the paranormal realm.

It is encounters like this, that elementals are often thought of as negative entities. It should be mentioned that most hauntings, that contain an elemental presence, usually turn out to be frightening in the extreme to residents of the location. Although rare to come across, the uttermost caution needs to be used when dealing with a supposed elemental haunting.

DEMONIC HAUNTING

In the shadowed recesses of the abyss, where light dare not tread and whispers of ancient darkness echo through the void, lurk entities of malevolent intent, known to mortals as demons. Born of primordial chaos and fuelled by insatiable hunger, these infernal beings embody the very essence of dread and despair. Their presence, shrouded in the miasma of forbidden knowledge, casts a chilling pall over the hearts of those who dare to glimpse their sinister visage. Beware, for where demons tread, the boundaries between worlds fray, and the fabric of reality itself trembles in their wake.

Demons or lower-level entities, need little introduction. They are the subject of movies, documentaries, horror stories and Sunday morning sermons. Their form and definition vary, as the perception of demons is not a universal one. Interpretations differ greatly, depending on individuals' belief and cultural background. Some religions and belief systems, do not even recognise the existence of demons. This is true of some branches of Buddhism and Indigenous cultures, who do not recognise the 'western' concept of demons. Others place significant emphasis on their role in spiritual matters, such as Christianity and some have a supernatural entity that loosely resemble demons, such as the Jinn found in Islam. Jinn are considered to have free will, like humans, and are capable of doing both good and evil actions. Demons do not do good; they bring chaos and harm wherever they can.

Demons, considered to be spiritual beings, operate on our plain of existence, bringing temptation and misery. They are powerful and malevolent entities, that oppose good and can lead humans to behaviours that are destructive, harmful, or contrary to moral or ethical norms. Demons can attach themselves to people, places and objects and aim to inflict mental, emotional, spiritual, and physical torture, on the humans they encounter. They are often associated with influencing individuals or possessing them. What we do know is these lower entities, much like negative non-human hauntings, exploit weaknesses, desires, or vulnerabilities, to lure individuals into making harmful choices.

Paranormal investigators specialising in these darker occurrences are known as demonologists. Their expertise lies in the study, investigation, and resolution of demonic phenomena. Positioned at the intersection of theology, religious studies, and the occult, demonology encompasses a diverse array of topics. Having a team member with specialised knowledge in demonology can be invaluable, during paranormal investigations. Alternatively, reaching out to a local demonologist can provide valuable insights and assistance when delving into known demonic locations.

Despite the sensational portrayals often depicted in Hollywood, encounters with these entities are exceedingly rare. Should an individual encounter such an entity, the repercussions can be profound and enduring, if proper precautions are not taken. It is strongly advised against attempting communication with these entities, as the primary goal of the investigator should be the removal of the entity and the severance of any attachments it has, to those seeking assistance. Once suspicion arises that a demonic entity may be involved, all attempts at communication should cease, and specialist help should be sought without delay.

It is essential to recognise that while the Catholic Church offers blessings for homes, a full exorcism is a meticulous process that requires thorough investigation. Investigators are encouraged to familiarise themselves with the procedures and protocols relevant to their local area, reaching out to representatives of various religious denominations, to gain insights into their beliefs and practices. Attempting such endeavours without the guidance of experienced professionals, is strongly discouraged.

Identifying signs of a potentially demonic haunting can be challenging, as they may initially resemble those of a non-demonic haunting. However, demonic manifestations often escalate to the extreme end of the spectrum, similar to poltergeist activity. Such hauntings may involve manifestations that surpass the bounds of typical paranormal phenomena, such as objects levitating or being forcefully propelled and changes in the way a person acts or behaves. These extreme manifestations serve as potent indicators that specialised intervention may be necessary.

Physical manifestations of demonic activity often leave distinct and unsettling traces, serving as ominous indicators of their presence. Scratches, typically occurring in threes, are a common occurrence, symbolically mocking the trinity and signalling the malevolent intent of the entity. Additionally, unexplained burns, bruises, and other marks on the body can manifest, serving as tangible evidence of the entity's aggression.

Another tell-tale sign of demonic activity is the presence of extreme odours permeating the property, often reminiscent of sulphur or decomposing flesh, which can overwhelm the senses and create an oppressive atmosphere. Increased insect activity, such as swarms of flies congregating in the area or around individuals, serves as a chilling manifestation of the entity's influence.

Moreover, animals within the vicinity may exhibit signs of distress and agitation, becoming terrified and aggressive, or refusing to enter specific locations where the entity is present. In some cases, animals have tragically fallen victim to the entity's malevolence, succumbing to unexplained injuries or even death, as a result of its influence. These physical manifestations highlight the severity of the demonic presence and the urgent need for intervention and assistance, from experienced professionals.

The desecration of religious artifacts within a home, serves as a significant indication of demonic presence, often involving the inversion, defacement, or destruction of sacred symbols, such as crosses or religious imagery. Acts of blasphemy, intended to mock or challenge religious beliefs, frequently accompany such manifestations, signifying the entity's contempt for spiritual sanctity.

In a notable case, three priests embarked on an exorcism in the home of a young boy, following an investigation by the church that confirmed the presence of genuine demonic haunting and oppression. Despite their success in removing the demonic entity, upon retrieving a statue of the Virgin Mary, they had placed within the room, they discovered that its hands had been inexplicably burnt off. This statue later found its place in the John Zaffis Paranormal Museum in Connecticut, serving as a chilling reminder of the entity's malevolent influence.

Given the widespread familiarity with the Catholic version of demonic possession and exorcism rites, it serves as a primary point of reference for many. However, the approach to dealing with demonic entities may vary depending on individual beliefs and cultural contexts. For some, the Catholic framework resonates most strongly, due to personal upbringing and faith traditions, offering a sense of familiarity and efficacy, in confronting such malevolent forces.

There are considered 4 stages that can occur in a demonic haunting. This usually revolves around a person or persons. In his 1990 book "An Exorcist Tells His Story," Father Gabriele Amorth (1925 – 2016), chief exorcist of Rome, identified the following stages of demonic activity: This is the mostly agreed upon across denominations.

Infestation: This is your typical haunted house type stuff: You may hear footsteps, voices, see apparitions, furniture or other objects moving without explanation. odours with no discernible source. Rather than directly affecting people, infestations affect only property, objects, and animals.

Oppression: Activity steps up with physical attacks, sleep disturbances including horrific nightmares, frequent and severe illnesses, major depression, or anxiety, severe financial, employment problems and relationship troubles. While these things happen in the normal course of life, all of them happening at once or in rapid succession could be a sign of demonic presence. A person maybe in a constant state of fear for an unknown reason and their whole life seems to unravel at once. It is often at this point that people will contact a paranormal investigator to try to determine what is happening to them and their home.

Obsession: As the name implies, at this stage the person has a hard time functioning, being constantly preoccupied with thoughts of the demonic activity commandeering his or her life, and frequently with thoughts of harm to themselves or others as well as suicidal ideology. Sleep becomes nearly impossible at this stage for the person because of the mental torment.

Possession: Contrary to popular belief, possession is not demons entering a person's body and taking over his or her soul. A person's free will is never removed, only severely compromised. In possession, a person is so physically, emotionally, mentally, and spiritually broken down by going through the other three stages that demonic spirits can seize occasional control over that person's actions.

Signs of possession include superhuman strength, speaking in a language the victim does not know, including ancient dead languages, inordinate aversion to holy objects, knowledge of events or facts the victim could not possibly know, and, according to Diocese of San Jose exorcist Gary Thomas (whose story was made famous in the book and movie "The Rite"), changes in facial features and levitation.

Not included in this list are 360-degree head spins. However, the basis for this notion comes from an actual case. Our very first case study for this section, can be none other, than the case that inspired the film, the exorcist.

Worth noting that all the first three of these stages can be addressed by a competent deliverance minister or priest. You do not need Vatican permission for the local priest to act. However, the last stage of dealing with an actual possession, is reserved for official exorcists only, with Vatican approval. This is a very long process that involves psychological assessments.

The Exorcist Case

On August 20th, 1949, the Washington Post ran a story of the exorcism of a teenaged boy (now believed to be Ronald Hunkeeler of Maryland). Reading that article was a man by the name of William Peter Blatty, a student at

Georgetown University. He managed to gain a copy of the diary of the exorcism, which became the basis for his 1971 book, The Exorcist.

It all began in February of 1949, when Roland, a thirteen and a half year old boy, began exhibiting disturbing behaviour that left his parents baffled and terrified. He was calm and normal during the day, but at night, he would suddenly erupt into screaming fits and other wild outbursts. Meanwhile, he would enter a trance-like state, make sounds in a guttural voice, and break out in scratches and red lines all over his body. He was grieving the loss of his Aunit Harriet. Harriet was a spiritualist who'd taught him many things — including how to use a Ouija board.

The family approached Reverend Luther Miles Schultze. He was a minister of St Stephens Luteran church in Washington DC. They reported that there had been a lot of unexplained activity within their home. Reverend Luther was unsure of what to do with the reports, so he directed the family to Father Edward Albert Hughes, of St James Catholic Church.

The family reported that they would hear knocks and raps and items were picked up and thrown. By January 1949, scratching noises in the walls and roof were heard almost consistently. They called in pest experts who could find no reason for the scratching, although they did hear it. The noises eventually centred around the room of Rolands room.

This activity increased to furniture moving, Water dripped inexplicably from pipes and walls. His mattress would suddenly move, and they claimed that the boy's bed moved on its own, slid violently across the room, and knocked them over. Footsteps, stomping in empty rooms and hallways and when they sent the boy away the activity followed him.

The Reverend and the priest decided to take the boy into a mental hygiene clinic. At the time these clinics specialised in the care of mental health. This one, was run by the church so, as part of the treatment, prayer circles were held daily around the boy. The reverend was present when many of the disturbances occurred and even took him back to his home to see if the disturbances followed. They certainly did, even though there had never been any kind of activity in the home previously. In one instance, the child unable to sleep due to the bed moving, sat in a chair, which promptly threw itself back against the wall, by itself. It then went forward, throwing the boy to the floor.

For the exorcism, Father Hughes strapped the boy to the mattress and began his recitations. But he had to stop the rite when Ronald broke off a piece of mattress spring and slashed the priest across his shoulders, leaving the exorcism unfinished.

A few days later, red scratches appeared on Rolands body. One of the scratches formed the word 'LOUIS,' which indicated to Ronald's mother, that the family needed to go to St. Louis, where the Hunkelers had relatives, to find a way to save their son.

A cousin put the Hunkelers in touch with Father Walter H. Halloran and Rev. William Bowdern. These two Jesuits, agreed to perform an exorcism on young Ronald with the help of several others

In early March 1949, the men gathered at the residence on Roanoke Drive. There, the exorcists witnessed scratching on the boy's body and the mattress moving violently.

Bowdern and Halloran, according to their reports, noticed a pattern in Ronald's behaviour. He was calm and normal during the day. But at night, after settling in for bed, he would exhibit strange behaviour, including screaming and wild outbursts. Ronald would also enter a trance-like state and start making sounds in a guttural voice. The priests also said they saw objects mysteriously flying in the boy's presence and noted that he would react violently when in proximity to any sacred object, presented by the attending Jesuits.

At one point a pitchfork-shaped pattern of red lines moved from the boy's thigh and snaked down towards his ankle. These types of things happened every night for more than a month. Once, a red X appeared on Ronald's chest, leading the priests to believe he was possessed by 10 demons.

The two priests never gave up, as they continued the exorcism night after night. On the night of March 20, the exorcism reached an unhealthy new level. Ronald urinated all over his bed and began shouting and cursing at the priests. Now, Ronald's parents had had enough. They took him to Alexian Brothers Hospital in St. Louis, for more serious treatment.

Finally, on April 18, a "miracle" occurred in Ronald's room at Alexian Brothers. It was the Monday after Easter, and Ronald awoke with seizures. He yelled at the priests, saying that Satan would always be with him. The priests laid holy relics, crucifixes, medals, and rosaries on the boy.

At 10:45 p.m. that evening, the attending priests called on St. Michael to expel Satan from Ronald's body. They shouted at Satan, saying that St. Michael would battle him for Ronald's soul. Seven minutes later, Ronald came out of his trance and said, "He's gone." The teenager recounted how he had a vision that St. Michael vanquishing Satan, on a great battlefield.

According to Bowdern and Halloran, the strange occurrences and behaviour ceased after that. And, despite providing the true story of The Exorcist, Ronald Hunkeler went on live a completely normal life from that moment forward.

Although the scratches, shouting, spitting, and cursing in the movie mimicked what Ronald had experienced, the boy's head never turned 360 degrees like Regan's did in the film. Similarly, Ronald never vomited green matter.

Following the exorcism of Roland, his family moved back to the East

Coast. Sources claim that he found a wife and started a family. He named his first son Michael, after the saint believed to have saved his soul. If Roland is still alive today, he would be in his mid-80s.

Many of the actual events seen in the film, 'The Exorcist', with the exception of the head spinning, come directly from another Exorcism case. One I believe is far more terrifying then even the film depicted. It is one of the most well documented and detailed exorcisms of all time. The case of the Marianne Hill Mission Possessions is indicative of a true demonic haunting and possession.

Marianne Hill Mission Possessions and Exorcisms

In 1906, the possession of a Zulu girl who had been taken to Marianne Hill Mission, is one of the most spectacular and well documented cases ever published by the Catholic Church. Much of what is seen in the film, The Exorcist, is a retelling of this disturbing possession manifestation. At the centre of the story is Clara Germana Tele, a Zulu girl who had been taken, baptised and retained at the mission.

Clara was described by the mission as an intelligent, quiet girl who was honest and caused no trouble. She was extremely well liked by both students and staff at the Mission. She was also described as devoutly religious having been converted away from her native religion, at a young age. By all accounts she was a poster success story for the Catholic Mission with their outdated, ethically questionable practices. It is worth mentioning that her parents were deeply committed to their indigenous beliefs and rituals, which some involved in the case cited as a contributing factor to the events that transpired on the peaceful night of August 20th, 1906.

It was in the early hours of that morning when Clara started showing sudden signs of agitation and possession. Over the following week it got progressively worse, with more extreme manifestations. The most extraordinary part of her possession, was her levitation, five or six feet into the air which occurred on a daily basis, in front of hundreds of witnesses. Anyone trying to pull the girl down, were lifted as well. She was also purported to be able to move up walls at will.

Although her native language was Zulu and she did speak a little English, during this time she spoke a number of other languages fluently. She understood and could speak Latin, German, Polish, Hebrew and many more. She would often mock God, religion and those present in multiple languages she was not capable of knowing. She acquired superhuman strength and it took 5 men or more to hold her down. When she was administered opium in order to sedate her, it had no effect, which at the time, the medical doctors who attended, could not explain. She was able to extend her neck and limbs that defied medical science. (This is where the head spinning idea came from).

She was able to recite information she could not possibly know, like the location of clergy in Rome, down to the very address where they resided. She was able to tell the priests exactly what others were doing that were not present in the room, or even the country, down to the very minute. One of the more interesting accounts, was that she had the ability to sense religious objects. She could tell which was holy water and which was normal water, even when the Priests tried to trick her. (She reacted violently when sprinkled with holy water and would laugh when they used normal water). Likely the oddest of all, is she could pick up dust off the floor throw it to the ground again and it would turn into a swirling moving ball of dust bigger than what she had thrown down.

At this point they had seen enough and got permission for a full-blown exorcism to take place. Fr Erasmus lead the exorcisms. Also present were eight school girls who were strong in order to help hold Clara down. It was also witnessed by three priests, fourteen sisters and over 150 natives over a three day period.

The exorcism rite began, and instantly the chair Clara was in, and the school girls who were trying to hold the hissing girl down, levitated clear off the ground. They described Claras face as distorting, she was howling and hissing and hitting out at anyone who she could. There was the report that Clara hit Sister Luitgardis in the arm so hard, it swelled up and turned blue from the bruising. Still the exorcism continued. The next thing was that Claras body began to swell, as if she was being blown up somehow. She went into a full rage at the room. Again, she and the other girls were lifted clear off the ground before being dropped. The priest ordered her hand and feet bound, quite a task within itself. It took them 3 hours just to get handcuffs on her.

When they tried to get her hand into handcuffs, Clara shot out her hand and grabbed the throat of one Sister Anacleta, with such force, the nun began to lose consciousness. It was then that both Clara and the nun were levitated, so that Sister Analetas feet were off the ground. It took every person in the room to be able to free the sister, from Claras grasp.

Finally, the sisters were able to bind her feet and arms to the chair. It took over 12 people. But that was not the end, Clara was able to snap the rope with pure strength, that bound her feet. By this time, the nuns decided to use their own body strength to weigh her down. This accomplished nothing, as Clara and the nuns again levitated off the floor together.

During all this, Father Erasmus had continued with the prayer of exorcism. Clara at this point tried to bite anyone who was near her, as she swore and cursed in multiple languages. The priest warned a nun standing next to her, to be careful, but the sister challenged the devil to try it. With that challenge, Claras head shot around, and sunk her teeth into the sister's arm.

On initial examination there were red bruise marks where the bite had occurred, but it had not ripped the sister's habit. The only oddity was, in between the reddened teeth marks on the nun's arm, was a small wound where Clara's tongue should have been. It was described almost like a snake bite, or if a needle had been stabbed into the nun's arm, with considerable force. This was seen to have somehow pierced the skin. The next day large blisters filled with a yellow substance, that burnt when touched, appeared on the arm where the teeth marks and wound were. It took days of extreme pain, for the nun's arm to even start to recover.

The end came as quickly as it had begun. The following words are the account of Father Erasmus himself. "I felt that finally the decisive moment had come. Once more Germana plainly soared aloft above all those around her. She screamed and howled in a manner beyond words to describe, and again sank to the floor. There she writhed and twisted like one in the agony of death and then stretched out full length. All was over. Germana was free from the terrible demon. The struggle ended at half past nine in the morning September 13th, 1906, in the mission Church at St Michael.".

Clara herself was very thankful and took communion and prayed fervently, after her ordeal. To make sure that the demon was gone, after some rest they resumed the exorcism. Clara remained calm and showed none of the abilities she had previously shown. Neither could she speak in anything but her native Zulu and broken English. Now during this exorcism, the demon would repeat again and again, that it would return, and that the next time would be much worse. The demon also predicted, correctly, things that were to later come to pass.

The demon kept its word, in so much as this is not the end of the story. At the end of January 1907, Clara began behaving in a very distressed manner. She started telling the missions workers, that she would become possessed again, as the demon had announced it coming to her in voices and dreams. During this time, her demeanour was described as desperate, frightened and withdrawn.

Fr Erasmus had to leave to go to Rome and a Fr Leonhard took over his duties. In mid-April Claras condition suddenly changed, and she started displaying the same symptoms as before, however, this time they were more extreme. The demon had returned but, it had returned with company. Shortly after Clara again began showing signs of possession, another girl at the mission, Monica Mohletsche, also started displaying symptoms. The Bishop of Natal and five other priests came to St Michaels, to conduct a second exorcism, this time of both girls, in separate rooms of the mission, over the same period of time. It went on from early morning to late at night, and took 2 days, to finally exorcise the demon from Clara successfully.

Monica took much longer than Clara, as she was so unmanageable. When 8 to 10 people could not manage her, or hold her down, they had to call for reinforcements. Her eyes, it was noted by the bishop, had an almost fiery orange glow, that raged and sent shivers of cold down his spine. Eventually, they were successful in driving the demons out. The priest noted that in Monicas case there was more than one, which made the exorcism harder to manage and perform. Monica went on to live a normal life and never experienced the same occurrences in her lifetime.

Sadly, Clara lived only six years after the exorcism and died in 1913, of consumption, which is tuberculosis in today's terms. She had no more possessions or symptoms after the second exorcism, and "died peacefully and resigned to the will of god," according to those who attended her, in her final moments. This case is well documented in The Penguin Book of Exorcisms which includes further reports, which go into the exorcism and manifestations, in much more detail.

It appears appropriate now to explore a contentious case, when allegations of demonic possession and influence, garnered global attention. The renowned "Devil Made Me Do It", case was adapted into a movie within the Conjuring cinematic universe. A series of films that I personally enjoy watching. Beyond the Hollywood portrayal, numerous documentaries have examined the case, and it unfolded in real time, through both national and international media coverage.

The Devil Made Me Do It

The case begins the year my sister Louise was born in 1981, Connecticut, USA. It involves the Glatzel family, brothers David, Alan, and Carl, sister Debbie and their parents. This was an average family, living an ordinary life, there is nothing to suggest what was about to happen.

Debbie decided to move in with her boyfriend, Arne Cheyenne Johnson, into a house they had found and rented, the next town over. Debbie's family helped her move and during this transition David, who was 10 at the time, and the youngest, was given the job of sweeping an upstairs bedroom. It is in this bedroom, that young David first encounters a presence that he says, overcame him and started pushing him around the room. In terror he leaves but does not tell his family, for fear of ridicule.

Over the next few days, David claimed to have experienced this entity in his parents' home and started behaving oddly and unpredictably. This convinced some, not all, members of the household, to believe that Dvid needed an exorcism. The Catholic church does not just perform exorcisms at will, there is a process and investigation. The Child was sent by the church to a psychiatrist who said there was nothing wrong with him. The church sent a Cardinal to investigate the claims. There was a deliverance performed (kind of similar to an exorcism, performed in Latin, but not the complete exorcism ritual).

91

Now Judy, Davids's mother, had attended a seminar at a library that Ed and Lorraine Warren had given, and became sure her son was possessed. She then contacted the Warrens, who attended the house and the ritual with the Cardinal.

The inclusion of the Warrens in this case warrants scrutiny due to their history. As self-proclaimed demonologists, they were known for detecting demonic activity in various situations. Their involvement in numerous controversial cases, has sparked accusations of fearmongering, fabrication, and exaggeration. David's own relatives, have accused the Warrens of exploiting his mother's fears and influencing David's behaviour. According to his brother, in a recent documentary, upon the Warrens' arrival, they allegedly suggested to David what he should experience, and he complied. His mother and sister primarily believed in the possession narrative propagated by the Warrens. While there is no concrete evidence of the Warrens fabricating stories, these accusations persist among those directly involved in these cases. Additionally, some families portrayed in the Conjuring films, claim that the Warrens persuaded them to embellish their accounts, promising financial gain, yet they received minimal compensation, if any. While the veracity of these claims remains uncertain, the Warrens' involvement, warrants a cautious examination of the purported phenomena.

As the Cardinal and the Warrens performed the deliverance rite, the boy began thrashing about wildly, and screaming profanities. There was none of the other signs that we would expect to see in a demonic possession. The tapes of the possession are in the public domain and are quite disturbing, all spoken in English, apart from the cardinals' prayers.

It is intriguing that David's brother, recalled a moment when David was unruly and shouting at his mother, attributing it to the entity's influence. However, when David's father intervened, and firmly instructed him to stop, David complied and ceased his disruptive behaviour, for the rest of the night. This incident is noteworthy, because it is uncommon for a demon to obey parental commands, but entirely plausible, for a misbehaving child who fears their parents' reaction. Once more, this raises doubts regarding the authenticity of the purported possession.

At this juncture, Arne intercedes during the ritual. Chris Holt, director of the documentary "The Devil on Trial," elaborates, "It was at that point that Arne gripped David and allegedly said, 'Leave the boy alone. Come on, take me on, take me on.' What [supposedly] happened next was a thing called transmigration where the evil entity can leave the possessed person and enter any number of people who are involved in the exorcism. It could be the priest; it could be a family member. It is just whoever it really decides to latch onto. And because Arne had challenged the demon, it went for Arne. Allegedly." The full interview is available on the podcast 'You Can't Make

This Up'.

Months following David's exorcism, Johnson engaged in a heated altercation with their landlord, 40-year-old Alan Bono, while intoxicated. Debbie and Arne's sister were also present. Police reports shed light on the ensuing events: inebriated, Bono behaved inappropriately and forcibly grabbed Arne's sister. Arne claims to have blacked out, only to regain consciousness, holding a knife after fatally stabbing Alan Bono. Debbie asserted that Arne's eyes turned black, and he erupted into a violent rage. Until her passing, Debbie maintained her belief, that Arne was possessed that night. Following Johnson's arrest for Bono's murder, his lawyer, Martin Minella, sought to employ demonic possession as an alibi defence—a first in US legal history. However, the trial judge dismissed demonic possession as a viable defence, leading to media labelling the case as "The devil made me do it." David's brother, Carl Glatzel, holds a sceptical view of the Warrens, branding them as con artists. He questions the alleged possession of both David and Arne, citing Arne's possessive behaviour toward Debbie and rumours of her involvement with Alan Bono. Referring to his mother's records, Carl alleges that she administered Sominex sleeping pills to the family to control them, suggesting that these pills may have induced David's hallucinations. David maintains his belief that his experiences were genuine, and not drug-induced hallucinations. He attributes Arne's actions to possession. What are your thoughts on this? I'd love to hear. Here are some other cases involving demonic entities or spirits.

The Smurl Haunting:
During the 1970s and 1980s, the Smurl family, residing in West Pittston, Pennsylvania, found themselves ensnared in a harrowing ordeal. They were besieged by inexplicable occurrences, ranging from foul odours permeating their home to physical assaults and chilling apparitions. With their lives turned upside down by these unsettling events, they turned to renowned paranormal investigators Ed and Lorraine Warren for help. The Warrens, well-versed in confronting the supernatural, delved into the case and concluded that the family was grappling with the malevolent grip of demonic or negative spirit. After years of enduring the torment inflicted by the malevolent entity in their home, the Smurl family's ordeal eventually subsided. The exact circumstances surrounding the cessation of the haunting are not extensively documented, but it appears that the intensity of the paranormal activity diminished over time. Following the conclusion of the haunting, the Smurl family sought to move on with their lives and put the traumatic experiences behind them. Despite the challenges they faced, they persevered and continued to live their lives to the best of their ability.

The Entity of Bill Ramsey:

During the 1980s, a British man named Bill Ramsey found himself thrust into the spotlight due to a series of alarming incidents that suggested he might be possessed by a demonic entity. The case took place in the seaside resort of Southend on Sea, when a mild mannered carpenter called Bill Ramsey became known in the press as the `Werewolf of Southend. Ramsey's story captivated the public as he recounted terrifying episodes in which he underwent startling transformations. Bill had been suffering since he was 9 years old with bouts of weird behaviour that people described as being wolf or animal like and accompanied allegedly by a foul smell.

Witnesses reported seeing Ramsey display superhuman strength, ripping posts from concrete and smashing them in front of his parents' home. He would adopt animalistic behaviour during these episodes, leading many to believe that something supernatural was at play. When he committed himself to hospital, he bit a nurse and ransacked the hospital before being sedated.

It was clear that Bill had lost self- control of his condition and on the night of 22nd July 1987, he decided to visit Southend Police Station and asked to be locked up for his own and the public's safety. During the course of a conversation with a police officer, Bill suddenly became enraged and `wolf-like` and physically attacked the 6` tall, 14 stone (196 lb or 89 kg) officer by hurling the him across a car park it took no less than six police officers to bring him under control  Bill`s enraged `werewolf like` behaviour did not cease under lock and key, as at one point Bill was able to wedge his head and arm through a cell door inspection hatch and whilst still snarling and snapping at   officers.

Police then were forced to call a doctor who administered Bill with a powerful sedative whilst the fire brigade were able to free him from the hatchway.

Bill`s case went global, and in the USA, Ed and Lorraine Warren the well-known demonologists, flew over to Southend to investigate his case. Suffice to say Bill was later taken to America and his condition was proscribed as `demonic` and later exorcised in a church ceremony in the USA. To date Bill has not suffered with any more bouts. Was Bill possessed? Or was Bill suffering from a rare mental condition known as Lycanthropy where the term is used in medical circles as reference to a mental illness in which a patient believes he or she is or has transformed into an animal and behaves accordingly. This is sometimes referred to as `Clinical Lycanthropy` to distinguish it from it use in legends.

Intrigued by Ramsey's claims, paranormal researchers delved into the case, conducting investigations to unravel the mystery behind his affliction. As media coverage intensified, Ramsey's story became a topic of widespread interest and debate, with some convinced that he was indeed experiencing spirit attachment. Yet, despite the attention his case garnered, the true nature of Ramsey's experiences remained shrouded in mystery, leaving many questions unanswered.

Distinguishing between paranormal phenomena and mental health issues poses a significant challenge for paranormal investigators. On one hand, genuine paranormal experiences can often mimic symptoms of mental illness, such as hallucinations or delusions. Conversely, individuals experiencing mental health issues, may interpret their symptoms as paranormal in nature. This overlap complicates the investigation process, as investigators must carefully evaluate each case, to determine the root cause of reported phenomena. Additionally, there is a stigma surrounding mental health, which can further obscure the distinction between paranormal and psychological explanations. Paranormal investigators must approach each case with sensitivity and a thorough understanding of both paranormal and mental health phenomena, to accurately assess and address the experiences, reported by individuals seeking assistance.

The likelihood of a paranormal investigator encountering a demonic haunting first hand, is exceedingly rare, unless specifically seeking out known cases of such phenomena. However, it is within the realm of possibility to encounter hauntings at various stages, such as infestation, oppression, or obsession.

It is essential to approach any claims of demonic activity with caution and scepticism. Human spirits may sometimes masquerade as demons or use terms like "legion" or "devil" to elicit reactions or instil fear. Additionally, homeowners, particularly those with strong religious beliefs, may be quick to label paranormal activity as demonic, leading to potential misunderstandings or clashes in belief systems, during investigations.

In cases where there is a strong suspicion of demonic activity, it is crucial not to provoke or confront the entity recklessly. Instead, investigators should regroup and formulate a plan of action. Familiarising oneself with protective exercises and establishing connections with local religious leaders, can provide valuable support and guidance, when navigating potentially dangerous situations.

As the veil between worlds grows thin and the darkness creeps closer, remember this: demons lurk in the shadows, ever vigilant, ever hungry. In the depths of the unknown, where fear and curiosity collide, tread carefully, for the whispers of malevolent entities echo through the darkness, beckoning the unwary into realms, best left unexplored.

In the realm of demons, the line between salvation and damnation is razor-thin, and to dance with darkness is to risk losing oneself to the eternal night. Proceed with caution, for in the depths of the abyss, even the bravest souls may find themselves ensnared, in the grasp of infernal forces, beyond their comprehension.

POLTERGEIST

**"Poltergeists are the wild children of the paranormal world,
disrupting lives with their unseen hands and mischievous antics."
Lloyd Auerbach**

The term "poltergeist" has its roots in the German language, stemming from two words; "poltern," meaning "to make noise," and "Geist," meaning "spirit" or "ghost." When combined, "poltergeist" translates to "noisy spirit" or "noisy ghost." Poltergeist phenomena are among the most widely recognised hauntings, alongside demonic hauntings, and possessions. Largely due to their portrayal in Hollywood films such as "The Amityville Horror" and "The Enfield Haunting." However, in reality, poltergeist hauntings are quite rare, and paranormal investigators are seldom called to investigate them. Nevertheless, for those experiencing them, poltergeist activity can be profoundly frightening. The nature of poltergeist phenomena is a subject of intense debate among paranormal researchers, with two main schools of thought emerging on the matter.

- That the activity is linked to the unconscious psychic energy of a living person, often a teenager or someone undergoing significant emotional distress. In these cases, the activity may not be caused by an external spirit or entity but by the individual's subconscious mind, projecting energy that manifests as physical disturbances. The living person is not aware of what they are doing.
- Intelligent entities or spirits are causing poltergeist activity. These entities are believed to have their own intentions and motivations, which could explain what seems like purposeful and sometimes malevolent behaviour associated with this phenomenon.

A third option, which is connected to the concept that it is caused by a living person, is that over time as it grows and gains more power. It then takes on a life of its own, becoming a sentient and often malevolent entity, in its own right. The concept of poltergeists "taking on their own life", is because poltergeist phenomena seem to exhibit a level of autonomy or independent existence and thinking. poltergeist activity can persist even after the initial circumstances or individuals, believed to be causing it, are no longer present.

If you were to ask various paranormal investigators what they think, I would suggest the answer would be, depending on the case, a bit of both. There are cases where the activity is caused by an intelligent spirit or entity that manifests by throwing things and causing havoc. These cases are not uncommon. True poltergeist activity, however, is in my belief, caused by a living person. What we can agree on, is that this kind of activity tends to occur around women more than men. The focus of a poltergeist tends to be, but not always, a female adolescent who is suffering from unresolved emotional turmoil. It is around this time when the activity begins. That said however, not all those who are the focus of such activity are teenagers. William G. Roll, a pioneer in poltergeist research, found the age of people reporting experiences of poltergeist activity, ranged from eight to 78 years. There was no data available, however, that detailed if these people were surrounded by someone of adolescent age.

William G. Roll, an American psychologist and parapsychologist affiliated with the Psychology Department of the University of West Georgia, is renowned for his study of poltergeist phenomena. He introduced the term "recurrent spontaneous psychokinesis" (RSPK) to characterize cases of poltergeist activity. While considered a pioneer in poltergeist research, Roll's methodologies and conclusions have faced significant scrutiny, from the scientific community. According to RSPK theory, unresolved stress accumulates and unconsciously projects outward as mental energy, influencing the physical environment and giving rise to poltergeist phenomena. This emotional turmoil can seemingly target individuals against whom the energy is directed, resulting in physical harm such as scratches, bruises, and even physical assaults. Typically, these hauntings escalate in severity over time. Initially characterized by knocks, bangs, and moving furniture, the activity intensifies, culminating in phenomena such as disembodied voices and the apparition of full-bodied entities. Furniture may slide across rooms, and beds may violently shake, amplifying the unsettling nature of the haunting.

In certain instances, poltergeist activity occurs in the vicinity of individuals who are stable and in a sound state of mind. Such hauntings defy easy classification due to their variability, with no two cases being identical. Typically, one individual within the household appears to bear the brunt of the poltergeist activity, which often revolves around them. Interestingly, disturbances tend to cease when this individual is absent from the premises. Poltergeist encounters frequently involve multiple individuals residing in or visiting a home simultaneously. The person who becomes the focal point of the activity may be grappling with significant emotional turmoil or confronting mental challenges. Resolution often hinges on this individual addressing and managing their emotional issues, which can lead to a reduction in poltergeist activity. Most poltergeist cases conclude as abruptly as they commence, without warning, spanning from mere days to weeks, or even extending over months to years.

The earliest recorded instance of poltergeist activity traces back to

AD 865 in Bavaria, Germany, within a small farmhouse near the Bingen-am-Rhein monastery, dubbed the Poltergeist of Bingen

. Initially, the farmer inhabiting this farmhouse, whose name has faded from history, attributed the disturbances to his children or mischievous neighbours. However, as the phenomena intensified—manifesting as knocking on walls, stones raining down, mysterious fires, and accusatory shouts from the poltergeist—the farmer recognized its paranormal nature and sought aid from the monastery. The disturbances grew more severe, resulting in injuries caused by stones, crops igniting spontaneously, and animals wasting away despite ample sustenance. Moreover, the poltergeist levelled accusations, insinuating inappropriate relationships and abuse by the farmer, leading to his ostracisation by the community.

The outcome of the haunting remains shrouded in uncertainty, with speculation suggesting that monks from the monastery may have conducted an exorcism, yet no records validate this or the cessation of the haunting. Speculation also arises regarding whether the farmer's alleged misconduct triggered the poltergeist activity directed at him. However, the absence of conclusive evidence renders this conjecture speculative, leaving the truth behind these allegations veiled in ambiguity.

Man in Blue Coat
George Inn (currently Lafferty's)

The owners, staff, and patrons of what was formerly known as The George, have frequently encountered poltergeist phenomena. These occurrences range from objects being forcefully thrown across the bar, resulting in the shattering of beer glasses, to lights flickering on and off and doors slamming shut. Additionally, there are reports of distinct footsteps and knocking sounds heard during the late hours. Some witnesses have even claimed to see the apparition of a man wearing a long blue coat and sporting a beard, often observed lingering on the staircase. Whether this spectral figure is connected to the poltergeist activity remains uncertain. Surprisingly, these incidents persisted well into the 2000s.

Bloxwich Lane
Walsall, Birmingham

From February to March of 1962, a private residence was plagued by intense poltergeist activity. Resembling the deafening noise of a pneumatic drill, the disturbances robbed both the family residing in the house and their neighbours of much-needed sleep. Additionally, objects within the home were reportedly thrown or displaced. Authorities, including housing officers and the police, were called to the scene, although their observations were not formally documented. However, a psychic visitor suggested that a deceased family member was attempting to communicate, although the outcome of this assertion was not recorded. The poltergeist activity abruptly ceased in 1963.

The Enfield Poltergeist (1977-1979):

This case unfolded at 284 Green Street, a council house located in Brimsdown, Enfield, London, England, spanning from 1977 to 1979. The focus was on the Hodgson family, particularly two of their children, 11-year-old Janet and 13-year-old Margaret. In August 1977, Peggy Hodgson contacted the police, reporting witnessing furniture moving by itself, accompanied by banging and scratching sounds emanating from the walls. A police constable witnessed a chair "wobble and slide" but could not ascertain the cause. The haunting escalated to include disembodied voices, loud noises, objects being thrown, furniture overturning, and instances of the children seemingly levitating. Over an 18-month period, more than 33 individuals, including neighbours, psychic researchers, and journalists, claimed to witness heavy furniture moving autonomously, objects being hurled across rooms, and the daughters levitating several feet off the ground. Janet asserted being possessed and communicating with a spirit named Bill, who purportedly died in the house years earlier, alleging he was murdered by his landlord, although this was never substantiated. Bill purportedly sought justice for his wrongful death. The case garnered widespread attention and remains extensively documented as one of the most notable instances of poltergeist activity. There is speculation that many of these occurrences were staged by the girls in front of the media, leading to debate among investigators about the authenticity of the haunting. The Enfield haunting served as the basis for the film "The Conjuring 2". As of October 2023, the current occupants of the property report no paranormal activity within the home.

When delving into the realm of poltergeist phenomena, caution is paramount for paranormal investigators. These investigations pose unique challenges and potential risks, necessitating careful consideration. Here are some precautions to heed: Approaching poltergeist investigations demands a delicate balance of courage and caution. Unlike other paranormal encounters, poltergeist activity can be unpredictable and potentially hazardous. Investigators must tread cautiously, recognising that their presence might escalate an already volatile situation. Always prioritise safety—both physical and emotional—and never underestimate the power of unseen forces at play. Remember, engaging with poltergeist phenomena entails inherent risks, including psychological distress and spiritual upheaval. Proceed with utmost respect for the unknown and be prepared to step back if the situation becomes overwhelming. In the quest for truth, let prudence be your guiding beacon, and may wisdom safeguard you from the shadows that lurk within.

PORTAL HAUNTING

"In the world of the paranormal, portals are the gateways through which the mysteries of the universe reveal themselves."

A portal haunting refers to a location where supernatural entities, such as ghosts, spirits, or even otherworldly beings, are able to manifest or pass through from another dimension or realm, into our own.

Portal hauntings are a fascinating and often unsettling phenomenon within the realm of paranormal activity. Unlike traditional hauntings, which are typically associated with specific locations or objects, portal hauntings are believed to occur at points where the barrier between our world and the spirit world, is particularly thin or porous, allowing entities to pass through more easily.

Portals are not a recent concept, as they have been depicted in numerous science fiction films and video games. However, in real-world scenarios, portal hauntings remain a contentious subject due to the limited understanding surrounding them. The concern with open portals, lies in their nature as unguarded gateways, providing unhindered entry to any entity or energy that wants to come through. It is akin to leaving your front door wide open, inviting anyone to enter at will. This vulnerability can cause disruption within a household, potentially resulting in what is commonly referred to, as a portal haunting.

Addressing these portals and their associated energetic disturbances is paramount, especially when considering their potential origins in magical practices or rituals gone awry. Priority lies in closing these gateways, clearly conveying one's intention for any lingering entities or spirits to depart. Once sealed, attention can turn to remedying any residual effects.

Critical to this process is introspection, regarding past actions that may have inadvertently facilitated the opening of these portals. This self-awareness forms the foundation for preventing their recurrence, ensuring a more permanent resolution to the haunting.

For those feeling uncertain or overwhelmed by the situation, seeking guidance from experienced practitioners of energy work, such as shamans, psychics, or spiritual healers, is advisable. These individuals can offer insights and assistance tailored to the specific circumstances, facilitating a more effective resolution.

Let us envision a scenario: An ordinary home, suddenly transforms into a hotbed of paranormal activity, following an incident involving a teenager, whom we'll refer to as Johnny, experimenting with a Ouija board and neglecting to properly conclude the session. This oversight likely results in the

100

opening of one or more portals, unleashing a barrage of unwanted phenomena into the household. Such occurrences underscore the inherent risks associated with practices like spirit communication, prompting many to steer clear of such activities within their homes. It is the very reason I do not use spirit boxes, or any other communication methods, within the confines of my home.

Locations experiencing a diverse array of anomalous phenomena, ranging from glowing orbs to peculiar entities and inexplicable atmospheric disturbances like mists or fog, often raise suspicions of portal activity. These manifestations hint at the existence of conduits through which various energies traverse, perpetuating the cycle of unexplained events. Identifying the presence of portals often transcends mere observation; it becomes a visceral experience for seasoned investigators. As they approach these gateways, individuals may perceive a sensation similar to the room spinning, accompanied by a palpable rush of swirling energy, enveloping their bodies. This dense concentration of energy in a confined space, often leads to feelings of sickness or headaches, earning these phenomena, the label of "vortexes."

Moreover, cleansing the affected space is often imperative, but it is crucial that this process be conducted by a knowledgeable practitioner. Improper cleansing rituals may inadvertently exacerbate the issue rather than alleviate it.

Addressing disturbances related to portals necessitates a nuanced approach, as solutions can differ significantly depending on the circumstances. Relying on one's intuition and seeking guidance from knowledgeable individuals is paramount. The ultimate objective is to restore harmony and equilibrium to the home, undertaken with respect, purposefulness, and an unwavering dedication to resolving the situation.

Here are the key points to glean from this section concerning Portal Hauntings: Portal hauntings often manifest certain shared characteristics, including unexplained temperature fluctuations, disturbances in electromagnetic fields, peculiar auditory phenomena like strange sounds or voices, and anomalous visual occurrences such as orbs or apparitions. While portals can theoretically manifest anywhere, they are frequently associated with specific types of environments, such as ancient ruins, burial grounds, intersections, or sites with a history of intense emotional or traumatic events.

Various theories endeavour to clarify the existence of portal hauntings. Some posit them as natural phenomena arising from geomagnetic anomalies or quantum fluctuations, while others attribute them to spiritual or metaphysical elements, such as the presence of ley lines or residual energy from past occurrences.

Encounters with portal hauntings can pose potential risks. Entities traversing through portals may not always be benign, and interactions with them can lead to adverse psychological repercussions, physical injury, or spiritual entanglement. Paranormal investigators and scholars often scrutinise portal hauntings, to gain deeper insights into their nature and potential ramifications. This may involve utilising an array of tools and methodologies, such as EVP (electronic voice phenomena) recordings, EMF (electromagnetic field) meters, and infrared cameras, to document and analyse paranormal phenomena. For individuals grappling with disturbances linked to portal hauntings, seeking assistance from experienced paranormal investigators or spiritual practitioners is always advisable.

Techniques like cleansing rituals, energy purging, and boundary establishment can aid in mitigating the impact of portal hauntings and facilitate resolution for affected individuals or locales.

HAUNTED OBJECT HAUNTINGS

Imagine a world where the ordinary becomes extraordinary, where the inanimate gains a life of its own, and where the seemingly innocuous harbours secrets beyond comprehension. Welcome to the realm of haunted objects.

In this reality, there exist fragments of the past that refuse to fade into obscurity. These fragments, these haunted objects, are not merely physical entities bound by matter and time; they are conduits between the realms of the living and the dead. Vessels that radiate with the residual energies of their often tumultuous histories.

A haunted object is more than just an amalgamation of wood, metal, or stone. It is a repository of memories, emotions, and experiences, each layer interwoven into its very essence like threads in a macabre tapestry. Within its silent confines lie echoes of laughter, whispers of despair and untold longings.

But it is not merely the past that haunts these objects; it is the unresolved, the unfulfilled, and the unredeemed. They are tethered to this world by the weight of unfinished business, by the echoes of injustices left unanswered, or by the longing for connection. Their presence lingers leaving an indelible mark on those who dare to come near.

A haunted object is a paradox—a relic of both the mundane and the supernatural, a bridge between the tangible and the intangible. It exists at the intersection of belief and scepticism.

To encounter a haunted object is to bear witness to the echoes of the past, to commune with spirits long departed, and to tread the thin line between fascination and fear. In the realm of haunted objects, ordinary becomes extraordinary. They are reminders that the past is never truly buried.

It baffles me, the amount of items on sale, on places like e bay or other online sources, claiming to be haunted objects. What baffles me even

102

more, is the amount of people that want to purchase a haunted object. Unless you are a serious paranormal researcher that has somewhere other than your house, to keep it, I cannot imagine why someone would think, seeking out a haunting, is a good idea. The majority, I am guessing, have no experience with the paranormal. Those that do, usually know better than to start collecting trapped spirits or even worse, angry, and malicious entities.

At this point it needs to be stated that a haunted object, is not to be confused with a cursed object. They are two different beasts entirely. Although we are not covering cursed objects in this book, understanding the difference is important.

In my experience, ghosts rarely hurt people. 99% of the time, the ghost story, and we are talking real-life ghost stories, ends with "we ran away" or "we moved" or "then the priest came". Ghosts rarely harm, and for a cursed object to be a cursed object, it has to harm someone.

I believe it is important to clarify that we're not solely discussing objects (haunted or cursed) that possess an inherent eerie quality, like creepy old Edwardian dolls and the equally creepy people who collect them. These objects may seem ordinary, such as chairs, lamps, beds, and vases. Yet they have the peculiar trait of bringing about misfortune or being the focus of otherworld companions. Typically, this misfortune manifests as death, financial loss, or conflict in a cursed item. A haunted items leads to typical haunting manifestation.

If a haunted object does cause serial harm, and it hurts more than one person, then it becomes a cursed object as well. That is a possibility, as the terms are not mutually exclusive, it is however, rare. It is more likely an object is a hunted object.

Probably most well known of cursed objects, are Annabelle the ragdoll and the doll Robert. Though they are technically attached to a spirit (though it more likely a non-human entity) they are both haunted and cursed. Cursed objects are, in their very nature, inherently dangerous. Haunted objects are generally not. I could literally, write a whole new book on cursed object. Maybe I will.

Now we have made the distinction, our primary focus in this section is to look at hauntings that are caused by bringing in, haunted objects.

Haunted objects essentially involve a spirit attachment, wherein a spirit or entity, forms a non-physical bond with the object. This attachment may stem from previous ownership or through a phenomenon known as spirit displacement, where the energy of a spirit becomes absorbed by an object, located near a traumatic event. From my own perspective, I believe that haunted objects present a range of potential explanations.

- Its Residual energy left over following an event, which caused heightened emotions to manifest (think suicide, murder etc). Residual cases can also be associated with a profound emotional connection to an object. For instance, a wedding ring that held significant meaning for someone, worn daily, might possess the capacity to absorb and preserve some of its owner's energy. Take, for instance, a case in Western Australia where clients believed their deceased mother's clock was haunted. The clock consistently stopped at 2:45 a.m., the precise time of her passing, repeating this occurrence once every 24 hours. Given that no other paranormal activity was reported, it is more plausible to interpret this as a residual haunting, of the object.

- In some cases, there exists an intelligent and interactive spirit or essence of a person, with a profound attachment to a particular item. They may have devoted countless hours to meticulously crafting something beautiful, that held immense sentimental value. Even after passing, the spirit revisits what they cherished in life. For instance, an old chair that served as their favourite spot. While this scenario might be labelled as "haunted," it essentially acts as a magnet, stimulating activity within the home.

- A spirit becomes attached to the energy of the person who owns the object. This often happens with items that have been passed down through generations or have been owned by one person for a long time.

- The emotional state of the owner when they were using the item is absorbed into the item (Think stone tape theory), that item could pick up on that emotion and attract a spirit, that is also experiencing that emotion. An item that has absorbed angry energy, may attract a spirit that feels angry that is not in fact, connected to the item itself.

- If someone passed away while wearing a certain piece of jewellery, that jewellery could hold on to the energy of the person and their passing.

There is much debate within the paranormal field as to what is the very nature of a haunted object. I personally do not believe an object can be, in and of itself, haunted. I believe that possessing a haunted object can cause the manifestations that a haunted house would have—things moving on their own, strange noises, seeing apparitions, hearing voices and so forth. I strongly believe that it either residual or there is an external intelligent spirit, that has an attachment to the item. So, when it comes to this kind of haunting it is generally an attachment issue. I would say a cursed object is more likely to be a non-human entity attached to an object.

104

The truth is paranormal researchers simply do not know for certain how an object becomes haunted. We can speculate as to why there is a spirit attached and resolve the haunting, the way we would any trapped spirit haunting. What are the signs you have a haunted object. Shortly after bringing a new item home you may experience the following.

- Strange sounds such as footsteps, knocking, or whispers may be heard, often emanating from the vicinity of the haunted object.
- Objects may appear to move on their own or be found in different locations without any logical explanation.
- Some individuals claim to witness apparitions or shadowy figures associated with the haunted object.
- Cold spots or sudden changes in temperature can be indicative of paranormal activity.
- Lights flickering, appliances malfunctioning, or electronic devices behaving erratically may occur in the presence of the haunted object.
- Occupants may experience feelings of being watched, a sense of dread, or discomfort when near the object.
- Some individuals may report experiencing vivid dreams, anxiety, or mood swings correlated with the presence of the haunted object.
- Pets may exhibit unusual behaviour, such as barking or growling at seemingly empty spaces or avoiding the area where the object is located.

If you think an object is Haunted, the first thing you should do is try to figure out what kind of haunting it is. If it is determined that it is a human spirit, then finding out why the spirit is attached to the object, would be the next step. This can be done by researching the history of the object or talking to a medium.

If it is a non-human entity, then we do not communicate with it, the best thing to do is call in specialist help.

Once you know why the spirit is attached to the object, you can try to help move them on, if that's what they want.

If you are successful in helping the spirit move on, be sure to bless the object so that it does not become Haunted again.

- Do not attempt to remove a spirit from an object without knowing why they are attached to it. This can agitate the spirit and make them angry. spirits that are angry can lash out if they feel threatened.

- Do not attempt to perform a cleansing ritual without first doing your research. Cleansing rituals can be dangerous if not performed correctly.

Some case examples of haunted objects are as follows:

The Hands Resist Him Painting

"The hands resist him" painting was painted by artist Bill Stoneham in 1972 and is considered one of the most haunted pieces of art. Every time the painting is sold the seller will warn the buyer that the figures in the painting will move or disappear altogether. Sometimes the people or objects will appear in the room in which it was displayed. Many people that have simply viewed the painting, have complained about immediately feeling sick or weak.

Bunk Bed

In 1987, Allen and Deborah Tallman of Horicon, Wisconsin, purchased a bunk bed from a thrift store for their children. Shortly thereafter, strange occurrences ensued: mysterious noises, a snow blower inexplicably moving, and unexplained illnesses. Gradually, the parents became convinced that the bunk bed was haunted. They ultimately disposed of the bed by burying it in a landfill and reported no further activity thereafter.

Anna Baker

The wedding dress of Anna Baker, housed at Baker Mansion, is rumoured to be haunted. In the mid-1800s, Anna was engaged to a man her father disapproved of, leading to his dismissal. Consequently, the wedding was called off, and the dress remained unworn. Anna lived out her life unmarried and passed away as an old maid. Since the dress was acquired by a historical society, visitors to the mansion in Altoona, Pennsylvania, have reported witnessing the dress fluttering in its glass case. Speculation arises: does Anna's spirit yearn to wear the dress, or perhaps she desired to be laid to rest in it?

The Anguished Man

The Anguished Man is an enigmatic painting of unknown origin. Its owner, Sean Robinson of Cumbria, England, asserts that he inherited it from his grandmother, who shared a chilling tale: the artist, driven to despair, allegedly mixed his own blood into the paint before taking his own life shortly after completing the piece.

This painting has garnered notoriety for its purportedly haunted nature. Reports abound of eerie phenomena accompanying it, including mysterious crying, and moaning sounds, as well as sightings of a spectral figure

106

resembling a man that seemingly trails the painting wherever it is displayed.

The Case of the Artifact:
In 2017, a museum curator in England, claimed to have experienced supernatural phenomena, after acquiring a voodoo artifact from Africa. The artifact, believed to be used in voodoo rituals, was said to be haunted by its previous owner. Following its acquisition, the curator reported experiencing unexplained disturbances, including objects moving on their own and strange noises. Some speculated that the artifact was inhabited by a malevolent entity seeking revenge for its removal from its original context.

The mystery of a haunted object has a great many ideas attached to it. But what of inanimate objects that become a manifestation within itself?

In conclusion, distinguishing between cursed and haunted objects is crucial for understanding the nature of paranormal phenomena, and determining appropriate courses of action. Cursed objects are imbued with malevolent energy or intentions, often leading to negative consequences for those who come into contact with them. Haunted objects, on the other hand, are items that are inhabited or influenced by spirits or entities, resulting in paranormal disturbances or manifestations.

When encountering a haunted object, it is essential to approach the situation with caution and respect for the spiritual realm. Here are some steps to safely deal with a haunted object:

- Assessment: Begin by carefully evaluating the object and documenting any paranormal activity associated with it. This includes strange sounds, movements, or other unexplained occurrences.
- Protection: Prioritise your safety by establishing spiritual protection measures before interacting with the object. This may involve using protective symbols, prayers, or rituals to shield yourself from negative energy.
- Communication: If possible, attempt to communicate with the spirit or entity attached to the object. Respectfully ask questions and listen for responses, but be prepared for varying forms of communication, including EVP recordings or psychic impressions.
- Respectful Removal: If the haunting is causing distress or disruption, consider removing the object from your home. However, do so with care and respect for the spirit attached to it. Perform a cleansing ritual to ensure that any residual energy is released, and the spirit is allowed to move on peacefully.

107

- Disposal or Containment: Depending on the severity of the haunting, you may choose to dispose of the object in a respectful manner or contain it in a designated space, such as a protective box or consecrated area.

- Seeking Assistance: If dealing with a haunted object becomes overwhelming or beyond your expertise, seek assistance from experienced paranormal investigators, psychics, or spiritual practitioners. They can offer guidance and assistance in safely resolving the situation.

In all cases, approach dealing with haunted objects with reverence, empathy, and a commitment to resolving the situation peacefully. By respecting the spiritual entities involved and taking appropriate precautions, you can navigate these encounters safely and effectively.

INANIMATE OBJECT HAUNTINGS: VEHICLES

It is not solely entities and individuals that can be the origin of a haunting. Inanimate objects are also known to imbue specific areas with a haunting presence, whether through residual energy or some form of intelligent or animated manifestation. Examples of this phenomenon, include vehicles such as planes, cars, boats, and horse-drawn carriages. This is also sometimes referred to as an animated haunting.

Over time, there have been numerous reports of phantom horse-drawn carriages, frequently driven by unidentified spirits, that have become enmeshed in local folklore. However, the most frequent sightings involve phantom planes, especially occurring on the anniversaries of battles or in specific areas.

These types of hauntings often lend themselves to rational explanations through critical thinking and investigation. Take, for example, the instance of phantom oncoming train lights, appearing on abandoned railway lines. With diligent examination and practice, many of these phenomena can be debunked.

The Saint Louis train lights serve as a captivating illustration of this concept. This phenomenon ranks among Saskatchewan's most renowned unexplained occurrences—a mysterious light that appears nearly every night near the central Saskatchewan community, seemingly along an old railway line. Witnesses commonly describe the light resembling that of an approaching train, emanating from the south. However, the perplexity arises from the fact that the railway line has long been abandoned, with its tracks removed years ago. Naturally, such occurrences come with their own legends, and this one revolves around the spirit of an old train conductor who purportedly lost his head, during a routine track inspection, a century prior.

The case garnered widespread attention, drawing crowds of people eager to witness and report on this extensively documented paranormal phenomenon. Yet, scepticism persisted, prompting two schoolgirls to take matters into their own hands, with the assistance of one of their fathers. Together, they embarked on an hours-long expedition, driving from various vantage points at night, to ascertain if they could replicate the effect. Ultimately, they succeeded in demonstrating that the phenomenon was merely the headlights of a distant car, cresting a hill. Despite its initial mystique, the phenomenon was debunked by their diligent investigation.

However, it is worth noting, that not all cases of paranormal phenomena are as readily explained.

The paradox inherent in hauntings involving inanimate objects, lies in the challenge of reconciling the seemingly static nature of these objects, with their ability to manifest paranormal phenomena. Unlike entities or living beings traditionally associated with hauntings, inanimate objects lack consciousness or agency. Yet, they can become focal points for residual energies or serve as conduits for spiritual activity.

This paradox raises questions about the mechanisms by which inanimate objects can retain and transmit, spiritual energy as well as the nature of their interaction with the physical world. It challenges our understanding of the boundary between the material and the spiritual realms and the complexity, of paranormal phenomena.

Moreover, the investigation of hauntings involving inanimate objects, often requires careful consideration of various factors, including the object's history, the context of its presence, and the cultural beliefs surrounding it. Debunking such phenomena can be particularly challenging, due to the potential for psychological and perceptual biases, as well as the influence of local legends and folklore.

In essence, the paradox of inanimate object hauntings highlights the mysterious and multifaceted nature of the paranormal, urging us to approach such phenomena with a combination of scepticism, open-mindedness, and rigorous inquiry.

Small Pick Up
On the M6 motorway, near Birmingham, author Paul Devereux had a remarkable encounter. While driving, he found himself overtaking a pickup truck, seemingly unmanned, along this particular stretch of road. After completing the manoeuvre, Devereux glanced at his side mirror only to witness the truck inexplicably vanish into thin air, leaving him astounded by the surreal nature of the experience. This encounter adds to the lore of inexplicable phenomena along the M6, prompting speculation and fascination

about the mysteries, that may lie hidden within its lanes.

Wellington Bomber
Aberdare (South Glamorgan) - Sky over Cwmbach estate
In approximately 1979, a witness outside their home, experienced a perplexing event. While hearing the sound of engines, they initially could not discern any visible aircraft. Intrigued, they stepped into their doorway. However, as the sound of the engines intensified, the witness ventured back outside. To their astonishment, they observed a twin-engine, dark-coloured Wellington bomber soaring overhead, appearing as tangible and audible as any actual aircraft. Curiously, the witness didn't find the encounter peculiar at the time, unaware that there were no airworthy Wellington bombers still in existence.

Lancaster Bomber
Barnoldswick (Lancashire) - Area near Rolls Royce's Bankfield factory, and area towards Craven
In January 2004, an extraordinary incident seized the attention of approximately thirty witnesses, who all claimed to have seen a peculiar sight: a silent, grey-coloured aircraft bearing a striking resemblance to a Lancaster Bomber, gliding noiselessly across the sky. These accounts, though scattered, shared remarkable consistency, and persisted over the span of a month before abruptly ceasing. When authorities consulted local air traffic control, to probe the matter, it was confirmed that no bombers were airborne during the reported sightings. This left the phenomenon unexplained and enveloped in enigma, leaving those who witnessed it baffled by the inexplicable occurrence.

Spitfire
Biggin Hill (Kent) - Biggin Hill Airport & village
Every year around the 19th of January, residents of Biggin Hill report sightings and occasionally the sound of, a Spitfire plane flying overhead. This spectral Spitfire seems to favour the month of January for its appearances, adding to the mystique surrounding its haunting presence in the skies.

In addition to the phantom aircraft, sightings of airmen dressed in trench coats have been reported in the village. These ghostly figures are said to approach people, asking for directions before vanishing into thin air, leaving witnesses bewildered. Such phenomena contribute to the richness of legends and folklore surrounding Biggin Hill, keeping alive the memory of its wartime history and the brave individuals who served.

Location: Ash (Surrey) - Ash Rectory
In 1938, the rector of the area had a chilling encounter that he documented: he was roused from sleep by the thunderous sounds of galloping. Upon

110

opening his eyes, he beheld a spectral coach being pulled by a team of horses passing through his very bedroom. Astonishingly, similar eerie phenomena had reportedly been witnessed by previous rectors as well. These unsettling occurrences were attributed to the rectory's location, perched atop an ancient road, steeped in mystery and folklore. Such tales continue to fuel the haunting legacy surrounding the rectory, captivating both residents and visitors with its spectral past.

The phenomenon of phantom vehicles, including ghostly horse-drawn carriages and spectral planes, has captured the imaginations of people around the world. While these sightings are often intertwined with local legends and folklore, they can often be rationalised through critical thinking and investigation.

Whether it is the appearance of phantom trains on abandoned tracks or mysterious planes on significant anniversaries, these occurrences prompt us to delve deeper into the mysteries of our surroundings. By applying careful consideration and diligent research, we can often uncover the truth behind these spectral apparitions, shedding light on the unknown and enriching our understanding of the paranormal realm. Yet, even as we strive to debunk these phenomena, the allure and intrigue of phantom vehicles continue to captivate our curiosity, reminding us of the enduring fascination with the unexplained.

OTHER PARANORMAL ENTITIES

Numerous cases of non-human paranormal entities exist, each steeped in its own lore and sightings. These entities defy explanation and elude classification within known categories of paranormal phenomena. I will leave it to the reader to decide whether they wish to embark on investigations into these mysteries. If you happen upon answers or embark on intrepid expeditions into the unknown, please reach out to the author of this book, as I am deeply intrigued.

Mothman
One notable example is the Mothman, a creature reportedly sighted in Point Pleasant, West Virginia, in the late 1960s. Described as a large, winged humanoid with glowing red eyes, the Mothman was associated with a series of strange occurrences and sightings, leading up to the tragic collapse of the Silver Bridge, in 1967.

In the late 1960s, the small town of Point Pleasant, West Virginia, became the centre of a series of strange events surrounding a mysterious creature known as the Mothman. Described as a large, winged humanoid with glowing red eyes, the Mothman was reportedly sighted by numerous witnesses in the area. These sightings were often accompanied by feelings of dread and unease.

The Mothman sightings coincided with other bizarre occurrences in Point Pleasant, including mysterious lights in the sky, strange animal behaviour, and reports of electrical disturbances. The climax of these events came with the tragic collapse of the Silver Bridge, in December 1967, resulting in the loss of dozens of lives.

Many locals began to speculate that the Mothman was somehow connected to these events, with some believing it to be a harbinger of disaster or an omen of impending doom. Others dismissed the sightings as hoaxes or misidentifications of known animals.

Despite various investigations and theories attempting to explain the Mothman phenomenon, the creature remains enigmatic, its true nature and origins shrouded in mystery. The legend of the Mothman continues to captivate the imagination of believers and sceptics alike, leaving unanswered questions lingering, in the minds of those who encounter its story.

Jumping Grey Thing
Birmingham-Icknield Street, Hockley

This one comes from my own hometown and occurred after I had left England, for Australia. In April 2014, a couple in their car, watched in disbelief, as a grey humanoid like creature jump across the road in front of their car, causing them to slam on the breaks. They described a kangaroo-like creature with glowing eyes, that seemingly gaining momentum by swinging its long extended inhuman arms. The entity stopped in the middle of road and looked at the car and them, before turning and moving back into the grounds of the cemetery.

The Dover Demon

In 1977, residents of Dover, Massachusetts, reported sightings of a strange, humanoid creature with glowing eyes and a large, hairless head. Descriptions of the Dover Demon vary, but witnesses reported feelings of unease and fear during their encounters. Despite extensive investigation, the true nature of the Dover Demon remains unknown. Speculation in the paranormal field tend to point to some sort of elemental being.

The Hopkinsville Goblins

In 1955, a family in Hopkinsville, Kentucky, reported a bizarre encounter with small, humanoid creatures that they described as resembling goblins or aliens. The creatures were said to have glowing eyes and to exhibit supernatural abilities, such as floating and disappearing.

The Unnamed Thing of Berkly Square

Ever since House No. 50 was erected, there had been strange tales of something strange lurking on the second floor. The place has always had a dark reputation for hauntings and supernatural mischief.

Built in 1740 by English architect William Kent, 50 Berkeley Square has gained a reputation as one of the most haunted buildings in London. Around 1741 occupants began complaining of phantom footsteps and something being dragged across the floor. Although dates vary according to different sources, the stories remain generally unchanged.

The first death to be blamed on the "thing", was an occupant named Mr. Thomas Myers in the early 1800s (some sources say he lived there between 1859 and 1874). Mr. Myers and his fiancée planned to be married in the house, but on the day of the wedding, the bride sent a note calling it off. Distraught, Mr. Meyers shut himself away on the 4th floor and became a recluse. He lived the rest of his life, only leaving the house at night and was eventually found dead on the 4th floor, his expression was frozen in terror. The house fell into disrepair and people were scared of the strange lights and noises at night and its mad inhabitant. Myers was even sued during his lifetime, by the local council for not paying his rates. When he did not appear in court, the magistrate excused him, because he was known to live in a haunted house.

The most famous of the reports occurred in 1840. Twenty-year-old Sir Robert Warboys was drinking in Holborn Tavern and declared the rumours to be "poppycock". He was then dared by his companions to spend the night to show them he wasn't afraid. Eager to prove that it was nonsense, he tracked down the landlord, who allow him to spend the night. The landlord laid out some conditions; that he bring a pistol and a candle, and in the event that anything happening, he was to pull a cord that would ring a bell in the landlord's quarters. The landlord showed him to a room, and he was last seen, sitting at a table around midnight.

At around 12.45am, the landlord was awakened by furious ringing of the bell. A few seconds after that, a gunshot rang out. The landlord raced upstairs and found Sir Robert Warboys, laying crumpled in a corner of the room. His pistol still smoking. His lips peeled back in a horrified grimace; his eyes appeared to be bulging. On the opposite wall, was a single bullet hole, but there was no sign of whatever he had shot at.

Three years later, in 1843 or possibly 1880, two sailors, Robert Martin and Edward Blunden, also spent the night, with deadly consequences. The men had lost their money and were looking for a place to spend the night. Coming across 50 Berkeley Square, the building appeared unoccupied, so they broke in through a basement window. Finding the basement damp, they ventured upstairs. They were fast asleep when Blunden woke to the sound of the door creaking open and something being dragged across the floor. He woke Martin after seeing what he described, as something grey crawling toward them. Suddenly, the creature leaped and wrapped itself around Blunden's throat. Panicked, Martin bolted from the house and soon stumbled across a policeman, patrolling the area. The policeman followed Martin back to the house. They found the room empty, but when they went to the basement, Blunden's corpse lay at the bottom of the stairs. His expression was that of unadulterated terror.

Another encounter involved Thomas Lyttleton, who spent the night in an upstairs room. During the night, he shot the creature and was convinced he had killed it. However, when he searched the house the next morning, he could find no trace of it.

An article in *Mayfair* Magazine in 1879, claimed a maid who stayed there, was found acting mad and died the next day, in an asylum. In her terror, she was never able to say, what had scared her so badly. Another story involves a nobleman who stayed there and was so scared that he became mute. Many who claimed to have seen the creature, compared it to a deformed octopus, because of its slimy tentacles.

In the late 1930s, the Maggs Brothers acquired the building, and the ground floor was turned into a bookshop. No employees or guests are allowed upstairs, and no happenings have been reported since.

. That being said, many theories are passed around on what the Nameless Thing could of been, with answers ranging from a poltergeist, a demon, extra-dimensional beings to an unknown supernatural energy. Either way, this is one location, the author will NOT be sleeping in.

The realm of non-human paranormal entities presents a captivating and often mysterious frontier for investigation. From ancient folklore to modern-day encounters, stories of spectral beings, demonic hauntings, and otherworldly phenomena persist, beckoning intrepid investigators to delve deeper into the unknown. As witnesses recount chilling encounters and unexplained events, the call to explore these realms grows stronger. By venturing forth with an open mind, rigorous methodology, and respect for the unknown, investigators have the opportunity to shed light on the enigmatic forces, that may lie beyond our comprehension. With each investigation, we inch closer to unravelling the secrets of these non-human entities and expanding our understanding of the supernatural world, that surrounds us. So let us heed the call and embark on a journey of exploration, for in the pursuit of truth, we may uncover answers that have eluded us for generations.

3 OTHER PARANORMAL PHENOMENA

In addition to hauntings, the paranormal realm encompasses a diverse array of phenomena that defy conventional explanation. From sightings of unidentified lights to encounters with temperature fluctuations, and from the mysterious phenomenon of phantom odours to reports of electrical interferences, the world of the paranormal is vast and multifaceted. These phenomena captivate the human imagination and challenge our understanding of reality. Exploring these enigmatic occurrences can lead to profound insights into the limits of our knowledge.

ORBS

Paranormal orbs are typically small, circular shapes that appear in videos and photographs at supposed haunted locations. There is a lot of controversy in the field of paranormal research regarding orbs.

There is no shortage of people who believe that any strange balls of light caught on still images or video cameras, are the embodiment or early manifestation of a spirit. Although this may bring a lot of comfort to someone who is grieving over a recent death, it is almost always not the case.

The truth of the matter is that many, if not most, can be explained away as dust, insects, mould spores, pollen, or water droplets in the air. It is believed that when a spirit or entity begins to manifest or is highly active in the area it produces visible balls of energy, in the form of orbs. A full manifestation is rare and takes a lot of energy for a spirit to achieve.

The number of photos I have been sent or seen, where someone claims it is a paranormal orb is so common, it borders on a cliche. However, with respect to those who do this, it does take a significant amount of experience and practice, to identify the difference between an actual paranormal orb or something like dust or even a simple flying insect. What often appears to be spirit orbs are 99% of the time, not anything paranormal.

I have over the years seen some amazing orbs both through the lenses of a camera and with my own eyes. The ones I believe are connected to the spirits that inhabit a place, that I have seen with my own eyes, have been a vivid blue, or white colour. The blue is almost always identical to the blue I saw surrounding my doctor friend, at the quarantine station.

They can in fact be several colours, blue, green, and gold to name but a few. They range in size and shape and can be fast or slow, some almost morphing as they go. Most often caught on video or camera, occasionally the energy is so strong, you can see them with your own eyes.

This is certainly true of highly active paranormal places. Sceptics suggest that orbs are simply artefacts caused by dust, moisture, insects, or reflections of light off particles in the air, particularly when using flash photography in dark environments. It has been my experience that they can actually be both.

The debate over the true nature of orbs continues among paranormal enthusiasts and sceptics alike. It is really when we come to interpret the data, we have analysed that we can make a determination if what we are looking at are explainable or fall into the realms of the paranormal.

PIN PRICKS OF LIGHT

Haunted locations often exhibit various light phenomena, adding to their mysterious allure. One notable example can be found at Tutbury Castle in Staffordshire, a site with a rich history dating back to the 1080s. Tutbury Castle, not far from where I lived and grew up, holds a special significance to me. Despite being mostly ruins today due to damage sustained during the English Civil War, it remains a captivating destination for paranormal enthusiasts.

Tutbury Castle holds a significant place in history due to its association with Mary Queen of Scots during her captivity under the reign of Elizabeth I of England. Mary arrived at the castle on February 4, 1569, and was subsequently transferred between Tutbury Castle and other locations multiple times. Her imprisonment at Tutbury Castle lasted until 1585, when she was relocated to Fotheringhay Castle. Sadly, just a month after her departure from Tutbury, Mary Queen of Scots was executed at Fotheringhay Castle, marking a tragic end to her tumultuous life. The castle's connection to such a pivotal figure in history adds to its intrigue and historical importance.

The castle's paranormal reputation is further enhanced by reports of unusual light displays witnessed by both visitors and investigators. These spectacles are described as spectacular and add to the mystique surrounding the location. The origin of these lights is a matter of debate among enthusiasts, with some attributing them to natural phenomena while others speculate about possible paranormal causes.

Exploring Tutbury Castle for signs of the supernatural offers a captivating and immersive experience. As visitors navigate through the ancient ruins, they are transported through centuries of history, providing ample opportunity to seek out evidence of paranormal activity and perhaps encounter unexplained phenomena first hand.

During my time living in England many years ago, I had the opportunity to attend ghost hunting nights and historical re-enactments at Tutbury Castle.

One particularly memorable story involving witnessing the director, Leslie, dressed as Mary Queen of Scots, deliver a speech with such authenticity that it felt as though people were transported back in time. As Leslie embodied the role, small pinpricks of gold lights would mysteriously appear around her, visible to the naked eye. These lights would flicker and dance throughout the duration of the speech, adding an eerie and enchanting element to the performance. However, once the speech concluded and the performance ended, the lights would vanish without a trace. This phenomenon was unique to Leslie's portrayal of Mary Queen of Scots and added an extra layer of intrigue to a ghost hunting night at Tutbury Castle.

I had heard about this phenomenon and was determined to witness it first-hand. So, I embarked on a late-night ghost hunting excursion in a remote location. I can attest that the reports of these pinpricks of light are indeed genuine. It is undeniably spiritual energy, responding to the events of the performance. However, such occurrences are rare. I have personally witnessed this phenomenon only twice in my life, at different locations. Interestingly, we have captured similar occurrences on video at other sites, although they were not visible to the naked eye, at the time.

As a side note, Tutbury Castle harbours a particularly ominous entity. During guided tours when a specific room is showcased, visitors often report feeling unwell, with some even fainting. The seriousness of these reactions necessitates the presence of medical personnel on-site. It is a chilling testament to the castle's haunted reputation. True Story.

HOT AND COLD SPOTS

Hot and cold spots reported at places where paranormal activity occurs, is almost as common as the occurrence of orbs.

Temperature fluctuations are attributed to the presence and interaction of spirits or entities, with the physical surroundings. Investigators use tools such as thermometers and infrared cameras to record these fluctuations. More often than not, the first indicator is that you feel the temperature change with your body. This generally occurs when there is other paranormal activity happening around you. When we talk about temperature fluctuations, we are talking big changes in the environment. I have been outside on investigations, in the cold and the cold spot is ten times that of the surrounding temperatures. Indoors a warm room, can become icy cold in one area, that tends to be fluid not static. The same applies to hot spots where a very cold room can become almost overheated.

So, how do spirits influence temperature? The concept of cold spots revolves around the idea that a spirit draws thermal energy from its surroundings to manifest. It is believed that spirits require energy to materialise or manipulate electromagnetic sources, for communication. When a spirit draws thermal energy from the environment, it creates cold spots, which can be detected by investigators' equipment.

Similarly, hot spots are thought to occur for similar reasons. When a spirit attempts to manifest, it heats the surrounding area, contrasting with cold spots where the spirit draws energy from its surroundings. Both hot and cold spots are frequently observed at haunted locations, reflecting the energetic interactions between spirits and their environment.

It is worth noting that within the paranormal field, there is often an association between the presence of hot spots and more negative hauntings. While cold spots are linked to common, everyday human hauntings. However, in my experience, I have not found this correlation to be consistent. I believe, that the concept of heat may be influenced by individual belief systems, regarding the afterlife and notions of punishment, rather than being rooted in empirical evidence.

Hot spots, are not exclusive to negative hauntings; they can also occur in positive human hauntings and non-human hauntings. Additionally, some suggest that these temperature anomalies may be influenced by a person's psychology and emotions. For instance, stress and fear can elevate heart rate and body temperature. Therefore, it is essential to corroborate personal experiences with equipment and the observations of others.

In my experience, hot and cold spots can be verified using instruments and are characterised by small areas, that are either cooler or warmer than their surroundings. These anomalies persist even after a thorough debunking process, suggesting that they cannot be attributed to natural causes alone. There have been many documented cases of these changes in temperature at various locations or associated with specific hauntings, here are a few notable ones.

The Brown Lady of Raynham Hall
One of the most renowned ghostly images in history, is said to have been taken at Raynham Hall in England, purportedly capturing the spectral figure known as the "Brown Lady." Witnesses who claim to have encountered her,

118

have reported sudden decreases in temperature when she appears, accompanied by various other paranormal occurrences. These shifts in temperature are frequently cited as supporting evidence of her otherworldly presence.

The Bell Witch Haunting
Witnesses claimed to have experienced cold spots and fluctuations in room temperature, particularly in the Bell family home, when the haunting took place.

The Enfield Poltergeist
During the Enfield Poltergeist case in the late 1970s in London, England, the Hodgson family reported experiencing a variety of paranormal phenomena, including unexplained temperature changes. Witnesses claimed to have felt sudden cold drafts and drops in temperature, in specific areas of their home, coinciding with other paranormal activity, such as objects moving on their own.

The Myrtles Plantation
The Myrtles Plantation in Louisiana, is renowned as one of the most haunted sites in the United States. Numerous visitors and staff members have recounted encounters with cold spots and dramatic temperature shifts within the plantation house, especially in areas with a documented history of paranormal activity. Many attributes these fluctuations to the presence of spirits, particularly those of former slaves, believed to linger on the property.

The Stanley Hotel
The Stanley Hotel in Colorado, famously known as the inspiration for Stephen King's novel, "The Shining," has a reputation for paranormal activity, including ghostly temperature changes. Guests and employees have reported sudden drops in temperature, especially in areas like the infamous Room 217, where paranormal occurrences are said to be particularly intense.

ODOURS

Odours present a fascinating and common phenomenon in various haunting experiences. In old buildings believed to be haunted, descriptions often include a lingering trace of aged odours, drifting down corridors or through rooms. Alternatively, individuals may encounter unexpected scents, such as a grandmother's perfume, while performing mundane tasks like washing dishes, even though their grandmother has been deceased for decades.

Sceptics often attribute these experiences to sensory hallucinations or wishful thinking. However, phantom odours are commonly associated with both residual and intelligent hauntings. Individuals may suddenly detect scents like perfume, cigarette smoke, or pipe tobacco, often coinciding with the sensation of a breeze or the sound of footsteps. In many cases, these encounters are not frightening; instead, they evoke feelings of comfort by triggering memories of loved ones. Scientifically, there is a strong correlation between odours and memory recall.

When I visited The Churchill War Rooms the smell of cigar smoke wafted past us while we completed the tour. It is reputedly haunted by the sounds of footsteps, feelings of "unease" and from experience the smell of cigar smoke. The hands of one of the clocks are said to move mysteriously by themselves.

Only a few nights ago, while doing an investigation of Swan View Station, here in Perth, some team members we got the strong smell of old floral perfume.

However, not all olfactory experiences are benign. Certain scents, such as sulphur (reminiscent of rotten eggs), or those of decay and decomposition, should raise red flags, as they are often indicative of negative or non-human hauntings.

The manipulation of odours by spirits remains a mystery, as the sense of smell is challenging to measure and record, in paranormal investigations. In cases of intelligent hauntings, it is believed that certain odours may be triggered as a form of communication, particularly those associated with loved ones who wish to convey their presence, to their families. However, our understanding is limited, and often we must rely on our own senses and witness reports, to comprehend these phenomena.

It is not uncommon for only one person in a room to be affected by an odour, while others may not detect anything. Conversely, odours may also be experienced by everyone present. These olfactory manifestations often dissipate as quickly as they appear, adding to the enigmatic nature of paranormal odours.

The Scent of Roses
In a famous case from the late 19th century, the spirit of St. Thérèse of Lisieux, a Carmelite nun, who later became a Saint in the Catholic Church, was said to have visited individuals and left behind the scent of roses. This phenomenon, known as the "odour of sanctity," is often associated with spiritual experiences and has been reported by numerous devotees of St. Thérèse.

The Ghostly Smell of Cigars
The White House in Washington, D.C., is said to be haunted by several spirits, including that of former President Abraham Lincoln. Visitors and staff

120

members have reported smelling the distinct aroma of cigar smoke in various rooms of the White House, particularly in the Lincoln Bedroom. Many believe this to be evidence of Lincoln's lingering presence in the historic residence. Sir Winston Churchill is said to haunt several locations and his presence is often accompanied by the smell of his cigar.

The Stench of Sulphur:
In cases involving demonic entities or malevolent spirits, witnesses often report encountering foul odours reminiscent of sulphur or rotten eggs. These odours are commonly associated with demonic manifestations in religious and paranormal literature. One famous example is the case of the alleged possession of the Lutz family, which inspired the book and film "The Amityville Horror." The family reported experiencing strong odours of sulphur during their time in the supposedly, haunted house.

The Smell of Decaying flesh
In locations associated with tragic, traumatic, or violent events, witnesses have reported detecting the smell of decaying flesh, even when there is no apparent source for the odour. This phenomenon is often linked to residual energy or a residual haunting, where past traumas or events leave an imprint on a location. One example is the case of the Tower of London, where visitors have reported smelling the scent of blood or rotting flesh, believed to be associated with the site's violent history as a prison, with torture and executions being commonplace.

As we complete this dialogue about the intriguing world of phantom odours, we have explored the mysterious occurrences of scents that seemingly manifest, without any discernible source. From the lingering perfume of a departed loved one, to the unsettling stench of decay in seemingly pristine environments, phantom odours challenge our understanding of the senses and the nature of reality itself. As we continue our journey through the realm of the paranormal, let us remain open to the possibility that there are phenomena beyond our current comprehension. Perhaps these elusive scents are reminders that there are still mysteries waiting to be unravelled, inviting us to explore the depths of the unknown with curiosity and wonder.

ELECTRICAL INTERFERENCE

When I think electrical interference, my mind is drawn to the film White Noise, a 2005 supernatural horror thriller, directed by Geoffrey Sax and starring Michael Keaton and Deborah Kara Unger. It is a film, I do not care to watch again, as it is quite disturbing in nature. In reality, and thankfully so, the incidents captured in the film are not common occurrences. What is common and is something that I have experience at almost all haunted sites, is electrical interference. This could be to gain energy to manifest activity, or it could be to manipulate electrical energy, in order to communicate.

It is a common occurrence for spirits to draw energy from electrical items, to facilitate interaction with the physical world. Instances such as TVs turning on and off, lights flickering, and electronic devices being drained of power, are frequently reported in haunted locations. Anything that emits energy can potentially be utilized by spirits present at the site. It is not uncommon for investigators to enter a location, only to find that the batteries in their equipment have been completely drained. This depletion may occur repeatedly throughout the course of a single investigation, this reminds us of the importance of bringing several extra battery packs.

This phenomenon is believed to stem from the idea that spirits have the ability to influence electric fields, causing disturbances or malfunctions in electronic devices. It is also theorised that spirits use this energy manipulation to leave behind EVPs (Electronic Voice Phenomena), further demonstrating their interaction with the physical world.

Electrical energy is considered one of the more accessible mediums for spirits to utilize in manifesting their presence. However, it is important to recognise that not all electrical disturbances are necessarily paranormal in nature. Factors such as faulty wiring, power surges, or environmental conditions like storms, can also contribute to disruptions in electrical systems. Additionally, electromagnetic interference from other electronic devices can sometimes be responsible for anomalies.

In one particular case, we encountered an instance where a guest investigator, carried an EMF meter in one hand, near his phone, which was located in his shirt pocket. This proximity caused the EMF meter to register what appeared to be large electromagnetic fluctuations, but it was actually reacting to the electromagnetic energy emitted by the phone. This highlights the need for careful consideration and thorough investigation to distinguish between paranormal activity and mundane factors, in cases involving electrical disturbances.

Let us dive into the intriguing cases where electrical interference seemingly caused by the paranormal, has left investigators and witnesses baffled. These incidents involve unexplained disruptions in electronic devices and power systems, often occurring in conjunction with paranormal activity. From sudden power outages during ghostly encounters, to mysterious malfunctions in electrical equipment during investigations, these cases challenge our understanding of the relationship between the supernatural and the technological.

The Borley Rectory Haunting (1929-1939)

Borley Rectory in England earned the moniker, "The most haunted house in England" due to its history of reported paranormal activity. Among the documented phenomena, were disturbances to electrical appliances, adding to its eerie reputation. Witnesses recounted instances of lights flickering on and off autonomously, doorbells ringing without any visible cause, and servants' bells chiming, despite the absence of occupants in the rooms. Additionally, unexplained electrical occurrences, such as the wireless device activating and deactivating on its own, were reported.

Tragically, the rectory met a fiery end, believed to be caused by spirits, when it was consumed by an electrical fire, further cementing its association with inexplicable phenomena and haunting experiences.

The Black Monk of Pontefract (1966)

The haunting in Pontefract, West Yorkshire, England, stands as one of the most notorious cases of paranormal activity, with its focal point being disturbances attributed to a malevolent entity, known as the Black Monk. Witnesses recounted a series of unsettling occurrences that plagued the household, leaving residents and investigators alike, shaken to the core. Among the reported phenomena were inexplicable flickering lights, the erratic behaviour of electrical appliances, seemingly influenced by unseen forces, and instances where investigators found their equipment inexplicably drained of power, upon visiting the property.

What sets this haunting apart is its enduring nature; these disturbances have persisted over time, defying attempts to explain or alleviate them. Even in the present day, reports continue to surface of strange happenings within the Pontefract property, serving as a chilling reminder of the lingering presence of the malevolent entity known as the Black Monk. Such cases challenge our understanding of the paranormal and the extent to which unseen forces can influence the physical world, leaving those who encounter them, grappling with fear and uncertainty.

The Sallie House Haunting (1990s)

Nestled in the quaint town of Atchison, Kansas, the Sallie House has earned a notorious reputation as one of the most haunted locations in the United States. Legend has it that the spirit of a young girl named Sallie roams its halls, but many suspect that this haunting is far from benign, and may involve a malevolent entity, of non-human origin.

Witnesses and paranormal investigators alike have recounted chilling encounters with unexplained phenomena within the Sallie House. Among the most common occurrences are eerie electrical disturbances that seem to defy rational explanation. Electronic devices often malfunction in the presence of this unseen entity, with lights flickering erratically and audio and video recordings plagued by strange interferences.

Despite its idyllic exterior, the Sallie House has become a focal point for paranormal investigations and documentaries, seeking to unravel its dark secrets. Yet, the mysteries surrounding this haunted dwelling persist, leaving those who dare to enter its confines, gripped by fear and uncertainty. The chilling tales of electrical disturbances serve as a haunting reminder of the otherworldly forces that may lurk within the shadows of this seemingly ordinary house in Atchison.

The Amityville Horror (1974)

The Amityville Horror stands as one of the most infamous cases of alleged paranormal activity, with residents of the house reporting a myriad of disturbing occurrences, including a series of unexplained electrical disturbances that defied rational explanation.

Witnesses to the haunting described a phenomenon where lights would inexplicably flicker on and off, seemingly without any human intervention. Electronic devices, ranging from kitchen appliances to televisions, were said to malfunction unpredictably, exhibiting erratic behaviour that could not be attributed to any technical issues. Additionally, there were accounts of strange electrical noises emanating from the walls of the house, adding to the atmosphere of dread and unease that permeated the dwelling.

These unsettling electrical disturbances added a sinister dimension to the already chilling atmosphere of the Amityville house, leaving residents and investigators alike baffled and unnerved. Despite attempts to rationalise or explain away these phenomena, the inexplicable nature of the electrical disturbances only served to deepen the mystery, surrounding the infamous Amityville Horror.

As we conclude our exploration into the intriguing intersection of ghosts and electrical disturbances, we are left with more questions than answers. The phenomena of lights flickering, electronic devices malfunctioning, and strange electrical noises accompanying ghostly encounters, challenge our understanding of the paranormal realm and its interaction with the physical world.

What does this mean for paranormal investigation? It underscores the importance of employing a multidisciplinary approach, combining traditional investigative techniques with an understanding of electrical engineering and environmental factors. By meticulously documenting and analysing electrical disturbances alongside reported ghostly activity, investigators may uncover patterns or correlations, that provide valuable insights into the nature of hauntings and the entities behind them.

Moreover, the prevalence of electrical disturbances in ghostly encounters, highlights the need for caution and discernment in interpreting evidence. While these phenomena can be compelling indicators of paranormal activity, they can also be influenced by mundane factors, such as faulty wiring or environmental conditions. Paranormal investigators must approach each case with an open mind and a healthy scepticism, rigorously testing hypotheses and ruling out alternative explanations, before reaching conclusions.

Ultimately, the convergence of ghosts and electrical disturbances offers a tantalising glimpse into the mysterious and often elusive world of the paranormal. By embracing a spirit of inquiry and collaboration, researchers may unlock new insights into these enigmatic phenomena, bringing us closer to unravelling the age-old mysteries of the afterlife.

GHOST LIGHTS

Ghost lights that seemingly follow individuals have long intrigued and mystified both paranormal enthusiasts and sceptics alike. These elusive phenomena, often reported in various locations around the world, involve mysterious lights that appear to trail behind or accompany individuals, as they move. Though their origins and nature remain uncertain, accounts of these spectral illuminations have sparked curiosity and speculation, leaving many to wonder about the possible explanations, behind their haunting presence.

The phenomenon of the Min Min lights in Australia, comes with a ghostly narrative that enhances its allure. These inexplicable lights, which roam the desert landscape, have woven themselves into local folklore, captivating those who chance upon them.

The legend surrounding the Min Min lights is shrouded in enigma and tradition. According to Australian Aboriginal lore, these ethereal lights represent the spirits of ancestors or mythical beings, wandering the vast expanse of the Outback. It is said that these spectral manifestations lead travellers astray or entice them into the wilderness, never to return.

Despite modern attempts to explain them as geological or atmospheric occurrences, or even optical illusions, the fascination with the Min Min lights endures. Numerous locals and visitors alike recount eerie encounters with these elusive apparitions, in the remote reaches of the Australian Outback, perpetuating their mystique.

In a 2016 article titled "Beware of The Ghost Lights Of The Outback" by Justin Meneguzzi, a story recounted by Bill Beatty in The Sydney Morning Herald on January 25, 1947, unveils intriguing origins behind the name "Min Min." According to legend, it is rumoured to trace back to a notorious outback hotel renowned for its wild and tumultuous atmosphere. This establishment, dubbed a "notorious shanty," allegedly supplied drugs and alcohol to local shearers and station-hands, who purportedly met their demise in a chaotic brawl or were targeted for their wealth. Adjacent to this infamous hotel stood the Min Min graveyard, where unfortunate patrons were laid to rest without proper funeral rites.

It is believed that the restless and vengeful spirits of those who met tragic ends at Min Min haunt the area, manifesting as the floating lights witnessed in the Outback. Some interpret sightings of these ethereal lights as a foreboding omen, signalling impending doom.

Further adding to the mystique surrounding the Min Min lights, Perth's Western Mail published an article detailing these mysterious, almost sentient orbs of light. The response was overwhelming, with numerous readers sharing their own encounters with this phenomenon.

Writer Bill Bowyang, in his regular column "On The Track," recounted his chilling brush with the outback lights and narrowly escaping a fate worse than death. "We were all sitting looking into the darkness, well away from the dying campfire and enjoying the cool air after the heat of the day, when suddenly I saw a light. At first, I thought it was someone waving a lantern, but it suddenly rose higher in the air, danced a few jigs, and hovered about, first high and then low, but always keeping at about 50 yards distant. Asking his companions where the lights came from and suggesting that they follow it, he was warned: "It'll lead ye to destruction. Where that light is, it leads right into a chasm with a drop of three or four hundred feet, and as soon as ye gets close to the light, out it'll go over the abyss. "Ignoring the warning he set off after the floating lights "I strode on into the darkness. I had got to within perhaps twenty yards of the peculiar light, which was still hovering like some huge ball of glowing embers in mid-air about seven or eight feet from the ground, when suddenly it swerved abruptly to one side. A man's warning voice came through the darkness. 'The abyss ain't a dozen yards from where ye are; come back, come back.' I stopped, but not before I had seen true to the old fellow's words – that the strange light had indeed drifted out over the great chasm. As I watched, the light hesitated, floated back a little towards me, then as though tempting me to follow, but at the same time annoyed at the possibility of losing a victim, it glided back again over the chasm where, with a few final erratic movements, it dropped from sight."

Justin Meneguzzi's account echoes similar tales of ghost lights, reported from various parts of the world. These spectral phenomena seem to exhibit a peculiar awareness of observers, often appearing to follow and then stop, maintaining a tantalizing distance from the viewer. Some witnesses even describe these lights as actively chasing them, with erratic movements and sudden disappearances adding to their mystique.

While these ghost lights exhibit similarities to the natural phenomenon, known as Bog or Marsh lights, often colloquially referred to as will-o'-the-

126

wisps, there are notable distinctions. Will-o'-the-wisps are commonly attributed to the spontaneous ignition of marsh gas, predominantly methane, generated by the decomposition of organic material. However, the observed behaviour in encounters with ghost lights, implies a more elusive, deliberate and mysterious origin, setting them apart from conventional explanations of marsh gas ignitions.

Introducing other cases similar to the Min Min lights opens a doorway to the exploration of spectral phenomena across diverse regions and cultures. These elusive lights, reminiscent of the Min Min light, have fascinated and perplexed observers worldwide. Among them are eerie manifestations such as the Marfa Lights in Texas, the Hessdalen lights in Norway, and the Brown Mountain Lights in North Carolina. Each of these phenomena shares commonalities with the Min Min lights, yet possesses its own unique lore and mystique Here are some more well known cases of spectral and scientifically explainable spectral lights.

Will-o'-the-Wisps

These atmospheric ghost lights, commonly observed in marshy areas, swamps, and bogs, have long been subjects of fascination and speculation. Their ethereal glow and mysterious behaviour captivate observers, sparking curiosity about their origins and significance.

One prevailing explanation attribute these ghostly illuminations to the spontaneous combustion of marsh gases, notably methane. As organic matter decomposes in the oxygen-deprived environment of marshlands, it releases methane gas. Under certain conditions, such as fluctuations in temperature or pressure, methane can ignite spontaneously, creating luminous orbs of light that dance eerily across the landscape.

However, the phenomenon is not without controversy and debate. While the marsh gas theory offers a plausible scientific explanation, some argue that it fails to fully account for the observed behaviour of these ghost lights. Witnesses often describe the lights as exhibiting purposeful movements, appearing, and disappearing in seemingly deliberate patterns, which some find difficult to reconcile with purely naturalistic explanations.

Moreover, cultural, and folkloric interpretations of these ghost lights vary widely. In some traditions, they are seen as omens or spirits, guiding lost travellers or warning of impending danger. Stories and legends abound, weaving tales of spectral entities or restless souls, haunting the marshlands.

Regardless of their origins or interpretations, atmospheric ghost lights continue to intrigue and perplex researchers and enthusiasts alike. Their enigmatic presence serves as a reminder of the mysteries that still linger in the natural world, inviting further exploration and inquiry into the unknown.

Hessdalen Lights

Nestled within the picturesque Hessdalen Valley of Norway, these enigmatic lights have captured the imagination of locals and scientists alike. Manifesting as luminous orbs suspended in the night sky, they defy conventional explanation and have become the focus of rigorous scientific inquiry.

The phenomenon's prevalence and persistence in the Hessdalen Valley, have spurred extensive research efforts aimed at unravelling its mysteries. Scientific expeditions equipped with advanced instruments and monitoring devices have been deployed to observe and analyse these baffling lights. Despite decades of study, however, their origin and behaviour remain shrouded in mystery, sparking speculation and intrigue among researchers and the broader scientific community.

What sets the Hessdalen lights apart is not only their frequency of occurrence but also their striking appearance. Witnesses describe them as radiant orbs, emitting a soft, ethereal glow that hovers gracefully in the night sky. Their movements are often unpredictable, defying the laws of physics and prompting questions about their underlying cause.

Numerous theories have been proposed to explain the Hessdalen lights, ranging from geological phenomena to extra-terrestrial visitations. Some researchers suggest that ionized gas or plasma, generated by geological processes or atmospheric conditions, may be responsible for their luminous display. Others speculate that the lights could be the result of unknown natural phenomena or even advanced technological experiments, conducted in secret.

Despite the proliferation of theories, the true nature of the Hessdalen lights remains elusive. Their continued presence in the Hessdalen Valley serves as a reminder of the mysteries that still permeate our understanding of the natural world, urging scientists and enthusiasts to delve deeper into the unknown, in search of answers.

Paulding Light

Situated in the vicinity of Paulding, Michigan, this captivating phenomenon revolves around a perplexing light that materializes along a desolate stretch of road. Eyewitness accounts depict the light's mesmerizing behaviour, as it manoeuvres, shifts hues, and vanishes abruptly, leaving observers in awe of its elusive nature.

The allure of this mysterious light has attracted visitors and researchers alike, drawn to the remote locale in hopes of witnessing its enigmatic spectacle first hand. Despite numerous sightings and attempts at investigation, the origin and purpose of the light remain cloaked in uncertainty, fuelling speculation and curiosity among those intrigued, by the unexplained.

Accounts of the light's movements vary, with some describing it as gracefully gliding along the road, while others attest to its sudden shifts in colour and intensity. Witnesses often recount feeling a sense of awe and wonderment upon encountering the phenomenon, prompting further intrigue and fascination with its inexplicable presence.

Brown Mountain Lights

Within the rugged terrain of the Brown Mountain region in North Carolina, these captivating lights have long fascinated both locals and researchers alike. Described as ethereal orbs or luminous streaks of light, they materialise and dissipate without warning, defying conventional explanation and sparking intrigue among those, who behold their elusive spectacle.

Rich in folklore and legend, the Brown Mountain lights have woven themselves into the fabric of local mythology, with tales of spectral apparitions and mysterious phenomena dating back generations. Yet, alongside their cultural significance, these enigmatic lights have also attracted the attention of scientists and researchers, keen to unravel their secrets.

For decades, scientific investigations have sought to shed light on the origin and nature of these elusive phenomena. Equipped with advanced monitoring equipment and research methodologies, experts have endeavoured to capture and analyse the lights' fleeting appearances. Despite rigorous study, however, the true cause of the Brown Mountain lights remains elusive, leaving researchers with more questions than answers.

Witnesses recount mesmerising encounters with the lights, describing their movements as fluid and unpredictable, with some reporting sightings of multiple orbs dancing across the night sky. These first hand testimonies, coupled with scientific scrutiny, underscore the enduring mystery surrounding the Brown Mountain lights and the allure they continue to hold for those drawn to witness them.

Naga Fireballs

During the culmination of the Buddhist Lent period, a mysterious phenomenon unfolds along the Mekong River in Thailand, captivating onlookers with its otherworldly display. These luminous orbs, said to emerge from the depths of the river, cast an eerie glow against the night sky, igniting speculation and wonder among those who bear witness to their spectacle.

The origins of these glowing orbs remain a topic of fervent debate, with various theories vying for explanation. Some propose that natural gases released from the riverbed could be responsible for the phenomenon, creating a luminous display as they rise to the surface. Others, however, attribute the lights to supernatural or spiritual causes, interpreting them as manifestations of divine or mystical forces.

Regardless of the explanations put forth, the allure of these mysterious orbs persists, drawing crowds of curious observers each year to witness their enigmatic emergence.

The origin of these enigmatic lights, which seemingly pursue and entice unsuspecting bystanders, remains shrouded in mystery. It is evident that the nature of this phenomenon defies conventional understanding and falls outside the recognised bounds of paranormal inquiry. As such, further research is imperative to unravel its origin and essence. However, this writer harbours no plans to venture into the Australian outback anytime soon, to trace the path of these mysterious lights. I find greater comfort exploring abandoned asylums than risking a foray into the unknown, following lights that appear to possess a will of their own.

ELECTRONIC VOICE PHENOMENON

when the world is shrouded in darkness and silence reigns supreme, there exists a realm where whispers from the beyond pierce the veil of reality. These ethereal voices, borne on the faintest breath of air, defy rational explanation, echoing through haunted corridors and deserted spaces. They are known as Electronic Voice Phenomena (EVPs), spectral utterances captured on recording devices, hinting at messages from realms unseen. In the eerie tapestry of the paranormal, these disembodied voices serve as a chilling reminder of the mysterious forces that dwell beyond the grasp of mortal comprehension.

Electronic Voice Phenomenon (EVP) constitutes a captivating aspect of paranormal investigation, encompassing voices or sounds recorded on electronic devices, such as audio recorders, in allegedly haunted locations. Often imperceptible to those present at the time of recording, EVPs are believed to originate from otherworldly sources, such as spirits or entities, serving as potential messages or evidence of paranormal activity.

In my extensive experience, EVPs have emerged as a personal favourite among the many phenomena encountered. Over the years, I have amassed thousands of recordings from diverse locations, seemingly spanning epochs. These recordings range from what I interpret as ancient languages spoken by Roman soldiers to chants in Latin by mysterious monks. I have even received EVPs in languages unknown to me, including those of local indigenous peoples and World War II veterans. Yet, amidst these intriguing messages, lie disturbing growls, screams, and vulgarities, demonstrating the spectrum of experiences encountered, in haunted environments.

However, scepticism regarding EVPs persists, with doubts cast on their validity and interpretation. Critics often attribute them to natural or artificial

130

sources, such as radio interference or pareidolia—the tendency of the human brain to perceive patterns in random stimuli.

Nevertheless, for those meticulously documenting and analysing EVPs, their enigmatic origins remain inexplicable. I urge readers to explore haunted locations armed with recording devices, allowing first hand experience of this phenomenon. Yet, be forewarned—some messages received may be less than courteous, revealing the diverse and sometimes unsettling nature of spirit communication.

As investigators delve into this mysterious phenomenon, they employ various tools and techniques, including digital voice recorders, specialized EVP recording devices, and electromagnetic field (EMF) meters. These tools serve to amplify and detect subtle auditory and electromagnetic anomalies that may signal the presence of paranormal activity, providing valuable insights into the unseen forces at play in our world.

Digital Voice Recorder

The fundamental tool for capturing Electronic Voice Phenomenon (EVP) is a digital voice recorder, recognised for its simplicity and effectiveness in paranormal investigations. When selecting a recorder for EVP research, it is advisable to prioritise sensitivity and recording quality, to ensure optimal performance in capturing faint or subtle sounds. Many investigators favour devices equipped with noise cancellation features, which help mitigate background noise interference, enhancing the clarity of recorded EVPs. By investing in a reliable digital voice recorder, with these key attributes, paranormal researchers can elevate their EVP capture capabilities and delve deeper into the mysteries of the unseen realm.

Digital Audio Recorder Apps

If you prefer to consolidate your tools, utilising a smartphone with dedicated EVP recording apps, offers a convenient alternative to standalone devices. These apps typically boast features such as noise reduction and voice activation, enhancing the quality of recorded EVPs. However, it is mindful to note, that smartphone microphones may have limitations in sensitivity, compared to specialised recording devices, potentially affecting the clarity of captured audio. Additionally, interruptions from incoming calls, notifications, or background apps can disrupt recordings, posing a challenge to uninterrupted EVP capture. Despite these drawbacks, smartphone EVP recording apps provide a cost-effective and accessible option, for amateur investigators or those seeking simplicity in their paranormal exploration endeavours.

131

Microphones

For those seeking to enhance their EVP recordings, incorporating external microphones can significantly improve audio quality and sensitivity. By connecting an external microphone to your recording device, you can capture EVPs with greater clarity and precision, thereby increasing the likelihood of detecting subtle paranormal phenomena. When selecting an external microphone, consider opting for omnidirectional models, which excel at capturing sounds from all directions. This ensures that no potential EVPs go unnoticed, as the microphone effectively captures audio from every angle. With the enhanced capabilities afforded by external microphones, paranormal investigators can elevate their EVP capture experience. I use an external microphone on my multi spectrum camera as well.

EMF Detectors

Some believe that paranormal activity is associated with electromagnetic fields (EMFs). While controversial, some investigators use EMF meters to detect changes in electromagnetic fields during EVP sessions. There are other tools that investigators use when trying to capture EVPs. The two main ones are as follows:

- White Noise Generators: Some investigators use white noise generators to create a consistent background noise during EVP sessions. The theory is that spirits may use this noise to manifest their voices.
- Infrared Cameras and Night Vision Equipment: Although EVPs are audio phenomena, having visual recording equipment can complement your investigations by capturing any visual anomalies that may occur simultaneously.

As we conclude this exploration of Electronic Voice Phenomenon (EVP), it is clear that EVP research, stands as one of the most captivating and intriguing facets of paranormal investigation. With its ability to potentially bridge the gap between the material world and the realm of spirits, EVP holds a special place in the hearts of many investigators, me included. Through the meticulous use of recording devices and dedicated tools, we endeavour to capture and analyse the enigmatic voices and sounds, that may hold clues to the mysteries of the afterlife. As we continue our journey into the unknown, EVP remains my favourite tool—a beacon of hope in our quest to unlock the secrets of those who have gone forth before us.

RESIDUES AND SUBSTANCES

In haunted locations, phantom substances materialize, defying the laws of nature, a spectral residue of unseen forces at play.

In some cases of active hauntings, investigators have reported discovering mysterious substances or residues, seemingly linked to paranormal activity. These substances often defy conventional explanations and contribute to the eerie atmosphere, surrounding haunted locations. Examples include ectoplasm-like substances, unexplained bodily fluids, or strange powders appearing without any rational cause or origin. These mysterious findings add an extra layer of intrigue to paranormal investigations, prompting researchers to delve deeper into the nature of this phenomena.

While the spiritualist movement's assertions, regarding ectoplasm have long been discredited, reports of mysterious substances persist in various cases globally. However, due to the scarcity of documented instances and rigorous scientific examination, little is definitively known about this phenomenon, leaving many questions unanswered.

Instances of peculiar substances have been recorded in notable cases, such as the Borley Rectory haunting, where an unexplained substance coincided with the appearance of a nun apparition. Similarly, during the Amityville Horror and Enfield Poltergeist incidents, families reported encountering unexplainable odours and slimy substances, seeping from walls and surfaces.

In the Entity case, concerning Doris Bither in Culver City, California, researchers observed inexplicable substances on her skin and clothing during investigations into her haunting. Similarly, the San Pedro Haunting and Sallie House Haunting in California, also involved reports of strange oily substances appearing on walls and floors, defying conventional explanations.

Theories regarding residues and substances found at paranormal locations vary widely, reflecting the diverse interpretations of paranormal phenomena. Here are some theories commonly discussed in the paranormal community in regards to residues and substances, appearing in haunted locations:

- Psychokinetic Manifestation: One theory posits that the human mind, particularly in states of distress or heightened emotion, can influence the physical environment through psychokinesis. This could result in the manifestation of substances like ectoplasm or mysterious residues, as a tangible expression of psychic energy.
- Spiritual Residue: Another idea suggests that intense emotional experiences, traumatic events, or repeated rituals in a location may

leave behind a residual imprint on the environment. This residual energy could manifest as substances or residues that are perceptible to sensitive individuals or equipment.

- Interdimensional Interaction: Some theories propose that paranormal entities or phenomena originate from alternate dimensions or realities. Substances found at haunted locations could be remnants or manifestations of interactions between these dimensions, leaving behind physical traces in our reality.

- Environmental Factors: Natural environmental elements, such as geological features, electromagnetic fields, or chemical substances present in the location, may influence paranormal activity. These factors could potentially interact with human perception or contribute to the formation of mysterious substances.

- Psychological Projection: Certain paranormal researchers suggest that individuals experiencing hauntings may unconsciously project their own fears, beliefs, or expectations onto the environment. This psychological projection could influence the perception of substances or residues, shaping the narrative of the haunting.

- Spiritual Entities: Believers in spiritual or religious interpretations of paranormal phenomena, may attribute the presence of substances to the actions or manifestations of spiritual entities, such as ghosts, demons, or other supernatural beings.

- Hoaxes and Contamination: Sceptics often point to mundane explanations for substances found at haunted locations, such as hoaxes perpetrated by individuals seeking attention or contamination from natural or man-made sources.

The Myrtles Plantation Haunting
the Myrtles Plantation stands as a renowned hotspot for paranormal enthusiasts, reputedly one of the most haunted locales in the United States. Amidst tales of apparitions and spectral whispers, reports abound of inexplicable phenomena encountered by visitors and staff alike. Among these eerie occurrences, sightings of mysterious substances or residues in select rooms of the plantation have captured the imagination of many, adding to its mystique as a hub of supernatural activity. These unexplained findings only deepen the enigmatic aura surrounding the Myrtles Plantation, inviting further investigation into the spectral secrets.

Occurrences of materialisations within haunted sites frequently align with occurrences of adverse hauntings, commonly associated with non-human entities. Such events commonly manifest in cases of poltergeist activity and what is often labelled as demonic hauntings. Nonetheless, the essence and source of these materials largely elude comprehension. It is imperative for the scientific community to reorient its attention towards scrutinising this occurrence, examining the nature of these substances, and conducting tests to broaden our comprehension of their role within our existing framework of understanding paranormal activity.

As we transition from exploring the various types of hauntings to discussing the equipment utilized in paranormal investigations, it is essential to understand the symbiotic relationship between the two. Hauntings manifest in diverse forms, ranging from residual echoes of the past to interactive spirits, engaging with the living. Each type presents unique challenges and requires specialised approaches for investigation. It is through the careful deployment of advanced equipment, that paranormal researchers can delve deeper into these mysteries, capturing evidence and shedding light on the supernatural realm. In the chapters ahead, we will delve into the tools and technologies employed by investigators, illuminating how they aid in unravelling the enigmatic phenomena that permeate haunted locations.

4 EQUIPMENT USED FOR PARANORMAL INVESTIGATIONS

Welcome to the intriguing world of paranormal investigation, where the veil between the known and the unknown is pierced by the quest for understanding the unexplained. In this chapter, we embark on a journey into the realm of paranormal equipment – the tools of the trade for those who seek to uncover the mysteries that lie beyond our ordinary perception.

As we delve into the exploration of paranormal phenomena, it becomes evident that traditional scientific methods often fall short in capturing the nuances of these elusive occurrences. Yet, armed with a diverse array of specialized equipment, paranormal investigators endeavour to shed light on the inexplicable, striving to unravel the secrets of haunted locations, apparitions, and otherworldly encounters.

Within these pages, we will uncover the purpose, mechanics, and potential insights offered by various pieces of paranormal equipment. From electromagnetic field (EMF) meters to thermal imaging cameras, each device serves as a conduit between the tangible and the intangible, enabling us to detect anomalies, measure fluctuations, and document phenomena that defy conventional explanation.

But beyond the technical specifications lies the essence of paranormal investigation – the profound human endeavour to bridge the gap between the known and the unknown, to confront the mysteries that linger in the shadows, and to seek answers to age-old questions about the nature of existence itself.

We embark on the use of paranormal equipment, where science and spirituality converge in the pursuit of truth, and where the boundaries of reality are challenged by the tantalizing prospect of the paranormal. Through the lens of these tools, we peer into the abyss of the unexplained, driven by curiosity, wonder, and a relentless quest for understanding.

Embarking on a journey into paranormal investigation, necessitates the

136

appropriate tools to effectively gather evidence. However, it is important to exercise caution and discernment, as acquiring all the equipment showcased on popular ghost hunter programs can be costly. Instead, a prudent approach might involve starting with basic essentials like a camera and voice recorder. In particular, the voice recorder holds a special place among my preferred tools due to its affordability and versatility. Fortunately, most modern smartphones are equipped with both a voice recorder and video camera, making them readily accessible to aspiring investigators. Let's delve into an overview of commonly utilized equipment by contemporary ghost hunters and their significance in the field.

KII EMF METER

The K2 meter stands as one of the most iconic tools within a paranormal investigator's arsenal. This handheld device is instrumental in detecting fluctuations in electromagnetic fields (EMF), a pivotal aspect of paranormal investigations. Named after its manufacturer, K-II Enterprises, the K2 meter operates by measuring electromagnetic activity in units of Milligauss (mG).

Typically, the K2 meter comprises a plastic handheld unit adorned with lights arranged either in a row or a circle on its front face. However, digital versions of these detectors are also available on the market, albeit lacking the traditional light display. These lights illuminate sequentially, indicating the strength of the detected electromagnetic field. In most models, green lights signify low or normal EMF levels, while yellow, orange, and red lights denote progressively higher levels of electromagnetic activity.

But why is the detection of electromagnetic fields so crucial in the realm of the paranormal?

Electromagnetic energy, propagated through mediums such as air or water in wave form, underpins the functioning of the universe. The electromagnetic spectrum encompasses an extensive array of energy types, spanning from longest wavelengths with the lowest frequencies to shortest wavelengths with the highest frequencies, surpassing even visible light. Here's a breakdown of the most common forms of electromagnetic energy:

- Radio Waves: These have the longest wavelengths and are used for various forms of communication, including radio broadcasting, Wi-Fi, and radar.
- Microwaves: With shorter wavelengths than radio waves, microwaves are used in microwave ovens, telecommunications as well as communications done by satellite.
- Infrared Radiation: This type of electromagnetic energy is just beyond the visible spectrum and is felt as heat. Infrared radiation

is used in night-vision technology and thermal imaging.

- Visible Light: This is the portion of the electromagnetic spectrum that is visible to the human eye. It includes the colours of the rainbow, from red to violet.

- Ultraviolet (UV) Radiation: UV radiation has shorter wavelengths than visible light and is responsible for sunburn and tanning. It is also used in sterilization and fluorescent lighting.

- X-Rays: X-rays have even shorter wavelengths and higher energies than UV radiation. They are used in medical imaging, airport security scanners, and for industrial inspection of products.

- Gamma Rays: Gamma rays have the shortest wavelengths and highest energies of all electromagnetic waves. They are produced by radioactive decay and nuclear reactions and are used in cancer treatment and sterilization. Most people are more familiar with the term as it applies to Astronomical Phenomena.

Indeed, the spectrum of electromagnetic energy encompasses a wide array of sources, ranging from natural phenomena to human-made technologies. Notably, our own Sun emits nearly all types of wavelengths across this spectrum, highlighting its profound influence on the electromagnetic environment of our planet.

Natural sources of electromagnetic energy include celestial bodies such as stars, including the Sun, which emit a broad spectrum of wavelengths, as part of their natural processes. Additionally, phenomena such as lightning and geomagnetic activity, generate electromagnetic fields that permeate the Earth's atmosphere.

On the other hand, human activities contribute significantly to the electromagnetic landscape. Man-made sources of electromagnetic energy range from everyday appliances like refrigerators and televisions, to more complex systems, such as power lines, radio towers, and cellular networks. These artificial sources can create localised electromagnetic fields, that intersect with the natural environment.

The interplay between natural and man-made electromagnetic fields, forms a complex mesh of energy that permeates our surroundings. Understanding and detecting these electromagnetic fluctuations are essential in paranormal investigations, as anomalous readings may indicate the presence of supernatural phenomena or environmental factors, influencing perceived paranormal activity.

Putting aside astronomical bodies for now, many objects and phenomena emit or produce electromagnetic energy across the spectrum. Light bulbs, Incandescent bulbs and fluorescent lights emit visible light, while some types of bulbs also emit small amounts of ultraviolet radiation or infrared radiation.

Electrical Devices that operate on electricity, generates electromagnetic fields. This includes household appliances such as TVs, computers, microwave ovens, and tablets. Fans, as discussed previously, will come under this category. These devices emit electromagnetic radiation, usually at very low levels. However, research has shown even low levels can have an effect on people in the vicinity. Radio and television broadcasting stations emit electromagnetic waves in the radio frequency range to transmit signals across space or wires. Cell phones and Wi-Fi routers emit electromagnetic radiation in the microwave frequency range to transmit data wirelessly. During storms, lightning produces intense bursts of electromagnetic energy, including visible light, radio waves, and other frequencies.

An often overlooked source of electromagnetic energy is living organisms, including animals and humans. The electrical activity in nerves and muscles within the body generates a weak electromagnetic field. Although these fields are typically subtle, they can be measured using specialized equipment.

Now that we have explored what the K2 meter detects, you might wonder why this is significant in paranormal investigations.

The belief that spirits or entities emit electromagnetic fields (EMF) is widely held among paranormal investigators. As mentioned earlier, spirits are thought to manifest by manipulating or emitting electromagnetic energy. Does the presence of high electromagnetic fields facilitate an environment in which spirits can more readily manifest? Or do spirits themselves cause electromagnetic fields to spike? The exact mechanism behind this phenomenon remains unknown, but what we do observe is a correlation between high electromagnetic field readings and spirit activity. This raises intriguing questions about the relationship between electromagnetic energy and the paranormal.

Apart from detecting potential spirit activity, there are several other reasons why EMF meters are indispensable tools in paranormal investigations:

- Correlation with Paranormal Reports at a specific location: EMF fluctuations have been reported in conjunction with alleged paranormal activity and experiences. By using EMF meters, we aim to correlate these fluctuations with reported phenomena such as apparitions, strange sounds, or feelings of being watched. This gives us a better idea as to why EMF is present and what baring, if any, they have on reported experiences.
- Baseline Measurements: Before conducting any investigations, paranormal investigators will take baseline readings of electromagnetic fields in the environment. These baseline measurements serve as a reference point for comparison during the investigation. Significant spikes or general deviations from the

139

baseline readings, may indicate the Prescence of spirit activity.

- Documentation and Evidence: EMF meters provide quantitative data that can be documented and analysed as potential evidence of paranormal activity. This data adds a level of objectivity to paranormal investigations and can be used to support or refute claims of paranormal occurrences.

- Experimentation and Research: Some paranormal investigators use EMF meters as part of experimental or research-based approaches to studying paranormal phenomena. By systematically measuring electromagnetic fields in various locations and under different conditions, investigators seek to better understand the nature of these phenomena.

We have all witnessed the scenes on paranormal investigation shows, investigators wandering through darkened buildings, K2 meters held aloft, eagerly awaiting the tell-tale jump of lights to red, signalling the presence of a spirit. Yet, behind these dramatic moments, lie a deeper rationale for the use of EMF meters, in paranormal investigations.

Many paranormal investigators and psychics adhere to the belief that energy, once generated, persists in some form. It is theorised that this energy lingers with the spirit, even after physical death, serving as a potential marker for their presence. Hence, EMF meters are employed in the hope of detecting this residual energy or the spirit itself.

However, sceptics are quick to point out that fluctuations in EMF can stem from various natural and man-made sources. Electrical wiring, appliances, radio frequency interference, and other environmental factors can all influence EMF readings, complicating the interpretation of results.

As a seasoned investigator, I am mindful of these factors and exercise caution when relying solely on EMF readings for conclusions. While I typically carry the KII meter during investigations, I do not make it a habit to wander throughout the night, with it constantly in hand. It is essential to consider multiple factors and corroborate evidence before drawing any definitive conclusions.

A case study serves as a perfect illustration of the nuanced interpretation required, when dealing with EMF readings. In this case I was part of, we will begin to explore how EMF fluctuations can be subject to differing interpretations and how it is incumbent upon us as investigators, to arrive at sound conclusions, based on the evidence at hand.

We received a call to investigate a house where the owners suspected a ghost was haunting their converted attic. The room, once a bedroom for one of their children, had become a source of unease. Their pets avoided entering, and anyone who dared to step inside felt an overwhelming discomfort. We felt

140

the energy shift the minute we entered, the oppressive feeling room. The child, who previously occupied the room, confessed to sensing a constant presence, feeling watched from the doorway, and experiencing bouts of fear bordering on panic, when asked to enter. She had refused to sleep there and was sleeping on a mattress, in her sister's room.

Despite no other reported paranormal incidents in the house, the family's distress was palpable. The child's claim of seeing a figure standing in the doorway, only heightened their concerns. Convinced that a spirit had taken residence in their home, the parents sought our assistance to rid their dwelling of this unsettling presence and restore peace to their family and calm to their children.

Armed with our trusty KII meter, we embarked on the investigation. Within minutes, we identified the source of the disturbances. Positioned just outside the doorway, to the left, loomed a sizable electrical box. Placing the EMF meter near it revealed an unusually high reading, with lights flashing orange and red—an aberration not commonly encountered in a residential setting, especially near a junction box.

High EMF readings can affect the human body in various ways. One thing it can do is give the person the feeling of being watched or the sensation of being anxious and fearful. People who have experienced high EMF over a period of time, sometimes report hallucinations as well. This may account for the belief that the child had seen a figure in the doorway. Health-wise, it is not good either, as high EMF has been linked to cancers and other health issues. Since high EMF (as a form of radiation), can reduce the melatonin levels in the brain, which is the hormone that stimulates sleep, it can also cause sleep disorders. We all know that you can get a visit from a rather unpleasant entity, when you have sleep disorders, encouraging the idea a location is haunted.

The owners were promptly advised to contact their electrician upon discovering the unusually high EMF readings. Such elevated levels could signify a range of electrical issues, including frayed or damaged wiring, electrical arcing, overload, or faults within the electrical box components. In this particular case, investigation revealed frayed and exposed wires, leading to electrical arcing and the alarming EMF levels observed.

Left unchecked, these electrical abnormalities posed a significant fire hazard, presenting a potentially catastrophic situation. Following repairs to the electrical box, all signs of paranormal activity ceased entirely, confirming the correlation between the high EMF readings and the perceived haunting.

Although we remained on-site to conduct further investigation, no additional paranormal activity was detected throughout the house. Our conclusion was clear: the reported haunting was solely attributable to the high EMF readings, caused by faulty wiring.

This incident highlights the practical role of EMF meters in paranormal investigations. They serve not only to validate paranormal claims but also to debunk them, by identifying mundane explanations. Obtaining accurate EMF readings is therefore paramount, for discerning the true nature of reported phenomena, ensuring thorough and credible investigations.

DIVINATION RODS

Like a silent whisper, the divination rod guides us through the unseen currents of the unknown, revealing secrets hidden beneath the surface of reality

Dowsing, also known as the use of witching rods or divining rods, entails employing a rod, stick, or similar tool to locate underground water, minerals, or other substances emitting energy. Notably, dowsing can also be utilized to detect high levels of energy fields, such as electromagnetic fields, which forms the basis for its application in paranormal investigations.

Recently, during an investigation with a different paranormal group, here in Perth, I encountered the use of dowsing rods as a means of communication with the deceased, for the first time in quite a while. However, the practice of divination or dowsing dates back centuries and finds mention in various historical records. Ancient civilizations such as Egypt, Greece, and China are believed to have employed divining rods, for diverse purposes, including locating water sources and precious minerals.

During medieval Europe, dowsing emerged as a crucial practice, particularly in times of drought when accessing water sources became a matter of survival. Known as "water witches" or dowsers, practitioners played a vital role in aiding communities with this essential task. However, as the Renaissance unfolded, dowsing faced scepticism and condemnation from religious and scientific authorities, who deemed it as superstition or even witchcraft.

The association of dowsing with occultism during this era, posed significant risks, as it could result in accusations of witchcraft. Instances of dowsing being used as evidence of involvement in occult activities. During this time mass hysteria and organised witch hunts were not uncommon, tragically leading to the wrongful deaths, of accused individuals.

Dowsing made its way to America through European settlers, who relied on it to locate water sources, for agricultural purposes and settlement, particularly during the westward expansion. Despite technological advancements, dowsing experienced a resurgence in the 19th and 20th centuries, notably in rural areas lacking modern water detection methods.

Today, dowsing persists globally, although it remains subject to scepticism from the scientific community. While some attribute successful dowsing to chance or suggestion, proponents firmly believe in its efficacy, especially in contexts like paranormal investigations.

While some investigators employ them alongside other equipment, others rely solely on divining rods for their investigations. Although I personally do not use them, their use in conjunction with other tools can yield intriguing results, offering potential insights into paranormal phenomena.

Rods are a simple form of paranormal tool in that it is limited with what you can do with them. They can be used to guide towards a spirit's specific location and can also be used as a communication tool. These tend to be answers to simple yes and no questions. In this case you could ask the spirit to cross the rods if they are male or separate if they are female.

The paranormal investigator who was using them asked the spirit to point the rods in the direction that the spirit was standing. The rods 'pointed' to where the proximity sensor was and then, the proximity sensor was activated! As with most equipment, they are used in conjunction with others in order to be effective. The dowsing pointing in a direction can be discounted as the user moving them. The proximity sensor going off and later EVPs at this time, saying, "I'm here", would indicate something more interesting is taking place.

PENDULUMS

Pendulums have been used in paranormal investigation for centuries and was one of the first recorded piece if 'equipment' used. Primarily they were used as tools for divination and communication with spirits. Their effectiveness is largely considered subjective and is debated among sceptics and users alike. They can be used in various ways within paranormal investigation practices:

- Divination: Pendulums are commonly used for divination purposes, where practitioners believe the swinging motion of the pendulum can provide answers to questions or reveal hidden truths. The pendulum is believed to tap into the subconscious mind or spiritual energies to provide guidance. Often, they are used on a map to locate where a missing person or body might be located.

- Communication with Spirits: Some paranormal investigators use pendulums as a means of communicating with spirits or entities. They ask specific yes or no questions with the pendulum's movement indicating the answer. This is similar to use of divining rods are used.

- Energy Detection: Advocates of pendulum use in paranormal

143

investigation claim that the movement of the pendulum can detect subtle energies in the environment, such as electromagnetic fields. The direction and intensity of the pendulum swing are interpreted as indications of the presence or nature of these energies. There may be some science behind this as we know energy, like electromagnetic energy, as the ability to interfere with physical objects in high enough levels.

- Mapping Energy Fields: In some cases, investigators use pendulums to map out energy fields in a particular location. By moving the pendulum around a space, they claim to be able to identify areas of high or low energy, which they may associate with paranormal activity. This is an alternative to using the KII meter to map electromagnetic energy at a location.

- Personal Sensitivity Calibration: For some the use of pendulums serve as a tool to calibrate their own sensitivity to subtle energies. By practicing with a pendulum, they believe they can hone their intuitive abilities and become more attuned to paranormal phenomena.

Critics of pendulum use in paranormal investigation, raise valid concerns regarding the potential influence of subconscious cues, hand movements, or external factors, such as air currents on the pendulum's movements. They argue that the interpretations derived from these movements may be subjective and susceptible to confirmation bias, rather than indicative of genuine paranormal forces at work.

Indeed, the pendulum's use in paranormal investigation is a contentious issue, with beliefs and interpretations varying widely among practitioners. While some swear by its accuracy and view it as a valuable tool for uncovering paranormal phenomena, others remain sceptical of its utility.

In the realm of paranormal investigation, pendulums are often wielded by mediums or spiritualis,ts to locate energy blocks within a location or on a person, or to assist in healing or separating spiritual attachments.

Ultimately, the use of pendulums in paranormal investigation hinges on personal belief and interpretation. While some may find them indispensable in their work, others may view them with scepticism and opt for alternative methods of investigation.

MOBILE PHONES

One of my early encounters at the Woodman Point Quarantine Station in Fremantle, Perth, around 2008, serves as a reminder of the often overlooked potential of mobile phones in paranormal investigations.

144

Mobile phones are frequently underestimated in their role as paranormal investigation aids. Beyond their conventional functions, they offer numerous capabilities for documenting and capturing paranormal phenomena. For example, the video recording feature enables investigators to chronicle their exploration of a site, providing visual evidence of any encountered phenomena. This feature proves particularly valuable when investigating spiritually significant locations.

Furthermore, smartphones come equipped with audio recording capabilities, which can be utilized to capture Electronic Voice Phenomena (EVPs) — alleged voices or sounds from the spirit realm. One effective technique involves using the smartphone's audio recorder in tandem with a dedicated voice recorder during EVP sessions. Simultaneous activation of both devices offers two distinct advantages:

- It is another recording device that can corroborate what happens.

Often spirits when there are multiple recording devices available, will only be heard on one of the devices, even if the others are very close. It might be your mobile is the one that picks it up.

When utilising your mobile phone during paranormal investigations, it is essential to make a note of its usage, whether in written or verbal form, particularly if you're also employing K2 meters. These notes can later be considered during the analysis phase of the investigation.

There is a plethora of ghost apps available for smartphones, ranging from entertainment-focused to those claiming to aid serious paranormal investigation. These apps fall into several common categories:

- Ghost Detector Apps: These apps purportedly detect ghosts or spirits by analysing environmental factors such as electromagnetic fields, temperature fluctuations, or audio frequencies using the smartphone's sensors.
- Spirit Communication Apps: These apps facilitate communication with spirits through EVP recordings, spirit boxes (scanning radio frequencies), or ghostly messages displayed on the screen, allowing users to ask questions and interpret responses based on audio or visual cues.
- Ghost Hunting Tools: These apps provide a range of tools for paranormal investigation, including EMF meters, EVP recorders, infrared cameras, and motion detectors, aiming to equip amateur ghost hunters with professional-grade equipment.

While these apps may be entertaining, it is important to note that they are

145

generally not scientifically validated tools, for genuine paranormal investigation. Many operate on principles of randomisation, pre-programmed responses, or simple sensor readings, which do not accurately reflect authentic paranormal activity. Therefore, scepticism is warranted when using these apps for serious investigation purposes, and their use is not advisable if they can be avoided.

A mobile phones' cameras are commonly used in paranormal investigations due to their accessibility and ability to quickly capture visual evidence. Here are some key advantages to consider when using phone cameras for paranormal investigation:

- Visual Documentation: Phone cameras allow investigators to document their surroundings in real-time, capturing any anomalies or unexplained phenomena that may occur during an investigation. Photos taken with phone cameras can serve as potential evidence of paranormal activity, providing visual documentation that can be analysed and scrutinised.

- Instantaneous Capture: Phone cameras enable investigators to capture potential paranormal phenomena as they happen, without the need for additional equipment or setup time. This instantaneous capture can be crucial in capturing fleeting events or unexpected occurrences that may occur during an investigation. I have caught bright blue orbs this way by clicking the camera immediately. By the time I have gone for a different camera the phenomenon had already gone.

- Convenience and Portability: Phone cameras are lightweight, portable, and easy to use, making them ideal for on-the-go paranormal investigation. People often carry their phone with them at all times, ready to capture any paranormal activity that may occur, without the need for bulky camera equipment. You can literally run an investigation anytime anywhere that you feel the need to.

- Night Vision and Low-Light Capabilities: Many modern smartphones are equipped with advanced camera features, including night vision and low-light capabilities. This can be beneficial for paranormal investigation in dimly lit environments or during night time investigations. These features allow investigators to capture clear images and videos in low-light conditions, potentially revealing paranormal phenomena that may not be visible to the naked eye. I had a lot of luck doing this on my smartphones 'night' settings when I was recently on night time investigation of Sunset Hospital Perth. However, phones have

146

their limitations, and it is advised if you are doing many night time investigations to save up and invest in some proper night vision equipment.

Spirits can also use phones, and the energy from phones to interact, in unexpected and sometimes very frustrating ways. During an investigation of the Woodman Point Quarantine Station, I relied solely on my digital camera and phone, along with a voice recorder. Following the advice of the tour guides, I made sure to bring along extra sets of batteries. This experience serves as a valuable lesson, emphasising the importance of always having an abundance of fresh batteries on hand, for your equipment during any investigation.

My camera, armed with brand new batteries, was zapped of life within minutes of stepping foot into one of the eerie buildings. It seemed our tour guide's warning about a camera-shy spirit, was not just a spooky tale. I swapped out the batteries, only to watch them drain once again in record time. With a third set of batteries in tow, my camera stubbornly refused to cooperate, leaving me feeling more than a tad frustrated. And I wasn't alone—others were experiencing the same battery-draining phenomenon.

Out came my trusty Apple iPhone, gleaming with a full charge and seemingly impervious to the spirit's antics. I snapped away eagerly, envisioning the treasure trove of evidence awaiting me once I could analyse the photos. I could not help but jest with my friend, boasting about how my unyielding iPhone had outsmarted the ghostly troublemaker. What I should have known was, our camera shy spectral friend, was probably listening in.

As we piled into the car to leave, I could not resist one final act of bravado. I asked my friend to pull over so I could snap a cocky photo of the building's exterior. But as I tried to click away, my phone remained obstinately unresponsive. Oddly enough, the temperature inside the car seemed to plummet, sending shivers down our spines. It was clear we had company—and it was not pleased with my bravado.

With my phone's battery rapidly draining to zero percent, I quickly apologised to the unseen presence for my disrespectful behaviour. Tail tucked firmly between my legs; we made a hasty retreat back home. But the supernatural surprises did not end there.

Upon returning home and recharging my phone, I discovered that the entire cache of photos had mysteriously vanished, as if they had never existed. Spirit: 1, Suzanne: 0.

But the saga did not end there. Years later, upon revisiting Woodman Point, I received a chilling EVP: "No Photos," accompanied by a sinister chuckle. It seems some spirits have a long memory—and a mischievous sense of humour.

OTHER PHOTOGRAPHY

Photography is one of the primary sources of evidence in paranormal Investigation. It is also one of the mediums that can be altered or misinterpreted. Cameras are capable of capture visual anomalies we can see with our naked eyes and things invisible to us at the time of the photograph. The types of evidence that can be caught on cameras are diverse. Over the years some of the things I have personally caught on photograph are listed, as well as those that can be caught on camera.

- <u>Apparitions or Ghostly Figures</u>: One of the most sought-after forms of evidence in paranormal photography is the capture of apparitions or ghostly figures. These may appear as translucent or solid human-like. I have caught figures at Aston Hall, Warwick Castle, Woodman Point Quarantine Station, Culloden Battlefield, Scotland, and Lancaster Castle. These images are very rare, they are the holy grail of paranormal Investigation.

- <u>Orbs</u>: Orbs are circular or spherical anomalies that appear in photographs, often characterised by a glowing or translucent appearance. Some believe that orbs represent the presence of spirits or energy manifestations, while sceptics attribute them to dust particles, moisture, or lens flare. These are commonly caught on camera because their cause is so varied and can be found everywhere.

- <u>Ectoplasm</u>: Ectoplasm is a term used to describe a substance or energy purportedly emitted by spirits or entities, during paranormal manifestations. In photographs, ectoplasm may appear as wispy or misty formations, often in conjunction with reported paranormal activity. This is the exception, I have never seen or caught any form of ectoplasm on video, tape or otherwise. Ectoplasm is often associated with very negative hauntings.

- <u>Light Anomalies</u>: Unexplained streaks of light, beams, or flashes captured in photographs are sometimes interpreted as evidence of paranormal activity. These anomalies may manifest in locations associated with reported hauntings or during paranormal investigations. These can be distinguished from orbs which tend to be small and spherical in shape. I have caught many light anomalies on camera over the years, some explainable, some simply light flares.

- <u>Shadow Figures</u>: Photographs may capture shadowy or dark figures that appear to have a humanoid shape but lack distinct features. Shadow figures are often associated with reports of paranormal phenomena and are believed by some to be manifestations of spirits or entities. I have never been able to capture a shadow figure at a location, but I have been on investigations where others have. The Shadow Person that resides near the gallows at Pentridge Prison, Voctoria Australia, has been photographed on many occasions during ghost tours of the building. Derby Gaol is another location where a large shadow man has been seen and photographed. Although this is most likely the old Jailer than a genuine shadow being.

- Temperature Anomalies: Infrared or thermal imaging photography can capture temperature anomalies that are not visible to the naked eye. Cold spots or areas of temperature variation may be interpreted as evidence of paranormal activity, as fluctuations in temperature are often associated with reported hauntings. This is very common and should be analysed next to other evidence presenting at the time.

When using any type of photography, it is important to make note of the environmental factors that might affect the visuals within a photograph. This was especially important, in winter, in the UK when our breath could make wispy patterns on photos look like ghostly beings, jumping out to make themselves known.

Having a camera at the ready is always a wise move. Take, for instance, an experience I had at Woodman Point—again! I spotted a mesmerising blue ball of light with my own eyes hovering next to my now husband's leg, and instinctively snapped a photo. Though. I excitedly informed him of the luminous orb hovering by his leg, my husband, not particularly keen on the paranormal, could not see it at that moment. Lo and behold, upon examining the photo, there it was: a perfect blue orb of energy captured in all its glory. And wouldn't you know it, this was right around the time we were experiencing strange movements and disembodied whistling, in the room. Talk about capturing the magic in the moment!

Aston Hall, nestled in Aston, Birmingham, is a majestic stately home boasting over four centuries of history. With its striking Gothic architecture, it is no wonder it feels like it stepped right out of the pages of Bram Stoker's Dracula. And let me tell you, once the sun sets, the atmosphere becomes even more chilling. Despite its eerie aura, I have a soft spot for Aston Hall—it is a fantastic place to visit. In fact, one of my closest friends tied the knot there!

But amidst its grandeur, lies a trove of ghostly tales. If you ever find yourself in England's bustling second city (sorry, Manchester), I highly recommend paying a visit to Aston Hall, especially if you have a penchant for the paranormal. And here is a tip: make sure to wander down the corridor I am about to tell you about and snap plenty of photos. I would love to hear about your experiences in this part of the building and see anything you manage to capture!

You will recognise it immediately when you encounter it—the sudden shift in atmosphere to an oppressive heaviness, that seems to weigh down on you, lets you know you are not alone. There is a similar spot at Sunset Hospital, where the change is so abrupt and tangible, that it almost knocks the wind out of you, prompting an instinctive deep breath.

This particular location is a long, dimly lit corridor that stretches past the children's nursery—a stark contrast to the light and airy long gallery, which is also haunted. It is here, in this confined space, where I once captured, what appeared to be a wispy white figure, on an old film camera, back in the late '90s. There is a palpable sense of presence, perhaps that of an aggressive female—possibly a governess or an unfriendly housekeeper, who passed over three centuries ago. The truth remains unknown, but there is no denying that something watches over those who traverse this corridor. If you are fortunate, you may catch a glimpse of her, and if luck is truly on your side, you might even capture her image on camera.

Photographs serve as invaluable evidence both for your personal records and for your clients. When clients reach out to you seeking answers about potential paranormal activity in their homes or workplaces, they are looking for verification—proof that something is there or not.

Having multiple shots of the same scene is crucial. It allows you to determine if an anomaly is consistently present across images, whether it remains static or exhibits fluid movements. This comprehensive documentation enables you to thoroughly analyse and potentially debunk what you are seeing. For example, if an anomaly appears in one photo but not in others, or if it shifts its position between shots, it can provide important insights, during your later analysis.

Consider the scenario where you capture a dense, white, human-shaped mist in a photo, despite standing two feet away from your friend in a chilly room. This could likely be debunked as breath condensation, especially if temperature readings taken throughout the investigation confirm the cold environment. Similarly, external factors like humidity can lead to misinterpretations, such as mistaking flying insects, for orbs.

Combining still images with video footage can yield even more comprehensive results. By observing the movement patterns of anomalies captured on video, you can differentiate between potential explanations, whether they are insects, water droplets, or indeed something paranormal. However, without reference points or multiple photos to compare, drawing conclusions about the origin of anomalies, becomes challenging.

150

In my experience, there is often a correlation between sensing "something", and capturing evidence, so don't hesitate to take a series of photos in such instances. I have learned to take hundreds of photos at any given location, because you never know what you might uncover.

Effective paranormal research is not just about exploring dark locations at night and calling out into the void—it is also about adhering to scientific methods and maintaining integrity.

TRIGGER OBJECTS

Trigger objects are indeed a popular tool among paranormal investigators and enthusiasts, as they can potentially attract the attention and interaction of spirits. While the televised paranormal investigations often showcase high-tech teddy bears, that light up in response to spirit activity, the truth is that fancy and expensive trigger toys are not necessary.

When we talk about trigger objects, we are referring to any item that might elicit a response from the spirits present at a location. However, it is essential to approach this practice with care and respect. I firmly believe in avoiding any actions that could provoke or disrespect spirits or entities. Such behaviour can not only be irresponsible and negligent but also potentially dangerous.

Choosing the right trigger object for a location requires consideration and sensitivity. For instance, in a place known for child spirits, simple toys like balls or dolls can be effective triggers. You might invite the child spirits to play and observe any responses, such as the ball being rolled back to you—an experience I have witnessed first hand. My team and I are about to do an investigation, in less than a week, of Swan View Tunnel and station, based at John Forrest National Park, Perth. As we believe some of the workers may have died building this now disused train tunnel, we have chosen a shovel for our trigger object as well as water and cigarettes.

Similarly, when investigating old monasteries or churches, appropriate trigger objects might include crosses, Bibles, or rosary beads, especially in Catholic locations where these items hold significance.

Ultimately, the goal is to engage respectfully with the spirits present and to create an environment conducive to communication, rather than provocation.

By selecting suitable trigger objects and approaching the interaction with care, investigators can potentially establish meaningful connections with the spirits, located at the premises. This is great if you intend on going back when they spirits tend to refer to you by name.

There is a lot to be said for knowing your location before you get there. Do the historical research or even designate a team member to be the researcher for your group. When you are planning an investigation, this knowledge will come in handy to know what kind of trigger objects to take.

Taking time to do this research, can be something that keeps you from making a mistake with the kind of trigger you use.

I recently received a message from an individual telling us that we are compromising the integrity of an investigation, by doing research and therefore creating expectation. There are many reasons, most of which I will not go into, why this statement is just not correct. Although site bias is a concern, integrity comes from the way you collect, analyse, and interpret data. I cannot magic a person there, that is not. Our job is to go in to learn, prove or disprove experiences. It is also a matter of safety, as we will explore through this next, true story.

A cautionary tale unfolds in the form of an unfortunate incident involving my dear friend and fellow investigator, James. Over time, James had grown somewhat complacent in his approach to investigative research, preferring the excitement of on-site exploration and post-analysis of evidence, over the meticulousness of paperwork or library research.

One day, James extended an invitation for me to join him at a set of ruins near Southampton in Hampshire. He had been informed of alleged rituals conducted by satanic worshippers at the site, and the alleged presence of a malevolent, non-human entity that stalked the ruins and people who dare go there. However, such entities were not exactly my cup of tea, so I declined the invitation. Unfortunately, James failed to conduct thorough research into the location, focusing instead on the sensational aspects of the story.

Armed with a pentagram, black candles, and various other occult paraphernalia, James ventured forth to provoke the dark entity, purportedly lurking within the ruins. His actions were met with a violent response—he was knocked to the ground by unseen forces and received what he perceived to be a hit by unseen hands and a scratch across his chest, which appeared in the dimensions of the cross. Had he delved deeper into his research, James would have discovered that the ruins belonged to Netley Abbey, a significant historical site, with ties to Henry VIII's dissolution of the monasteries, in the 16th century. Many such dissolved monasteries are rumoured to be haunted, and Netley Abbey is no exception. However, there is no evidence of satanic rituals ever occurring there; the known hauntings, are attributed to devout monks.

It became evident that the violent reaction James experienced was likely triggered by a monks spirit, feeling offended by the intrusion of occult items into a consecrated and holy space. This hypothesis was supported by James capturing ghostly singing and the audible displeasure of a male voice, shouting phrases like "unholy objects" and "Get them out." It was the first time James had ever been physically attacked. He now does his appropriate research.

This unfortunate incident serves as a stark reminder of the importance of mindfulness and respect when selecting trigger objects and researching your location. Proper research can transform trigger objects into invaluable tools for fostering positive interactions with spirits. Complacency, on the other hand, can lead to unpleasant encounters, that are entirely avoidable with due diligence.

For residual hauntings utilising music as a trigger, is a strategy often endorsed by paranormal investigators, for its potential effectiveness. The rationale behind this approach lies in the belief that specific sounds, particularly music, possess the ability to evoke memories or emotions tied to past events. Here is a closer look at why music is considered a viable trigger, for residual hauntings:

- Emotional Resonance: Music has a powerful ability to evoke emotions and memories. Certain songs or melodies can transport people back to specific moments in their past, triggering vivid recollections of associated events or emotions. In the case of residual haunting, playing music that was present during significant events in the location's history may evoke the emotions and energy associated with those events, which in turn will manifest as residual phenomena. It is advised to be site specific and take into account the time period that applies to the property. This would focus on the time of an event or period that would have emotional significance.

- Psychological Association: People often associate songs or a particular type of music with specific times, places, or experiences in their lives. Similarly, individuals who lived or spent time in a particular location may have strong psychological associations with certain types of music. Playing music that was popular or commonly heard during a specific historical period in the location may evoke a sense of nostalgia or familiarity, potentially intensifying the residual energy as well as any resident spirits.

- Frequency and Vibration: Another theory that some consider is that it is suggested sound waves, in this instance produced by music, can interact with the energy present in a location. It is theorised that certain frequencies or vibrations may resonate with the energy patterns associated with past events, potentially triggering residual phenomena.

Trigger objects serve as valuable tools in paranormal investigations, offering a means to evoke responses from spirits and entities. While their effectiveness may vary, they provide investigators with a tangible point of focus and experimentation. By carefully selecting trigger objects relevant to the location or history being investigated, researchers can potentially facilitate communication and interaction with the supernatural realm. However, it is essential to approach their use with caution, recognising that results may not always be definitive, and interpretations may vary. Nonetheless, trigger objects remain an integral part of the paranormal investigator's toolkit.

THERMAL IMAGING CAMERA

Thermal imaging technology operates by detecting changes in infrared light, which is imperceptible to the naked human eye. Infrared radiation, also known as thermal energy, plays a pivotal role in emitting heat. When utilising an infrared camera, this thermal energy or heat is captured and converted into an electronic signal, which is then processed to generate a thermal image. Modern infrared cameras boast remarkable precision in measuring heat, rendering them indispensable tools for paranormal investigators.

Although thermal imaging equipment represents a significant investment, its capabilities are unparalleled. It has the capacity to identify both hot and cold spots, as well as reveal phenomena that elude human sight, such as apparitions or moving objects. These attributes make thermal cameras invaluable assets in open environments, where they can provide tangible validation of phenomena reported by investigators or homeowners.

The benefits of incorporating thermal imaging into paranormal investigations are manifold. While the following list is by no means exhaustive, it highlights some key advantages:

- Detecting Temperature fluctuations: Thermal cameras can detect variations in temperature, which are often attributed to the presence of spirits or other entities. Sudden cold spots or unexplained heat signatures could be indicative of paranormal activity.
- Evidence Collection: Thermal imaging provides visual evidence that can be captured and analysed and in today's time very accurate. This can be valuable for documenting phenomena that investigators experience during an investigation that cannot be seen with the naked eye.
- Corroboration of Personal Experiences: People at haunted locations often report feeling sudden drops or increases in temperature during paranormal encounters. A thermal camera can corroborate these personal experiences by providing visual evidence of temperature fluctuations in the environment or airspace around a person.
- Identifying Potential Hotspots: Thermal cameras can help identify potential areas of interest within a location by highlighting unusual

154

temperature patterns. Investigators can then focus their attention on these hotspots to gather further evidence, or where they should start their investigation.

- Objective Data Collection: Thermal imaging provides objective data that can be analysed scientifically. This can add credibility to paranormal investigations by offering measurable evidence of unusual phenomena.

- Enhanced Safety: Infrared cameras can help investigators navigate dark environments more safely by providing a clear view of their surroundings, even in low-light conditions.

- Increased Credibility: Incorporating advanced technology like thermal cameras can enhance the credibility of paranormal investigations by demonstrating a commitment to thorough and objective exploration of alleged phenomena. Thermal technology can be used to locate and debunk phenomenon by locating the sources of any temperature fluctuations.

Eastern State Penitentiary

One notable case where thermal imaging technology was instrumental in a paranormal investigation occurred at the Eastern State Penitentiary in Philadelphia, Pennsylvania. This historic prison, known for its haunting reputation, was the subject of an intensive investigation by a team of paranormal researchers equipped with thermal imaging cameras.

During the investigation, the team captured compelling thermal images that revealed unexplained cold spots and fluctuations in temperature throughout the prison corridors and cells. These anomalies were particularly pronounced in areas associated with reported paranormal activity, such as the cellblocks and solitary confinement areas.

One of the most significant findings came when the team detected a distinct human-shaped heat signature in an empty cell. Despite no visible presence to the naked eye, the thermal imaging camera clearly captured the outline of a figure standing in the cell, suggesting the presence of a ghostly entity.

These thermal imaging results provided compelling evidence of paranormal activity within the Eastern State Penitentiary, corroborating eyewitness testimonies and historical accounts of ghostly encounters at the site. The case highlighted the effectiveness of thermal imaging technology in documenting and validating supernatural phenomena.

Thermal imaging technology has revolutionised paranormal investigations, providing researchers with a powerful tool to detect and document anomalous thermal signatures. By capturing heat signatures invisible to the naked eye, thermal cameras offer valuable insights into potential paranormal activity, allowing investigators to identify unexplained cold spots, apparitions, or other thermal anomalies. As this technology continues to advance, it promises to further enhance our understanding of the unseen forces that exist beyond the realm of conventional perception.

DIGITAL OR ANALOG AUDIO RECORDING

Voice recorders are my very favourite tool for any paranormal investigation. Using voice recorders at haunted locations is a common practice among paranormal investigators and enthusiasts seeking to capture audio evidence of supernatural phenomena. There are many reasons why the use of recording devices is encouraged. There are also used and trusted methods for the deployment and use of audio recorders.

Voice recorders stand out as one of the most essential tools in my paranormal investigation kit. Their role in capturing audio evidence of supernatural phenomena makes them indispensable for both seasoned investigators and enthusiasts alike. Let us explore why recording devices are widely embraced in paranormal investigations, along with some established methods for their effective deployment and use.

The primary objective of employing digital voice recorders in haunted locations is to capture Electronic Voice Phenomena (EVP). EVP refers to purported voices or sounds of spirits or entities that are typically inaudible to the human ear but can be picked up by recording devices. There are two primary approaches to EVP capture: continuous recording over extended periods and targeted EVP sessions conducted in real-time. In my experience, EVPs constitute one of the most compelling forms of evidence supporting the existence of life after death.

Digital and analog voice recorders differ primarily in their method of recording and storing audio data:
Recording Method:

Digital Voice Recorder:
Digital recorders convert sound waves into digital data using an analog-to-digital converter (ADC). This process involves capturing sound as a series of numerical values, which are then stored in digital format on memory chips or internal storage.

Analog Voice Recorder:
Analog recorders use magnetic tape or other analog media to directly record

156

and store sound waves. The recording process involves imprinting the variations in sound amplitude onto the recording medium, preserving the analog signal for playback.

AUDIO QUALITY

Digital Voice Recorder:
Digital recording technology typically offers higher audio quality and clarity compared to analog recordings. Digital recorders can capture a wider frequency range and produce clearer sound reproduction, making them suitable for professional use.

Analog Voice Recorder:
Analog recordings may exhibit some degree of signal degradation, noise, or distortion inherent to analog media. While analog recorders may impart a unique warmth or character to recordings, they generally offer lower fidelity compared to digital recordings.

STORAGE AND PLAYBACK

Digital Voice Recorder: Digital recordings are stored as files in a digital format, allowing for easy playback, editing, and transfer to other devices such as computers or smartphones. Digital recorders often feature built-in storage or removable memory cards for storing recordings.

Analog Voice Recorder: Analog recordings are stored directly on the recording medium, such as magnetic tape or cassette tapes. Playback requires a compatible analog playback device, such as a tape recorder or cassette player. Analog recordings cannot be easily edited or transferred without additional analog-to-digital conversion.

CONVENIENCE AND FEATURES

Digital Voice Recorder: Digital recorders offer various features and functionalities, such as USB connectivity, file management, voice activation, built-in microphones, and editing capabilities. They are often more compact, lightweight, and user-friendly than analog recorders.

Analog Voice Recorder: Analog recorders may lack some of the advanced features and conveniences of digital recorders. However, they may appeal to users seeking a simpler, more nostalgic recording experience or those working in environments where digital technology is not feasible or preferred.

157

Overall, the choice between digital and analog voice recorders depends on factors such as audio quality requirements, desired features, ease of use, and personal preference. Digital recorders are generally preferred for professional applications and modern recording needs, while analog recorders may be favoured for their nostalgic appeal or specific use cases.

STRATEGIC PLACEMENT

Strategic placement of digital recorders in areas of reported paranormal activity is crucial for maximising the chances of capturing EVP. Recordings may be conducted during both daytime and night time investigations to cover a range of potential phenomena. This approach is particularly effective for large locations, allowing investigators to leave recorders unattended while exploring other areas.

USE OF RECORDING DEVICES

Recording sessions typically last several hours, during which investigators engage in communication with any spirits present, prompting responses in hopes of eliciting EVP. Following the recording session, investigators meticulously review the audio recordings, listening for anomalies or voices that cannot be readily explained. Software tools may be employed to enhance and analyse recordings further, focusing on noise reduction and amplification.

While compelling EVP recordings can offer valuable insights into paranormal phenomena, it is crucial to approach them with a healthy dose of scepticism and consider alternative explanations. Environmental noise, equipment malfunctions, and pareidolia can sometimes account for sounds heard on EVP. However, distinct responses and clear voices often suggest paranormal activity.

In my experience, EVP sessions have yielded a diverse range of phenomena, from growls and hisses to crystal-clear responses to direct questions. Software tools may be used to enhance audio clarity, ensuring accurate interpretation during analysis.

Maintaining recording integrity is paramount during EVP sessions, requiring investigators to stand still or place recorders in stationary positions to minimise background noise. Any noises made by team members or potential rational explanations should be verbally acknowledged on the recording to facilitate later analysis.

Paranormal investigators employ a classification system to categorise audio evidence, a topic we'll delve into further when discussing evidence analysis.

In 2023, Jack and I embarked on an investigation at the renowned haunted

Kenwick Pioneer Cemetery. As we traversed the grounds, examining the various graves, my recorder was diligently capturing our surroundings. Suddenly, Jack voiced his concern, fearing he had inadvertently stepped on a grave. Little did we anticipate the response that awaited us upon reviewing the recording.

At the precise time stamp of Jack's remark, a distinct female voice resonated through the audio, sternly admonishing, "Shame on you." With no other living souls present in the cemetery besides us, the source of the voice remained a mystery. Was it the spirit of an aggrieved soul, disturbed by our presence, or perhaps a poignant reminder of the sanctity of the final resting place?

Throughout my paranormal investigations, I've encountered a myriad of eerie sounds, from guttural growls to spine-tingling hisses and blood-curdling screams. Yet, amidst the cacophony of supernatural phenomena, crystal-clear responses to our direct inquiries have left an indelible impression. Often, the subtle nuances of these recordings require meticulous enhancement and audio processing to discern their true significance, underscoring the importance of specialised software tools in our analysis.

Maintaining the integrity of our recordings is paramount during EVP (Electronic Voice Phenomena) sessions. Whether standing motionless or positioning the recorder in a stationary location, minimising extraneous noise is essential to capturing pristine audio evidence. Any incidental sounds or rational explanations, such as footsteps or whispers, should be promptly acknowledged on the recording to ensure accuracy during subsequent analysis.

As paranormal investigators, we adhere to a rigorous classification system when evaluating audio evidence, meticulously categorising each recording based on its characteristics and context. This systematic approach is fundamental to our evidence analysis, providing a framework for interpreting and drawing conclusions from the wealth of auditory phenomena encountered during our investigations.

TEMPERATURE GUN

Temperature guns are simple handheld devices that measure the temperature of surfaces using infrared radiation. They are non-contact devices, meaning they can measure temperature from a distance without physically touching the object or surface. Paranormal investigators use temperature guns to scan various areas within a haunted location, looking for deviations from the ambient temperature that cannot be readily explained by conventional means.

During the investigations, investigators use the temperature guns to scan walls, floors, doorways, and other surfaces where paranormal activity has been reported or is suspected to occur. Temperature readings are often recorded, in the initial walk through along with the corresponding weather, location and time for later analysis.

Digital Thermometers are also a great tool for recording sudden drops or raising of temperature, they tend to record the ambient temperature. Using any kind of thermographic cameras, Infrared Thermometers and infrared temperature sensors only measure surface temperature and not ambient temperature. It is good to keep this in mind when choosing which equipment to buy.

Critics of using temperature guns in paranormal investigations argue that temperature fluctuations can be caused by various factors and are not indicative of paranormal activity. They emphasise the importance of conducting controlled experiments and ruling out environmental variables before attributing temperature changes to unknown causes. Additionally.

Temperature guns have limitations, such as their sensitivity to distance and surface emissivity, which can affect the accuracy of readings.

- Temperature guns measure the surface temperature of objects or surfaces they are directly pointed at. They do not measure the air temperature or the temperature of objects beyond the surface. This limitation can make it challenging to accurately assess the overall thermal conditions of a room or space. For example, a wall may be warm when a reading is taken compared to the ambient temperature. However, behind the wall, beyond the scope of the temperature gun is extremely hot because there is a water heater there.

- The accuracy of temperature measurements can be affected by the distance between the temperature gun and the surface being measured. This also applies to the angle at which it is pointed. The further away the surface is, the larger the area being measured becomes, leading to less precise readings.

- Different materials emit and absorb infrared radiation differently, affecting the accuracy of temperature readings. This is called surface emissivity: Most temperature guns allow for adjustments and calibration to account for surface emissivity, but this requires knowledge of the material being measured. A highly reflective or shiny surfaces, like a mirror or metal, can produce inaccurate readings if their emissivity is not properly accounted for.

- Temperature readings can be influenced by environmental factors such as nearby heat sources, drafts, sunlight, or reflective surfaces.

These factors can cause false temperature readings and may lead to misinterpretation of data if not properly investigated at the time of observation,

- The most frustrating part of using a temperature gun is response time, especially when measuring rapidly changing or moving temperatures. Sometimes the readings have a delayed response time. This delay can result in inaccurate readings if the target temperature changes before the device registers it.

Like all measurement instruments, temperature guns require regular calibration in order to ensure the accuracy of the reading. Without proper calibration, temperature readings, leading to unreliable readings. Temperature guns typically have a limited temperature measurement range. Extreme temperatures outside of this range may not be accurately measured. However, this has never really been too much of a problem in my experience. Most temperature guns have a temperature measurement range between approximately -50°C to 550°C (-58°F to 1022°F), sometimes wider. There has never been a scenario where I have encountered such temperatures at any location.

If investigators believe they have captured significant temperature fluctuations that align with reported paranormal phenomena, they document these findings in their reports or presentations. Temperature readings may be presented alongside other evidence, such as EVP recordings or EMF, photo and video evidence, to build a case for the presence of paranormal activity at that location.

MOTION DETECTORS

Motion detectors are commonly used as a tool to detect any unexplained movement or activity at supposedly haunted locations. These detectors typically work by sensing changes in infrared radiation or microwaves, triggering an alarm or the more advanced versions a recording when such changes occur.

They are often place them in areas where paranormal activity is reported or suspected, such as hallways, doorways, or areas with a history of experiences. There are a number of different types of motion detectors on the Market. I have a particular like of Infrared motion detectors during our investigations.

- Infrared Motion Detectors: These detectors work by sensing changes in infrared radiation emitted by an object. When an object, spirit or entity moves within the detector's field of view, it interrupts the infrared beams, triggering the sensor to detect

161

motion. These are the ones we use on our investigations and the field of view is you have to be almost on top of it, to break the beams. I have found these motion detectors to be very reliable during investigations and rarely do they go off from outside interference. You do still need to be mindful of where you place them.

- Microwave Motion Detectors: Microwave motion detectors emit microwave signals and measure the reflections to detect movement. When an object moves within the detection zone, it disturbs the microwave signals, causing the detector to register motion. These detectors are commonly used in security systems. Paranormal Puck 2 EMF/Microwave Sensor combines electromagnetic field (EMF) detection with microwave sensing capabilities. This device was marketed explicitly for paranormal investigations. The great advantage to using microwave detectors is there are many varied options for both indoor and outdoor use, given the main purpose of these detectors are security monitoring.

- Ultrasonic Motion Detectors: Ultrasonic motion detectors emit ultrasonic waves. Any moving object within the detection range changes the pattern and direction of the reflected waves signalling the presence of motion.

- Passive Infrared (PIR) Motion Detectors: PIR motion detectors detect infrared energy emitted by objects in their field of view. They are often used in security systems to detect human movement. In paranormal investigations, PIR detectors can be deployed to monitor areas for any sudden changes in infrared radiation, potentially indicating the presence of a paranormal entity moving through the space.

- Vibration Motion Detectors: These detectors are sensitive to vibrations or movements in the environment. They can be placed on floors, walls, or other surfaces to detect any subtle movements that might occur. Vibration motion detectors are less commonly used in paranormal research because they are just not that reliable and can be set off by the slightest movement.

Motion detectors in paranormal investigations capture evidence of paranormal phenomena, such as apparitions or entities moving through a doorway, corridor, or space. If a motion detector is triggered without any apparent cause, it could suggest the presence of a spirit in that area. It is essential to approach the use of motion detectors in paranormal investigations with a healthy dose of critical thinking. While they are undoubtedly valuable tools for detecting physical movement, they can also be triggered by other environmental factors such as drafts, animals, and vibrations. Sometimes new sensors can malfunction and go off by themselves or stay on because they are new. They should be used alongside other tools and methods, and their findings should be interpreted alongside corroborating evidence to prevent the investigator from misinterpretation when the alarm sounds.

When a motion detector is triggered, it can be the first indication that there is something present. Once this occurs an investigator can then decide to conduct an EVP or Spirit Box session. Sensor detectors play a crucial role in paranormal investigations, but they also have limitations that investigators should consider:

- Environmental Interference: Sensor detectors can be affected by environmental factors such as temperature fluctuations, humidity, electromagnetic interference, and ambient noise. These factors may produce false readings or obscure genuine paranormal activity.

- False Positives: Sensor detectors may register false positives, detecting mundane phenomena or natural occurrences that mimic paranormal activity. For example, fluctuations in electromagnetic fields can be caused by household appliances, wiring, or nearby electronic devices, leading to erroneous interpretations.

- Sensitivity Settings: Some sensor detectors allow users to adjust sensitivity settings to filter out background noise or enhance detection capabilities. However, improper calibration or sensitivity settings may result in missed opportunities to detect genuine paranormal phenomena or an increased likelihood of false alarms.

- Limited Range and Coverage: Sensor detectors have finite detection ranges and coverage areas, which may restrict their effectiveness in large or complex environments. Investigators must strategically position detectors to maximise coverage and ensure that potential paranormal hotspots are adequately monitored.

- Power Source Dependence: Many sensor detectors rely on batteries or external power sources to operate. Battery-powered detectors may experience power drain or require frequent battery replacement, impacting their reliability and usability during extended investigations.

- Interpretation Challenges: Sensor data collected during investigations may be open to interpretation, requiring careful analysis and contextual understanding. Investigators must exercise discernment to differentiate between genuine paranormal activity and ordinary environmental fluctuations or equipment

163

malfunctions.

Equipment Limitations: Some sensor detectors have inherent limitations in terms of sensitivity, accuracy, or detection capabilities. Investing in high-quality, specialised equipment can mitigate these limitations but may come at a higher cost. Integrating multiple sensor detectors into a cohesive investigative setup may pose challenges in terms of compatibility, synchronisation, and data management. Investigators must ensure that their equipment is properly configured and coordinated to yield meaningful results.

Despite these limitations, sensor detectors remain valuable tools in paranormal investigations when used judiciously, in conjunction with other investigative methods, and with a critical understanding of their capabilities and constraints.

MEL METER

The Mel Meter is unique piece of paranormal equipment in that combine multiple functions, namely temperature and EMF, recorded onto a single device. It was developed by Gary Galka, who was inspired to create the device after the tragic loss of his daughter, Melissa Galka, who was a well-known paranormal investigator.

Melissa Galka was a paranormal investigator who gained recognition through her appearances on the television series "Ghost Hunters Academy" and "Ghost Hunters International." She was born on May 5, 1984, in New Jersey, USA. Melissa had a passion for the paranormal from a young age and became actively involved in investigating hauntings and supernatural phenomena.

Melissa then appeared on "Ghost Hunters International" which focused on investigating paranormal activity and haunted outside of the United States. Melissa contributed her expertise as a member of the team impressing watches and paranormal investigators alike as she went.

Melissa Galka's passion for the paranormal and her contributions to the field of ghost hunting made her a respected figure among fellow investigators and fans of the genre. She brought a combination of enthusiasm, professionalism, and empathy to her work, always striving to uncover the truth behind reported hauntings and provide closure to those affected by paranormal experiences.

Tragically, Melissa Galka passed away on November 2, 2019, at the age of 35 in a car accident near to her home. Her untimely death was a loss to the paranormal community and utterly devastated her family.

Melissas story, however, continued, in true paranormal investigator style, when she began contacting her parents through the ghost box, EVP and any possible way that she could. In fact, they still hold birthday celebrations for her and she still shows up. They have recorded 100s of messages from Melissa over the years. This inspired her father to find better ways to detect the Prescence of his daughter.

the Mel Meter is designed to provide paranormal investigators with a tool for monitoring environmental conditions and detecting potential signs of paranormal activity. Some versions, as well as detecting changes in temperature and EMF, also contains a flashlight, data logging and audio alerting to any changes when they are detected.

The Mel Meter, like any paranormal investigation tool, has its limitations and drawbacks:

- Cost: The Mel Meter can be relatively expensive compared to other EMF meters or paranormal investigation equipment, making it less accessible to some investigators, especially those on a tight budget.

- Complexity: Some users may find the Mel Meter's interface and functionality complex or challenging to navigate, particularly if they are new to paranormal investigation or not familiar with technical equipment.

- Limited Features: While the Mel Meter is designed specifically for measuring EMF levels and temperature fluctuations, it may lack additional features found in more advanced paranormal investigation devices, such as data logging, audio recording capabilities, or connectivity options.

- Sensitivity Variations: Like all EMF meters, the Mel Meter's sensitivity may vary depending on factors such as calibration, environmental conditions, and proximity to electromagnetic sources. Users must calibrate the device properly and account for potential interference to obtain accurate readings.

- Single Functionality: The Mel Meter primarily focuses on measuring electromagnetic fields and temperature changes, which may limit its versatility compared to multifunctional paranormal investigation tools that offer a broader range of features and capabilities.

- Reliability Concerns: Some users have reported issues with the reliability and durability of Mel Meters, including malfunctioning displays, inconsistent readings, or premature device failure. Ensuring the device is properly maintained and periodically calibrated can help mitigate these concerns.

- Interpretation Challenges: Interpreting the data collected by the

165

Mel Meter requires knowledge and expertise in understanding electromagnetic fields and temperature fluctuations in the context of paranormal investigation. Users must exercise caution to avoid misinterpreting normal environmental fluctuations as paranormal activity.

- External Interference: The Mel Meter, like any EMF meter, may be susceptible to external interference from nearby electronic devices, power sources, or environmental factors. Users must minimise potential sources of interference and validate readings through multiple measurements and cross-referencing with other equipment.

Despite these drawbacks, the Mel Meter remains a popular choice among paranormal investigators for its reliability, accuracy, and specialised functionality in measuring EMF levels and temperature changes during investigations. One last note, If I should die an untimely death, you can bet all of your money, that I will return to let you all know that I am ok via EVP, and yes, I still want cake!

LASER GRID

Bill Chappell is a revered figure in the realm of paranormal investigation, celebrated for his ground breaking contributions to the field through innovative equipment designs. Among his notable inventions stands the Laser Grid, a revolutionary tool designed to facilitate the detection and visualisation of paranormal activity within a given location.

The Laser Grid functions by projecting a meticulously arranged grid pattern of laser beams onto a surface, typically a wall or other flat surface. This grid pattern comprises an array of luminous dots, intricately arranged to form a matrix resembling a grid. When deployed during a paranormal investigation, the Laser Grid is strategically positioned in dimly lit or darkened areas where reports of paranormal phenomena have been documented.

Operating in tandem with motion detectors or other sensing devices, the Laser Grid serves as a proactive sentinel, poised to detect any disruptions or anomalies within its field of illumination. As spirits or entities traverse the environment, their presence may perturb the laser beams, inducing perceptible alterations in the grid pattern. These visual disturbances offer tangible evidence of paranormal activity, enabling investigators to corroborate their findings through visual documentation.

One of the most compelling attributes of the Laser Grid is its ability to provide a dynamic visual reference that can be captured in real-time through video recordings or photographs.

Pros of using a laser grid in paranormal research:

- Visibility: Laser grids provide a visual reference point for detecting subtle movements or anomalies in the environment during paranormal investigations, enhancing the visibility of potential paranormal activity.
- Real-time Monitoring: The grid's pattern allows investigators to monitor changes or disruptions in the laser beams in real-time, providing immediate feedback on any disturbances in the area being monitored.
- Object Tracking: Laser grids can be used to track the movement of objects or entities within a space, helping investigators to capture evidence of paranormal phenomena such as apparitions or shadow figures.
- Controlled Environment: Laser grids create a controlled environment for conducting experiments or observations, minimising the impact of external factors and providing a standardised framework for paranormal research.
- Documentation: The grid pattern creates a visual record of the investigation, enabling investigators to document and analyse any observed phenomena or anomalies captured on video or camera footage.

Cons of using a laser grid in paranormal research:

- Limited Coverage: Laser grids have a finite range and may not cover large areas effectively, limiting their utility in monitoring expansive spaces or environments during paranormal investigations.
- Interference: External factors such as dust, smoke, or air currents can interfere with the laser beams, causing false positives or obscuring genuine paranormal activity from detection.
- Calibration Challenges: Ensuring the accurate alignment and calibration of the laser grid setup can be time-consuming and may require technical expertise, leading to potential inaccuracies or inconsistencies in the data collected.
- Safety Concerns: Laser beams used in grid setups can pose a safety risk if not handled properly, especially when pointed directly at the eyes. Investigators must take precautions to prevent accidental exposure and ensure the safety of themselves and others present during the investigation.

167

- Environmental Limitations: Laser grids may be less effective in outdoor environments or locations with high ambient light levels, diminishing their visibility and reducing their effectiveness in detecting subtle movements or anomalies.
-

Overall, while laser grids can be valuable tools in paranormal research for enhancing visibility and detecting potential activity, they also have limitations and considerations that investigators must account for when using them in investigations.

REM POD EM

The "Radiating Electromagnetic Pod," commonly known as the REM-POD EM, stands as a staple sensor and communication tool within the realm of paranormal investigation. Its mechanism revolves around the generation of its own electromagnetic field, with the primary function being the detection of any disruptions within this field.

Equipped with specialised EMF sensors, the REM Pod EM is finely tuned to detect fluctuations in electromagnetic fields, offering a heightened sensitivity to subtle changes in the surrounding environment. Additionally, the device features a proximity sensor that specifically identifies alterations in the electromagnetic field proximate to the device itself.

Upon detecting any significant changes in electromagnetic activity, the REM Pod EM promptly triggers audible and visual feedback mechanisms. This may manifest as distinct beeping sounds, flashing lights, or a combination of both, depending on the model being utilised. Such responsive features serve to alert investigators to potential paranormal phenomena, prompting further investigation and documentation.

Like other paranormal investigation equipment, the REM Pod EM serves as a crucial tool for documenting anomalous activity. Investigators often utilise video or audio recording devices to capture the device's reactions in real-time, providing tangible evidence of any observed interactions or events. The interpretation of such activity is frequently cross-referenced with data from other investigative mediums, such as audio and video recordings, to corroborate findings and enhance understanding.

Pros of using a REM Pod EM (Electromagnetic) device in paranormal research:

- EM Detection: REM Pod EM devices are designed to detect electromagnetic fluctuations in the environment, which are often associated with paranormal activity. This capability allows investigators to monitor changes in electromagnetic fields that

168

may occur during ghostly manifestations or disturbances.

- Immediate Response: REM Pod EM devices provide immediate audible and visual feedback when detecting changes in electromagnetic fields, allowing investigators to react in real-time to potential paranormal phenomena.

- Portable and Easy to Use: REM Pod EM devices are typically compact and portable, making them easy to transport and set up in various locations during paranormal investigations. They also usually feature simple controls and interfaces, allowing for straightforward operation by investigators of all experience levels.

- Data Logging: Some REM Pod EM devices come equipped with data logging capabilities, allowing investigators to record and analyse fluctuations in electromagnetic fields over time. This feature can be valuable for documenting and reviewing evidence obtained during investigations.

- Correlation with Other Evidence: By correlating data from REM Pod EM readings with other forms of evidence, such as EVP recordings or temperature fluctuations, investigators can establish patterns or connections that may support the presence of paranormal activity in a particular location.

Cons of using a REM Pod EM device in paranormal research:

- False Positives: REM Pod EM devices may be susceptible to false positives caused by environmental factors such as electrical wiring, nearby electronic devices, or radio frequency interference. Distinguishing genuine paranormal activity from these false readings can be challenging and may require careful analysis.

- Limited Range: REM Pod EM devices have a limited detection range for electromagnetic fields, which may restrict their effectiveness in monitoring larger areas or environments during paranormal investigations.

- Sensitivity Issues: Some REM Pod EM devices may have sensitivity issues, either detecting too many minor fluctuations or failing to register significant changes in electromagnetic fields. Calibrating the device appropriately and adjusting sensitivity settings may help mitigate this issue.

- Reliance on Interpretation: Interpreting the data obtained from REM Pod EM devices requires subjective judgment and interpretation by investigators. Without corroborating evidence or additional context, fluctuations in electromagnetic fields detected by the device may not necessarily indicate paranormal activity.

- Battery Dependence: REM Pod EM devices typically rely on batteries for power, and their operation may be affected by battery life or performance. Investigators must ensure that the device is adequately powered and that spare batteries are available to prevent interruptions during investigations.

Overall, while REM Pod EM devices can be valuable tools for detecting electromagnetic fluctuations associated with paranormal activity, they also have limitations and considerations that investigators should be aware of when using them in their research.

SLS CAMERA

The SLS Camera, also known as Structured Light Sensor Camera, is based on structured light technology, originally conceived through the x box Kinect system.

The SLS Camera emits a grid or pattern of infrared light into the environment that is not visible with our eyes. This grid serves as a reference for the camera to detect depth and spatial information. As the infrared light interacts with an object, the camera captures the reflections and uses them to create a depth map of the reflected object. This allows the camera to detect and measure distances to objects within its field of view.

The SLS Camera's software analyses the mapped data and identifies any anomalies or shapes that deviate from the expected background. It then highlights or represents these anomalies on the camera's display, often as stick figures or skeletal outlines.

The SLS Camera provides real-time visualisation of any detected spirits with the camera's live feed. Investigators can observe and interact with these representations visually on the screen.

Many SLS Cameras feature the ability to record video or capture images for further analysis and documentation later. I personally do not use the SLS in investigations as I have found them to be unreliable, however each person should at the very least, try it out and see what they feel.

Pros of using an SLS (Structured Light Sensor) camera in paranormal research:

- Real-time Visualisation: SLS cameras provide real-time visualisation of the surrounding environment, allowing investigators to observe any anomalous figures or entities that may appear. This immediate feedback can be valuable for documenting paranormal activity as it occurs.

- Three-Dimensional Mapping: SLS cameras use structured light patterns to create three-dimensional maps of the environment, enabling them to detect and track objects in space. This capability allows investigators to capture detailed representations of any entities or phenomena present, enhancing the quality of evidence obtained during investigations.
- Non-Invasive: SLS cameras are non-invasive tools that do not require physical contact with the subject or environment being monitored. This characteristic makes them suitable for use in a variety of locations and situations without causing disruption or interference.
- Portable and Easy to Use: Many SLS cameras are compact and portable, making them easy to transport and set up for paranormal investigations. They often feature user-friendly interfaces and controls, allowing investigators of all experience levels to operate them effectively.
- Corroboration of Evidence: SLS camera footage can provide corroborating evidence for other forms of paranormal phenomena, such as EVP recordings or EMF fluctuations. By capturing visual representations of anomalous figures or entities, SLS cameras can help validate the presence of paranormal activity in a particular location.

Cons of using an SLS camera in paranormal research:

- Cost: High-quality SLS cameras can be expensive, making them inaccessible to some paranormal investigators or research teams operating on limited budgets. The initial investment required to purchase an SLS camera may be prohibitive for some individuals or organisations.
- Scepticism and Criticism: SLS camera footage is often met with scepticism and criticism from sceptics and debunkers within the paranormal community and beyond. Some critics argue that anomalies captured by SLS cameras may have natural or technological explanations rather than being evidence of paranormal activity.
- Interpretation Challenges: Interpreting SLS camera footage requires subjective judgment and interpretation by investigators, as anomalies captured on camera may have alternative explanations. Without additional context or corroborating evidence, it can be difficult to determine whether anomalies are genuinely paranormal

or the result of environmental factors or technical artifacts.

- False Positives: SLS cameras may generate false positives or artifacts due to environmental conditions, lighting effects, or technical limitations. Distinguishing genuine anomalies from false readings can be challenging and may require careful analysis and validation.

- Limited Field of View: Some SLS cameras have a limited field of view, which may restrict their effectiveness in monitoring larger areas or environments during paranormal investigations. Investigators must carefully position and adjust the camera to capture relevant activity without missing any potential phenomena.

Overall, while SLS cameras offer unique capabilities for capturing visual evidence of paranormal activity, they also have limitations and considerations that investigators should be aware of when using them in their research.

FLIR SCOUT TK THERMAL MONOCULAR

The FLIR Scout TK Thermal Monocular is a handheld thermal imaging device and was designed for various outdoor applications. These include surveillance, search and rescue, and wildlife observations. It uses thermal imaging technology to detect and visualise heat signatures emitted by objects and living organisms.

With similar functionality to the previous camera, but in a much smaller and easier to handle form. It has a wide -4 to 104-degree operating temperature, and IP-67 dust- and waterproof rating, make it ideal for paranormal investigations in less-than-ideal weather conditions.

The camera has a detection range of up to 100 meters (approximately 328 feet), allowing users to observe objects from a distance. However, on the downside this is quite a limited distance when you are outside or in large open environments.

The monocular offers multiple viewing modes, including white hot, black hot, and InstAlert, which highlights the hottest objects in the scene in bright red for quick identification. The Scout TK is powered by a built-in rechargeable lithium-ion battery, which provides several hours of continuous use on a single charge. Users may need to carry spare batteries or recharge the device frequently, particularly during extended outdoor excursions.

It can be conveniently recharged via a standard USB cable bur compared to higher-end thermal imaging devices, the Scout TK has a lower resolution, which may result in less detailed images and reduced clarity at a distance.

he effectiveness of thermal imaging devices like the Scout TK depends on temperature differences between objects and their surroundings. In environments where there are minimal thermal contrasts, such as on hot days or in areas with uniform ambient temperatures, the device has limited effectiveness in detecting objects.

I have known a few investigators that do not like using FLIR for this very reason. I also know many that make the decision to use it as a normal part of any investigation. The reader must make up their own mind.

Advantages of FLIR thermal cameras in paranormal research:

- Detection of Temperature Anomalies: FLIR thermal cameras can detect temperature variations in the environment, allowing investigators to identify cold spots, heat signatures, and other anomalies associated with paranormal activity. This capability enables them to capture potential evidence of ghostly manifestations or energy fluctuations.

- Non-Visual Detection: Unlike traditional cameras, FLIR thermal cameras do not rely on visible light to capture images. Instead, they detect infrared radiation emitted by objects based on their temperature, making them effective for detecting entities or phenomena that may not be visible to the naked eye.

- Real-Time Monitoring: FLIR thermal cameras provide real-time monitoring of temperature changes, allowing investigators to observe anomalies as they occur. This immediate feedback can help guide investigations and capture evidence of paranormal activity in the moment.

- Versatility: FLIR thermal cameras are versatile tools that can be used in various environments and conditions, including low light or complete darkness. They are suitable for indoor investigations, outdoor explorations, and confined spaces, making them adaptable to different paranormal research scenarios.

- Documentation and Analysis: FLIR thermal cameras allow investigators to document and analyse temperature data over time, providing a comprehensive record of paranormal phenomena. This data can be reviewed, compared, and analysed to identify patterns or correlations associated with haunted locations.

Disadvantages of FLIR thermal cameras in paranormal research:

- Limited Detail: FLIR thermal cameras produce images based on temperature variations rather than visual detail, resulting in less detailed images compared to traditional cameras. This limitation may make it challenging to discern specific shapes or features of paranormal entities captured on camera.

- Environmental Interference: FLIR thermal cameras may be susceptible to environmental factors that can affect temperature readings, such as air currents, reflections, or nearby heat sources. These factors can introduce noise or false positives into thermal imaging data, complicating the interpretation of results.

- Cost: High-quality FLIR thermal cameras can be expensive, making them inaccessible to some paranormal investigators or research teams operating on limited budgets. The initial investment required to purchase and maintain FLIR thermal cameras may be prohibitive for individuals or organisations with financial constraints.

- Learning Curve: FLIR thermal cameras require training and experience to use effectively, particularly in interpreting thermal imaging data and identifying potential anomalies. Investigators may need to familiarise themselves with the operation of the camera and develop proficiency in analysing thermal images for paranormal activity.

- Subjectivity in Interpretation: Interpreting thermal imaging data obtained from FLIR cameras can be subjective, as anomalies may have alternative explanations besides paranormal activity. Investigators must exercise caution and critical thinking when interpreting thermal images to avoid misinterpretation or confirmation bias.

While the FLIR thermal cameras offer unique capabilities for detecting temperature anomalies associated with paranormal phenomena, they also have limitations and considerations that investigators should be aware of when using them in their research.

FULL SPECTRUM CAMERA

A full spectrum camera is a specialised device used in paranormal investigations to capture images across a broader range of wavelengths than standard cameras. Unlike traditional cameras that are designed to capture only visible light, full spectrum cameras are modified to also detect ultraviolet (UV) and infrared (IR) light, as well as visible light. I use the full spectrum on every investigation.

The concept behind using a full spectrum camera in paranormal investigations is rooted in the belief that paranormal phenomena may manifest in wavelengths beyond the visible spectrum. For example, spirits or energy anomalies may emit light or appear in forms that are invisible to the

174

naked human eye but can be detected by cameras sensitive to UV and IR light.

By capturing images across a wider spectrum, full spectrum cameras offer paranormal investigators the opportunity to potentially capture visual evidence of paranormal activity that may otherwise go unnoticed. This includes anomalies such as apparitions, light anomalies, or energy manifestations that may be present in UV or IR wavelengths but not visible in the visible spectrum.

Additionally, full spectrum cameras can be paired with other investigative tools such as infrared illuminators or UV lights to enhance their effectiveness in low-light or night-time environments. This combination allows investigators to explore and document paranormal phenomena in conditions where standard cameras may struggle to capture clear images.

Using a full spectrum camera in paranormal investigations comes with several pros and cons:

Pros

- Enhanced Sensitivity: Full spectrum cameras are capable of capturing light beyond the visible spectrum, including ultraviolet (UV) and infrared (IR) light. This increased sensitivity may help capture anomalies or phenomena that are not visible to the naked eye or traditional cameras.

- Increased Potential for Evidence: By capturing a broader range of light, full spectrum cameras may detect anomalies or energy sources that could be indicative of paranormal activity. This can provide investigators with additional evidence to analyse and assess.

- Flexibility: Full spectrum cameras can be used in various lighting conditions, including low light and complete darkness, making them versatile tools for paranormal investigations.

- Non-Invasive: Unlike some other paranormal investigation tools, such as EMF meters or EVP recorders, full spectrum cameras do not emit any signals or disturb the environment, making them non-invasive tools for capturing potential evidence.

- Documentation: Full spectrum cameras enable investigators to document visual evidence of paranormal activity, including apparitions, light anomalies, or energy manifestations, which can be analysed and shared as part of the investigation.

Cons:

- High Cost: Full spectrum cameras tend to be more expensive than regular digital cameras or even DSLRs. This cost may be prohibitive for some investigators or teams, especially those operating on a limited budget.

- Complexity: Operating a full spectrum camera may require some technical expertise, especially when it comes to post-processing and analysing the captured images. Investigators may need to invest time in learning how to use the camera effectively.

- False Positives: The increased sensitivity of full spectrum cameras may also lead to an increased likelihood of capturing false positives, such as lens flares, dust particles, or other environmental contaminants. Distinguishing between genuine paranormal phenomena and artifacts can be challenging.

- Image Quality: Full spectrum cameras may produce images with different colour tones or artifacts compared to standard cameras, particularly when capturing UV or IR light. This can affect the clarity and visual appeal of the images, making interpretation more challenging.

- Limited Scientific Validation: While full spectrum cameras can capture a broader range of light, their effectiveness in capturing paranormal phenomena has not been scientifically validated. As such, the evidence obtained from these cameras may not be considered conclusive by sceptics or scientific communities.

The use of full spectrum cameras in paranormal investigations provides investigators with a valuable tool for capturing visual evidence of potential paranormal activity across a broader range of wavelengths, thus expanding the scope of their research, and enhancing their ability to document unexplained phenomena. I personally would recommend this as something that you will eventually want to buy.

SAFE TRANSPORT AND STORAGE

Ensuring the safe transportation and storage of paranormal equipment is paramount for maintaining its functionality and longevity. Here are some guidelines to help ensure the safety of your paranormal equipment during transport and storage:

- Invest in sturdy, padded cases designed specifically to protect paranormal equipment during transportation. Cases with custom foam inserts provide a snug fit for each piece of equipment, reducing the risk of damage from impacts or rough handling during travel.

- Before transporting equipment, securely store all loose components such as cables, batteries, and accessories in their designated compartments within the cases. Proper organisation minimises the risk of damage or loss while in transit.

- Clearly label all equipment cases and individual pieces with their names and contents to facilitate easy identification and locate specific items when needed. This helps prevent misplacement or loss of equipment.

- Handle paranormal equipment with care during transportation, avoiding dropping or mishandling. Even minor impacts can potentially damage sensitive electronic components or affect calibration.

- Store paranormal equipment in a cool, dry environment away from direct sunlight and extreme temperatures, as exposure to heat, cold, or humidity can damage electronic components and compromise performance.

- Before storing equipment for an extended period, remove batteries to prevent corrosion and damage from leaking batteries. Store batteries separately in a cool, dry place.

- Conduct regular maintenance checks on paranormal equipment to ensure it remains in optimal working condition. Inspect cables, connectors, and components for signs of wear or damage, and address any issues promptly by replacing or repairing them as needed.

- Maintain a detailed inventory of all paranormal equipment, including serial numbers, specifications, and purchase dates. This documentation is useful for insurance purposes and in the event of loss or damage.

- If storing equipment in a shared space or facility, consider implementing security measures such as locks or surveillance cameras to prevent theft.

For expensive equipment, it is advisable to insure it against damage or theft, especially when taking it to locations where others may have access. Ensure compliance with any specific requirements set by the insurance company, such as securing the equipment with locks when not in use. Invest in a lockable yet portable solution if necessary.

5 COMMUNICATION TOOLS AND EQUIPMENT

As the moon cast its ghostly glow over the silent graveyard, the air thick with anticipation, the veil between the living and the dead seemed to shimmer. In this hushed realm where shadows danced with secrets, whispers of the past lingered like echoes in the night. It was here, amidst the gravestones weathered by time, that the intrepid seekers of the unknown gathered, armed with tools to bridge the gap between worlds

In the dim light, their hands trembled as they reached for the ancient artifact resting upon the table - a mysterious board adorned with cryptic symbols and letters. Known by many names - the talking board, the spirit board - its eerie presence seemed to beckon, promising a connection to realms beyond mortal comprehension

With bated breath, they dared to invoke the spirits, to seek answers from the other side. For in this twilight realm where the living and the dead converged, the journey into the unknown was about to begin

Communication tools for the dead, often refer to devices or methods believed to facilitate contact with the spirits or entities that inhabit the paranormal world. While these concepts are popular in paranormal and spiritual circles, they often typically lack scientific validation and are often viewed sceptically by mainstream science.

The use of communication equipment in paranormal investigations is a common practice among paranormal investigators and enthusiasts. These tools are employed with the aim of detecting, recording, or facilitating communication with spirits or other paranormal entities. However, it is important to note that the effectiveness and reliability of these tools are widely

178

debated, and their use often falls outside the realm of scientific inquiry. Here are some points to consider when discussing the use of communication equipment in paranormal investigations:

Some communication tools are specifically designed to facilitate communication with spirits or entities. Examples include the Ouija boards, EVP (Electronic Voice Phenomena) recorders, spirit boxes (or ghost boxes), and ITC (Instrumental Transcommunication) devices. These tools are believed to capture or facilitate messages from the spirit world, allowing investigators to ask questions and receive responses.

One of the main challenges in using communication equipment in paranormal investigations is interpreting the data or responses obtained. The interpretation of evidence obtained through communication equipment can be highly subjective and influenced by personal beliefs, expectations, and biases.

Confirmation bias, in particular, may lead investigators to interpret ambiguous or random phenomena as evidence of paranormal communication, reinforcing their preconceived ideas and beliefs. Confirmation bias is a "cognitive bias that refers to the tendency of people to search for, interpret, favour, and recall information in a way that confirms their pre-existing beliefs or hypotheses" In other words, individuals tend to seek out information that supports what they already believe and ignore or discount information that contradicts it.

Key aspects of confirmation bias include:

- Selective Attention: People are more likely to pay attention to information that aligns with their beliefs while ignoring or downplaying information that contradicts them. This is significant when an investigator chooses to ignore obvious signs of rational explanation.

- Selective Exposure: Individuals may seek out sources of information that reinforce their existing beliefs, avoiding sources that challenge or question them.

- Interpretation: When presented with ambiguous information, individuals may interpret it in a way that confirms their existing beliefs, even if other interpretations are equally plausible.

- Memory: People are more likely to remember information that supports their beliefs and forget information that does not, leading to a biased memory of past events.

This can often be the case for grieving family members who want so much to reconnect with their lost loved ones. Ethical considerations come into play when using communication equipment in paranormal investigations.

Investigators need to consider the potential psychological impact on clients or participants, especially if they are seeking closure or validation regarding deceased loved ones. Sensitivity, respect for privacy, and informed consent are crucial aspects of conducting ethical paranormal investigations. Something all investigators should be striving for, when dealing with the emotions of people.

Taking all this into account, communication almost always plays a big part in the paranormal investigations. It is at this point that I will reiterate that communication with Spirits, should always be done with the uttermost respect. There are several reasons why I strongly believe that this is the only way to conduct yourself, when using any method of communication. Here are just a few of those reasons.

Many cultures and religions have strong beliefs about the afterlife, spirits, and how to honour their dead. In these belief systems, it is common to show respect to the deceased out of reverence for their memory, their contributions during their lifetime, or their continued presence in the spiritual realm.

For individuals grieving the loss of a loved one, speaking to the deceased can be a way to process their emotions, find closure, and maintain a sense of connection in death. Showing respect during these interactions can contribute to the healing process and honour the memory of that person. Treating the deceased with respect is often considered a matter of personal ethical conduct and basic human decency. Regardless of one's beliefs about the afterlife, acknowledging the dignity of the deceased and their impact on the lives of others is a fundamental aspect being human. Recognising the grief and pain experienced by those who are mourning, speaking to the dead respectfully can be an expression of empathy and compassion. It acknowledges the significance of the loss and affirms the emotional bond between the living and the deceased.

Even for individuals who do not hold specific religious or cultural beliefs about the afterlife, speaking to the dead respectfully as opposed to provoking the dead, can avoid potential negative consequences. It is no different than if you were in a room with a living person.

Provoking the dead refers to intentionally instigating or antagonising spirits or entities in an attempt to elicit a response during paranormal investigations. Provoking the dead raises ethical questions about respect for the deceased and their potential spiritual state, not to mention the intentions of the investigator communicating. Many people believe that intentionally provoking spirits is disrespectful and may lead to negative consequences, including angering or disturbing the spirits or causing harm to those involved. There are safety concerns associated with provoking the dead for the living, as it may incite fear, anxiety, or emotional distress among participants. Not to mention will upset the spirit that you are communicating with, who could lash out and harm someone.

There is ongoing debate within the paranormal community about the ethics and efficacy of provocation techniques. While some investigators advocate provocation to elicit responses from spirits, others caution against antagonising entities and emphasise the importance of respectful communication. I am of the opinion the latter is the better option, both morally and ethically.

Whereas I am an advocate of firm boundaries, they can be put into place respectfully. Going into a communication session with something other than the best of intentions, is a recipe for trouble.

With that said, here is an introduction to some of the common communication tools, used by investigators and the methodology should you choose to try these yourself.

K2

The KII is versatile to say the least as it can be used to communicate with an intelligent spirit or entity at a location and is often utilised as such in paranormal investigations. Intelligent spirits or entities, communicate through the KII meter by influencing the electromagnetic fields around it. This could manifest as fluctuations in the lights or sounds produced by the meter, typically corresponding to yes or no questions posed by an investigator. An example of this would be, one flash for yes, two flashes for no). Another example would be to use the audio alarm on the KII. You can have several KIIs and ask a spirit to make one and not the other alarm to confirm they are present.

Using a K2 meter for communication during paranormal investigations can have both pros and cons:

Pros:

- Real-Time Detection: K2 meters provide real-time detection of electromagnetic fields (EMF), allowing investigators to potentially detect fluctuations or spikes in electromagnetic activity that could be associated with paranormal phenomena.
- Simple Operation: K2 meters are relatively easy to use and operate, making them accessible tools for investigators of varying levels of experience.
- Portable: K2 meters are typically small and lightweight, allowing investigators to easily carry them to different locations during investigations.
- Immediate Feedback: The visual and auditory indicators on K2

181

meters provide immediate feedback when electromagnetic fields are detected, allowing investigators to quickly respond to potential paranormal activity.

- Correlation with Paranormal Events: Some paranormal investigators believe that spikes in EMF detected by K2 meters correlate with the presence of spirits or other entities, providing a potential means of communication with the paranormal realm.

Cons:

- Limited Specificity: K2 meters detect a broad range of electromagnetic fields, including those generated by electrical wiring, appliances, and other mundane sources. As a result, it can be challenging to distinguish between natural and paranormal sources of EMF.
- Lack of Scientific Validation: The use of K2 meters for paranormal communication lacks scientific validation, and there is no conclusive evidence to support the claim that fluctuations in EMF indicate the presence of spirits or other paranormal entities.
- Susceptibility to Environmental Interference: K2 meters are susceptible to environmental interference, such as nearby electrical devices, radio frequencies, and other sources of electromagnetic noise. This can lead to false positives and inaccurate readings during investigations.
- Subjective Interpretation: The interpretation of K2 meter readings during paranormal investigations is subjective and can vary between investigators. Without standardised protocols or criteria for interpretation, there is a risk of bias and inconsistency in the assessment of evidence.

While K2 meters can be useful tools for detecting electromagnetic fluctuations during paranormal investigations, they come with limitations and considerations that investigators should be aware of when using them for communication or evidence gathering.

REM POD EM

Some paranormal investigators believe that spirits or entities can manipulate electromagnetic fields to communicate. The first thing to do is to establishing Baseline Readings before attempting any communication using a REM pod. In order to establish a baseline reading, take written note of the electromagnetic field fluctuations in the area. Make note of anything that may be causing fluctuations such as electrical devices and electric wiring.

Investigators will then communicate with spirits by asking questions aloud and interpreting any fluctuations or responses in the REM pod's readings, as answers. Investigators may use techniques such as EVP (Electronic Voice Phenomenon) recording to capture potential verbal responses while the REM pod is being used.

Before using a REM pod for communication, creating a welcoming atmosphere for spirits to communicate. This may involve verbalising intentions or using rituals or prayers, depending on personal beliefs.

Interpretation of REM pod readings is subjective and open to interpretation. Investigators look for patterns or correlations between changes in the electromagnetic field and their questions or prompts.

In all communication, REM pods are used in conjunction with other equipment such as EMF meters, temperature sensors, and EVP recorders. Correlating data from multiple devices can provide a more comprehensive picture of any anomalous activity and help distinguish genuine phenomena from environmental interference.

Whereas the pros and cons of the REM POD are the same as the K2 meter, there is one more con to consider. The effectiveness of REM Pods for paranormal communication relies on the belief that fluctuations in electromagnetic fields are indicative of supernatural activity. This belief is not universally accepted and lacks scientific validation, which can be a point of contention among sceptics and critics.

OUIJA BOARDS

The use of Ouija boards in paranormal investigations is a subject of much debate and contention among practitioners, enthusiasts, and sceptics alike. While some willingly incorporate them into their investigative methods, others, like myself., opt to steer clear of this form of communication.

Commonly referred to as talking boards or spirit boards, the term "Ouija" itself is derived from the French and German words for "yes" - "Oui" and "Ja" respectively. There exists a myriad of Ouija board designs, with some enthusiasts even curating collections in dedicated museums such as the Salem Witch Board Museum. Typically, these boards feature the words "Yes" and "No" positioned at the top corners, with "Goodbye" located at the bottom, although variations in layout do exist. Additionally, they typically include numbers 1 through 10 and all the letters of the alphabet.

The mechanics of a Ouija board involve the use of a planchette, a small heart-shaped or triangular device usually equipped with a small window or pointer. During a session, participants place their hands on the planchette,

183

which is then believed to be manipulated by spirits to spell out words or letters, facilitating communication.

The Ouija board has its origins in the wonderful spiritualist movement of the late 19th century. The modern Ouija board, as we know it today, is often credited to businessman Elijah Bond and lawyer Charles Kennard, who patented the concept and name in 1891. However, the exact origins of the board's design and name are still disputed. Some sources suggest that Bond and Kennard were inspired by earlier devices used for similar purposes which got its inspiration from automatic writing. Spookily others claim that the idea came to them through supernatural or spiritual means, during a séance.

In 1966, for some reason, known only to them, rights to the Ouija board were acquired by the toy and game manufacturer Parker Brothers and became a commercial success. Marketed as a form of child's entertainment rather than a tool for serious spiritual communication, this board has frightened children and teenagers ever since. I do not advocate the Ouija board as a children's game.

Today, the Ouija board holds a significant place in popular culture, appearing in various forms of media such as films, TV shows, and literature. Its widespread presence has turned it into a cultural phenomenon, with views on its use ranging from harmless entertainment to a potentially risky tool for paranormal communication.

For some, the Ouija board is seen as nothing more than a fun game, while others consider it a means to communicate with the deceased. However, there is a segment of believers who view it as a dangerous instrument that can attract malevolent entities. This concern, stems from the ease with which lower-level spirits can allegedly manipulate the board, posing as benign figures before revealing their true, malevolent nature.

Another aspect of concern is the belief among some, in the paranormal community, that using a Ouija board can open portals—doorways through which spirits or entities can pass. This perceived risk has led many to avoid using the board altogether, fearing the potential consequences of inviting unknown entities into their midst.

Despite these risks, paranormal investigators often utilise the Ouija board as a tool for communication during investigations. Each investigator must weigh the potential benefits against the perceived risks and make their own decision regarding its use.

For those considering using a Ouija board, it is essential to approach it with respect and caution. Here's a basic guide on how to use one:

- Find a quiet, dimly lit room where you won't be disturbed. Some people like to light candles or burn incense to create a more mystical atmosphere. Some like to go through their spiritual protections or say a prayer or recite a protective mantra before starting the session.

- Gather participants: It is usually best to have at least two people, though you can use a Ouija board alone if you prefer. Make sure everyone participating is calm and respectful.
- Lay the Ouija board flat on a table or another stable surface. Everyone should sit around the board comfortably, with their fingertips lightly touching the planchette.
- Take a moment to centre yourselves and focus your energy. Clear your mind of distractions and set your intentions for the session.
- Start asking questions: Once everyone is ready, begin asking questions aloud. You can start with simple yes or no questions, such as "Is anyone there?" or "Can you hear us?" Make sure to speak clearly and respectfully. It Is advised that you verbalise that only good/positive spirits are invited to communicate.
- Wait for a response: Keep your fingertips lightly on the planchette and wait to see if it starts to move. The planchette may begin to spell out answers or move to different letters or numbers on the board. Some people find that it moves quickly and smoothly, while others experience slower, more deliberate movements. It is a good idea to have someone who is taking notes not part of the physical session.
- As the planchette moves, pay attention to the letters or numbers it points to. Be open-minded and respectful as you interpret the responses and try not to force the planchette to move in a certain direction.
- End the session: When you're finished, thank any spirits or entities that may have communicated with you and say goodbye. Move the planchette to "Goodbye" on the board to officially close the session. Some people like to cleanse the space afterward with sage or holy water to remove any lingering energy.

The proper closure of a Ouija board session is crucial to ensure the safety and well-being of all involved. Whether ending communication or encountering any issues during the session, it is imperative to shut down the session correctly and close the circle. Failure to do so may result in unforeseen problems or unwanted attachments.

To close a Ouija board session correctly, it is believed that the spirit being communicated with must say goodbye and signal the end of the session. If the spirit refuses or fails to do so, the investigator should move the planchette to the word "goodbye," verbally state it, and then proceed to close the circle.

This step is essential to properly sever any connection established during the session and prevent lingering energies from lingering.

There have been reported cases where the use of a Ouija board is believed to have triggered haunting or other paranormal activity. While these cases vary widely in credibility and are often anecdotal, they serve as cautionary tales regarding the potential risks associated with Ouija board use. Here are a few examples:

The Belmez Faces:

In the 1970s, a Spanish family reported a peculiar phenomenon where faces appeared on the floor of their home. Some individuals speculated that their prior use of a Ouija board might have somehow triggered this occurrence. However, sceptics proposed alternative explanations, suggesting that the faces could have been either hoaxed or the result of natural processes. Despite the speculation, the exact cause of the phenomenon remained a subject of debate, with some attributing it to paranormal activity and others dismissing it as a fabrication or natural occurrence.

The Doris Bither Case:

The case that inspired the movie "The Entity" revolves around Doris Bither, a woman who claimed to be haunted by malevolent entities in her home during the 1970s. Bither allegedly engaged in occult practices and used a Ouija board, leading some to speculate about a connection between these activities and the reported hauntings. However, the validity of Bither's claims and the extent of any association with the Ouija board remain subjects of intense debate. Critics question the reliability of the evidence and suggest alternative explanations for the reported phenomena, such as psychological factors or environmental influences. Despite the controversy surrounding the case, it remains a prominent and often-discussed example in paranormal research and popular culture.

The Ammons Haunting:

In 2011, Latoya Ammons and her family from Gary, Indiana, made headlines when they reported experiencing a series of bizarre occurrences in their home, including claims of possession and levitation. While some reports suggest that the family had used a Ouija board before the disturbances began, this detail is subject to dispute and has not been conclusively confirmed. Nevertheless, the case garnered significant media attention and has been featured on various paranormal television shows, sparking widespread fascination and debate about the nature of the reported phenomena. Despite investigations by both paranormal experts and sceptics, the true cause of the

186

disturbances remains uncertain, leaving the case as a captivating enigma in the realm of paranormal lore.

The Exorcism of Roland Doe:
This case, which inspired the novel and film "The Exorcist," involves a boy named Roland Doe who allegedly became possessed in the 1940s after using a Ouija board. The details of the case are heavily embellished and debated, but it is often cited as an example of the dangers of using Ouija boards.

I believe that utilising Ouija boards in investigations can be beneficial if approached with caution and a thorough understanding of the potential risks involved. Properly closing the session, establishing clear spiritual protections, and setting boundaries are essential practices to mitigate any negative consequences. However, personally, I tend to avoid their use due to the inherent risk of inadvertently opening portals and the ambiguity of their function. Ouija boards lack specificity in their communication, and there is a possibility for any entity present to manipulate the board's movements. Engaging with the board under these circumstances may attract negative spirits or entities as the doorway remains open, effectively extending an invitation. Similar caution should be exercised with all forms of communication tools, emphasising the need for respectful and careful usage. I should point out that this is only the authors opinion and not shared by many who use them on every investigation they go to.

OVILUS

The Ovilus stands out as one of my preferred devices for paranormal investigations. This electronic tool, serves as a conduit for spirit communication, generating words or phrases based on environmental cues, such as, changes in electromagnetic fields and temperature. The belief is that spirits manipulate these environmental factors to select words from the device's database.

Equipped with various modes, including dictionary mode and phonetic mode, the Ovilus offers flexibility in its output generation. In dictionary mode, words are selected from a preloaded database, while phonetic mode generates words based on detected phonetic sounds in the surroundings.

While the device typically generates one word at a time, each output should be noted, as they may collectively reveal meaningful messages, especially when reviewed or analysed retrospectively, particularly in the context of historical research. Like any communication tool. using an Ovilus device in paranormal investigations, can offer several advantages and disadvantages:

Pros:

- Real-Time Communication: The Ovilus provides real-time responses in the form of spoken words or displayed text based on environmental data, such as electromagnetic fields or temperature fluctuations. This immediate feedback can facilitate communication with potential spirits or entities during investigations.

- Objectivity: The Ovilus operates independently of human influence, reducing the risk of subjective interpretation or bias that may occur with human mediums or investigators. This objectivity can lend credibility to the evidence collected during paranormal investigations.

- Versatility: Ovilus devices come in various models with different features, allowing investigators to choose the model that best suits their needs and preferences. Some models offer additional features such as data logging or customisable dictionaries, enhancing their utility in different investigative contexts.

- Non-Invasive: The Ovilus does not require physical contact or interaction with the environment, making it a non-invasive tool for paranormal communication. This can be particularly useful in situations where investigators are unable or unwilling to directly engage with potentially hostile entities.

Cons:

- Lack of Scientific Validation: The effectiveness of the Ovilus in facilitating communication with spirits or entities has not been scientifically validated. Sceptics argue that the responses generated by the device are likely random or influenced by environmental factors rather than indicative of paranormal activity.

- Interpretation Challenges: The responses produced by the Ovilus are often cryptic or ambiguous, requiring interpretation by investigators. This can lead to different interpretations of the same data and make it challenging to draw meaningful conclusions from the device's output.

- Environmental Interference: The Ovilus relies on environmental sensors to generate responses, making it susceptible to interference from external factors such as electromagnetic fields, temperature changes, or radio frequencies. This can result in false positives or inaccurate readings during investigations.

- Reliance on Belief: The effectiveness of the Ovilus in paranormal

188

investigations often depends on the belief system of the investigators and participants involved.

The Ovilus device has been used in numerous paranormal investigations and has been featured in various cases where it was purportedly used to facilitate spirit interaction. While the validity of these cases is often debated and sceptics argue that the responses generated by the device may be influenced by environmental factors or random chance, proponents believe that the Ovilus has provided meaningful communication with spirits or entities. Here are a few examples:

Trans-Allegheny Lunatic Asylum
The Trans-Allegheny Lunatic Asylum in West Virginia is known for its alleged paranormal activity. During investigations at this location, paranormal teams have reportedly used the Ovilus to communicate with spirits believed to haunt the asylum. The device has generated responses that investigators interpreted as relevant to the location's history and the experiences of former patients.

Villisca Axe Murder House
The Villisca Axe Murder House in Iowa is the site of a gruesome unsolved murder that occurred in 1912. Paranormal investigators have used the Ovilus at this location in attempts to communicate with the spirits of the victims or the perpetrator. Some have claimed to receive responses that they believe are indicative of intelligent communication.

Waverly Hills Sanatorium:
Waverly Hills Sanatorium in Kentucky is another notorious location for paranormal activity. During investigations at Waverly Hills, paranormal teams have employed the Ovilus to communicate with spirits believed to linger in the abandoned hospital. The device has purportedly produced responses that investigators interpreted as relevant to the location's history of illness, death, and tragedy.

While the Ovilus offers promising possibilities for paranormal communication, its use requires a critical approach, acknowledging both its potential benefits and limitations in facilitating meaningful interactions with the spirit world.

SPIRIT BOX

The Spirit Box, sometimes called a Ghost Box, is a device used in paranormal investigations to communicate with spirits or entities from the other side. There are several options available on the market, each with its own features and capabilities. When choosing a Spirit Box, it is important to consider factors such as budget, features, user reviews, and personal preferences. There are a number of different types of spirit boxes and in the following, we will focus on the most commonly used.

- Radio Sweep Spirit Box: This type of Spirit Box scans through radio frequencies at a rapid pace, creating a constant stream of white noise. Spirits can manipulate this noise to communicate through snippets of radio broadcasts or by producing distinct voices or sounds. Users often listen for relevant responses to their questions amidst the noise. The most popular of this is the SB7.

- Digital Spirit Box Apps: With the rise of smartphone technology, there are numerous Spirit Box apps available for download from the google apps store. These apps usually simulate the functionality of traditional Spirit Boxes, using algorithms to generate random noise or audio fragments for potential spirit communication. I have never personally used these apps and many are for entertainment purposes only as opposed to serious spirit communication. Many of these apps generate set words and phrases to make a person believe they are communicating with a spirit.

- Custom-Built Spirit Boxes: Some investigators prefer to create their own Spirit Boxes using modified radios or electronic equipment. These custom-built devices may offer more control over the scanning speed, frequency range, and other parameters like removing sounds other than white noise allowing users to tailor their preferences.

Some Spirit Boxes come with additional features such as built-in recording capabilities, temperature sensors, and EMF (Electromagnetic Field) detectors. These extras can enhance the investigative process by providing more data for analysis and correlation with potential paranormal activity. However, they tend to be on the more expensive end of the market. The most popular by far in the SB7 Spirit box.

SB7 SPIRIT BOX

The spirit box is a compact handheld device that operates by scanning through radio channels, generating white noise in the process. Users have the ability to adjust the sweep speed and direction, allowing for a customisable experience. While using the spirit box, spirits are believed to communicate directly in real-time, though it may require practice to discern their messages. These communications can range from single words to complete phrases or sentences.

As the spirit box sweeps through radio frequencies, users may hear various noises, but the rapid scanning speed prevents complete words or sentences from being heard from the radio channels it traverses.

The SB7 model, for instance, features two outputs, enabling investigators to connect it to a voice recorder while simultaneously using headphones. This setup allows for a comprehensive recording of the session while providing the user with real-time auditory feedback. In my experience, when using the SB7 without an external speaker, headphones offer the optimal listening experience.

During our recent investigation at Sunset Hospital in Perth, we encountered several pertinent responses on the SB7 device, primarily concerning World War II. Notably, the SB7 also mentioned our individual names and accurately indicated the number of investigators present. This trend persists across various locations, where we have received site-specific details and relevant responses to our inquiries. Personally, I incorporate the SB7 in every investigation I undertake.

It is recommended to invest in quality headphones for clear audio reception from the voice box, along with a compact external speaker to enhance real-time listening capabilities.

6 OTHER INVESTIGATIVE TOOLS

Although we focus our attention on the use of equipment that can be quantified and recorded, there are other tools, paranormal investigators use. These tools are said to add another dimension in the quest to understand the paranormal. Many investigators use mystical methods to investigate the paranormal, involving and incorporating practices, beliefs, and tools traditionally associated with mysticism, spirituality, and the occult.. While these methods often diverge from conventional scientific approaches, they can provide unique perspectives and insights into the investigative process.

Mystical methods often rely on alternative modes of perception beyond the five recognised senses of sight, hearing, smell, touch, and taste.

sensory perceptions or tools to detect and interpret potential paranormal phenomena. Some of these include:

- Sixth Sense or Intuition: Many investigators believe in the existence of a "sixth sense," an intuitive feeling or gut instinct that guides them to areas of interest or alerts them to the presence of paranormal activity.
- Empathy or Sensing Emotions: Some individuals claim to have empathic abilities, allowing them to sense or feel the emotions or energies of spirits or entities present in a location.
- Psychometry: Psychometry is the ability to perceive information about an object or location by touching it. Paranormal investigators may use psychometry to gain insights into the history or energies associated with certain items or places.
- Remote Viewing: Remote viewing involves the ability to perceive or gather information about a distant or unseen target without the use of the physical senses. Some paranormal investigators practice remote viewing as a means of accessing information about

haunted locations or events.

- Mediumship: Mediums claim to have the ability to communicate with spirits or entities and may serve as intermediaries between the physical and spiritual realms during paranormal investigations.

- Aura Reading: Some investigators claim to be able to perceive and interpret auras, or energy fields surrounding living beings or locations, which may provide insights into paranormal activity.

While these senses and techniques are widely used in paranormal investigations, it is important to approach them with critical thinking and scepticism, as their validity is often debated within the scientific and paranormal communities. We are not going to focus on all these methods, just the main ones used in paranormal investigations.

SIXTH SENSE OR INTUITION

This is something that to a degree, we all do every day. When you spend enough time dealing with the paranormal you tend to fine tune this ability. Paranormal investigators often rely on their sixth sense or intuition as a valuable tool during investigations. This intuitive ability is subjective and can vary greatly among individuals. I cannot explain how it works, but I can confirm it does work. Here's an overview of how paranormal investigators use sixth sense and intuition:

- Sensing Energies: Many investigators claim to have a heightened sensitivity to energy, allowing them to perceive subtle changes in the environment that may indicate the presence of paranormal activity. This can include feelings of heaviness, cold spots, tingling sensations, or sudden shifts in mood.

- Guiding Investigation: Intuition often guides investigators to areas of interest within a haunted location. This may involve feeling drawn to specific rooms, objects, or areas where paranormal activity is suspected to occur.

- Assessing Atmosphere: Intuition helps investigators gauge the atmosphere or "vibes" of a location, providing insights into whether it feels peaceful, neutral, or charged with paranormal energy. This assessment can influence how investigators approach their investigation and interact with the environment.

- Interpreting Evidence: Intuition plays a role in interpreting evidence collected during investigations. Investigators may rely on their gut instincts to determine whether a phenomenon is paranormal in nature or can be attributed to natural or

193

environmental factors.

- Safety Precautions: Intuition also helps investigators assess the safety of a location and determine whether it is advisable to proceed with an investigation. This may involve sensing potential risks or negative energies that could pose harm to themselves or others.

While many paranormal investigators believe in the existence of a sixth sense or intuitive ability, it is important to note that not everyone experiences or interprets these sensations in the same way. Some individuals may have a natural predisposition towards intuitive perceptions, while others may need to develop and hone their intuitive skills over time through practice and experience. I have found the latter to be truthful for my work.

Additionally, scepticism and critical thinking are essential in paranormal investigation, and investigators should always strive to balance their intuitive impressions with empirical evidence and rational analysis. While intuition can be a valuable tool, it should not be relied upon exclusively, and investigators should remain open-minded and willing to consider alternative explanations for phenomena encountered during investigations.

EMPATHY OR SENSING EMOTIONS

Empathy and sensing emotions can play a significant role in paranormal investigations by providing investigators with insights into the emotional energies present in a location. I have always been a highly empathic individual which has helped me over the years with dealing with people in my personal and professional life. Here's how empathy and emotion sensing can aid paranormal investigations:

- Understanding the Environment: Empathy allows investigators to pick up on the emotional residue or energy imprints left behind by past events or individuals in a haunted location. Sensing the emotions associated with these imprints can provide clues about the history of the location and the experiences of those who have passed through it.
- Connecting with Spirits: Empathic individuals may be able to establish a connection with spirits or entities present in a location by tuning into their emotional state. This can facilitate communication with the spirit world and provide insights into the motivations or intentions of the entities encountered during an investigation.
- Validation of Paranormal Activity: Sensing emotions associated

194

with paranormal phenomena can validate the presence of spirits or entities in a location. For example, feeling a sudden wave of sadness or fear may coincide with the detection of EVP (Electronic Voice Phenomenon) or other evidence of paranormal activity.

- Providing Comfort: Empathic investigators can offer comfort and reassurance to clients or occupants of haunted locations who may be experiencing distress or fear due to paranormal phenomena. By validating their experiences and offering support, empathic investigators can help individuals feel heard and understood.

- Enhancing Communication: Empathy can enhance communication between investigators and spirits by fostering a deeper understanding of the emotions and intentions of the entities present. This can lead to more meaningful interactions and potentially facilitate the resolution of unresolved issues or conflicts.

- Assessing Energy Levels: Empathic individuals may also be sensitive to fluctuations in energy levels within a location, including changes in mood or atmosphere. This awareness can help investigators gauge the intensity of paranormal activity and determine the best course of action during an investigation.

For empaths participating in paranormal investigations, there are several potential risks and challenges to consider:

- Emotional Overwhelm: Empaths may be more susceptible to becoming overwhelmed by the intense emotions and energies present in haunted locations. Experiencing a flood of emotions from spirits or residual energies can be emotionally taxing and may lead to feelings of distress, anxiety, or even physical symptoms such as headaches or nausea.

- Absorption of Negative Energy: Empaths may inadvertently absorb negative energy from spirits or entities present in a location, leading to feelings of sadness, fear, or agitation. This can result in emotional and psychological distress, particularly if the empath is unable to effectively manage or release the absorbed energy.

- Boundary Issues: Empaths may struggle to establish and maintain boundaries between themselves and the spirits they encounter during investigations. Without proper boundaries, empaths risk becoming too deeply entangled in the emotional experiences of spirits, which can negatively impact their well-being and mental

195

health.

- Psychic Attack: In rare cases, empaths may be vulnerable to psychic attack or manipulation by malevolent entities seeking to exploit their empathic abilities. This can manifest as intrusive thoughts, nightmares, or feelings of being spiritually drained or overwhelmed.

- Secondary Trauma: Constant exposure to traumatic or distressing energies in haunted locations can take a toll on an empath's mental and emotional well-being over time, potentially leading to secondary trauma or burnout. It is essential for empaths to prioritize self-care and engage in practices that promote emotional resilience and healing.

To mitigate these risks, empaths participating in paranormal investigations should take proactive steps to protect themselves and manage their empathic abilities effectively, we will go into these techniques in a later chapter of this book,

- Grounding Techniques: Engage in grounding exercises before, during, and after investigations to anchor yourself in the present moment and release excess energy.

- Shielding: Visualise a protective shield or barrier around yourself to filter out negative energy and prevent psychic intrusion.

- Setting Intentions: Set clear intentions for the investigation and establish boundaries with spirits to maintain control over your empathic experiences.

- Self-Care Practices: Prioritise self-care activities such as meditation, exercise, journaling, and spending time in nature to replenish your energy and maintain emotional balance.

- Seek Support: Connect with fellow empaths or experienced investigators who can offer guidance, validation, and support in navigating the challenges of paranormal investigations.

By taking proactive measures to protect themselves and manage their empathic abilities, empaths can participate safely and effectively in paranormal investigations while minimising the potential risks to their well-being.

USE OF PSYCHICS AND SENSITIVES

Many Paranormal groups use the services of psychics or sensitives when investigating a location or resolving a haunting.

Psychics are individuals who claim to have extrasensory perception (ESP) abilities or heightened intuitive faculties that enable them to perceive information beyond the ordinary five senses. These abilities may include clairvoyance (clear seeing), clairaudience (clear hearing), clairsentience (clear feeling), or other forms of psychic perception.

Psychics claim to be able to perceive information about the past, present, or future, as well as insights into the thoughts, emotions, or experiences of others. They claim to be able to see, hear or feel the emotions of those who have died. They may use various methods such as meditation, or a trance like states to access and interpret this information.

Psychics are commonly consulted for guidance, advice, or insight into personal matters, as well as for paranormal investigations or spiritual communication. However, it is important to note that the claims of psychics are highly controversial and subject to scepticism, with many sceptics challenging the validity of their abilities and the scientific basis for their claims.

The term Medium and Psychic are often used interchangeably, however, there is a distinct difference between the two.

- Psychic: A Psychic is usually a person who claims to have ESP or extra sensory perception or heightened intuition. They take information about the past, future and present from the environment. They can intuitively connect to a person's thoughts and emotions.
- Medium: A medium on the other hand, are those that specialise in communicating with the spirits and entities that reside in the spiritual realm. They claim to be able to relay messages and information between the spiritual realm and the physical one.

Mediums often use psychic abilities to process and interpret the information that they are receiving. More often than not, you will get a psychic medium that does both. It should be established what abilities the person joining the investigation has, that way you can assess the information that they receive and manage the expectations of both the team and the client.

Although we as a Paranormal Group do not discredit the use of psychics, we instead tend to use both simple and high tech electronic equipment to document and substantiate our experiences. That's not to say the use of a psychic cannot enhance the investigation process and there may be times that the best course of action is to bring a psychic or medium into the investigation. In fact, one of our team member sis a psychic medium. Often a paranormal group will have a psychic or mediums (sometimes referred to as sensitives) as part of their team.

There are many advantages to having a psychic medium as part of your team. They can often access information that our instruments and equipment cannot. Here are some of the advantages to using Sensitives to aid an investigation.

- Communication with Spirits: In some cases, mediums have communicated directly with the spirits believed to be causing the haunting. Through their abilities mediums may help to understand the underlying reasons for the haunting, such as unresolved issues or emotional trauma experienced by the spirits during their lives.

- Clearing Residual Energy: Mediums may also assist in clearing or releasing residual energy associated with a haunting. By connecting with the spiritual realm, mediums may perform rituals, prayers, or energy work to cleanse the space and encourage any lingering spirits to move on peacefully.

- Providing Closure: Mediums may offer comfort and closure to individuals experiencing hauntings by providing messages or insights from deceased loved ones or by helping to resolve any unfinished business or unresolved emotions connected to the haunting. This can bring a sense of peace and resolution to those affected by the paranormal activity.

- Identifying Triggers: Through their intuitive abilities, mediums may help to identify triggers or factors contributing to the haunting, such as traumatic events, emotional distress, or environmental factors. By understanding the root causes of the activity, individuals or investigators can take steps to address and mitigate the haunting.

Cases where mediums were called in to try to resolve the hauntings.

The Amityville Haunting:
One of the most famous cases involving a medium is the Amityville haunting. In 1974, the Lutz family moved into a house in Amityville, New York, where a gruesome murder had taken place the year before. They experienced a series of terrifying paranormal phenomena, prompting them to seek the help of psychic medium Lorraine Warren. Warren claimed to have communicated with the spirits in the house and conducted a cleansing ritual to rid the home of negative energies. While the veracity of the haunting remains controversial, the Lutz family reported a decrease in paranormal activity after Warren's intervention.

The Rosenheim Poltergeist:
In 1967, the offices of a law firm in Rosenheim, Germany, became the focus

of a series of unexplained phenomena, including flickering lights, flying objects, and malfunctioning electrical equipment. The disturbances attracted the attention of parapsychologist Hans Bender and psychic medium Erika Dannhoff, who conducted investigations and attempted to communicate with the alleged poltergeist. Dannhoff claimed to establish a connection with the spirit responsible for the activity and helped to calm the disturbances through her interventions.

The Sally House:
homeowners, Tony, and Debra Pickman, enlisted the help of psychic medium Peter James to investigate the haunting. James conducted séances and communicated with the spirit believed to be haunting the house, allegedly helping to calm the activity and bring closure to the Pickman family.

The Chase Vault Mystery:
In the early 19th century, the Chase family vault in Barbados gained notoriety due to reports of coffins mysteriously moving and rearranging themselves inside the sealed tomb. Mediums were consulted to investigate the haunting, including the Reverend Thomas B. Cumming. Cumming claimed to have communicated with the spirits of the deceased, discovering unresolved family disputes and grievances. While the Chase Vault mystery remains unsolved, Cumming's involvement added to the intrigue surrounding the case.

The Stanley Hotel:
The Stanley Hotel in Colorado, famously known as the inspiration for Stephen King's novel "The Shining," is believed to be haunted by several spirits. Mediums and psychics have visited the hotel to communicate with these spirits and provide insights into their presence. Some claim to have helped the spirits move on to the afterlife or find resolution for any lingering issues they may have had.

Private Residences:
Many private residences around the world have reported hauntings and paranormal activity, prompting homeowners to seek the assistance of mediums and psychics. These mediums may conduct investigations, communicate with the spirits believed to inhabit the property, and perform rituals or ceremonies to help resolve any disturbances.

Historical Sites and Battlefields:
Historical sites and battlefields often have a reputation for being haunted due to the tragic events that occurred there. Mediums and psychics have been brought in to communicate with the spirits of those who died in these

locations and provide insights into their experiences. Some claim to have helped the spirits find peace or closure.

CHANNELLING

In paranormal terms, channelling refers to the practice of an individual acting as a conduit for spiritual entities to convey information. Those who engage in channelling often claim to receive messages, guidance, or insights from deceased individuals and other supernatural entities. The channeler typically enters into a meditative trance or altered state of consciousness to facilitate communication with these entities, allowing them to speak through them. Channelling can take various forms, including verbal communication, automatic writing, or non-verbal impressions It is suggested by some, that a person channelling can take on the physical characteristics of the spirit they are channelling, as well as their emotions. Though this Is highly debated They often have no memory of their interactions during this time. I am personally on the fence as far as changing physical attributes for reasons we shall explore later.

I personally do not advocate for or permit the practice of full physical channelling during any of our investigations, even if an individual claims to possess the ability. While channelling can be an intriguing method for spirits to communicate and interact through a medium, it can also be highly unpredictable. I have witnessed individuals who are typically composed, and calm become unexpectedly hostile and threatening during channelling sessions. Given the potential risks and unpredictability involved, I prioritise the safety and well-being of both investigators and clients. Additionally, the lack of verifiable evidence or validation further reinforces my decision to avoid unnecessary risk and disturbance during investigations.

There are lots of forms of channelling that I will allow, as long as it does not proport to allow a spirit to take control of a medium's thoughts and actions. Each team leader of an investigation needs to weigh up the benefits as opposed to the negatives, when working with this kind of method.

Cases where channelling a spirit went wrong often involve situations where the channeler loses control, experiences negative or harmful effects, or encounters deceptive entities posing as benevolent spirits. The results have ranged from psychological harm, attachment, possession and the physical manifestations of a haunting.

Charles Webster Leadbeater
Charles was a prominent Theosophist. Theosophy teaches that the purpose of human life is spiritual emancipation, and the human soul undergoes reincarnation upon death according to a process of karma who claimed to

channel spiritual entities, there are accounts suggesting that his continued channelling led to a mental health deterioration over time. This led to erratic behaviour and questionable teachings.

Anneliese Michel

In some cases of attempted spirit channelling, individuals have reported experiencing demonic possession or influence. One of the saddest and most well-known was the case of Anneliese Michel, which inspired the movie "The Exorcism of Emily Rose," Anneliese and her family believing she was possessed after she underwent a series of exorcisms, due to what they perceived as demonic influence, resulting from her involvement in channelling sessions. Most priests, bar one said she should carry on with medical treatment for epilepsy except one. Anneliese underwent 67 Catholic exorcism rites by this priest during the year before her death. her cause of death as malnutrition and dehydration resulting from almost a year in a state of near starvation while the rites of exorcism were performed. She weighed 30 kilograms, suffered broken knees from continuous genuflections, was unable to move without assistance and was reported to have contracted pneumonia Her parents and two priests were convicted with the coroner noting she could have been saved up to a week before she died. She was diagnosed with epileptic psychosis (temporal lobe epilepsy) and had a history of psychiatric treatment. This case is almost certainly a case of misidentified mental illness.

Channelling supernatural entities or spirits have played a large role in mass killings involving religious cults. In both the Jonestown Massacre and The Heaven's Gate Cult, their charismatic leaders were able to manipulate the vulnerability of their follows because they claimed to be able to channel. David Jones claimed he could communicate with spirits and channelled divine messages and visions to his followers. Over 900 people, 300 children and infants died at Jonestown either willingly ingesting poison or were forced to if they refused.

Marshall Applewhite and Bonnie Nettles, leaders of the Heaven's Gate Cult, claimed to channel messages and teachings from extra-terrestrial beings. Applewhite had been recruited after a near death experience by his nurse Nettles. He convinced his followers to commit mass suicide on March 6th, 1997, following the appearance of Hallie's comet. resulting in the deaths of 39 people initially and 3 former members in the months following the mass suicide.

These tragic events shocked the world and raised questions about the dangers of charismatic leaders and belief systems based on channelled messages. If anything, these cases illustrate the need for critical thinking, ethical consideration, and responsible practice when exploring paranormal phenomena.

Where these are extreme cases of where channelling or the belief thereof, has played a part in tragic outcomes, there are advantages to using some forms of channelling. Channelling, when conducted with care and proper understanding, can offer several potential positives in paranormal investigation:

Direct Communication: Channelling allows for direct communication with spirits or entities, providing insights, information, or messages that may not be accessible through traditional investigation methods such as EVP or EMF readings.

- Personalised Insights: Channelling can provide personalised insights tailored to the specific questions or concerns of investigators or clients. This can offer a deeper understanding of the paranormal activity present in a location and its potential significance.
- Emotional Healing: In some cases, channelling sessions may facilitate emotional healing or closure for individuals affected by paranormal phenomena. Messages from departed loved ones or spirits may provide comfort, validation, or resolution to unresolved issues.
- Validation of Experiences: Channelling can validate the experiences of individuals who have encountered paranormal phenomena, offering reassurance that their encounters are real and acknowledging their concerns.
- Investigative Leads: Information obtained through channelling sessions may provide valuable leads for further investigation, guiding investigators to specific areas of interest or uncovering hidden aspects of a location's history.
- Spiritual Growth: For individuals involved in the channelling process, it can serve as a means of spiritual exploration and growth, fostering a deeper connection to the spiritual realm and expanding their understanding of consciousness and existence.
- Bridging Worlds: Channelling bridges the gap between the physical and spiritual realms, facilitating communication and interaction between the living and the deceased. This can promote a greater sense of interconnectedness and understanding between different planes of existence.

While channelling presents certain risks and challenges, it can also offer unique opportunities for communication, insight, and healing in paranormal investigation when approached with respect, caution, and a discerning mindset.

AUTOMATIC WRITING

Automatic writing, also known as psychography, is where a person allows their subconscious mind to take control of their writing hand, producing words, phrases, or even entire texts without apparent conscious thought or control.

The history and application of automatic writing is a varied one and has changed over time. It is used in both therapeutic psychologies, to mysticism and esoteric traditions. For the purposes of this book, we are only focusing on its use as a tool in spiritualist practices.

Automatic writing, as with most practices gained prominence during the Spiritualist movement of the 19th century. Spiritualism emerged in the mid-1800s, primarily its focus was on communication with the spirits of the deceased. Mediums would often enter trance states and allow spirits to communicate through them, sometimes through writing. Automatic writing was seen as a way for mediums to convey messages from the spirit world to those ready to hear them in the physical world.

In more modern times there are paranormal investigators who use automatic writing as part of their investigation. Some mediums claiming to receive messages, use automatic writing as a tool to focus their minds to be able to get clarity and streamline their interpretation of said message. Put simply a medium will channel the spirit by using a meditative or trance like state, then allow a spirit to take control of their motor functions. This is mainly their arm and hand to write messages or draw.

How this happens is up for much debate in the paranormal field. However, our bodies are made up of electrical energy, this is a known fact. It is generated through our nervous system that includes the brain and spinal cord. The body relies on electrical impulses to transmit information between cells.

It is widely accepted that spirits or entities can interact with electrical outputs We see this in their manipulation of our electrical devices. The same applies to the body. It is believed that the energy of the spirit and medium, merge and the spirit use these electrical impulses to manipulate the arm and hand. The body of the medium is used almost like an electrical conduit for the energy of the spirit of entity.

. This theory is what those who practice automatic writing believe and is not proven by science. There are other theory's that are possibilities. One is that spirits or entities telepathically transmit a message to the medium who in turn interprets the message which is then expressed in the form of writing. This of course is problematic as it is open to the subjective interpretation of the medium doing automatic writing.

In many examples of automatic writing the messages seek to provide guidance, comfort, or reassurance to the living, offer insights into spiritual matters, convey messages of love or forgiveness, or even impart practical advice relevant to the recipient's life circumstances.

Sceptics may attribute automatic writing to a subconscious processes or suggestion that it is a result of what is called ideomotor movements. Ideomotor movements are involuntary or unconscious movements made by a person in response to a suggestion. These movements occur without the individual's awareness or intention. Ideomotor movements are often claimed by sceptics for many reported paranormal phenomena, including automatic writing, dowsing and Ouija board use.

However, for those who believe in the spiritualist perspective, automatic writing represents a direct form of communication between the living and the spirit. In some instances, psychic mediums claim to have used automatic writing to provide information related to unsolved crimes or missing persons cases.

Pearl Curran and the spirit of Patience Worth

In the, a woman named Pearl Curran started using her neighbours Ouija board. She then claimed to have received messages from a deceased 17th Century woman named Patience Worth. Fischer's automatic writing sessions produced poems, stories, and other writings attributed to Patience Worth. Patience continued to communicate through Pearl until November 25, 1937, when she gave her final communication. Pearl had apparently received warning from Patience that she was going to die. Even though Pearl had not been in ill health, she developed pneumonia late in November and died on December 3, 1937, While the case is controversial, some argue that the content of the writings demonstrated knowledge beyond Fischer's capabilities given she had left school at only 14 with a minimal education.

The Helene Smith Case:

In the late 19th and early 20th centuries, Helene Smith, a Swiss medium, claimed to have contacted beings from Mars and other planets, through the use of automatic writing. Smith produced detailed accounts of Martian landscapes, civilisations, and entire languages, which she claimed were communicated to her by the extra-terrestrial entities. While her case was famous in her time, it is a strong example of subconscious ideomotor movements influence by suggestibility.

For those interested in trying automatic writing in the course of an investigation there are a number of ways to facilitate it.

- Preparation: Before attempting automatic writing, it is essential to prepare yourself mentally and emotionally. Relaxation techniques such as deep breathing or meditation may help you enter a focused state of mind conducive to receiving intuitive impressions. There are many techniques available, and courses should one choose to explore this medium further.

- Environment: Find a quiet and comfortable space where you can work without distractions. minimise external noise and create a calm atmosphere conducive to concentration. If there are others present, you will want them to be silent while you are preparing.

- Intentions: As with all communications you should clearly state your intentions for the session. If you're conducting a paranormal investigation, you may intend to communicate with any spirits or entities present in the location and seek answers to specific questions or requests for guidance. Being specific minimises the risk of any entity coming through. Though there is no guarantee of safety with communication of any kind.

- Writing Instrument: Choose a writing instrument such as a pen or pencil and hold it lightly in your dominant hand. Relax your hand and arm muscles, allowing the pen to move freely without conscious effort.

- Focus Your Attention: Clear your mind of distractions and focus on a specific question, topic, or individual you wish to communicate with.

- Allow the Writing to Flow: Begin writing without consciously controlling the movements of your hand. Let the pen move across the paper freely, allowing words, symbols, or images to emerge spontaneously. Avoid analysing or censoring the content as it comes through.

- Interpret the Results: Once you feel that the automatic writing session is complete, review the content that has been produced. Pay attention to any recurring themes, symbols, or messages that may provide insights into the paranormal activity, or the entities involved.

Approach the results of the automatic writing session with caution and scepticism. Automatic writing is a subjective process that may be influenced by various factors, including the subconscious mind, suggestibility, and external influences. Always seek corroborating evidence where possible. Any significant findings or impressions that may be relevant to the paranormal investigation should be documented. This takes a great deal of practice, and some find it easier than others. It is highly recommended, before attempt any kind of channelling you become particularly good at using spiritual protection.

While automatic writing may hold personal meaning and significance for the individuals who practice it, its effectiveness in providing reliable information or solving real-world cases is subject of great debate. Still, it is a tool used by many paranormal investigators throughout the world today who believe it has the power to bring meaningful communication and bridge the gap between life and death.

SCRYING

Scrying is a form of divination or fortune-telling that involves gazing into a reflective surface to perceive information. This surface can be anything reflective, such as water, mirrors, crystals, and glass balls. Practitioners state while staring at the surface, they can receive visions, symbols and other information pertaining to a situation or persons life. It is an ancient practice that is found in various cultures and is often associated with mysticism and the occult.

Otherwise referred to as seeing or peeping, most people are familiar with the technique, in regard to fortune telling that utilises a crystal ball. Everyone has an image of a Romani mystic staring into her crystal ball for answers about the future or someone's fortune. Although, still a favourite in spiritual circles in more modern times, mirrors are the preferred medium to use by most paranormal investigators. The technical name for mirror or crystal ball scrying, is catoptromancy.

I am by no means suggesting you run off and buy a crystal ball for your next investigation, though that might be a bit of fun, as any mirror at a location can be used if you want to give it a try.

Mirrors play a significant role in beliefs about the afterlife. Superstitions surrounding mirrors and the dead, are prevalent in various cultures and traditions up until today. In many cultures, it is a tradition to cover mirrors in a house where someone has died. This superstition stems from the belief that mirrors can trap the soul of the deceased or attract negative energy. By covering the mirrors, it is thought to prevent the deceased person's spirit from being trapped in the mirror or from lingering in the house.

In Jewish, Irish and Chinese practices, mirrors are either covered or turned to face the wall, to prevent a spirit becoming trapped. This was also very common during the Victorian era. While this may seem irrational to some, they hold significant cultural and psychological significance for many people, across the globe.

Many paranormal Investigators believe that mirrors act as portals or gateways in some locations, allowing the dead and other entities, to freely move around.

Ancient civilisations such as those found in Egypt, Greece, and China, mirrors were often used in rituals and were believed to have special magical properties. Some cultures thought mirrors could capture and reflect the true soul of a person, making them potential portals into the spirit world.

Many aspects of folklore and urban legends focus on the use of mirrors. There are Legends that talk about mirrors being portals to spirits telling a person's future. In more modern urban legends, mirrors are the focus of summoning ghosts or malevolent entities. Bloody Mary is a good example of this, practiced today by many a teenager. Bloody Mary is a legend of a ghost, phantom, or spirit conjured to reveal the future. She is said to appear in a mirror when her name is chanted repeatedly. Some superstitions warn against looking into a mirror at night or seeing your reflection in a darkened room. It is believed that this could invite supernatural entities or spirits, to appear in the reflection or behind you. The start of any good horror movie or book!

As captivating as these sometimes terrifying stories are, there is nothing magical about a mirror and most of the superstitions around them are based on mythology and folklore, rather than fact. However, in some locations as at Meryl's Plantation, a mirror on the property is widely believed to act as a portal.

The practice of mirror scrying is really very simple. A person sits at eye level to a mirror in a dimly lit room (we will touch on this in a minute) to begin the session. They may enter a meditative state or 'trance' and then focus their attention onto the surface of the mirror. The belief is that symbols or insights might appear in the mirror or provide answers to questions.

The second thing that is claimed is that a person's face will change to the face of the spirit, that is in that location. This one has always caused some amusement to me. It is true, and I recommend you trying it after this chapter, that if you stare, without blinking into a mirror at a fixed location, the image will appear to change. This disappointingly, is not due to a spirit jumping into where your face should be, in order to communicate. It is a simple case of Troxler's Fading.

The Phenomenon, rather than being paranormal, is actually a psychological affect. It is called Troxler's Fading or Troxler's effect and is well documented and researched. It is all to do with how our brains process visual stimuli. Troxler's fading occurs when your eyes are fixated on a point for an extended period, the surrounding visuals will become either distorted or it will completely fade away, creating blurred edges. Couple this phenomenon, with the brains ability to create faces and patterns when it cannot make sense of stimuli, you have the perfect ingredients to create an unknown face. To prove my point, I want you the reader to try this technique. Once you see your face begin to change, and you will, I want you to then avert your eyes from the fixated point. You will find the effect disappears and your face, is your face again. I would not necessarily try this if you were in an extremely haunted location right now.

Now let us get into the reason this is so often done in low light or even worse, red light. Red light, a particular favourite of our less than honest 19th century mediums and is still being used frequently today.

In low light conditions, our pupils expand (Dilate) to allow more light to enter the eye. This can improve our ability to see in dimly lit environments but also make us more sensitive to subtle changes in lighting and visual stimuli. Red light, in particular, causes less constriction of the pupils compared to other colours, which can further enhance sensitivity to light in low-light conditions. When transitioning from a brightly lit environment to a dimly lit one, our eyes undergo a process called visual adaptation. This involves adjustments in the sensitivity of our retinas to various levels of light. In low light, our eyes become more sensitive to dim stimuli, which can amplify the perception of subtle changes in lighting and visual cues. This causes our eyes to often distort the images that we are seeing.

A particularly good, real world example of this occurs in the morning and evening. Dusk and dawn, also known as twilight, are transitional periods between day and night when the sky is partially illuminated. During these times, the quality of light can have a significant effect on visibility and visual perception, especially while driving. During these hours a driver will notice the following conditions:

- Reduced Visibility: The low angle of the sun during dusk and dawn can create glare and shadows on the road, making it more challenging to see clearly. Glare from the sun or headlights of other vehicles can obscure objects and reduce visibility, particularly if driving directly into the sun.
- Decreased Contrast: The soft, diffused light of twilight can lead to decreased contrast between objects, making it harder to distinguish between different elements on the road, such as pavement markings, signage, and pedestrians.
- Impaired Depth Perception: The changing light conditions during dusk and dawn can affect depth perception, making it difficult to judge distances accurately. Objects may appear closer or farther away than they actually are, increasing the risk of misjudging braking distances or the speed of approaching vehicles.

The combination of reduced visibility, glare, and impaired depth perception during dusk and dawn can elevate the risk of collisions and accidents, especially if drivers are not alert and cautious. As the light changes rapidly during twilight, drivers may need to adjust their eyesight and adapt their driving behaviour accordingly.

The same thing happens in low light and especially red light. As our brains try to focus better you usually inadvertently set off an occurrence of Troxler's Fading, which is why mediums face, seems to change.

In low light conditions, our brains may rely more on contextual cues and previous experiences to interpret visual stimuli. This can make us more susceptible to visual illusions and perceptual distortions, as our brains attempt to make sense of ambiguous or incomplete visual information. There is no question, scientifically that low light and red light can influence our visual perception by affecting pupil dilation, visual adaptation, colour perception, and susceptibility to visual illusions. This is exactly why I personally, do not trust the practice of low light scrying or red light scrying during any paranormal investigations.

I was recently on a small private investigation, as a guest, at a well-known location in Perth with my husband. My husband had been dragged, kicking, and screaming as he is not, as I mentioned previously, at all into the paranormal. He certainly would rather spend an evening doing anything but ghost hunting.

We were locked down in the small building and my husband had been the one chosen, to lock the doors of the building and make sure that everyone was accounted for. It was late at night, and this was the small building we would be sleeping in overnight He was the last person to enter the little room we were holed up in. The well-known psychic medium that runs these tours, did a scrying session in front of the group, under red light. She had someone at the back of the room, who claiming that the psychics face was changing into various people. An old woman, a young soldier, a nurse. the list went on. As she faced her audience, I was seated, with my husband and a few others, facing the double doorway. The doorway had a large glass distorted window panel for privacy. You could see into the square hallway, but not see detail, because it was not a transparent glass window. As I was staring into the hallway through the glass panel, a full blown, male shaped, black shadow, walked right past the door. Much to the shock of my husband and the others who had also seen this figure. There was no living person outside the room we were in or in fact, the rest of the building. My husband had seen his first, and last, apparition as he no longer accompanies me on events.

The irony of this situation, while these guests were staring straight at her with scientifically distorted vision, they missed the full blown apparition that walked across the hallway. The figure was seen by only a few of us, that were facing the doorway. We searched the and everyone was accounted for. Everyone except the tall dark, unknown figure, which appeared and disappeared into an area of the building, where there were no exits.

Now that we have covered the majority of the equipment and methods of paranormal investigators it is not suggested you run out and buy super expensive equipment. These are just tools and not many groups have all the equipment. A great suggestion is to connect with other groups and merge investigations. That way you have access to more equipment.

Other than that, I just started with a voice recorder. If you are going to invest in some equipment I would advise an EMF meter, Professional voice recorder (which is more sensitive), an IR motion detector or full spectrum camera or a REM-POD EM.

When working with psychics or engaging in practices like channelling, scrying or automatic writing, it is essential to maintain a critical mindset, with the way you approach the information obtained. Not all claims made by psychics or through these practices can be verified empirically. There can be psychological or subjective factors at play. We strive as investigators to corroborate our findings. I am not saying that these methods should not be used. Just used in collaboration with other measurable equipment. Mediums and psychics can sometimes offer valuable insights or perspectives that complement other investigative methods. This in turn, contributing to a more comprehensive understanding of paranormal phenomena, at any given location. But they are not to be taken as necessary fact. As with any aspect of paranormal investigation an open mind, taking the pros and cons into account when giving evidence weight, is essential to maintain the integrity of an investigation.

- Protective Tools
  Other tools not used necessarily for investigating the paranormal but more for protection, may also be included in a paranormal Investigators kit. Here are the two main examples from our own paranormal investigations.
- Sage and Incense:
  Burning sage or incense is a ritualistic practice believed to cleanse spaces of negative energy and promote spiritual clarity. Many investigators use these tools to prepare a location before investigating, and certainly to cleanse themselves, their cars and their equipment, afterwards.
- Holy Water or Blessed Objects:
  For investigators who incorporate religious or spiritual beliefs into

210

their practice, holy water or blessed objects, such as crucifixes or rosary beads, may be used for protection against malevolent entities. They can also be used to bless spaces, before or during investigations. This can be adapted to whatever belief system that a person may follow.

7 SPIRITUAL PROTECTION METHODS FOR INVESTIGATIONS

SPIRITUAL PROTECTIONS

Spiritual protection is a concept that revolves around safeguarding yourself from negative energies and maintaining a state of positive vibrations. It involves various practices, aimed at creating a shield against harmful influences, such as harmful spirits, which is crucial for paranormal investigators.

Negative energies can come from various sources, such as people, environments, and spirits or even our own thoughts and emotions. These energies can affect our mental, emotional, and physical well-being, if not addressed correctly.

We know that when dealing with the paranormal, we are not dealing with the physical, we are dealing with energy.

The law of conservation of energy says that energy is neither created nor destroyed. When people use energy, it does not just disappear. Energy changes from one form of energy, into another form of energy. For example, in an electric kettle, electrical energy is transformed into thermal energy. The thermal energy is then transferred into the water heating it up. Although energy cannot be created or destroyed it can be moved around and transformed. Everything around us is made of energy, including our own bodies.

Let us apply this concept to paranormal investigation. We are dealing with energy all the time. As paranormal investigators, we know that ghosts can manipulate our energy, energy in the environment and our equipment. We have seen it happen over and over again. Our phone and camera settings get inexplicably drained, during an investigation and lights or television sets get turned on and off. These are just a few examples of how spirits can manipulate energy. Spirits can pull energy from these devices. Think back to my camera at woodman point that drained 3 times in one evening. They can also do the same to our bodies.

When jaunting into the world of the paranormal, as a paranormal investigator, it is crucial to prioritise your personal safety and well-being and that of the team. One important aspect of this, is by familiarising and practising spiritual protections. This should be your number one priority to learn and master, if you take nothing else from this book.

Engaging with supernatural entities and investigating haunted locations, can expose investigators to various energies and potential risks. Spiritual protection serves as a safeguard against negative forces and psychic attacks, which may occur during investigations. These kinds of attacks are not to be taken lightly and can significantly disrupt a person's wellbeing, long after an investigation ends.

Our aim by practicing spiritual protection is to prevent unwanted attachments or influences, from lingering supernatural beings.

It is important to note that while spiritual protection, is in my opinion, necessary for paranormal investigators, it does not guarantee complete immunity from all paranormal phenomena.

Spiritual Protections are also good for teaching clients how to protect themselves, from any harmful influences, during and after a hunting. I make it a habit to teach all our clients if they are willing, at least some of the techniques we are about to explore.

In many cases, clients will complain of medical issues, headaches and exhaustion that has no medical cause. This is likely being exposed to dead energy, or from energy from the living. We will explore the issues around attachments shortly.

Symbolism plays a significant role in these practices, and rituals, are often used to create a conducive environment, for safe and positive spiritual communication or exploration. Rituals may involve the use of sacred objects, incantations, or prayers, believed to invoke spiritual energies or protection against malevolent forces.

Many of these methods, are deeply rooted in spiritual and religious traditions, drawing upon personal beliefs about the nature of the soul, the afterlife, and the spirit world. Practitioners may invoke deities, angels, or spirit guides as intermediaries in their investigations, seeking their guidance or protection. It is up to everyone to find a method that works for them personally. This is because intent, and belief, play a large part in how effective a method is. There are, as a general rule, a number of stages, to the technique of spiritual protection. There are also lots of variations to this technique, but they all revolve around the concepts of:

- Grounding
- Centering
- Shielding
- Filtering

Warding is another method used by some investigators when they are at a location.

By grasping these methodologies and fundamental principles of spiritual safeguarding, the aspiration is for you to enter the realm of the paranormal securely and assuredly, minimising any potential risks. While we can never guarantee our safety when delving into the unknown, it is equally crucial not to be complacent or expose ourselves to unnecessary hazards. Engaging with the paranormal should never be trivialised or treated as a game, as disregarding its seriousness can result in enduringly unpleasant consequences. Not all shadows harbour benevolent intentions or friendliness.

GROUNDING AND CENTERING

In a spiritual context, grounding refers to practices that help individuals connect with the Earth's energy, establishing a sense of stability, and maintaining a balanced state of being, within oneself. It is considered a fundamental aspect of spiritual protection. It is also one of the easiest to learn. The other aspect of grounding is that it encourages mindfulness, helping individuals stay rooted in the present. This can lead to increased clarity, intuition, and insight. Our aim with grounding is to maintain mental, emotional, and spiritual well-being, preventing the infiltration of harmful energies. It can also be practiced, in your day to day life.

At any time during the investigation, if you are feeling overwhelmed by the energy or affected by the energy in any way, it is a good idea to ground. The following techniques should be learnt, and practiced often, for them to be effective in the field. Some of the signs that you are ungrounded are as follows:

- Feeling disoriented, overwhelmed, light-headed, or dizzy.
- Having a strong need to get away from other people.
- Finding yourself daydreaming and losing touch with reality.
- Being agitated or feel a sense of anxiety.
- Craving sugar and starches.

- experiencing strong emotions that come from nowhere.
- Inability to focus.
- Headache or nausea for no specific reason.

If you are already in an investigation, the first thing you are going to do is to remove yourself from that environment. This could be stepping outside the room, into another room or even walking completely outside, away from the building. This happens frequently on investigations with even the most experienced of investigators. Often if it is just residual energy and by removing yourself from the situation, you will immediately begin to feel better. Even if this is the case, I would still suggest following through with your chosen grounding technique. Here is the process I personally use and find works for me.

- Find a quiet location and stand with your legs slightly apart in a firm stance.
- Start by taking three deep breaths and close your eyes.
- Imagine your body and your energy as a bright white light.
- The bad energy are black water globules stuck over your body.
- Start to imagine this bad energy is coming together and slowly moving down your body into your legs.
- Continue taking relaxed breaths and picture every time you breath in you are being filled with white healing light and every time you exhale you are pushing the bad energy down.
- Imagine the bad energy now seeping through your legs and being pushed into the ground until they are gone.
- At this point I want you to imagine that white light growing roots and grounding your body to the earth.
- When you are feeling better, I want you to then imagine the flow of energy is reversing from the ground up.
- Reach up and imagine roots extending into the sky and which in turn sends bright white light down.
- Then retract all the energy from below and above to form a ball of white light in the centre of your stomach just underneath the rib cage perfectly centred and balanced.
- Then end the session with 4 deep breaths.

There are lots of other variations out there and once you grasp the basic concept, you can form any visualisations that works well for you. You should start all your investigations, with a team grounding exercise.

It is important to note that spiritual protection is not limited to any specific religious belief system but can be practised by anyone of all backgrounds.

SHIELDING

Paranormal investigations involve exploring places or situations where there may be encounters with spirits or entities. Some of these entities may carry negative energy or intentions. Spiritual shielding is used to protect investigators from potential harm or negative influences, which may be directed at them.

Spiritual shielding techniques can help investigators maintain their mental and emotional well-being by creating a sense of protection and stability, preventing them from being overwhelmed by the energies or experiences they encounter.

Spiritual shielding allows investigators to establish and maintain boundaries, between themselves and any spiritual entities that they may encounter. This helps prevent unwanted intrusions into their personal space or energy field and ensures that they can interact with spirits or entities, in a controlled and safe manner.

Some individuals involved in paranormal investigations may be particularly sensitive to spiritual energies or psychic phenomena. Spiritual shielding techniques can help minimise their psychic sensitivity and prevent them from being overwhelmed, by the energies they encounter during investigations.

While there are many techniques to shield, I found the following method to be effective for me personally.

- Firstly, you need to complete your grounding and centering technique as discussed above. Shielding is an expansion of grounding and centering.
- Imagine the bright white, pure energy ball forming at the centre of your stomach under the ribs.
- Imagine that this bright white ball it is expanding out creating a perfect bubble encasing your entire body.

The frequency of spiritual shielding during a paranormal investigation can vary, depending on the preferences of the investigators, as well as the specific circumstances of the investigation. However, I would recommend doing it as frequently as you can. Here are the times that would be recommended, to go through your visualisation process.

- Before the Investigation:
- During Breaks or Rest Periods:
- When Feeling Vulnerable or Drained:
- When Entering New Locations or Areas:
- Based on Intuition or Sensitivity:

It is best practice to learn to trust your instincts and prioritise well-being. It is always better to take proactive measures, to ensure your safety and protection throughout the investigation process. It is the one lesson you do not want to learn the hard way.

ADVANCED SHEILDING

For the advanced level of shielding, we go through the same process as with normal shielding, except we add a few more visualisations.

visualise the outside of your shield being completely covered in a mirror to reflect the negative emotions back towards the sender. Sometimes I imagine myself surrounded by a giant disco ball which was a suggestion from a fellow investigator. This visualisation helps me hold the shield in place longer and raises the vibrations by being amusing.

Shielding takes practice and must be kept up in order to work effectively. This takes some practice when your mind is elsewhere on the investigation. It is best to try to form the habit, by repetition and before you know it, it becomes second nature. I know a few investigators that set an alarm for every hour to re visualise and renew their shielding.

FILTERING

Once the investigator has learnt and practiced shielding and advanced shielding there is one more step, a more intuitive investigator, may like to practice. This is called filtering and can apply to sensitives as much as it can apply to those who are not.

The shielding, is designed to keep energy and influence out, especially the advanced shielding techniques. It is designed to really protect the investigator from any and all, kinds of energy that may have a negative effect.

What if you're a sensitive individual who seeks specific information without welcoming negativity? Alternatively, you may aim to enhance your intuition and explore the paranormal safely, avoiding potential harm. In such instances, we employ the concept of filtering, to complement our shielding techniques. This process requires precise, transparent, and positive intentions.

Filtering allows for a protective barrier, but it is a selective energy barrier.

You choose what you allow in, while protecting yourself from the more extreme energies, that you may encounter. I would not advise this method for new investigators; it is more suited to those with experience in the kids of energies out there and what they are capable of. I mainly have seen this method used by those that are psychic, or in some way extremely intuitive. A shield does not allow them to receive the information they want, selective filtering does.

The visualisation in this instance, is identical to the idea of a mirrored bubble. Instead of this bubble being a complete barrier or disco ball, imagine it as made of something more breathable. Something that allows for the transfer of energy backwards and forwards. A good example of this is a material such as a knitted blanket. The idea, is it surrounds us and protects us from the extreme energies, but we can still get some information through. It is not a solid barrier.

In the 'Ghost Hunters Survivors Guide', written by Michelle Belanger, she compares the ideas of a paranormal filter to that of a coffee filter. Water is allowed to flow freely through the filter, but all the bigger ground coffee is prevented from access to the cup. This is the concept we are striving for. Again, it is about having a clear idea and throwing out the intentions of what kind of energy you are willing to receive. I would advise people who have an interest in spiritual protections, to invest in this book.

I always start with the intention that only love and light may be transferred into my bubble. Anything that may do me harm, cannot cross the barrier. This is verbally reiterated, throughout the investigation.

In conclusion, there are varying beliefs and practices that people use for protection when investigating the paranormal. The above example is just one of countless variations. In other beliefs and practices, people use prayers and mantras, crystals, and Holy Water. I have known people to carry amulets and Talismans, of various religions and faiths.

The most important thing is to know your boundaries, to be firm with your boundaries, and to go into any investigation with a positive frame of mind and good intentions. It is also knowing when to call it a night, to leave an area or stop an interaction that is becoming overwhelming or negative.

8 INVESTIGATION DOCUMENTATION

Whether you are a novice enthusiast or an experienced investigator, meticulous documentation is essential for analysing and interpreting collected data. Professionalism and credibility are closely linked, to effectively capturing, analysing, and debunking information. It is crucial to have documentation procedures in place for each stage of the investigation, from initial planning and client contact to witness statements, on-site documentation, analysis, final report generation, and any necessary follow-up.

Documentation is essential for paranormal investigators for several reasons. Firstly, it provides a systematic record of the investigation process, including the methods used, the evidence collected, and the observations made. This documentation serves as a reference point for the investigators themselves, ensuring consistency in their approach and helping them to track their progress over time.

Secondly, documentation enables investigators to analyse and interpret their findings objectively. By documenting details such as the location, time, environmental conditions, and any equipment used, investigators can identify patterns or correlations that may shed light on paranormal phenomena. This data-driven approach, enhances the credibility of their findings and allows for more rigorous scrutiny by peers or sceptics.

Moreover, documentation facilitates collaboration and communication within the paranormal research community. By sharing their findings and methodologies, through written reports, presentations, or online platforms, investigators can contribute to the collective knowledge and understanding of the paranormal. This exchange of information encourages peer review, constructive feedback, and the advancement of research in the field.

Additionally, documentation plays a crucial role in fostering transparency

219

and accountability. By keeping detailed records of their investigations, including any limitations, uncertainties, or alternative explanations, investigators demonstrate integrity and professionalism in their work. This transparency builds trust with clients, stakeholders, and the broader public, helping to dispel scepticism or misconceptions surrounding paranormal research.

Lastly, documentation serves as a historical archive for future reference and analysis. Even if a paranormal investigation does not yield conclusive results or immediate answers, the documented data and insights may prove valuable for future research endeavours. By preserving this information for posterity, investigators contribute to the ongoing quest for understanding the mysteries of the paranormal realm.

In conclusion, documentation is necessary for paranormal investigators to maintain accuracy, objectivity, collaboration, transparency, and the advancement of knowledge in their field. By meticulously documenting their investigations, investigators enhance the credibility of their findings, facilitate collaboration with peers, and contribute to the ongoing pursuit of understanding.

We use the following in all our Investigations as a minimum:

- File Front Sheet with open and close dates.
- Client Contact Log.
- Investigation Plan.
- Investigation Report.
- Debunk Report.
- Investigation Observations.
- Environmental Observations.
- Equipment Investigation Log.
- Evidence reviews pages for Audio, Video and Photo.
- EVP Session Log.
- Final Report.
- Consent Form.
- Confidentiality Form.
- Eyewitness Account Form.

Its good practice to get into the habit of following through with the paperwork even when conducting investigations without a client. You cannot properly interpret or analyse data without complete records.

It is also a great tool for later sharing the information with other Paranormal Groups or enthusiasts that may be interested in a location.

Making notes also gives the ability to be open to scrutiny and accountability by your peers and team members. It contains all the evidence you need to back up your conclusions and show the methods used to reach those conclusions. It bolsters your credibility as a scientific investigator of the paranormal and makes it easier to come to a determination.

The paperwork need not be overly elaborate, although when corresponding with clients, I recommend using a letterhead featuring your brand or name for a more professional appearance. Demonstrating organisation and competence instils confidence in clients. Every detail is meticulously documented: phone calls, emails, statements, and narratives linked to the location. We meticulously record the roles each individual plays during an investigation, along with obtaining signed consent and confidentiality agreements from all involved parties. This is especially crucial for private homeowners or businesses seeking discretion regarding their paranormal issues. Nothing goes unrecorded; every observation or event is documented. Detailed documentation is vital because the volume of information and factors to consider can overwhelm memory. This ensures accuracy in interpreting the data collected. Our documents are compiled into a file, easily accessible to any team member needing information on a specific case or location. Typically, this file is managed by the Team Leader or Senior Investigator.

Many inexperienced investigators, encounter difficulties during data analysis due to inadequate record-keeping. I recall an instance where an investigator, while analysing EVPs, neglected to note the timestamp for each audio clip. Despite capturing remarkable EVPs, the problem arose when other team members sought to review recordings surrounding the EVPs for context but could not locate them. Often, revisiting context or correlating timestamps with other mediums becomes necessary. Ensuring meticulous documentation of every detail not only saves countless hours of rework but also facilitates thorough data analysis and comprehensive case recording. Although documentation may seem tedious and occasionally frustrating, it is indispensable for conducting a thorough analysis of data. Moreover, it proves invaluable when collaborating with other groups for comparison of investigations. By maintaining detailed records, such as names consistently captured on audio at the location or similarities in EVPs' wavelength, frequency, and tone, we can draw inferences about the spirits involved. Consequently, other groups often approach us, having seen our posted evidence or heard of our investigations, to incorporate our findings into their own evidence gathering. With everything meticulously organised in the associated file, I can readily provide any information requested.

221

9 HOW TO RUN A PARANORMAL INVESTIGATIONS

PICKING YOUR TEAM

I often say to anyone wanting to get into the field, who approaches us, why do you want to be a paranormal investigator? What are your intentions and frame of mind? On our website, we ask that individuals write us a little about themselves, so that we can better judge if we are dealing with someone serious about the scientific method or someone who is not. Intention matters a lot when dealing with the paranormal, as your frame of mind can influence the spirits that you deal with. There is no space in serious investigations for nonsense behaviour. I never encourage a person to go out alone on paranormal Investigations, especially to more isolated areas. This is purely for safety reasons. If anything happens there is no one there to assist, in an accident or other emergency. This is another reason to find or start your own group.

As an investigator that thinking of starting a team, you need to have answered the above questions. Why do you want to investigate the paranormal and what do you hope to achieve. Expanding on these questions will tell you the kinds of people you want on your team.

Many people are drawn to paranormal investigations, out of sheer curiosity and a sense of adventure. Exploring supposedly haunted locations, using equipment like EMF detectors and EVP recorders, and trying to capture evidence of paranormal activity, can be thrilling and entertaining. For some paranormal investigations are a form of recreational activity, similar to attending ghost tours or watching horror movies. It is a way to experience a thrill and even get an adrenaline rush.

In this context, the focus may be more on the experience itself, rather than rigorous scientific research. There might be a playful or light-hearted atmosphere among participants, with storytelling and sharing of first hand experiences, taking centre stage.

I have been on those tours and have a wonderful time. I have also seen people leave those tours early. The theory of seeing a ghost and hunting shadows is fun, having an actual paranormal experience, is sometimes not.

On the other hand, there are those, like my team and I, who approach paranormal investigations with a more serious and scientific mindset. They see it as an opportunity to explore unexplained phenomena and possibly uncover new insights about the nature of life and death.

Genuine paranormal researchers often employ scientific methods and principles in their investigations. This might involve conducting controlled experiments, gathering data, and analysing evidence in a systematic manner.

These researchers are typically motivated by a desire to understand the unknown and to contribute to our knowledge of the world. They may be more sceptical and critical of evidence, striving to rule out natural explanations before considering supernatural ones.

While still acknowledging the potential for fun and excitement, their primary goal is to conduct legitimate scientific inquiry and potentially advance our understanding of the paranormal.

The difference between fun and real research in paranormal investigations, reflects the diverse motivations and intentions within the field. Some may engage in it purely for entertainment, while others are committed to rigorous exploration. It is up to you the reader, to decide which of these categories you choose to fall into, in deciding the people best suited to your team. Either is perfectly acceptable.

Individuals seeking entertainment are not an ideal fit for our specific group. Similarly, I am incompatible with groups whose primary objective is entertainment rather than serious investigation.

There is no right or wrong way when it comes to the motivation, as long as you are careful and respectful. The wonderful thing about the paranormal field is there is a group and place for anyone, who is interested to participate. Whether its curiosity, scientific research, spiritual advancement, there is a place for everyone to experience the paranormal in the way they feel most comfortable. And that is a wonderful thing. There are some, things to take into consideration when picking a team regardless of your motivations.

For my team we tend fit the rigid scientific methodology. That is not to say, we do not a have a lot of fun, but our primary motivation is research and experience.

Whatever the motivation there are certain characteristics you do not want in a group member. You do not want one of your investigators going in all bravado and provoking the spirits that are there. This can lead to attachments and attacks, not to mention trouble for the homeowners when you leave. Likewise, if you want to gain access to locations and especially people's homes, you need a team that conducts themselves appropriately. This is especially true when dealing with people's belief systems and managing expectations. Sometimes, dealing with the living, is the hardest part of an investigation. In most instances, if you are dealing with private clients, you are dealing with people who are grieving or frightened. Someone who cannot take that seriously is not an asset.

Two of the most important words to remember when setting up a team is Safety and Respect. You want people that will take the safety of themselves, the team and client, as a top priority. You also want someone who is respectful of the team and living people you encounter and also the dead. A small team can be truly cohesive but can just as easily fall apart if there is a disrespectful member A person's conduct can either make or break your team. I have found over the years, that if your methodology and intention is in agreement, differing views and techniques are not really an issue. If, however, there is no agreement on how things should be done, then differing belief systems and views can be exceedingly difficult to manage.

In one instance an investigator and good friend of mine, recently set up a new team in the US, because he moved states. He made a bad choice when he invited a new friend to join his team. His friend did not necessarily have bad intentions, but certainly did not take the situation seriously. His disrespectful behaviour towards other members caused issues within the group. It was the provocative and disrespectful behaviour towards the spirits at a certain location, in the mid-west, that had serious consequences. It led to an attachment of an angry and aggressive male spirit. The incensed spirit did not attach to the friend who was disrespectful, as one would suppose, but to another team member, who was going through some emotional turmoil, and was simply the easier target. It took her six months to sever that negative attachment and emotionally recover from the trauma it caused her and her family.

When looking for a team or team member, reliability and most importantly responsibility are necessary traits. Hauntings often occur in isolated locations. Maybe you are investigating that old, abandoned asylum or prison that's been deserted for years. Maybe it is an old, abandoned factory, built in the middle of nowhere or a reputedly haunted deserted house in the middle of the woods. In these places, working as a team is imperative for the physical safety and wellbeing of all involved. There is no place for egos or maverick behaviours.

There should be clear roles for all your investigators and a clear chain of command. Remembering there is a significant difference, between being in charge and being a leader. A cohesive team should have a strong leader who has a clear expectation of what people are doing. This is for the safety of all involved. For example, I do not want any of my team members to just go and wander off on their own. It is simply not always safe to do that, especially in large or dilapidated locations. An investigation should have a plan and each

224

member assigned a roll.

Your team should be positive people, have good intentions and have particularly good mental health. The reality is spirits can manipulate the emotions of people. I have seen it countless times where a specific spirit has the ability to make a person feel sick, upset, or anxious. Most often than not it is not deliberately malicious it is just a reflection of their emotional state. Some spirits can and will, in some cases, use emotional turmoil to their advantage. The same applies for places with extremely high residual energy, it can have an impact on people who enter that area, physically and emotionally. I do not know any long term paranormal investigator that has not experienced this. Many in the paranormal field, me included, also believe that an investigators mental health and emotional state, can attract spirits and entities that share that state, leading to emotional attachments.

There is a theory on why it seems, that like energy can attracts like energy. If you have negative energy going in, there is a good chance you are going to attract negative energy back. The same applies with living people, you tend to attract people, who have the most in common with you. I am not saying that if there are things going on in your life, you cannot investigate the paranormal safely. You just must be mindful of how people are doing before going out on an investigation. If there are problematic mental health issues, there are 101 reasons why that person should not be attending, until they are in a better frame of mind, or they are getting appropriate treatment.

There should never be any drugs or alcohol involved or in the system of someone going out on an investigation. This may alter people's perceptions and particularly their reactions. The other reason is physical safety, as many locations can be unsafe if you are not paying attention. Anything that can slow reflexes or alter perception, is just a plain safety risk. Lowered inhibitions can increase the risk of attachments from negative spirits or entities. Likewise, we do not allow people under the age of 16 on our tours, courses or investigations.

There are several reasons why children should not attend paranormal investigations: Paranormal investigations can involve encountering unsettling or frightening experiences. Children may not have the emotional maturity to cope with such situations, leading to anxiety, nightmares, or other negative effects. Investigations often take place in unfamiliar or potentially hazardous environments, such as abandoned buildings or remote locations. Children may be more prone to accidents or injuries due to their curiosity and lack of awareness of potential dangers. Paranormal investigations may involve discussions or encounters with sensitive topics, such as death, trauma, or spiritual beliefs. It is important to consider whether children are ready to engage with such content and whether their presence is appropriate in these contexts.

225

In some jurisdictions, there may be legal restrictions on involving children in activities that involve potential risks or exposure to disturbing content. Additionally, it is essential to respect ethical guidelines regarding the participation of minors in paranormal research.

This maybe obvious to many reading this book but I have been asked on numerous occasions if children could attend an investigation the adults wanted to participate in.

Having team members with the ability to visualise protections, stay calm and collected is necessary. As exhilarating as investigations can be, the fact of the matter is, it can also scare even the most seasoned of investigators. Nothing is going to get your heart beating like suddenly being touched by unseen hands or coming face to face with an apparition, who intends to scare you. Working well under pressure helps when dealing with clients and in potentially stressful situations.

Conducting a paranormal investigation can offer a deeply rewarding and intriguing experience. Personally, I have always found joy in visiting familiar haunts or exploring new locations. Through my website, I am available to suggest destinations based on individuals' past encounters. Nowadays, there is no shortage of ghost tours and paranormal excursions for those seeking something unique, and I wholeheartedly support enthusiasts indulging in such experiences.

However, while these activities are undeniably enjoyable, true paranormal investigation centres around rigorous research. As investigators, our primary objective is to meticulously document and scientifically validate the existence of ghosts. We aim to enlighten the public and provide assistance to those grappling with paranormal phenomena.

The reality is, a considerable amount of paperwork accompanies this endeavour—countless hours spent sifting through audio and video recordings, documenting and researching locations, individuals, and occurrences. The actual investigation itself constitutes only a fraction of our responsibilities. Connecting with like-minded individuals can enhance the experience, regardless of the investigative approach one adopts.

With this in mind, you have your team established and a wonderfully eerie and mysterious location in mind. What is the next step in the Investigative process?

PREPARATION

Preparing for an investigation is personally one of my favourite things to do. That is because at heart, I love history and I love research, a trait that I have always had. I love getting to the truth of the matter. I tend to be as meticulous as I can about the data I gather. Post investigation I relish the idea of ending up with more data to cross reference. It is something I personally enjoy doing, which might not be suited to all. It is always a clever idea to designate one or two people to the role of researcher.

The researcher, is really the one who initially prepares the investigation. There are two main ways to do this. they differ, only in so much as, one is a general location and the other involves a little extra, because you are dealing with a personal client. the methodology really stays the same.

Let us look at the two scenarios in a little more detail. Firstly, let us say that you are attending a location that does not have a client and there is no need for a resolution. Let us examine a real world example, I have just finished sending out the details of an upcoming investigation to my team members. The location we will be going out to in the next three weeks, is the Swan View train tunnel at John Forrest National Park, here in Perth, Western Australia.

I like to prepare my cases in as much detail and corroborating evidence as I can. I want my team, to have as much information as possible before we go out there. The second part of this, and the one that really takes the research, is that I want the information to be accurate.

Now I have visited the train tunnel previously but none of my team members have. Let me explain little about the place we are going and why. It is a place many paranormal investigators have been, and although I have walked through this abandoned train tunnel numerous times, I have never conducted a paranormal investigation there.

PREPARING FOR THE SWAN VIEW TUNNEL INVESTIGATION

The Swan View Tunnel has an interesting history and is the only historical railway tunnel in Western Australia, that you can actually walk through. Construction started in 1894 and it took 300 men until 1896 to complete the dangerous work. They used only picks, dynamite, and shovels at that time. It is also known as the darling range tunnel as it is on the edge of the Darling Scarp. It cost $12,000 to build, which in its time was a lot of money. It was designed by the famous West Australian, C.Y O'Connor. What we do know, is that construction workers, lived in tents by the tunnel and worked 24 hours a day, except Sundays, to ensure that the tunnel would be completed, on time. Little to nothing, can be found on the men, who built the tunnel. We do not know if any men died during its construction.

The tunnel is 340m long and there is a bypass around the tunnel that was completed in 1945 for reasons that shall soon, become obvious. The line was completely closed in 1966.

What has caught our interest, is the intriguing history of this location. A quick search of its haunted past will reveal captivating ghost stories. Dating back to its opening in 1896, a significant design flaw was immediately

227

apparent in the tunnel's construction. Its narrow and low dimensions caused the smoke from steam trains to accumulate within, leading to hazardous levels of carbon monoxide. The trains traversed the tunnel at a crawl, allowing the toxic atmosphere to envelop the entire passage before reaching the other side.

There have been many paranormal groups that have gone to the tunnel to collect evidence of the countless men, who are supposed to have been killed in the tunnel, when they suffocated due to the effects of carbon monoxide poisoning. This is where our preparation begins, with an initial story.

When preparing for an investigation there are a number of things you are going to want to do. Firstly, you want to get any appropriate permissions to be at a location. This is especially true if you are dealing with private property or someone's home or place of business. In this case I do not need any permissions as this is in a national park, open to the public.

UNDERSTAND THE ALLEGATIONS

Ensure you fully understand the nature of the allegations or complaints being investigated. This includes gathering all relevant documents, statements, or evidence, related to the case. The following applies to both a public and private location.

I do prefer to get first-hand accounts where possible of any alleged experiences. This can take time.

When investigating private property, it is advisable to request the person who contacted you to compile a list of individuals they know who might be open to discussing their sightings and experience Be respectful, for some these paranormal experiences can be frightening. Some people do not want to be involved with the paranormal let alone an investigation. Their experience is something they may not want to revisit. Whatever it is, be respectful if someone does not want to talk. Document everything you hear in written form to review later. This is when often you will get second hand accounts from the owner.

If it is a public place and well investigated, like the swan view tunnel, approach other paranormal groups that have investigated the location first hand. Get their accounts and evidence of what they have found.

In this case I have spoken to a few first hand witnesses and compiled several website articles in relation to investigations from other groups. I have spoken directly to two other paranormal groups and one amateur group to collate their evidence and get first-hand accounts. They sent me their videos, EVPs and photographs of interest.

All the groups I spoke to, tell the story of men that died in the tunnel. None of these groups had done any proper research, to see if the story was correct. However, they were able to give me a list of Some of the reported phenomena. They are the following:

- Phantom Footsteps: when walking through the tunnel, 3 people have claimed to have heard footsteps run up behind them suddenly, only to turn and find no one there.
- There have been countless photos and more recently a video released those shows what looks like a shadow figure. This shadow figure is always encountered inside the tunnel.
- He has been reported in the tunnel countless times. This is backed up by other accounts online of people seeing or being startled by this shadow figures.
- There are orbs reported and two separate incidents of light, almost like a lantern light that appears and disappears in the centre of the tunnel.
- EVPs have been recorded and the name 'Frank' has come up twice.
- Orbs have been photographed inside the tunnel. Though these appear to more likely dust orbs.
- The ghost that haunts there, has been reported as telling investigators to "sush". by attending mediums, as he does not appreciate noise.
- There is said to be a young woman spirit that is in the tunnel, confirmed by EVP of a woman's voice.
- Keys have been heard jingling.
- Hair gets pulled.
- Multiple EVPs
- Electrical Interference.
- High EMF readings, even though there is no power in the tunnel.

GATHER EVIDENCE ABOUT THE LOCATION

The next step is seeing if there is any data to corroborate these claims. The most obvious point to start, is confirming how many deaths, if any occurred within the tunnel.

I have in this instance, gathered all the evidence I could find from first-hand accounts by others, newspaper articles, written histories, coroner reports and railway incident reports. This is where the story behind the reason for the haunting, begins to unravel.

Since its opening in 1896, the tunnel has experienced numerous incidents of near-asphyxiation from carbon monoxide poisoning. However, it wasn't until 1942 that a fatal incident occurred. On November 5th, 1942, during a slow transition through the tunnel, two drivers and several firemen were overcome by carbon monoxide poisoning while aboard their train. Sadly, one of the drivers passed away, while the others fortunately survived. Research into this incident revealed newspaper articles, coroners' reports, and accident records, all documenting the single recorded death. Additionally, it was discovered that the men were rendered unconscious by the poisoning, leading to a subsequent train crash further along the line by Swan View station. The circumstances surrounding the driver's death were heavily debated, with questions arising as to whether it was a result of injuries sustained in the crash or from the carbon monoxide exposure.

I learnt that the deceased drivers name was Spencer Trobridge BEER known as Tommy. There was a man names Clement Fredrick Dove, known as frank who was injured in the 1942 incident. It is not known if this man is still alive or if he maybe the Frank referred to, in the EVP. This information could warrant further investigation whilst there.

Swan view platform is now no longer operational, but still stands. It is about a 20 minute walk from the tunnel. We know that the death was discovered and may have occurred nearer the station. With this information we will now be conducting a twofold investigation. One at the station platform, the other at the tunnel.

Well known athlete Thomas Moloney lost a leg in the tunnel in 1914 after being overcome by fumes, falling out and being run over by his train. he survived. He was a fireman on the train at the time, stoking the fires and keeping them running.

Speculations circulated regarding a driver's death in 1903, yet my search yielded no death records for such an event. No additional records surfaced indicating multiple deaths or any fatalities within the tunnel. However, given the era, it is improbable that deaths during the tunnel's construction would have been documented. The story of multiple deaths inside the tunnel are just not accurate and appear to be more urban legend than fact.

The images and videos capturing the shadowy figure are quite compelling, accompanied by EVPs and disembodied voices. During this preparatory phase, I have meticulously documented all available information about the tunnel, including its history and the allegations surrounding it. Through this process, I have gained insights into the equipment necessary for our investigation and have successfully debunked several prevalent stories circulating on various platforms. As of now, there are no recorded deaths directly associated with the tunnel, leaving the question of its haunting unexplained. However, there are gaps in our knowledge that require further research, particularly regarding the alleged 1903 incident, which may necessitate a visit to the state library or railway museum. Despite extensive reporting on other incidents, I remain sceptical of the purported death, in 1903, as its absence in contemporary newspapers and coroners' reports raises doubts. Nevertheless, I cannot entirely dismiss the possibility and intend to

230

explore this further.

Additionally, considering the likelihood of fatalities among the tunnel's construction workers, who remain unidentified in public records, suggests avenues for investigation, possibly through EVP questioning. Furthermore, we possess pertinent names of individuals involved in these incidents, which may prove valuable in our inquiry.

DETERMINE WHAT EQUIPMENT YOU ARE TAKING

The investigation approach should be tailored to the unique characteristics of the site. Considering the abundance of recorded voice phenomena at this particular location, we will employ our voice recorders and utilise the SB7 camera equipment for capturing still photos. Additionally, the inclusion of an IR camera is warranted, given that the shadow figure is frequently captured on both video and still camera footage. Given we know the tunnel was dug out with picks, shovels and dynamite, a shovel would be an ideal trigger object.

ESTABLISH AN INVESTIGATION PLAN

Outline the investigation's scope, including the timeline, necessary resources, and key personnel involved, adhering to relevant laws, regulations, and company policies. Prepare written investigation plans to be provided, to the client/location and the team. Ensure all insurance and paperwork, such as confidentiality and consent forms, are prepared, if applicable.

For this investigation, I have compiled and distributed all available documentation and information to each team member for review and familiarisation prior to our fieldwork. We have scheduled a meeting to develop the investigation plan, including EVP session topics, a week before our departure. During this meeting, tasks will be assigned, and a team leader will be designated.

Although confidentiality and insurance documents aren't pertinent to this investigation, they've been organised for other cases as necessary.

Given the nature of this tunnel location, where information is limited, it took approximately a day and a half to gather research and witness statements. Some investigations, involving multiple sources and lengthy histories, may require more time. We only finalise the date for the on-site investigation after thorough research and discussion. Final preparations involve equipment checks, ensuring everything is fully charged, and all devices have accurate time and date stamps—essential for the analytical stage. Occasionally, an initial site visit may be conducted to familiarise ourselves with the location and interview any witnesses.

ATTENDING THE LOCATION

SPIRITUAL PROTECTION

Prior to embarking on any investigation or when the team convenes, it is essential to engage in grounding, centering, and shielding exercises collectively. This practice fosters inclusivity and cohesion within the team. Each team member takes turns leading the others through these exercises, offering valuable experience, and fostering a sense of belonging within the team for those who choose to participate.

MAKING YOURSELF KNOWN TO THE SPIRITS

I have emphasised the importance of respect and intention in paranormal investigations. Just as with interactions among the living, initial impressions carry weight. It is certain that the spirits at the location are aware of our presence, observing us from the moment we arrive, and in some cases, even before. While this practice may not be adopted by all groups, I strongly advocate for budding paranormal investigators, to incorporate it into their standard procedure, regardless of the location.

Upon arrival at a location following our protection exercise, we introduce ourselves to the resident spirits. Subsequently, we explain the purpose of our visit and assure them of our positive intentions. This practice is not only a matter of good practice but also of good manners. By conveying our respect and expectations for respectful behaviour in return, we establish a mutual understanding. Additionally, if there are areas of the building inaccessible to us, we inform any spirits present that they can venture into those areas, ensuring they won't be disturbed, if they so choose. This approach is particularly beneficial in locations frequently investigated, where spirits may become agitated or reactive due to the constant attention.

At certain locations, you might find it necessary to provide an explanation of the equipment being used, especially in very old sites like those commonly found in the UK. For instance, a ghost from 1066, such as one from the Battle of Hastings, might be hesitant to interact with modern equipment like a voice recorder developed 811 years after their death. In some cases, the spirits will ask what the equipment is through EVP or the spirit box.

At this juncture, we also emphasise to the spirits that they do not have permission to attach themselves to us or our equipment. It is a standard practice for us to reiterate this point when we conclude our investigation. As an investigator, you may have personal boundaries that differ from others. For instance, I once accompanied an investigator who preferred not to be touched by spirits. She made her preference clear from the outset, and while the rest of us were open to interaction, the spirits respected her wishes and refrained from touching her that night. During active investigations where numerous events are occurring, it may become necessary to remind certain spirits of the ground rules. Younger spirits, in particular, can become overly excited. In such instances, it is crucial to assert and reinforce boundaries. Do not hesitate to assert your boundaries verbally and reiterate them if a spirit crosses the line. Maintain a matter-of-fact demeanour and then swiftly move on to the next task. It is important to handle these situations with respect; if necessary, you can always disengage from contact if a spirit fails to respect your boundaries.

THE WALK THROUGH

The first thing you are going to do is a walkthrough of the location or the building, to familiarise yourself with the layout and take the necessary readings and ambient noise levels. This is not only for research and verification purposes, but safety. If you are investigating at night, then you want to make sure that you are familiar with the layout of the building. Especially if you are wondering around in the dark. This is especially true for older buildings where some of the stairs or areas have hazards.

This is also the point where you make clear to the team which areas are off limits, regardless of what happens. Often, owners will almost always restrict areas and we need to respect their instructions. It is a great chance to get your own impressions of the building as you go through. Pay close attention to what your own body is telling you. If you have a medium on the team, this is a good opportunity to get their impressions. Make sure any findings or impressions are documented and written down.

EMF BASE READINGS

During your initial walkthrough, one of the earliest steps is to record the baseline readings for the property or location. These baseline readings are crucial as they establish the natural levels of the environment. While conducting the walkthrough, make note of any fluctuations, as they may indicate the presence of electricity or other significant factors that require attention. This practice is particularly important for two main reasons.

- Base readings throughout the property can be recorded.
- Any sudden spikes can be documented – This is important later when your wandering around, possibly in the dark and your K2 spikes. You realise then it is just the owner microwave that's setting it off: Debunked.

- EMF fluctuations at the location between the natural EMF field and the non-paranormal EMF fields can be written down. - That way you when you get much bigger spikes you can pay attention.

Take note of any particular high readings that may cause the feelings or sensations associated with a paranormal presence. It is super important when on an investigation to make sure your phones and other equipment is not influencing the EMF readings.

THERMAL READINGS

Both the ambient temperature readings and specific surfaces temperature readings are going to be recorded. Thermal baseline readings help establish what is considered, "normal" in terms of temperature fluctuations in the environment being investigated. This allows investigators to distinguish between natural temperature changes and potentially paranormal phenomena.

By establishing baseline temperatures, investigators can easily identify significant temperature variations during the investigation. Having baseline readings helps eliminate false positives that may occur due to environmental factors, such as drafts, heating systems, or fluctuations in weather conditions. It allows investigators, to attribute temperature changes to paranormal activity, only after ruling out mundane explanations.

Baseline readings serve as a reference point for comparison throughout the investigation, providing a scientific basis for interpreting temperature fluctuations. This helps investigators quantify and document changes in temperature, adding objectivity to their observations. By analysing baseline temperature readings alongside other evidence, such as paranormal phenomena picked up by other equipment, investigators can evaluate their significance comprehensively, enhancing the credibility of the investigation.

I find it beneficial to commence with these readings to promptly identify and address any temperature measurements that may be misleading. For instance, during one investigation, we detected a heater concealed behind a wall solely through our thermal baseline readings. This discovery prevented any potential misinterpretations, as the heater's presence created an anomalous human torso-like image on the thermal camera.

ENVIRONMENTAL OBSERVATIONS

At the beginning of an investigation, Environmental Observations play a critical role. Environmental conditions can directly influence various

234

phenomena that may manifest during the investigation. For instance, heightened humidity may result in an increase in orbs due to moisture in the air, while humid conditions can also lead to heightened insect activity. These factors are important considerations for investigators during the analysis and interpretation of video and photographic evidence later on. Similarly, extremely frigid air, is more likely to produce visible breath on camera, which could be misinterpreted by individuals reviewing the photos afterward.

For my group environmental observations include, but are not limited, to the following:

- Ambient Temperature: Both indoors and outdoors taking note of any anomalies.
- Weather Observations: Is it cold, sunny, hot, raining or snowing. Is it particularly windy or still. On an investigation in England the team of investigators heard what they believed were bangs and rapping coming from the attic. Turned out it was an overhanging tree on a very windy day hitting the roof of the property, debunked.
- Humidity: Important to determine moisture and insect activity in the air, Important especially for outdoor locations.
- Any Other Noteworthy Observations: Including sunrise, and sunset times, important to note because of the casting of shadows that could be misinterpreted on photographs.
- Sun position and Moon phase if applicable for the exact same reasons.

Top Tip: This practice should be conducted either at the outset of the investigation or just prior to commencing an EVP session or setting up video equipment. Use your video camera and/or voice recorder to capture a minimum of a 20-second recording. Ensure that the rooms are silent during this process to capture background ambient sounds. This step is crucial for noise reduction during the analysis of your video and audio recordings. It is often necessary to record a sizeable portion of the noise you intend to reduce, ultimately saving valuable time during the analysis phase.

SETTING UP YOUR EQUIPMENT

The extent of setup required depends on the equipment being used, varying among different groups and individuals. Some investigation teams employ elaborate camera and computer setups for real-time observation, while others opt for simpler arrangements, such as a single static camera and a trigger object. It is crucial to have a predetermined plan for equipment placement based on prior information regarding areas of heightened activity.

Always ensure that the lenses of your cameras and video cameras are clean and free from dust, as smudges and debris can compromise the integrity of photograph or video evidence. If you have a base station for monitoring in real-time, ensure it is operational and tested before beginning. Activity may become apparent at this stage, so be prepared to document any unusual occurrences promptly.

During equipment setup, it is advisable to have a team member equipped with a voice recorder, EMF meter, and spirit box present. It is not uncommon for activity to manifest as setup progresses, even during initial site visits or witness interviews. Spirits are often aware of your presence and may seek to communicate immediately. Be ready to conduct impromptu EVP sessions during setup to capture potential evidence.

While planning is essential, flexibility is equally crucial, as the spirit world operates unpredictably. Remain adaptable to unexpected manifestations, seizing opportunities to gather evidence even amid structured setup routines.

STILL PHOTOGRAPHS

While others are busy setting up equipment and taking baseline measurements, if the location is not overly spacious, we conduct a walkthrough and capture a series of still photographs. Typically, we take these photographs in sets of three. Every empty room, corridor, hallway, and entrance is photographed. Various types of cameras can be utilised for this purpose, with the IR camera often revealing more details than a regular vision camera. Before commencing, ensure that each photograph includes a date and timestamp.

COMMENCING THE OFFICIAL INVESTIGATION PLAN

Entering a paranormal investigation, it is advisable to have a comprehensive written plan outlining the placement of equipment and intended actions, prior to the investigation. The written plan also encompasses a detailed breakdown of our activities, which may include vigils in specific locations, EVP sessions, Spirit box sessions, or trigger object sessions. This ensures that upon arrival, there are clear expectations regarding the activities planned for the night. However, it is essential to acknowledge that paranormal investigation is inherently unpredictable, and the plan serves as a rough guideline rather than a rigid schedule. Adaptability is key when navigating the uncertainties encountered during on-location investigations. I distribute this plan along with an explanation of why certain areas of the location are deemed more significant, based on factors such as previous evidence or eyewitness reports. However, it is not uncommon for this plan to be adjusted based on the activity observed during the walkthrough and setup phase. Sometimes, the walkthrough itself yields intense activity, such as disembodied voices or heavy footsteps. In such cases, the team leader must make on-the-spot decisions regarding the direction of the investigation. This flexibility ensures that the team can adapt to unexpected occurrences and maximise their chances of capturing compelling evidence.

At this stage, you'll determine which equipment to bring with you to the specific area of the location you're heading towards. Essential items include a still camera, video camera, and a voice recorder. Before each session, it is imperative to record temperature and EMF readings for comparison with baseline measurements, ensuring thorough documentation of all findings.

To prevent interference with the equipment or readings, ensure that everyone's phone is set to airplane mode. Additionally, it is recommended that the individual handling the K2 or EMF reader does not have their phone on their person; they should either turn it off or pass it to another team member. If necessary, one phone at the base location can remain operational to ensure communication in case of emergencies.

SMALL SESSIONS

A Paranormal Investigation is most effectively conducted in shorter, concentrated sessions to avoid exhaustion. Based on my experience, sessions lasting approximately half an hour to a maximum of 45 minutes in any given area prove to be sufficient.

Clear delineation of roles is essential for smooth operation. Each team member should be aware of their responsibilities, as outlined in the pre-investigation plan. This includes tasks such as note-taking, questioning, EMF meter operation, and temperature readings at the outset of each session. I strongly recommend assigning specific roles, such as video recording and photography, prior to commencing the investigation. This minimises planning time and maximises active investigation time.

Following each session, it is crucial to take breaks to recharge and regroup. This interval also presents an opportunity to review and perform protection exercises. Taking breaks allows for discussion of next steps and ensures proper hydration, which is particularly vital for individuals who may find paranormal investigation emotionally or energetically draining.

EVP SESSIONS

An EVP session can occur spontaneously or be planned, depending on the evidence of spirit presence. Prior to commencing, it is customary to express gratitude to the spirits present, explain the equipment and its function, and articulate positive intentions if desired. During an EVP session, designate one person to ask questions at a time, typically in 2-minute intervals, allowing all participants an opportunity to engage. It is advisable to have at least two individuals ask questions, as spirits may be more receptive to certain individuals. If known, spirits can be addressed by name. Questions should be specific and allow sufficient time for responses. Playback during the investigation is recommended, focusing on two or three questions at a time before reviewing. Maintain respect throughout the session, refraining from asking questions that would be inappropriate for a living person. Upon concluding the session, express gratitude to any interacting spirits and formally close the session. If a spirit clearly indicates a desire to discontinue or vacate an area, respect their wishes and conclude the session, expressing gratitude before moving to the next location. Additionally, maintaining respect is crucial, as returning to a location may be necessary, and spirits are less likely to engage with individuals who were disrespectful during previous encounters.

OBSERVATION SESSIONS

If you have a comprehensive setup with multiple cameras and a centralised base camp for live monitoring, I recommend dedicating a 20-minute session to simply observing the environment. Gather at your base and attentively monitor the cameras for any anomalies, unusual sounds, or visual phenomena.

In some cases, spirits may be disinclined to communicate with yet another investigator visiting the location. By refraining from active interaction and instead focusing on observation, we have experienced notable success. Visual anomalies, movement of trigger objects, and voice phenomena have been captured during these observation sessions. This strategy is often overlooked but can yield valuable results. Therefore, I advocate for the inclusion of a 20-minute observation session as a standard component of all investigations.

SPIRIT BOX SESSIONS

Spirit box sessions can occur spontaneously or be planned in advance for specific areas of a location. There are several stages and techniques employed by paranormal investigators during these sessions.

Firstly, ensure that the spirit box is functioning properly and fully charged, especially if it is battery-operated. Select a quiet location with minimal radio interference to conduct the session and bring along extra batteries as a precaution. It is not uncommon for batteries to drain unexpectedly during sessions.

If conducting the session with a group, gather everyone together and explain the purpose and guidelines. Emphasise the importance of respect, open-mindedness, and focused attention. Participants should remain as still as possible and listen attentively for responses, particularly through the spirit box.

Set a clear intention for the session, whether it is inviting spirits to communicate, establishing ground rules for interaction, seeking answers to specific questions, or remaining open to any messages that may come through.

When ready, turn on the spirit box and adjust the scan rate to a speed that allows for clear and audible communication. Begin scanning through the frequencies, listening for any anomalous voices or messages. The ideal scan rate is a matter of personal preference and may vary between individuals and devices. Experimentation with different speeds and directions (forward or backward) can help determine the most effective settings for communication. Ultimately, select the settings that make it easiest for you to hear and identify potential messages from spirits.

Encourage participants to ask open-ended questions aloud, leaving pauses between each question to allow time for potential responses. Questions can range from general inquiries about the presence of spirits to more specific queries related to the location or situation. I find the majority of the sessions will be specific questions about the location or nay activity that has occurred. It could be to ask if they know the names of those participating, the owner of the location, if they could tell you something specific in the environment, such as what the trigger object is. The entire purpose of the conversation is to establish and document intelligent responses to specific questions. I had one spirit tell me the colour of the scarf I was wearing and the fact I was wearing a cross around my neck. This is the most exciting part of the investigation for some, having a real time conversation with a spirit or entity in real time.

Pay close attention to the voices and sounds coming through the spirit box. Spirits may communicate in various ways, including direct responses to questions, relevant words or phrases, or even manipulating the scan rate or static to convey messages.

Record the session using a voice recorder or digital device to capture any

239

responses or messages that come through the spirit box. Some have this built in or allow for you to connect a voice recorder, such as the SB7. Take note of any significant words, phrases, or patterns that emerge during the session. All words and phrases are relevant as they may make sense at a later point in the investigation. We have had a spirit repeat the word alarm to us and then 1 hour later the alarm was sounded in the building, we could find no cause.

Once the session is complete, thank any spirits who may have communicated and respectfully close the session. Offer gratitude for any messages received and express openness to future communication. You never know if you might return to the location.

THE ESTES METHOD

Another favoured method among paranormal investigators is the Estes Method, which combines sensory deprivation with a spirit box to facilitate communication with potential spirits.

In this method, one team member wears noise-cancelling headphones connected to the spirit box, often while blindfolded, to reduce sensory stimuli and enhance focus on the messages coming through the device. Meanwhile, another team member, usually from a separate area or room to avoid suggestion, asks the questions.

During the session, the team member with the spirit box calls out any words, phrases, or sentences received, which are then noted down for later analysis. This method effectively hones in on messages from the spirit box, providing a more focused communication experience.

Notably, there have been instances where the spirit box referenced objects held by an investigator in another room, unbeknownst to the operator. I highly recommend trying this method for those seeking a concentrated spirit box experience.

Addressing the possibility of encountering disrespectful or aggressive spirits, it is essential to maintain boundaries similar to interactions with the living. If a spirit displays disrespectful or disturbing behaviour, the team may remind it to be respectful or choose to ignore it. However, if the behaviour persists or becomes excessively negative, the session is promptly terminated, and focus shifts to another activity.

Ultimately, it is crucial to prioritise personal boundaries and not tolerate any disrespectful or unpleasant behaviour, whether from the living or the spirit realm.

TRIGGER OBJECT

It is customary to utilise objects or devices, carefully selected as trigger objects, to attract or engage with spirits at the location. These trigger objects can vary widely, ranging from toys for child spirits to items directly or symbolically linked to the location.

Setting up a trigger object can be approached in different ways, with two primary methods being static and interactive configurations.

STATIC TRIGGER OBJECTS

Carefully position the trigger objects in a section of the location where paranormal phenomena have been observed. Various techniques are employed by investigators when arranging a static trigger object. The choice of method is contingent upon the nature, dimensions, and form of the trigger being utilised.

- Place the trigger object on a piece of white paper and use a pen to draw around the object.
- Place the Object on a piece of black or dark paper or card. Draw around the object in visible pen. Sprinkle flour over the top of the object being careful not to move it. Sometimes you can get little finger prints or hand prints in the flour. Rember out of respect for the people who own the location to clean up afterwards.
- Tie a piece of cotton to the trigger object and then tie the other end onto something within the room that is stationary nearby. This could be an ornament or a chair etc (Any movement of the trigger object may cause the string to become taut, making the stationary object move. This in turn, provide a visual indicator of activity to the investigator) – This method needs to be set up carefully so there are no false positives.

Ideally, we position the object in close proximity to data collection equipment, such as cameras or EVP recorders. I always ensure there is a voice recorder and a proximity sensor placed alongside the static trigger object. This setup allows us to verify any interaction by capturing audio and detecting movement. Some investigators take it a step further by incorporating datalogging equipment capable of monitoring changes in temperature, humidity, or pressure around the trigger objects. Utilising equipment like a Mel meter or a thermal camera enhances our ability to monitor activity effectively, providing multiple layers of scrutiny to discern genuine paranormal phenomena from environmental influences or technical glitches.

Once the setup is complete, it is essential to mitigate any external factors that could compromise the results, including physical objects or environmental variables like vibrations and drafts. Following this, a camera is installed to visually monitor the object either in real time or for later analysis. While a standard visual camera suffices for this purpose, some prefer to employ thermal imaging or full-spectrum cameras for enhanced detection capabilities.

Subsequently, the static trigger object remains undisturbed within a securely locked room or an inaccessible location, ensuring its integrity throughout the experiment. All equipment must be accurately timestamped, and thorough documentation of observations and findings is imperative. Furthermore, it is vital to uphold objectivity and explore alternative explanations for any apparent movement of trigger objects.

USING A TRIGGER INTERACTIVELY

The interactive use of trigger objects can prove highly effective, especially when dealing with playful or mischievous spirits, such as child spirits. These entities often exhibit a desire to engage with trigger objects, commonly in the form of toys. Investigators employ these objects as focal points to communicate with any spirits or entities believed to be present. This interaction may involve posing questions or making requests for the spirits to manipulate the objects in specific ways.

Recreating familiar scenes or actions can prompt a response, particularly when utilising objects associated with the spirit's occupation, hobbies, or personal belongings. For instance, consider a scenario where you are investigating a Plane Museum reportedly haunted by a plane engineer named George. Bringing along some non-specialised tools, you could approach a plane exhibit and simulate repair work while engaging with the spirit, asking for assistance in fixing the aircraft. Although the spirit is aware of the simulation, witnessing the action may evoke memories of its occupation, potentially eliciting an emotional response or prompting nostalgic interaction.

Paranormal investigators utilise trigger objects not only for spirits to interact with directly but also to evoke emotional responses and elicit reactions. For instance, when dealing with child spirits or groups of children, investigators may place toys or sweets and invite the spirits to engage with them, offering treats and encouraging playful interactions.

Similarly, investigators can directly engage with the spirits by initiating games or activities. For example, rolling a ball and inviting the spirits to participate by rolling it back is a method observed at various locations. Another approach involves playing hide-and-seek, prompting the spirits to locate and touch any investigator they choose. By making these interactions enjoyable and light hearted, investigators aim to foster a comfortable atmosphere for the spirits to engage. Additionally, conducting such experiments without informing the team allows for spontaneous responses and observations.

One investigator showcased remarkable creativity during an investigation aboard the historic HMS Victory and HMS Warrior, moored in Portsmouth, England. The HMS Victory, famously Vice-Admiral Lord Nelson's flagship, offered a unique setting for paranormal exploration. Venturing aboard for a tour, the investigator settled into one of the rooms and began reading an account of the Battle of Trafalgar. As he recited, he felt an immediate response, experiencing an electrifying atmosphere in the room. Astonishingly, he witnessed a full-bodied apparition crossing the doorway, adding a surreal dimension to the encounter.

On the HMS Warrior, known for its significant role in history as the ship that escorted Princess Alexandra of Denmark to Britain in 1863, the investigator delved into another intriguing experiment. Recalling the ship's rich history, particularly the captain's gesture of engraving the princess's appreciation on a brass plate fitted to the ship's wheel, he devised a unique approach. Placing a photo of Princess Alexandra of Denmark upright on the floor, he recited her message of gratitude and congratulated Captain Cochrane and his crew by name. The response was immediate and intense, marked by a sudden drop in temperature, mysterious footsteps, and the unexpected toppling of the photo frame. These compelling experiences underscored the profound connection between historical context, intention, and paranormal phenomena aboard these iconic vessels.

This highlights the importance of direct communication with the presumed spirit, using their name if known, and making polite requests rather than demands. When addressing the spirit, request their interaction with the trigger object respectfully.

Ask the spirit to engage with the trigger object by moving it, altering its position, activating its lights or sounds, or any other manipulations. Offer clear instructions and allow sufficient time for the spirit to respond.

Consider offering incentives or rewards to encourage spirit interaction and invite them to physically touch or manipulate the trigger object. Use environmental cues or prompts relevant to the spirit's interests or experiences to facilitate interaction with the object.

It is essential to acknowledge that the effectiveness of these trigger objects can vary depending on the nature and willingness of the spirits present in that particular location.

Bobby Mackey's Music World:

Bobby Mackey's Music World in Wilder, Kentucky, is notorious for its alleged haunting by aggressive and demonic entities. Trigger objects like musical instruments, such as guitars and pianos, have purportedly been witnessed moving or generating sounds autonomously during paranormal investigations. Extreme caution is advised when visiting this establishment.

Eastern State Penitentiary:

Eastern State Penitentiary in Philadelphia, Pennsylvania, stands as a former prison with a rich history. Trigger objects such as prison uniforms, shackles, and various artifacts have allegedly been manipulated or disturbed during paranormal investigations at this location.

The Whaley House:

The Whaley House, nestled in San Diego, California, holds the reputation of being one of the most haunted residences in the United States. Trigger objects, encompassing antique furniture, toys, and personal items belonging to the Whaley family, purportedly experience movement or even being thrown by invisible entities during paranormal investigations. Visitors are urged to exercise caution when exploring this site, given its eerie reputation and reported paranormal activity.

Trans-Allegheny Lunatic Asylum:

The Trans-Allegheny Lunatic Asylum in Weston, West Virginia, is a historic psychiatric hospital with a reputation for intense paranormal activity. Trigger objects, including medical equipment, patient records have reportedly been moved or by unseen forces during paranormal investigations conducted at the asylum. These incidents have been documented by investigators and visitors alike for as long as there have been visitors.

10 EVIDENCE ANALYSIS AND INTERPRETATION

"Analysing evidence in paranormal investigations is akin to deciphering a complex puzzle. Each piece tells a story, but it is the astute interpretation that unveils the narrative hidden within the shadows."

Once the investigation phase concludes, the real work begins analysing the wealth of evidence amassed during your exploration. This phase is not only the most time-intensive but also the most critical. As an investigator, you must not only master the art of analysing the data but also possess the skill to interpret its significance. Evidence analysis and interpretation lie at the core of paranormal investigations. This intricate process involves collating, documenting, organising, analysing, and interpreting the evidence gathered during investigations. The ultimate goal is to ascertain the potential presence of paranormal phenomena. Through thorough and systematic analysis, paranormal investigators aim to gain deeper insights into these phenomena, thereby contributing to the advancement of paranormal research. Similar to any scientific discipline, this process requires several key elements to be diligently applied.

CLEAR OBJECTIVES

Before beginning the investigation. understand what you are trying to achieve and what specific phenomena you are investigating. Does your analysis back this up?

- Quality Data: Collect high-quality data using reliable equipment with standardised procedures. Your procedures could include making sure that equipment is calibrated correctly, checking their function, and

245

getting base readings as well as making sure they are all have a date and time stamp. Ensure that data collection methods are consistent.

- Comprehensive Documentation: Document all aspects of the investigation thoroughly, including the location, date, time, environmental conditions, equipment used, and any relevant observations or experiences. I cannot overestimate the importance of proper record keeping.

- Critical Thinking Skills: Apply critical thinking skills to evaluate evidence objectively and discern between genuine phenomena and potential natural or man-made explanations. Consider alternative hypotheses and explanations for observed phenomena. One of the big mistakes that is so easily made is letting our desire and excitement cloud our judgment.

- Scientific Method: Follow the scientific method, including forming hypotheses, designing experiments, collecting data, analysing results, and drawing sound conclusions. Approach every investigation with a healthy dose of scepticism.

- Analytical Tools: Utilise appropriate analytical tools and techniques to analyse data effectively. This may include using sound programmes when analysing audio evidence, or video programme that allows frame by frame analysis. Make sure you make a copy of the raw data to work on as we don't want the original data altered or compromised.

- Peer Review: Seek input and collaboration from other investigators, enthusiasts, and team members. Peer review helps ensure the integrity and accuracy of the analysis and can provide valuable perspectives. Peer review of raw data allows for things you missed the first time to be potentially picked up by others or can allow for the evidence to be rationally explained.

- Ethical Conduct: Conduct investigations with integrity, honesty, and respect for all parties involved, including clients, witnesses, and the general public.

- Transparency And Reproducibility Maintain transparency in your analysis methods and make your findings and methodologies reproducible. Document your analysis procedures thoroughly so that others can replicate your work and verify your results if they choose to. Keep all raw data.

- Open Mindedness Remain open-minded throughout the analysis process. Be willing to revise interpretations in light of new evidence or insights. Sometimes it really is nothing paranormal and this is as valuable a conclusion than any.

A thorough investigation entails analysing written notes, audio recordings, video footage, and digital photos, all of which can be quite extensive. It is a monumental task, and I recommend that each investigator analyse their own evidence, unless there is a designated team member responsible for data analysis. Personally, I am not fond of relying solely on one team member for analysis, as interpretations can be subjective. I prefer having multiple team members review the recorded data independently to identify any potential anomalies. Fresh perspectives and interpretations often uncover details that may have been overlooked during the initial review.

Another reason an investigator might delegate data analysis is if they lack the necessary skill set. Analysing data requires specific training and expertise. For instance, one investigator may excel at analysing EVPs, while another prefers scrutinising video evidence. In our team, Jack enjoys immersing himself in hours of video footage, whereas I find satisfaction in meticulously examining audio recordings for subtle whispers.

Ideally, analysis should occur in a quiet room devoid of distractions, allowing the analyst to focus intently. It is beneficial to have at least two people involved in the analysis process, either working together in pairs or separately but convening later to discuss their findings as a group. This collaborative approach ensures thorough examination and helps mitigate the risk of overlooking significant evidence.

Personally, we each analyse our own data and then swap. I cannot count the times something has been picked up by another investigator, that has been missed by me or vice versa. you can ask them for verification if you find something interesting or even have them go over an item you've looked at or listened to for anything you may have missed. In my team, my Co-founder Jack Bryant is much better at sound filtering background noise and clearing up background noise. You use the resources you have available and sometimes one team member is just better at certain parts of the analyses.

Above all else take your time reviewing your files. This is not at all a quick process in order to do it properly. There is nothing to be gained by rushing through the process. It takes patience, time and a lot of dedicated hours.

It is crucial to ensure that all equipment used during the investigation is properly timestamped with the date and time. This practice simplifies the analysis process and facilitates cross-referencing between different types of evidence. In my view, timestamping is indispensable for conducting a thorough investigation. Without accurate timestamps, it becomes challenging to establish temporal relationships between events and accurately correlate findings across various mediums.

As of the time of writing here are some of the software, we use that I would recommend.

247

- Audio: AVS Audio Editor or Audacity are a couple of good free audio analysers you can download. I have always personally found Audacity a little easier to use. Investing and using some good noise cancelling headphones will remove outside interference and allow you to hear any possible EVPs with more precision and less noise contamination.

- Video: AVS Video Editor is another great free program to use when analysing your data. Video analysis is time consuming and hard on the eyes. It is recommended that you do your visual analysis in short bursts to give your eyes a rest. Tired eyes can miss evidence. If you see an activity, you believe could be paranormal, document the time, date and time stamp on the program. Cut and copy the section for a more precise analysis.

- Photographic: An investigator can really use any graphics program to view your photos. Examine all areas of interest. Make sure you look at the whole picture. I tend to go edge-to-edge and top to bottom on the outside of the photo and then line by line left to right in the rest of the photo. If you find any type of anomalies, you want to come back to then put them in its own separate folder. Make sure that before you start manipulating a picture make sure to save a copy and work on that one.

I typically begin by duplicating all my files to preserve the integrity of the original data. From there, I meticulously sift through the copied data, extracting anything noteworthy and organising it into relevant folders. I also compile a detailed list indicating the medium, date, and timestamp for each piece of evidence. This written record serves as a guide as I delve into each item, cross-referencing them along the way. Before delving into the specifics of how we analyse different types of evidence, it is essential to discuss the concept of matrixing and its relevance to paranormal investigation data analysis.

MATRIXING

Pareidolia, commonly referred to as matrixing in the context of paranormal investigation, is a psychological phenomenon wherein the human brain interprets ambiguous or random sensory stimuli—such as patterns, colours, shapes, or sounds—as familiar objects or patterns. This phenomenon has a notable impact on how individuals perceive visual and auditory evidence in paranormal contexts. As we explore each type of evidence, we'll examine specific examples to illustrate this concept further.

Matrixing commonly manifests in paranormal investigations, whether

248

visually or audibly, through direct sensory perception or examination of photos and audio recordings. For instance, while peering down a dimly lit corridor, one may perceive a shape resembling a person, only to realise it is a trick of light and shadow upon closer inspection. Similarly, during EVP analysis, an investigator might discern what appears to be a distinct word, yet upon sharing the recording, others may only hear indistinct background noise. As investigators analysing data, it is crucial to recognise two primary types of matrixing:

- Visual Matrixing: In visual matrixing (pareidolia), individuals may perceive recognisable shapes, faces, or objects in random patterns or textures. For example, seeing faces in clouds, patterns in wood grains, or figures in shadows. During paranormal investigations matrixing may mistakenly be taken as evidence of apparitions or other supernatural phenomena when, in reality, it is a result of the brains tendency to find familiar patters where there are none. A perfect example of visual matrixing is seeing a face on the surface of the moon.

- Auditory Matrixing: Auditory matrixing (apophenia), occurs when individuals interpret random sounds or noise as meaningful words, phrases, or sentences. This can happen in situations where there is background noise or white noise, such as during EVP sessions. Investigators may perceive voices or messages in the static and attribute them to spirits or entities when they are likely the result of apophenia.

Environmental elements, encompassing factors like illumination, shadow play, reflective surfaces, and atmospheric variables such as humidity or mist, can exacerbate matrixing by generating visual or auditory illusions mistaken for paranormal occurrences. It is imperative for investigators to mitigate these influences throughout the data collection, analysis, and interpretation phases.

EVPS AND AUDIO ANALYSES

There are four classes assigned to an EVP that is based on the clarity and the quality. This is universal to the paranormal investigation community. As sharing our evidence with our fellow community and with the public is all part of being a paranormal investigator, it is a class system that the reader should familiarise themselves with defined requirements to help investigator's determine which category of EVP they've captured.

249

EVP CLASSIFICATIONS

There have been quite a few guidelines developed to help investigators to determine what class an EVP should fall into. We will go through some of the classifications and scales that investigators use. There is no real right one to abide by, I have known investigative groups that have used one or another over the years. You can choose which one you find most applicable and easy to use. We still Use Class A, B, C given the majority of Class Ds are discarded. I personally use the AA-EVP system as this is the most widely used and understood classification system today.

THE RAUDIVE SCALE

Konstantin Raudive was the first prominent EVP researcher to attempt to put categories to the voices he captured.
- Class A EVP: Voices Can be heard and identified by anyone in the vicinity without the use of any aids. The Language is easy to identify and is clear. There should be no confusion as to what the voice on the EVP is saying.
- Class B EVP: Voices speak more rapidly and more softly but are still easily audible to a trained and attentive ear.
- Class C EVP: Voices give us a great deal of information and much paranormal data Unfortunately, these can be heard only in fragments, even by a trained ear, but with improved aids these can eventually become possible to hear and demonstrate these voices, which lie beyond our range of hearing, without any trouble.

THE ESTEP SYSTEM

As technology improved it was not long before the Raudive Scale was soon replaced. This system was made popular in 1988 when it was published in a book by Sarah Estep. The Book 'voices of Eternity' made the scale the standard for all EVP classifications globally.

- Class A EVP: Voices are loud and clear; they can be duplicated into other tapes and can be heard without headphones.
- Class B EVP: Voices are not as loud o=and clear as a class A but can often be made out and heard without the use of headphones.
- Class C EVP: Headphones must be used to hear them and often the voices are faint and whispery. Not all words can be identified

and interpreted.

As with the previous attempt to classify EVPs this scale became outdated. It was replaced by the American Association of Electronic Voice Phenomena or the AA-EVP system.

THE AA-EVP SYSTEM

This system attempted to do what the others had not. It took away subjectivity which the other scales had not done. It focused instead on the clarity and the quality and consensus of what most people could agree on hearing. This is still used to day by many investigators.

- Class A EVP: People hearing will generally agree on the content and the message can be heard without headphones.
- Class B EVP: Not everyone will agree on the content of the message, and you will need headphones in order to hear the message.
- Class C EVP: EVP requires the use of headphones to hear the content message and will often need amplification and filtration. The content will seldom be heard by others listening.

THE KM SYSTEM

Named after EVP researchers Doug Kelly and Jari Mikkola this system goes one step further by also including the meaning of the message that corresponds and correlates to the meaning and relevance of the message.

Think back to the experience of the spirit person in the quarantine station here at Woodman Point. Had the lady asked, "What are you doing here?" and the word 'cabbage' came through, it would not have been as significant as the relevant "Haunting you" we received.

This system has four classes to them numbered 1 to 4 instead of the typical ABC.

- Class 1: This is an interactive spirit voice which is a direct response to a human statement, question, action, activity, or spirit voices responding to each other. All the words are clear and intelligible with or without headphones. Spirit communicates comprehensible and existentially meaningful expression of thoughts, feelings, actions, opinions, or intentions.

251

An example of spirits responding to each other was collected at Aston Hall, in Birmingham, England in the early 2000. We were on a ghost tour and a caught a female spirit on recorder responding to one of the investigators that she was present. This spirits response was following by a Class A EVP of an aggressive male saying, "don't talk!". It was a clear response to the female spirits interaction. We did not hear from her for the rest of the investigation.

- Class 2: Voice is a general statement and not a direct response to a statement, question, action, or activity by any humans. Most or all the words are generally clear and understandable, with or without the use of headphones. Spirit communicates comprehensible and existentially meaningful expression of thoughts, feelings, actions, opinions or intentions.

- Class 3: This is a non speech EVP. The spirit voice is a sound other than the spoken word, growls, singing, humming, hissing, screams are all included under this class. Things like musical Instruments, footsteps, rapping, banging etc are also covered under this classification.

- Class 4: Words are unintelligible, with or without headphones, and the EVP contains nothing of value understanding the spirit realm or spirit psychology. Spirit communicates comprehensible and existentially meaningful expression of thoughts, feelings, actions, opinions, or intentions.

Class D EVP

You may hear people mention Class D EVPs on occasion. This is the lowest form of clarity and are generally, similar to Class 4, disregarded by Investigators. This is because although you may hear something your mind can matrix audio. Much like how to can look at a photo and often see a face, the same applies to audio. Mostly these kinds of EVPs are debunked and disregarded. They are just not clear enough to come to any proper conclusion.

EVP CLASSIFICATION OVERVIEW

Class A recordings are so clear that these kind of EVPS are really what we strive for as Investigators. They are usually caught in highly active locations with a very Intelligent haunting.

Class Bs are in all the years of investigations at many locations are the most common EVPs that an investigator will capture. The audio may not be heard it in real-time; It is usually heard during audio playback. In most cases, you can make out the words after listening to the data a few times. You should not have to strain to understand the words. Often the voices are either more rapid or soft. They should still be quite plainly audible to a trained ear.

Class Cs are also very common on Investigations. These EVPs often are not clear and sound more like murmurs or whispering. Audio editing and using audio filters are usually the only way we can hear something legible.

EVP ANALYSES

During the investigation, capture brief recordings of ambient noise in each room visited, lasting between 10 to 20 seconds. These recordings are conducted in silence to provide ample background noise for later filtering during analysis. This step is vital for audio analysis, as insufficient background noise can hinder the accurate interpretation of potential EVPs. By ensuring these short recordings are taken in silence, investigators can gather adequate background noise to effectively filter out extraneous sounds and isolate any EVPs present.

Additionally, cross-check any potential evidence across multiple mediums. For instance, if an EVP is captured on audio, investigators should locate the corresponding segment in the video footage. This allows for comparison and verification of the evidence, ensuring its consistency and reliability across different formats.

When analysing evidence, it is essential to cross-reference findings across different mediums. If an EVP is detected in your video footage, it is valuable to compare it with the corresponding audio file. This comparison may reveal additional evidence such as orbs or, in fortunate cases, even figures or shadows.

I typically prioritise EVP analysis, noting any anomalies with their respective timestamps. Later, when reviewing video and photographic evidence, I pay close attention to these timestamps. Often, one piece of evidence can lead to others that either corroborate or debunk it. For instance, if audio captures footsteps and muttering, I check the video for the same timestamp, only to discover the source is another investigator in a different room. This process allows for the identification of significant findings while also filtering out explainable occurrences.

Similarly, if anomalies are captured in photographs, it is worthwhile to locate the corresponding frame in the video footage. Timestamp documentation proves invaluable here, facilitating easier identification of the relevant spot. Utilising the frame-by-frame function in video editing software aids in pinpointing the precise moment of interest.

Audio analysis demands a new skill set, including the ability to manipulate noise levels, understand frequency, range, and pitch, and navigate complex audio analysis programs. The goal of audio analysis is to discern whether an

EVP is genuine or a result of pareidolia or matrixing.

PHOTOGRAPHIC EVIDENCE ANALYSES

Repeatedly, the most common pitfalls in paranormal investigation emerge during the analysis of photographic evidence. This is primarily due to the phenomenon of matrixing, where the human brain interprets random patterns as familiar shapes or objects, often leading to misinterpretation. It requires skill and practice to discern between genuine anomalies and mundane explanations. Distinguishing between an orb and an insect or discerning a genuine face from matrixing requires a keen eye and experience. Ironically, despite relying on visual evidence, photography analysis proves to be the most challenging and time-consuming among all mediums.

It is not uncommon for paranormal investigators to be inundated with requests to examine photographs purportedly showing figures or faces in windows. These instances are prevalent and underscore the importance of thorough analysis.

In the subsequent sections, we'll delve into the most prevalent mistakes made during photographic analysis and provide insights to differentiate between genuine anomalies and explainable occurrences.

ORBS

This is perhaps one of the most ubiquitous phenomena encountered in haunted locations, yet it remains one of the most challenging to interpret, even for seasoned investigators. There is no shame in this, as discerning between an insect, dust, pollen, or a genuine orb can be exceptionally difficult. In many cases, such anomalies are debunked due to the inability to draw a conclusive determination.

The reality is that the majority of orb-like manifestations captured in photographs can be attributed to mundane sources such as dust, insects, mould spores, pollen, or other airborne particles. This underscores the critical importance of cross-referencing photographic or video evidence with audio recordings.

In the author's perspective, an "orb" captured in a photo simply represents a luminous anomaly, potentially with or without colour, within the atmosphere. However, if this luminous anomaly exhibits erratic movement or changes shape when observed in the accompanying video footage, it may indicate an insect rather than dust or another airborne particle. By examining the video footage further, if the anomaly is seen moving towards a specific point, such as a voice recorder, and coincides with the detection of a clear EVP in the audio recording at that precise moment, it adds depth to the investigation and enhances the potential significance of the anomaly.

Perhaps it zips through the air, unseen by the naked eye, heading towards an unsuspecting investigator who suddenly feels a touch. This kind of corroborative evidence adds depth to the investigation and makes for more compelling evidence compared to a solitary ball of light. Without corroboration, all that can be concluded is that it is intriguing.

Another common misconception about orbs is the belief that dust particles appear as white orbs, while paranormal orbs exhibit colour. However, this is far from accurate. Dust particles can manifest in a variety of colours, ranging from red, pink, blue, yellow to green, and beyond. The diversity of coloured objects in our environment means that dust particles can take on any hue imaginable.

Insects, on the other hand, often present as bright, elongated orbs. The challenge with flying insects is that their appearance may not resemble typical insect features on camera or in photographs. They may appear as spherical balls of light with no discernible features, or as balls with a tail of light trailing behind them. However, there are instances where insects are easily identifiable and can be promptly debunked.

Raindrops also have the potential to mimic orb-like anomalies, appearing as bright white comet-like shapes or small cylindrical orbs. Moreover, raindrops can exhibit colour, much like how rainbows are formed. The possibilities of what can be mistaken for orbs are extensive and varied.

So, how do we, as investigators, distinguish between genuine paranormal phenomena and other natural occurrences like insects or dust particles? If an anomaly is not immediately identifiable as an insect or dust particle—often discernible by factors such as density, shape, or movement—we rely on corroboration.

For instance, there have been numerous occasions where we captured an EVP and upon reviewing the video footage, observed what appears to be a genuine orb darting towards the voice recorder. Similarly, we have observed instances where investigators, on video, appear to be physically affected, coinciding with the appearance of an orb either emanating from or moving toward them. These occurrences often coincide with other activity happening around us at the time the orb is captured.

All other orbs, if they cannot be definitively identified, are considered interesting yet unidentifiable. Sometimes, it is easier to identify an orb of interest on video rather than in a photograph. The anomalous movement patterns, shifting shapes, or unusual colours may indicate something beyond ordinary. While such observations are intriguing and noteworthy, we approach them with scepticism unless there is additional context or evidence suggesting significance.

In our analysis, we prioritise explanations grounded in natural phenomena, unless there is compelling evidence to suggest otherwise. Given the multitude of variables at play, particularly in haunted locations, it is often challenging to draw definitive conclusions without corroborating evidence.

MIST LIKE ANOMALIES

Mist anomalies, often captured in photographs, can be easily mistaken for paranormal phenomena. When encountering such anomalies, it is essential to first rule out common explanations.

For instance, consider whether there was any cigarette smoke or other sources of smoke present in the vicinity. Environmental factors, such as weather conditions or humidity levels, could also contribute to the appearance of mist-like phenomena. In cold conditions, the breath of the person taking the photos may appear as mist in the images. Additionally, matrixing—a phenomenon where the brain interprets random patterns as familiar shapes—could also play a role, especially in misty environments.

Moreover, ensure that camera lenses are clean and free of dust, as contaminants can distort the appearance of photographs. Photographic contamination or movement may also create false mist-like effects. Sometimes, subtle smoke molecules become visible only when illuminated by the camera flash, especially in low-light conditions.

Considering factors like nearby fires or sources of heat, such as fireplaces or outdoor fires, is also important in assessing the origin of mist anomalies. By meticulously investigating these potential causes, investigators can more accurately determine the nature of the anomaly captured in the photograph.

These questions underscore the critical importance of accurately documenting your surroundings when collecting evidence. With the correct environmental data and awareness of who is present, many variables can be either ruled out or confirmed, helping to avoid misinterpretation of anomalies. Without such data, drawing conclusions about observed anomalies becomes impossible.

Once all possibilities have been meticulously examined and eliminated, any remaining anomalies become more intriguing. We follow a systematic process of cross-referencing all mediums of evidence to determine if there is any corroborating evidence indicating a presence at the time the photograph was taken.

To facilitate this process, it can be helpful to create a table with categories for video, audio, and photographic evidence, each with corresponding timestamps of findings to be examined in more detail later. By methodically going through each list and cross-referencing timestamps with other mediums, we can identify any anomalies that may have been overlooked initially. This method has often led to the discovery of interesting anomalies that were previously missed. We repeat this process for each type of evidence collected, ensuring thoroughness and accuracy in our analysis.

SHADOWS AND FIGURES

These come up less frequently but again they are easy for our minds to create if the circumstances are right. This is particularly true of things like doorways or darker crevices. This is because often there is different shades, uneven light or texture that is more observable in darker colours. Any kind of disturbance in shade can cause the mind to matrix to try to make sense of what it is seeing. And low and behold a shadow figure or person pops out of the photo at you.

Analysing these photos is the same as any others. You look at all the evidence in the photo to determine could it be matrixing. This can be very difficult if all your seeing is a creepy dark shadow hiding in the closet watching you. In these cases, it is often a good idea to have another team member look at the photograph to determine what they think they see. I always ask how they have come to that conclusion. Every team member should be held to the highest standard when it comes to the analysis of data. They should be able to explain their reasoning, methodology and conclusion before making a final decision.

In many cases the clients will talk about seeing a ghost or identify the ghost in the photo as great Aunt Mary or Grandpa Joe for example. We must take these things with a pinch of salt as sometimes its fear and wishful thinking on behalf of the client. Double exposure involving a team member can cause figures to appear in the photograph.

There is a famous photo of a woman sitting in a park. A family member took a photo straight on and all said that when the photo was taken there was no one behind her. When the photograph was developed, a man is seen standing behind her that has an exact and striking resemblance to her husband who had dies 18 years previously. This is an interesting photograph as in the trees behind them, most people see a scary looking cloaked figure. Think the movie scream and you get the idea. When analysing the photo, it would be hard to debunk the male behind whose family claim died 18 years previously. In fact, when you compare photos of her husband when living and the said photograph it does indeed look like her husband. On top of that no one at the table noticed the male. You would think that someone would have seen him given his proximity to the group.

The Hooded figure who appears to be watching on from the trees I a very sinister way is without doubt matrixing. I would invite the reader to go and have a look for yourselves and see what conclusions you can draw from the photograph itself. Its unusual in the fact you have the supposed dead husband in it and a perfect example of how our minds matrix images that simple are not there.

FACES

In almost 90% of cases, without question, the face or faces you see in a photograph is matrixing. Some can appear very convincing, and it will take close analyses of the photo to decide.

The first thing I assume is matrixing and it is only after very careful examination and peer review that we rule it out. Actually, determining a face is unexplained is an extremely rare and happy occurrence. This is where it is often a great idea to have someone else have a look at the photo to see what conclusion they come up with and why. Again, we go through the process of what has been listed under matrixing above, to determine if we feel we need to do a corroboration of our other mediums. Most often than not there is no need to go any further. If we all come to the same conclusion and then debunk. Eventually you get an eye for making a quick determination but like with orbs etc it can take time and practice.

There is also the very famous photo of Freddie Jackson who appears behind his friend during a full squadron photo. The only problem was allegedly Freddy Jackson had been killed two days prior. This is a verified fact although his death is not the same as is mentioned in the retelling of this story. The photo was taken around the time of the start of WWI. The interesting thing about this photograph is that his squadron identified him. His funeral took place the day of the photograph was taken. The other interesting thing about this photograph is that some said it could have been a double exposure. Now this is a possibility with cameras at the time however, everyone in the photo is wearing a hat. Freddy is not. Is this a soldier who did not know he had died and was attending the photo session? Was he coming to say one final farewell to his friends? Or is this a trick of outdated cameras. The difficult thing with this photo is that he was identified by those who know him and allegedly his family. I will leave it to the reader to make the decision.

ANALYSING LIGHT ANOMALIES: THE TWO R'S.

When examining photographs containing significant light anomalies, two key concepts to consider are refraction and reflection.

Light anomalies frequently appear in photographs submitted to investigators for analysis due to their potential to be caused by various explainable circumstances. Analysing light anomalies in paranormal investigation photos can pose several challenges due to various factors that can affect the appearance of light in images. Here are some common

259

problems encountered and ways to circumvent them:

- Natural Light Flares: Natural light flares from the sun or other light sources can create anomalies in photos. To circumvent this issue, investigators should be mindful of the position of the sun or other light sources when taking photos and avoid capturing images directly facing intense light sources.
- Unclean Camera Lenses: Dust, smudges, or fingerprints on camera lenses can distort images and create false light anomalies. Ensuring that camera lenses are clean before taking photos can help mitigate this problem.
- Reflections and Refractions: Reflections or refractions of light from external sources can cause unexpected light anomalies in photos. Investigators should be aware of reflective surfaces in the environment and consider whether external light sources could be causing reflections or refractions.
- Electrical Issues: Malfunctioning electrical devices or electrical disturbances can produce bursts of light that may appear as anomalies in photos. Investigating the location for potential electrical issues and ruling them out can help prevent misinterpretation of light anomalies.
- Close Objects Interference: Objects close to the camera lens, such as camera straps, hair strands, or dust particles, can create light anomalies when illuminated by the camera flash. Keeping objects away from the camera lens and ensuring a clear field of view can reduce the likelihood of such interference.
- Environmental Conditions: Environmental factors such as fog, mist, or precipitation can interact with light and create visual anomalies in photos. Understanding the prevailing environmental conditions during the investigation and considering their potential effects on light anomalies can aid in accurate interpretation.

To circumvent these challenges, investigators should exercise caution when analysing light anomalies in photos, thoroughly examine the environmental conditions and potential sources of interference and consider alternative explanations before attributing anomalies to paranormal activity. Additionally, capturing multiple photos from different angles and under different conditions can help validate the presence of genuine anomalies and differentiate them from mundane causes.

INTERPRETING TEMPERATURE READINGS

Interpreting temperature readings in paranormal investigations can yield valuable insights into potential paranormal activity, but it also comes with its own set of challenges. Here are some pros and cons of using temperature readings and ways to circumvent common issues:

Pros:

- Indicator of Anomalies: Sudden fluctuations in temperature, especially unexplained drops or increases, can be indicative of paranormal activity. This can provide valuable evidence to support claims of hauntings or supernatural occurrences.
- Corroboration with Other Evidence: Temperature readings can complement other forms of evidence, such as EVP recordings or visual sightings. When multiple forms of evidence align, it strengthens the case for paranormal activity.
- Objective Measurement: Temperature readings provide quantitative data that can be objectively analysed and documented, adding a level of scientific rigor to paranormal investigations.

Cons:

- Natural Factors: Temperature fluctuations can be influenced by natural factors such as drafts, HVAC systems, weather conditions, or the presence of nearby heat sources. Distinguishing between natural and paranormal causes can be challenging.
- Subjectivity in Interpretation: Interpreting temperature readings in the context of paranormal investigations can be subjective. Investigators may attribute significance to temperature fluctuations that could have mundane explanations.
- Equipment Limitations: Temperature measurement devices may have limitations in accuracy or sensitivity, leading to potential inaccuracies in readings. Use high-quality equipment and calibrate it properly to minimise errors.

Ways to Circumvent Issues:

- Baseline Measurements: Take baseline temperature measurements of the investigation area to establish a reference point. This helps

261

in distinguishing between normal fluctuations and anomalous changes.

- Environmental Assessment: Conduct a thorough assessment of the environment to identify potential sources of temperature fluctuations, such as drafts, heating/cooling systems, or external weather conditions.

- Multiple Data Points: Use multiple temperature measurement devices placed in different locations within the investigation area to gather comprehensive data. Corroborating readings from multiple devices can enhance the reliability of the findings.

- Control Experiments: Conduct control experiments in controlled environments to understand how natural factors affect temperature readings. This can help in distinguishing between natural and paranormal causes of temperature fluctuations.

- Contextual Analysis: Interpret temperature readings in the context of other evidence collected during the investigation, such as audio recordings, visual observations, and eyewitness accounts. Look for patterns or correlations that support the presence of paranormal activity.

By considering these factors and employing best practices in temperature measurement and analysis, investigators can mitigate potential challenges and derive more reliable conclusions from temperature readings in paranormal investigations.

EVIDENCE COLLECTION CASE STUDY

On 20th April 2024, My team and I accompanied another team to investigate the grounds of The Sunset Hospital in Dalkeith, Perth Western Australia. We arrived early just so we could get a feel for the location, prior to meeting the other team. In all there were 5 of us for that night. It should be noted, you cannot enter the hospital; it is being renovated and we did not have the appropriate permissions. However, security onsite was aware of us being there.

We stayed on location from 5.15pm and I did not get home till around 8:30pm that night. The equipment we had on us was simple, as we would be walking around most of the evening. An IR portable handheld camera and stand; Multiple Voice recorders; Dowsing Rods, Motions sensors, Headphones the spirit box, an Ovilus type device and photographic camera.

It took about two days to fully analyse all the data that we had captured. Here is How some of the mediums were used to corroborate some of our EVPs.

EVP Message – "Invasion" and "World War 2." And "Who shot me" – believed to be communicated by the same male spirit. We also received the words "Hitler" and "prisoner". The context was correct because the hospital was used as a psychiatric hospital to house soldiers returning from the Great War and WW2. When these EVPs were captured, we were outside the wing of the hospital these soldiers would have been treated. On the video at this time the motion sensors were going off and we viewed light anomalies shoot into the recorder. That shot away and the EVPs stop.

EVP Message – "Please don't go"
At this point we could see that this was in direct response to some of the investigators discussing moving to a different location because we were videoing the scene at the time.

EVP Message – "Please Go."
When reviewing the recorded SB7 material during the 5 minutes we received multiple requests to please go, the same message was received by the SB7 being used by a different investigator.

EVP Message – "She Cares."
on reviewing the time stamp on the video, we could see that this was in response to one of two possibilities. I had told my teammate Jack to be careful of some barbed wire I thought he might be getting close to. The second option was I has just called my husband to say goodnight to my 1 year old as I was not home to put her to bed which Jack had mentioned to the spirits moments before. On his video we could also see about this time that there was a light in the building that was flashing, which stopped shortly afterwards.

EVP Message – "Helen"
This name came up for separate investigators who were not together at the time. We do not know the significance of the name, but I believe it is one of the female spirits that reside there.

EVP Message "ineligible ... Baseball team"
At this point our video showed other investigators not far away discussing sports which had been mentioned on their devices.

EVP Message – "Guard" – shortly before this another investigator had let the security guard know we were with them as we were standing quite a distance away. I then received on my recorder the word Guard. I did not know the guard was just being discussed in an area a little farther away.

These are just some of the ways in which we look at multiple sources to determine the information we are receiving and the significance of those findings. Usually there is a reason why things are said, it might be in response to something they are seeing, hearing, history or some significance to them. By cross referencing our time frames across mediums we can put more weight when we have context to what we are seeing and hearing

CONCLUSION EVIDENCE ANALYSIS

The investigation of paranormal phenomena involves meticulous analysis of various types of evidence, including audio recordings, photographs, videos, temperature readings, and eyewitness testimonies. This phase of the investigation is crucial for discerning potential signs of paranormal activity and distinguishing them from natural or explainable occurrences. Here, we delve into the methodologies and considerations essential for effective evidence analysis.

- Approach to Evidence Analysis: Upon the completion of an investigation, the collected evidence undergoes comprehensive analysis to uncover any potential anomalies indicative of paranormal activity. This process requires a combination of technical expertise, critical thinking, and attention to detail. Investigators must remain objective and diligent in their examination to ensure the integrity of the findings.
- Challenges in Evidence Analysis: One of the primary challenges in analysing paranormal evidence lies in the subjective nature of interpretation. Phenomena such as orbs in photographs or unexplained sounds in audio recordings can have multiple possible explanations, ranging from natural phenomena to equipment malfunctions. Distinguishing between genuine paranormal activity and mundane occurrences requires careful scrutiny and corroborating evidence.
- Critical Considerations: To mitigate the impact of subjective interpretation, investigators employ several critical considerations during evidence analysis:
- Baseline Measurements: Establishing baseline measurements for environmental factors such as temperature, humidity, and electromagnetic fields provides a reference point for identifying deviations that may indicate paranormal activity.
- Corroboration: Cross-referencing multiple forms of evidence,

264

including audio, visual, and environmental data, helps corroborate potential paranormal phenomena. Consistency across different mediums strengthens the credibility of the findings.

- Controlled Experiments: Conducting controlled experiments in controlled environments enables investigators to differentiate between natural and paranormal causes of observed phenomena. By replicating conditions and monitoring variables, researchers can assess the likelihood of paranormal influences.

- Expert Analysis: In complex cases, seeking input from experts in relevant fields, such as audio engineering or photography, can provide valuable insights into the authenticity of the evidence. Expert analysis enhances the rigor and credibility of the investigation's conclusions.

Evidence analysis is the cornerstone of paranormal investigations, guiding researchers in their quest to unravel the mysteries of the unexplained. Through systematic examination and meticulous scrutiny, investigators strive to uncover compelling evidence of paranormal phenomena while remaining grounded in scientific principles. By embracing a rigorous analytical approach and adhering to best practices, the pursuit of understanding the supernatural continues to evolve, offering glimpses into realms beyond the ordinary.

EVIDENCE SHARING

Introducing evidence sharing involves preparing to disseminate findings from paranormal investigations to various audiences, including fellow investigators, clients, or the general public. It encompasses compiling, organising, and presenting evidence in a clear and accessible format, ensuring that the significance of the findings is effectively communicated. This phase of the investigation serves to foster transparency, collaboration, and knowledge exchange within the paranormal community, ultimately contributing to the collective understanding of supernatural phenomena.

SHARING WITH THE PARANORMAL TEAM

Once our evidence analysis is complete, the next step is to share our findings with team members before extending them to clients or the paranormal community. Given that each team member has been examining their respective data, this phase allows for a collective review of the investigation's discoveries. When streamlining the process, it is beneficial for each member to send their files to a designated person who can then consolidate them on a single computer. Subsequently, each team member takes turns presenting their findings, including any uncertainties or debunked elements. Ideally have a central coordinator prepared to organise all information post-presentation.

This may be your initial exposure to other individuals' EVPs, marking a pivotal moment in the analysis process. As you listen to their findings, connections may emerge between their evidence and your own discoveries. It is during these exchanges that messages can often be linked, shedding light on previously obscure elements. I've frequently observed instances where an EVP I captured gains clarity and significance, when juxtaposed with evidence provided by another team member, highlighting the collaborative nature of our investigations.

During a recent investigation with a new team, the name "Nicola" repeatedly surfaced, appearing four times through both the SB7 and voice recorder. It was not until we reached the stage of sharing evidence with the rest of the team that the significance of this name became apparent. To our surprise, we discovered that "Nicola" was the full name of the psychic investigator who typically accompanied the team on-site. This unexpected revelation added an intriguing layer of connection to our investigation, highlighting the mysterious ways in which information can manifest during paranormal exploration.

Once we have discussed all our evidence, which usually takes a while as there can be debate and discussion, now is the time to put it all together and decide what to do next.

In the case of Sunset, there are limited actions to take. Given its status as a public location rather than a residence or business seeking assistance. Our primary decision revolves around ensuring it remains a site for future investigation, with a focus on potential replication of results. Additionally, we aim to delve deeper into the history of Sunset, particularly regarding its association with programs at the WA State Library. Perhaps this research will shed light on activities such as baseball. Furthermore, I intend to pursue leads related to names encountered during our visit. For those in Perth, WA interested in exploring Sunset Hospital, we anticipate regular visits in the foreseeable future and extend an invitation to join us by contacting the author.

SHARING YOUR FINDINGS WITH THE PARANORMAL COMMUNITY

Engaging with the paranormal community involves delving into realms where the boundaries between fact and speculation blur, where the inexplicable often reigns supreme. It is a space where stories of ghostly encounters, UFO sightings, and cryptid sightings are not only accepted but eagerly sought. Within this community, there is a shared sense of curiosity, a hunger to explore the unknown and unravel the mysteries that elude conventional scientific explanation.

One of the most compelling aspects of engaging with the paranormal community is the opportunity to exchange experiences and theories with like-minded individuals. Whether discussing personal encounters with the supernatural or debating the latest findings in paranormal research, there is a sense of camaraderie that comes from sharing these experiences with others who understand and believe.

However, approach this engagement with an open mind and a healthy dose of scepticism. While the paranormal community is built on a foundation of belief in the extraordinary, it is also essential to critically evaluate evidence and consider alternative explanations. This balance between curiosity and critical thinking is what drives meaningful discourse and pushes the boundaries of our understanding of the unexplained.

Engaging with the paranormal community offers an opportunity to explore the cultural and psychological dimensions of belief in the supernatural. From the folklore and mythology that have shaped our understanding of ghosts and monsters to the psychological factors that influence our perceptions, there is a wealth of fascinating topics to explore.

In essence, engaging with the paranormal community is about more than just swapping ghost stories or debating the existence of non-human entities. It is about fostering a sense of wonder, curiosity, and intellectual curiosity in the face of the unknown. Whether you're a sceptic, a believer, or somewhere in between, there is a place for you in this diverse and endlessly fascinating community.

When engaging in paranormal debates, it is crucial to maintain ethical standards to ensure that discussions remain respectful, constructive, and grounded in integrity. Here are some key principles to consider:

- Acknowledge that beliefs about the paranormal vary widely among individuals. Approach discussions with an open mind, showing respect for differing viewpoints even if you don't agree with them.
- Present evidence accurately and honestly, avoiding exaggeration or distortion of facts to support a particular viewpoint. Misrepresenting evidence undermines the credibility of your argument and can harm the overall integrity of the debate.
- Thinking: Foster an environment where critical thinking is valued and encouraged. Encourage participants to question assumptions, evaluate evidence critically, and consider alternative explanations before drawing conclusions.
- Recognise that personal experiences with the paranormal can be deeply meaningful to individuals. Approach discussions with empathy

and sensitivity, avoiding dismissive or derogatory language that may belittle others' experiences or beliefs.

- Base arguments on empirical evidence whenever possible, relying on scientific research, eyewitness testimony, and other credible sources. Avoid relying solely on anecdotal evidence or unverified claims, as these can be unreliable and easily misinterpreted.

- Keep discussions civil and respectful, even in the face of disagreement. Avoid personal attacks, insults, or hostile behaviour toward others. Remember that productive debate is about exchanging ideas, not winning arguments at any cost.

- Maintain a healthy scepticism and be willing to challenge your own beliefs as well as those of others. Avoid accepting claims at face value without sufficient evidence and be open to revising your opinions in light of new information.

By adhering to these ethical principles, paranormal debates can become more enriching and productive exchanges of ideas, fostering greater understanding and appreciation for the complexities of the unknown.

Maintaining confidentiality regarding people's names and addresses is paramount when sharing supernatural cases, ensuring the protection of individuals' privacy. By withholding personal identifying information, such as names and addresses, investigators uphold ethical standards and demonstrate respect for those involved.

This safeguard not only prevents potential harm, such as unwanted attention or intrusion, but also fosters a safe environment for individuals to share their experiences without fear of repercussion or exploitation.

SHARING THE INFORMATION WITH YOUR CLIENT

Introducing the sharing of information with a client, especially when delving into profound topics, like the paranormal entity that has been appearing in the corner of their bedroom at night, requires a delicate balance of professionalism, empathy, and respect for their beliefs and boundaries.

It is an investigators job to creating a safe and supportive space where they can explore the depths of their experiences with sincerity and understanding.

Discussions will be guided by a mutual commitment to confidentiality, ensuring that personal information and stories are treated with the utmost respect and discretion. My goal is to empower you to navigate the mysteries of the supernatural realm, with clarity and confidence, while honouring the nature of the knowledge we uncover along the way.

As a professional investigator, it is crucial to transparently disclose, all notable evidence to clients, even those that have been debunked.

This can be an incredibly distressing time, for individuals experiencing haunting phenomena in their home or workplace. It is essential to be well-prepared and empathetic to the emotions your client may be experiencing.

While you may return to the safety of your own bed, your client may be left grappling with unsettling EVPs and other evidence you have presented.

Considering having a client liaison within your team, as this can be highly beneficial. However, when it comes to sharing information, I would advise for the Liaison and the Team Leader to take the lead in discussions. By this stage, a clear plan to address the issue, should have been established, or it should be determined if further investigation and research are required.

Make sure you make an official client report in writing that they can sit down and look at when they are calmer. Bombarding a person with evidence can be unsettling and difficult to absorb. Having it in writing for them to look at later is, in my belief, essential.

It should include all the details of the investigation and any relevant findings. You should write it on letterhead, with your name and logo if you have one.

People often inquire, about what goes into an investigation report. Essentially, we include all evidence, but it is not just the evidence that matters; it is the interpretation. Remaining objective and calm is crucial, especially when clients are anxious and fearing the worst. It falls upon investigators to be methodical, compassionate, and logical in their communication of information.

We include debunked elements and explain why, while significant evidence merits its own section. Providing reasons for conclusions or lack thereof is equally important, even if it is not always what clients want to hear, so tact is key in discussions. We present findings and interpretations, allowing clients to make their own decisions. The primary focus is on what, if anything, can be done to address the situation if resolution is desired.

Sometimes, it is complex, requiring further investigation or referral to specialists. It is crucial not to promise specific outcomes upfront; rather, the investigator's role is to investigate and draw conclusions based on evidence. While positive outcomes can be advised, no guarantees are made.

Organising evidence systematically is essential, ensuring efficiency during discussions. Occasionally, tough conversations are necessary, such as advising clients to seek other forms of help if occult practices, or substance abuse are involved. Refusal to assist until underlying issues are addressed may be necessary, with referrals provided if unable to help directly.

Sometimes, no firm resolution is reached; the absence of evidence may call for further investigation or alternative approaches.

Ultimately, empowering the client to take control of their situation is key, to respecting their decisions even if they differ from the investigator's perspective. Our group offers printable resources for investigators, available upon request.

11 HAUNTING RESOLUTIONS

In the quiet solitude of evening, where shadows dance and the curtain between the realms grows thin, let us embark into the domain of haunting resolution. Within the depths of our souls, we are often beckoned to confront the ghosts of our past, to reconcile the echoes of our choices, and to forge a path towards clarity and understanding

In this ethereal realm, resolution is not merely a destination but a melody that lingers in the corridors of our minds, urging us to confront our fears and embrace the truth that lies within. It is a journey fraught with uncertainty, where the line between reality and illusion often blurs, and where the echoes of our decisions reverberate through the corridors of time.

As we navigate the labyrinth of our innermost thoughts and emotions, we start to unravel the mysteries that bind us and discover the power that lies in embracing our shadows. For it is only through resolving the ghosts of the past, that we can truly find peace and forge a future illuminated, by the light of our own mortality.

As spectral earthbound guardians, we are called upon to navigate the currents that bind the living to the departed, to untangle the webs of regret and anguish that ensnare restless spirits. Through the eyes of mortality, we glimpse the untold stories, the sorrows unspoken, and loves left unfulfilled.

In this sacred undertaking, we tread the delicate balance between worlds, weaving threads of understanding and compassion to guide the lost souls towards their final peace. Each spirit we encounter bears a tale as old as time itself, a testament to the intricate tapestry of the human experience and the enduring power of redemption.

Paranormal Investigators seek solace for the departed, healing for the living, and resolution for the hauntings that linger in the shadows of our collective consciousness.

The idea of the living and dead coexisting in an ideal situation, is a concept that sparks profound contemplation. In such a scenario, the boundary between life and death becomes a harmonious and symbiotic relationship, between the two realms.

Picture a scenario where the veil separating the living and the dead is thin, where spirits freely wander among the living, and where the departed are not forgotten, but revered as guides and guardians. For many of the hauntings we, as investigators, encounter, this is the ideal scenario and not as far-fetched as one might think.

From my own spectral tales, there is a family in Western Australia who is living this tight rope, though tentatively. The current owners made it clear they were happy for their resident female ghost to stay. To live in the confines of the house, she had once called home, and still wished to call home. It was on the condition she did not appear or overly bother the living in her antics. Paranormal activity in the house stopped after this conversation, but I have no doubt the resident spirit is happily living, alongside the current owners. For now, in this home at least, there is a calm and a peaceful co-existence.

I know of another family here in Western Australia who, once being told their resident spirit was a happy former owner, were more than happy to co-exist. They have built up a lovely relationship over the years, with the resident ghost, even closing the garage and turning off lights, should the homeowner forget.

When the living and the dead reach an agreement to coexist, it marks a delicate balance between realms. It is a recognition that both have their place in the universe, with the living honouring the memories and legacies of those who have passed, while navigating their own existence in the present. The agreement entails a mutual respect for boundaries and a shared understanding that each has a role to play, in this life and beyond. This is the Holy Grail of haunting resolutions.

In a shroud of darkness, not all hauntings yield to reason or safety. Some defy explanation, lurking in the corners of our consciousness like shadows refusing to dissipate. Behind closed doors and within crumbling walls, shadows come, with the never ending feelings of dread and uncertainty.

In the depths of abandoned places and seemingly ordinary homes, there lies a truth far more chilling than the living can comprehend. These hauntings, untethered from the laws of the living world, possess a malevolent energy. This energy brings with it sinister intent, drawing the curious closer, with an irresistible allure.

But heed this warning: to confront such hauntings, is to dance with the unknown, where danger lurks in every corner and every flicker of unseen movement. For not all hauntings seek resolution; some exist merely to ensnare the unwary in their web of terror, leaving only darkness in their wake.

For the hapless paranormal investigator tasked with confronting these unyielding hauntings, each step forward is a plunge into the abyss of the unknown. Armed with only our wits and an arsenal of investigative tools, we tread cautiously into the realm of the supernatural.

Every creaking floorboard and flickering light becomes a harbinger of impending danger, a sign that we are not alone in the darkness. Yet, driven by a relentless pursuit of truth and understanding, we press on, our resolve tested with each passing moment.

It is often when we delve deeper into the heart of the haunting, the line between observer and participant blurs. We become entangled in a dance with forces beyond our control and often our understanding.

In this shadowy realm of uncertainty and fear, the paranormal investigator must navigate a treacherous path, where the price of discovery may exact a toll, too high to bear. And as we stare into the abyss, it is soon realised that some hauntings are not meant to be understood, but merely survived.

MOVING TRAPPED SPIRITS ON

Within the fabric of reality, lies the enigmatic phenomenon of spirits lingering between worlds. They are caught in a liminal space, caught in the earthly realm where they stay, caught in a realm they often wish to escape. It is within this landscape that the art of haunting resolution unfolds—a sacred duty undertaken by those who possess the unique ability and desire to bridge the gap between the living and the departed

In the pursuit of peace for restless souls and closure for the living, we embark on a journey fraught with emotion. in our quest to bring tranquillity to the tormented spirits, we may encounter malevolent forces that seek to thwart our efforts. Yet, armed with courage, compassion, and an unwavering resolve, it is our duty. For every soul deserves a chance to find peace in the embrace of the eternal realm.

Haunting resolution is really an odyssey of empathy, enlightenment, and transformation as we try to illuminate the darkness and guide lost souls to their final rest.

The key to helping a trapped spirit find their forever home, is to find out the reason why they are tethered to a location or a person. Helping these spirits let go, is a delicate and profound process that a deep connection to the spiritual realm.

In the case of unexpected deaths, often loved ones will stay with their family members, as they never had a chance to say their final heart wrenching goodbyes. It could be that they are angry or maybe they want to stay for a specific reason. A wedding is coming up, they want to witness the birth of their grandchild. It could be as simple as wanting some closure to an issue, whose resolution is now beyond their grasp.

In some cases, the problem comes from the living, who act like anchors, pulling the souls of their deceased ones near. In many cases the overwhelming grief of a loved one, can keep a spirit here, as they try to help their loved ones go on living the life, that now eludes them. Maybe the death was so sudden that they don't even know they have passed on. This can be the case for many child spirits, who may not understand what has happened to them. In many cases it can come down to a simple case of fear. Maybe they were not good in life, and they are afraid of possible repercussions in death. Maybe their wishes were not met on death or their final resting place disturbed. There are any number of reasons why a spirit could be trapped and not willing or able to move on. With each case as varied as the souls that linger there, resolution is often in the eye of the beholder. It can be long and complex process or short and simple.

From my own case load we had a case in Coventry, near Birmingham England, where a wife, Jenny, in her 60s, had reported she believed her late husband was causing issues within her home. They were an extremely religious, God fearing Catholic family. He had been a recreational diver and had gone missing, presumed drowned oversees. In the months after his disappearance at sea, there was angry unexplained banging's and activity within the home. Things being thrown, doors slammed, chairs were dragged by unseen hands across the kitchen, in front of truly terrified guests. Jenny was lost, frightened and confused, as there had never been any paranormal activity in the home. She had shared this home with her husband for 38 years and raised three children. Eventually, she had her answers, as to the cause, when she witnessed her husband standing in their living room, looking distressed, before vanishing. To say she was truly heartbroken as this sight, would be not to honour the 38 years, she was a devoted wife to this person whim she loved so much. There love was an enduring love story that had taken the worst kind of turn. She needed answers and called on us. to provide them.

Desperate and motivated to somehow save her husband's soul, she had confided in friends. She was advised to bring in her local parish priest. He could after all, send the dearly departed husband onto the blessed eternity, he had so adamantly believed in. Lingering between worlds made no sense to the family, who could not understand why his soul was not in heaven. He was a good man, and honourable man and loved by many. The priest came in and did a house blessing, praying for the deceased. For a week thing remained silent, until one night the banging's started again. At her wits end, a family member convinced her to contact our local paranormal investigator group. We were charged then, with uncovering why Jennys husband, was not at rest.

274

This was my very first case, in a private home. After two days, our paranormal group believed we had the answer and a plan of resolution.

It turned out, being very religious, the lingering husband was very upset he had not had his last rites and a proper Catholic service or place of rest, as such he could not go onto the next life. The words "grave", "Last rites", "Buried" "Missing", "Priest", "Say goodbye" and "remember" were all captured on EVP. As well as some loving messages for his distressed wife and children.

The family priest, who had not approved of the paranormal investigation, came in and reluctantly preformed last rites and a blessing. A memorial was held at his church two weeks later, for family and friends, to be able to say their goodbyes and I am sure allowed him to say his. For it is my strong belief that spirits attend the funeral of the earthly bodies.

Following the memorial and a promise of a memorial plaque later to remember him, all activity in the home completely ceased. In a sweet turn of events, a short time later, we were informed that he returned one last time, to visit his grieving wife. This time, however, he was standing in the kitchen, smiling, and nodded approvingly at his wife, before slowly dissipating. His last appearance gave Jenny and her family much comfort during their time of grief and was the bittersweet ending to their enduring love story.

This is a case, the deceased had a belief system and when his belief about what should happen around his death were not met, he was not able to move on to the next world.

By fulfilling those wishes, he was able to move on peacefully and remind his wife, through a final visit, how love endures, and the spirit continues, even in death. It is to this day, this is one of my favourite cases and one that brings me comfort when facing the deaths, of those I love.

The human soul is a complex and intangible essence that embodies the core of individual identity, encompassing emotions, consciousness, and spiritual beliefs. It is believed by many to be eternal, transcending physical existence.

Frequently, we encounter narratives of individuals nearing the end of their lives, clinging on until they are reunited with a cherished person. It is as if their souls yearn for one final connection before departing from their physical forms. Similarly, we hear accounts of individuals remaining in this world out of profound love for their families. Upon receiving reassurance from a loved one that it is acceptable to depart and that their family will endure, they peacefully transition from this life. These poignant stories underscore the profound impact of love and connection in both life and death.

This powerful connection can prevent a spirit moving on, because, of the intense grief of their loved ones. I have found this is more often the case with sudden deaths. Parents who lose their children, young adults who have passed on suddenly or children whose parents cannot let go, are prime targets for this kind of haunting. Often child spirits will remain with their grieving families because their grief acts as an anchor.

This is a very delicate kind of resolution because, you are most often than not, dealing with unimaginable pain and grief. There is no time limit on grieving, and you cannot just let go of the pain, you have to work through it, in order to come out the other side. For some, in the moment, it is impossible to imagine, and neither should we expect them to. The acute grieving period, unless absolutely necessary or requested, is not the time for resolution.

The key to this kind of haunting is acknowledgment and acceptance, that their loved one is gone. Often the spirit, just being told that they can move on that their living family is ok, is enough to resolve this kind of haunting. However, the reality with this kind of haunting, it can take years for the living to get to that point.

Sometimes it takes professional grief counselling, for the family to get to the point when they can release their loved ones to the other side. This is particularly true for parents who have lost their children, unexpectedly and tragically.

Helping spirits and living people let go, is a very delicate process and requires a lot of empathy, understanding, compassion and patience. The steps that may aid in assisting spirits to find peace and move on, can also apply to the living struggling to let go. This mainly pertains to human spirits who find themselves trapped, seeking assistance to liberate themselves from the confines of this realm and transition into the next phase of existence.

But what of other spirits whose needs and emotions are more complex? It all begins by actively listening to the spirit's story. Spirits often linger because they have unresolved issues or unfulfilled desires. By listening to their grievances and acknowledging their presence, you create a space for them to express themselves. This can take multiple visits, over a considerable amount of time, depending on the situation.

Show compassion and empathy towards the spirit, acknowledge, and understand their pain and struggles and let them know that you are there to help them find peace. Sometimes, spirits are holding onto guilt or regret, and offering forgiveness and understanding can be immensely healing. You may also bring in an appropriate religious or spiritual leader, who can help them find forgiveness and peace.

Once you know why they are still lingering here, help the spirit find closure by addressing any unresolved issues or unfinished business they may have. This could involve helping them communicate a final message to a loved one, fulfilling a last wish, or resolving a past trauma. We had a case up at a notorious children's institution, where child spirits abound, tethered by past traumas inflicted on them. Many have been able to be freed by simply acknowledging that what happened to them was wrong and telling their story, so that the wrongs that occurred are no longer a secret. Attempting to help a spirit with unresolved issues is not always possible

. There are many times where this is not possible and talking about the reasons why, with a spirit, maybe enough to allow them to let go and move on. Sometimes resolution is not possible because time has passed for justice to be served.

This is the very sad case of a spirit that lingers near to where I grew up. Her tale is a sad one and has one of the most bazaar twists, that I have ever come across. It is an unresolved haunting but a tale that I feel must be told. It involves two terrible murders that happened 157 years apart. And one oddly that I have a personal interest in due to proximity at the time of the second murder.

Erdington is a small suburb of Birmingham, England that dates back to the 9th century. The old English community, which has its fair share of ghosts, evolved from a rural village to a popular midway point for those traveling between Chester and London in the 18th and 19th centuries. Yet there is a dark chapter to Erdington's history that continues to haunt its residents. Both figuratively and as I found out, literally. It centres, for those who ever want to visit, around Kingsbury Road.

Our tale starts on Whit Monday, 26th May 1817, when 20 year old Mary Ashford, went out to a dance at Tyburn house.

At 6:30 a.m. on May 27, 1817, a labourer named George Jackson came across a bundle of clothing, a hat, and shoes near a water-filled pit. He alerted locals who dragged the pool and found the body of Mary Ashford with bruising on her arms, presumably raped before her death. Footsteps of a man and woman were found in a nearby field. Authorities scrutinised the events leading up to Mary's death and named one Abraham Thornton as the prime suspect.

Abraham Thornton was the son to affluent parents and hailed from Castle Bromwich, another Birmingham Suburb. Mary had met Abrham Thornton, the previous night at the dance and the two had danced well into the evening. Thornton claimed to have then escorted Mary accompanied Mary across the fields and lanes back to Erdington, where he left her alive and well. The evidence was overwhelming for the time, he was the last to be seen with her and he appeared to have blood on his shirt when arrested. However, he provided an alibi that was substantiated by 8 separate people. He was three miles away at the time the coroner put the time of death. Much to the anger of locals who believed he was guilty, at his trial in August 1817 at Warwick Assizes, he was acquitted of Marys Brutal murder.

Lawyers acting on behalf of Marys family, enacted an ancient Norman Law, which allowed those acquitted in the criminal courts, to be tried for the same crime in the civil courts. Thornton was re-arrested in October 1817 and sent for trial. Thorntons Lawyers, being ever versatile, decided to invoke another archaic Normal Law, which involved Thornton literally throwing down the gauntlet (glove) and challenging Marys semi invalid brother, to a duel to the death. The Ashford's withdrew their prosecution and Thornton walked free. Thornton was hounded out of town and eventually emigrated to the US never to return. Mary Ashford was laid to rest in Holy Trinity churchyard in Sutton Coldfield, a place I am very familiar with.

Marys spirit, still seeking justice, has been seen in and around the area since Thorntons acquittal. She is seen around the Penns Lane and Berwood Road area which is very close to where the pit, her body was discovered in, was located. She is also seen on a bench and on the road near the Tyburn House inn, at the junction of Kingsbury Road and Chester Road. Paranormal investigators have caught, what they believe, are her final screams for help, the words "justice" and "Thornton" have been captured. She has also told them her name is "Mary". The story doesn't end here, as there is an oddly coincidental (if you believe in coincidence) and tragic epilogue to this story.

On Whit Monday, 26 May 1974, a young nurse named Barbara Forrest, was murdered, her accused assailant was arrested but acquitted at trial.

The names of the victims and years of death are the only difference between the cases. Both women's deaths occurred on, or in the hours after, Whit Monday, in the Erdington area. Their bodies were found only 500 yards apart. They were both unmarried, aged 20, had been left for dead and there were attempts to hide the bodies. Both girls had visited a friend on the evening of Whit Monday, both had changed into a new dress that night, and both went to a dance. They were last seen alive on May 27 and the men charged, but acquitted of each murder, had the same surname, Thornton. Barbara had a premonition commenting to her friend she had a bad feeling about the month of May. As a sidenote Abraham Thornton was the last man in England to claim a TRIAL BY COMBAT and was acquitted of the charge as there was no suitable Ashford male relative to oppose him. The law of the land was changed as a result.

I used to belong to the choir of Holy Trinity Church, where Mary Ashford was buried. My mother would always be there early to collect me, as the entrance to the church is secluded up an alleyway called Trinity Hill. My mother never wanted me to be alone waiting, as she was concerned for my safety. Little did I know she had every reason to be.

As the year ended in Birmingham 1996, 17-year-old schoolgirl Nicola Dixon, had stayed at home, over the festive period to take her driving test on New Year's Eve. However, that day her test was cancelled because of snowy weather, leaving her disappointed. That night, she was ready to see in the New Year with a celebration. She was planning to flit between a couple of parties across the road from each other that was only a short walk from her home, in

Sutton Coldfield. Dressed in typical 1990's teenage style, Nicola went out with friends to dance.

Nicolas's life was tragically taken from her, by a sadistic murderer before the clocks chimed midnight. Nicola, was attacked in Trinity Hill alley, which ran by the Holy Trinity Church. She took a short cut to meet friends in the town-centre pub.

Her murder was brutal and extremely sadistic. The brave teenager managed to crawl across the snow to her final resting place, before eventually succumbing to her massive head injuries and dying alone in the grounds of the church. She was found crawling distance from where Mary Ashford is buried. Her Body was found by the Rectors wife the following morning. Luckily, in this case, there was not an acquittal and her murderer, who does not deserve naming, was convicted and imprisoned. Nicola was only a year older than I and died very near to where my mother would wait. Her death upset me greatly and I still think of her from time to time.

Nicola Dixons Memorial can be seen at the top of Trinity Hill. Not far from Holy Trinity Church Sutton Coldfield. Her memorial was unveiled by her parents in 2001, based on one her own pieces of artwork.

One can only hope and pray, that Nicolas spirit is at rest, however, for the Mary and Barbara, this is not the case. Both cases are considered unsolved, although it is believed that the right assailants were caught and then acquitted. Both women have been heard to say their names, on EVP, in the area where they were killed. The word Justice, comes up frequently. But for Mary Ashford, whose murderer has long been dead, there will be no earthly justice. For Barbara, the case is not actively being worked on, and therefore justice is unlikely to occur.

In order for these spirits to move on, there needs to be acceptance that an earthly resolution is not possible. A fact neither spirit, at this point, is willing to accept. As a result, their spirits are bound to the place they both perished.

It is my hope that one day, someone will be able to help release these souls, so that they can let go of the circumstances that lead to their deaths, and rest peacefully.

For some, like Mary and Barbara, resolution is not possible and so their spirits linger. In some cases, they can become angry and bitter. It is our job to sift through all the anguish. We want to encourage the spirit to let go of attachments to the physical world and transition towards the light. Remind them of the beauty and peace that await them on the other side and assure them that they will find solace and healing in the afterlife. This is especially important if fear plays a role in the reasons why someone does not feel able to move on.

Engage in rituals or ceremonies that are meaningful to the spirit's culture or belief system as needed. These rituals can help facilitate the transition

279

process and provide comfort and closure to both the spirit and the living. This was the case of Jennys husband, in that the final rite was part of what was needed for release.

While helping spirits transition, it is essential to protect yourself and the environment from negative energies. Use protective rituals, such as smudging with sage or calling upon spiritual guides and guardians, to ensure a safe and positive interaction. You can ask the spirits loved ones to come and collect them and guide them into the light. Often this is a great way to facilitate the crossing over in a peaceful, meaningful, and beautiful way.

Finally, always treat the spirit with respect and gratitude for allowing you to assist them in their journey. Express appreciation for their trust and courage in seeking help and honour their transition with reverence and dignity. It is a privilege to be part of the transition of a human soul and should be treated as such.

Remember, helping spirits let go for many, is considered a sacred responsibility. By offering your assistance with compassion and respect, you can guide spirits towards the peace that they seek and that every human soul deserves. spirits of a more benevolent nature often find solace in the presence of loved ones, guiding them through their final moments with reassurance and comfort. These spirits may linger briefly to offer words of encouragement or convey messages of love and support before peacefully departing to the next realm.

REMOVING NEGATIVE HUMAN SPIRITS AND ENTITES

In the realm of spiritual intervention, there exists A deep calling to aid those souls ensnared by negativity, trapped between worlds, or burdened by malevolent energies. With reverence and courage, we embark on a sacred journey of guiding these troubled spirits towards the light, offering them liberation from their torment, and restoring harmony to the spiritual balance.
The art of moving negative human spirits or entities on, considered a noble endeavour, demands empathy, discernment, and a steadfast commitment to the greater good. Our job is to become a beacon of hope and agents of spiritual release and transformation.

When dealing with negative entities or malevolent spirits that resist transition, the process becomes more complex. These entities may cling to the physical realm out of a desire to cause harm, wreak havoc, or feed off the energy of the living. Removing them requires specialised knowledge and techniques employed by experienced spiritual practitioners or paranormal investigators. It often involves rituals, blessings, or spiritual interventions aimed at breaking the entity's hold on the earthly plane and facilitating their transition to the afterlife.

In some cases, professional assistance from mediums, psychics, or clergy members trained in spiritual cleansing and exorcism may be necessary to effectively banish these entities and restore harmony to the affected environment. This is an entirely new book, and I am not really going to delve into the removal of malevolent entities here. We are focusing more on negative human entities.

Malevolent entities or spirits may often seek to prevent our efforts, testing our resolve, when clearing an area. Yet, armed with faith, wisdom, and the power of the human heart, we press forward, knowing that every human soul, no matter how tarnished, deserves redemption and release.

Our calling in amongst the darkness, dispels the shadows that cling to the human spirit. In the pursuit of release, we affirm the sacred interconnectedness of all beings and uphold this eternal truth. That love, and light prevail over darkness and despair.

Once malevolent entities have been identified and dealt with, if possible, the next crucial step is to cleanse and ward the property to prevent their return and restore positive energy. Property cleansing involves purifying the space of any lingering negative energies or residual effects from the entity's presence. We can also use these techniques to move on humans' spirits. This can be achieved through various methods such as smudging with sage, using protective crystals, or performing spiritual rituals aimed at banishing negativity. Additionally, warding techniques are employed to create a protective barrier around the property, preventing further intrusion by malevolent entities or negative influences. By combining thorough cleansing with effective warding measures, individuals can ensure a lasting sense of safety, tranquillity, and positivity within their home or property.

CLEANSING AND WARDING A LOCATION

We cleanse a home to purify its energy, remove negative influences, and restore harmony to the living space. Over time, homes can accumulate energetic residue from past events, emotions, and even the presence of negative entities. Cleansing rituals help to dispel these energies, creating a fresh and vibrant environment conducive to peace, clarity, and well-being for those who dwell within. Additionally, cleansing can serve as a symbolic act of renewal, inviting positive energy to flow freely and infusing the home with a sense of sanctuary and protection.

Cleansing a home can help guide a spirit to cross over by clearing away negative energies or attachments that may be keeping the spirit tethered to location. When a home is cleansed, it creates a shift in the energetic environment, making it less hospitable for lingering spirits or entities. This shift can help weaken the ties that bind the spirit to the physical world, making it easier for them to release any attachments and move towards the light.

Some cleansing rituals involve invoking protective energies or spiritual guides, which can offer guidance and support to spirits as they transition to the other side. These protective energies can help guide the spirit towards the light and provide a sense of safety and reassurance during the crossing over process.

Overall, cleansing a home can serve as a catalyst for spiritual transformation, helping to facilitate the journey of spirits as they transition from the earthly realm to the afterlife and removing negative entities.

There are many methods for cleansing a home and warding against further activity. This is something that really should only be done when you know what you are dealing with and most importantly, how to do it correctly. Many cultures have their own methods for clearing away negative energy, far too many to mention here. I am going to focus on the most common methods for cleansing a home.

It is an absolute must that before attempting any kinds of cleansing that you are familiar and practiced, in the art of grounding, centring, and shielding. Oftentimes earthbound spirits and certainly negative entities, are not happy you are trying to remove them from a location, they do not want to leave. They will try to affect a cleansing in any way that they can.

In this section, we are going to discuss four types of cleansings. One using a smudge stick, the second involves using our own energy, thirdly by using sound and lastly, using religious artifacts.

Here in Perth, Australia, about 6 years ago, we had a case of a Tenant Advocate whose client had a haunted house. The family that lived in the house, were first nations people and believed that the deceased was an angry loved one, who had died tragically. Not the kind of average case you get in that field of legal work.

The advocate with the help of elders, facilitated what is called a 'smudging ceremony' in the house as per their belief system.

Cleansing a home has more to do with intention and belief, than it does with anything else. This is why often the tools that you need for a cleansing, can vary depending on the spirit or people you are working with and what their belief systems are.

Often its good practice to discuss with the owners of the property, what their belief is, before you go ahead and do the cleansing. Often, we teach our clients how to cleanse their properties on a regular basis. If they are Catholic, maybe the local priest and holy water will be more effective, than a smudging ceremony. For some religious objects are the focus of their belief, for others it could be some other cultural or religious icon. For other cultures, they may have some form of cleansing ritual practiced by their peoples, which has more meaning and intent than some religious icon.

As clearing a home is not a religious action it can be something a person of strong religious conviction may not allow. I knew one investigator that was trying to remove a human spirit, but the owners did not believe in spirits, just demons. They were very black and white in their belief of the afterlife They wanted a religious exorcism, which just angered the spirit, who was also religious. A cleansing was the method the investigator wanted to go and what he believed would resolve the haunting. Neither could agree, so they went down the route of a religious house blessing instead. This did the trick and was acceptable to the living and the dead at that location.

The initial cleansing is often conducted without the presence of the family due to the potential for unpleasant or even threatening experiences, especially if there is an attachment to a living person. Spirits may manipulate emotions and pose risks to those conducting the cleansing. However, in some cases, having the family present during the cleansing may be necessary, as each situation varies based on the energy present at the location. Sometimes, the goal isn't to rid the space of spirits or entities but to clear accumulated negative energy that has led to a residual haunting. Regardless of the specific circumstances, any form of cleansing requires determination, positive intent, and focused concentration to be effective. Typically, the cleansing process involves working methodically from the top to the bottom of each room, starting from the back of the property and progressing towards the front. If the property has a basement, it is usually the last area to be cleansed.

After conducting a cleansing to rid a space of negative energy or malevolent entities, it is essential to implement warding techniques to prevent their return. These wards act as protective barriers, ensuring that the space remains free from unwanted influences and disturbances.

SMUDGING

Smudging is a traditional practice in many indigenous cultures. It involves burning sacred herbs, such as sage, cedar, or sweetgrass, to cleanse a space, object, or person of negative energy and to promote spiritual purification and harmony. The smoke generated from burning these herbs is believed to carry prayers and intentions to the heavens.

The concept of smudging embodies a profound beauty, both in its simplicity and in its deep spiritual significance. At its core, smudging is about the purification of energy and the creation of a sacred space, where one can connect with the spiritual realm, whether it is for personal reflection, prayer, or healing.

Smudging is traditionally used for purifying, cleansing the soul, and removing negative thought and energy from a person or place.

If we go back to the smudging ceremony that took place here in Perth, in the haunted rental house, the intent was to clear, purify and renew the space, remove the unwanted energy and to provide a scared space, in order for the angry spirit to move on. It is always advisable to have more than one person doing this kind of cleansing.

Remember to do your spiritual protections of grounding, centering, and shielding before you begin.

Once you have your intention in mind, light the smudging stick and hold at a 45-degree angle pointing the tip down towards the flame. Allow it to burn for about 20 seconds and then blow it out.

We first cleanse our hands with the smoke as if we were washing our hands. We then draw the smoke over our heads, eyes, ears, mouths, and our bodies. These actions remind us to think positive thoughts, see good actions, speak good words, and show the good of who we are and our positive and loving intentions. The following mantra of intent was created for a school where they use smudging as part of the curriculum. When the children and adults start the ceremony and smudge themselves, they recite the following.

- We smudge to clean our minds so that we will have good thoughts of others.
- We smudge our eyes so that we will only see the good in others.
- We smudge our ears so that we will only listen to positive things about others.
- We smudge our mouths so that we will only speak well of others.
- We smudge our arms to do the good work that we do in a loving and caring way.
- We smudge our feet so that we walk in a good way.
- •We smudge the bottom of our feet to cleanse the connection between ourselves and Mother Earth.
- We smudge our heart to cleanse it of negativity.
- We smudge our hair to cleanse away any negativity we may be carrying.
- We smudge our back to release any negativity we may carrying and let it go (turn clockwise and complete the circle once back is done).
- We smudge our whole being so we will portray only the good part of our self through our actions.
- We smudge to cleanse negative energy within our own being or any negative energy in a space.

I have replicated this here, so that you the reader, going into a situation where you maybe smudging a property or yourselves after an investigation, can focus your intent. These are not just empty word, they are the very essence of you, that you are putting into the atmosphere. Remember the concept that darkness cannot stand where there is light? Good intentions are the very light that we use, to remove the darkness from a place, restore harmony to the living, and peace to the souls that needs it.

There are several ways to progress once you have cleansed your own energy and you are ready to begin.

As stated previously work from top to bottom and from the back to the front of the property. If there are multiple levels to the home start from the top level and work your way down. If this is a home and it is possible to do so, open all the windows to the home and make sure any pets are secured safely.

Open windows to encourage air flow throughout the house. In this example we are going to work towards the front door of the property.

Use your hand to fan the smoke into every corner of the room. walk around the room, space, object, or person, fanning the smoke over its entirety. You can picture the smoke absorbing and removing the negative energy and it dissipates with the smoke, we want the smoke to drift into all of the corners, including closets and hidden spaces. Contemplate your wishes for the family, home, or location as you go, keep repeating this intention out loud if you choose.

IMPORTANT: As you are picturing the removal of negative energy, we are also replacing that negative energy with pure positive white light. This is very important to maintain spiritual balance.

Pay attention to how you feel in certain areas of the location. If the atmosphere feels heavier in some places than in other places, spend a little more time on that area. Imagine it filled with the bright white light and all the dark negative energy being removed.

Guide the smoke and the negative energy toward the open windows or a door, so it can escape. When walking round the property give special attention to areas in front of mirrors, in corners, and in spaces like hallways, and doorways, closets and dark recesses.

In the case of an intelligent negative haunting, by filling each room with light, we are pushing that spirit out of the space and into an uncleansed area. This is why it is done methodically, cutting of places to hide until the spirit has nowhere left to go.

Before and during the cleansing ritual set clear and compassionate intentions for moving the human spirit on. Focus on creating a peaceful and loving environment for both the spirit and you. We are not going to entertain any non-human negative energies that are there.

If you sense the presence of a spirit, acknowledge it with respect and kindness. You can verbally communicate your intentions to help it move on, expressing gratitude for its presence while gently encouraging it to transition to the next stage of its journey.

Call upon higher powers if that is your belief, such as spirit guides, angels, or ancestors, to assist in guiding the spirit towards the light. Ask for their support and protection throughout the cleansing process.

Visualise or physically offer light and love to the spirit, guiding it towards a place of peace and resolution. You can envision a beautiful, radiant light surrounding the spirit, providing comfort and guidance as it moves forward.

During the cleansing ritual, maintain an attitude of compassion and empathy towards the spirit. Avoid using harsh or forceful methods that may agitate or disturb it further.

Offer the spirit words of closure, reassuring it that it is safe to let go and move towards the light. Express gratitude for any lessons or blessings it may have brought and encourage it to find peace and fulfilment in its onward journey.

A word of warning some negative entities and even the spirits themselves can try to affect you during a cleansing. You may feel sick or like you are bring watched. Feeling suddenly anxious or afraid is common and do not be surprised if other activity occurs while you are doing the cleansing. In this case stop and do your grounding, centring and most importantly your shielding before continuing.

Do not rush a cleansing, take your time and be methodical. A property may take more than one cleansing over time. After completing the cleansing ritual, fill the space with positive energy and blessings to reinforce the sense of peace and harmony. You can use uplifting affirmations, blessings, or rituals to create a kind and supportive environment for yourself and any lingering energies.

Once you have completed the smudging it is important you close the session down with the right intention. Make sure all that positive energy has replaced all the negative energy to maintain balance. To do this, declare your intention out loud or silently in your head.

Some like to walk around the perimeter of the house outside to create a barrier. There are times that the human spirit has not left and may need a little more work. Creating an environment free of the negativity associated with any real negative energy can help the spirit heal and eventually move on.

Make sure you extinguish the stick by pressing it lightly into a heat proof container or into dry earth/sand. Never use water as this will result in you being unable to re-light the stick. I prefer to just gently dab it out (however in really thick sage bundles the flame can still smoulder inside unseen) so do be mindful that it is properly out.

USING YOUR OWN ENERGY TO CLEANSE

The concept of energy intertwining and its effect on cleansing a location, is often rooted in spiritual and metaphysical beliefs, rather than empirical science. However, let's explore it from a perspective that integrates both.

Many spiritual and philosophical traditions propose that everything in the universe is interconnected through energy. This energy can take various forms, such as vibrations or auras. According to this belief, individuals, objects, and places are all influenced by and connected through this energy.

Positive energy is often associated with feelings of peace, harmony, and togetherness. When a person enters a space with positive energy, they can uplift the atmosphere and influence those around them. Think of that one person you know that always makes you feel uplifted in their presence. Cleansing a location with positive energy involves intentionally imbuing the space with these uplifting vibrations to counteract any negative energies, that may be present.

Practitioners of cleansing may use various techniques such as meditation, visualisation in order to facilitate the cleansing of an area.

Even from a scientific perspective, there is evidence to suggest that our perception of spaces, can be influenced by psychological factors. For example, entering a clean and well-lit room may evoke feelings of comfort and relaxation, while a cluttered and dimly lit space, may induce stress or discomfort. In this sense, intentionally infusing a space with positive energy could have psychological benefits for those who reside, in that space.

Just as individuals can affect the energy of a space, collective energy can also have a profound impact. Group activities such as ceremonies, rituals, or shared moments of joy and celebration, can create a powerful collective energy that uplifts and cleanses a location on a larger scale. Think of how it feels to walk into a very old cathedral, which has had thousands of years of good intentions. This is often way people describe the feelings of peace, when they walk in a building used for worship.

Ultimately, whether or not one believes in the metaphysical aspects, the intention behind such practices can have real and tangible effects on persons or energies that lie within the bounds of that space.

The practice is identical to using the smudge stick, however this time we are using the theory of energy interconnectedness, rather than the cleansing powers of herbs.

The following is a simple technique, to use your own energy to cleanse a space.

Before you begin, take a moment to set your intention. Decide what energy

287

you want to bring into the space and what you want to cleanse or release. It could be negativity, stress, residual energy, removing a negative entity or helping a human spirit, move towards the light.

Find a comfortable position either standing or sitting. Close your eyes and take a few deep breaths to centre yourself. Visualise roots extending from the soles of your feet deep into the earth, grounding you and connecting you to the energy of the earth.

- Visualise a bright, warm light surrounding you. This light represents positive energy, love, peace, and good intention. Imagine this light filling your entire being, from your toes to the top of your head, until you feel fully immersed in its warmth and brightness.

- Take deep breaths and with each inhale, imagine drawing in more of this positive energy. With each exhale, visualise releasing any negativity, or unwanted energy from your body. As you continue to breathe deeply, feel the energy expanding outward from your body, filling the room with positivity and light.

- As you breathe and extend your energy, focus your intention on cleansing the room. Visualise the positive energy washing over every surface, corner, and crevice, clearing away any lingering negativity or heaviness. Many choose to do sweeping actions with their hands as if dusting. You do not need to touch the surfaces of the building for this process to work and I find it better if you do not. Our focus should be on intent not getting distracted by physical stimuli.

- Once you feel the energy of the room has been cleansed to your satisfaction, take a moment to express gratitude for the opportunity to cleanse and refresh the space.

- When you are ready, gently bring your awareness back to the present moment. Wiggle your fingers and toes, take a few more deep breaths, and slowly open your eyes. Trust that the positive energy you have infused into the room will continue to radiate and uplift those who inhabit it.

As far as moving on any spirits, the technique is identical in all the cleansing rituals, hence I have not repeated them here. This technique can be adapted and personalised to suit your own beliefs and preferences. Remember, that the most important aspect of a cleansing, is your intention, throughout the process.

Often you can feel the oppression in the atmosphere when there are layers of residual or negative energy present. After a successful cleansing ritual, you can often feel the difference at a property, with most people saying it feels 'lighter'.

288

USING HOLY WATER AND OR RELIGIOUS ARTIFACTS

In countless tales and legends worldwide, the concept of using holy artifacts to cleanse an area is deeply ingrained in cultural practices. These artifacts hold immense symbolic and spiritual significance, believed to possess powers capable of purifying spaces tainted by negative energies, malevolent entities, or spiritual disturbances.

Throughout history, various cultures have employed diverse holy artifacts in purification rituals. For instance, in Christianity, items such as crucifixes, holy water, and relics of saints are used to bless and sanctify spaces, driving away evil and malevolent spirits. Similarly, in Hinduism, objects like sacred ash (vibhuti), holy texts, and idols of deities, are utilised in rituals, to dispel negative forces and restore spiritual harmony.

The efficacy of these artifacts is frequently ascribed to faith, belief, and the divine energies they encapsulate. Whether it is the essence of revered figures like saints infused into relics or the symbolic potency of sacred symbols such as the sign of the cross, these artifacts act as channels for divine grace and safeguarding.

In modern times, the use of holy artifacts for cleansing purposes persists, albeit often within religious contexts. From purification ceremonies conducted by priests to personal rituals performed by individuals seeking spiritual cleansing and enlightenment. The practice endures as a means of invoking divine assistance, in warding off malevolent influences and restoring sacredness to one's person.

However, beyond religious beliefs, the concept of cleansing spaces with holy artifacts, also resonates with the universal human desire for purification and renewal. Whether through traditional rituals or personal preference, the act of using holy artifacts to cleanse an area represents a profound spiritual endeavour to create harmony, peace, and sanctity in ourselves and the world around us.

When people think of using holy artifacts to deal with negative spirits or entities, many people picture the film, the exorcist, or some similar horror film. Where good battles evil for control of a person or space. People's minds tend to go to head spinning and levitation.

Cleansing a place and possession of a place or person, are two distinct concepts and paranormal phenomena. Each involving different practices, beliefs, and manifestations.

Cleansing a place typically refers to the ritualistic or spiritual act of purifying a space from negative energies, malevolent entities, or spiritual disturbances. It often involves the use of sacred rituals, prayers, holy artifacts, or symbolic actions to remove or dispel any perceived negative influences. The purpose of cleansing a place is to restore harmony, balance, and positive energy to the environment, making it conducive to spiritual practices, well-being, and peace of mind.

Possession, on the other hand, refers to the phenomenon where an individual's mind, body, or spirit is believed to be controlled or influenced by an external entity, often of a malevolent or supernatural nature. In cases of possession, the affected individual may exhibit abnormal behaviour, personality changes, or loss of control over their actions, attributed to the presence or influence of the possessing entity. Possession is often associated with spiritual or religious beliefs, where the possessing entity is perceived as a demon, evil spirit, or other supernatural being.

Exorcism or spiritual intervention is commonly sought to free the possessed individual from the influence of the entity and restore them to their normal state.

While both cleansing a place and dealing with possession may involve spiritual beliefs and practices, they address different aspects of spiritual and supernatural phenomena. Cleansing focuses on purifying and sanctifying a space, whereas possession involves the intervention to release an individual from external spiritual influence or control.

A Catholic priest, for example, has permission to go ahead and cleanse a property. They need specialist permission from the Vatican to do an exorcism of a location. It is important to distinguish between the two.

For the purposes of this section, let us assume this is not a case that requires an exorcism, we just have unwanted activity within the home, which needs to be moved on or removed.

We'll take a cue from prior practices of traversing the property. Ahead of commencing the cleansing ritual, it is essential to prepare the space. Clear away clutter and ensure the area is tidied and pristine.

- Select Your Artifacts: Choose religious artifacts that hold significance to you and your beliefs or that of the homeowners. These could include items such as holy water, sage bundles, incense, blessed oil, religious symbols, or prayers from your tradition.
- Take a moment to centre yourself and set your intention for the cleansing. You might say a prayer or affirmation asking for protection, purification, and the removal of any negative energies from the space. Set the intention for any human spirits you wish to move on from the property.
- Begin the Cleansing Ritual: Light any candles, incense, or sage bundles you have chosen to use. As you move through the space, wave the smoke, or sprinkle the holy water while reciting prayers,

mantras, or affirmations that resonate with you.

- Focus on Problem Areas: Pay special attention to areas of the home where you feel negative or heavy energy is concentrated or where there have been reported disturbances. Spend extra time cleansing these spaces thoroughly.
- Visualise Protection as you perform the cleansing, visualise a protective barrier forming around the home, sealing it off from any negative influences and filling it with positive energy.

Once you feel that the cleansing is complete, offer a final prayer of gratitude for the purification of the space and the protection of those who inhabit it. Extinguish any candles or incense used during the ritual.

SOUND CLEANSING

In many spiritual traditions, including various world indigenous practices, sound is believed to have the power to clear negative energy and spirits. Different cultures have their own rituals and techniques involving sound to cleanse spaces and individuals of unwanted influences.

Sound cleansing practices are often accompanied by intentions set by the practitioner or participants. The focused intention to release negative energy or entities, coupled with the sound vibrations, is believed to create an environment that is less hospitable to such influences.

You will often hear paranormal investigators refer to lower or higher-level entities. This denotes the type of spirit or entity you are dealing with. It is believed more negative energies operate at a lower energy frequency and positive energies at a higher frequency. The Pure sound that vibrates and gives off a higher frequency, forcing lower frequency entities to leave.

Using sound to dispel negative energies and guide human spirits towards the light, is a fascinating concept that integrates elements of spirituality, energy work, and sound therapy. While the effectiveness of such practices can vary depending on individual beliefs and experiences, many people find resonance in the idea, that sound vibrations can influence emotions, thoughts, and even spiritual states. An example of this is someone feels emotionally better when they listen to their favourite music.

It is crucial to acknowledge the diversity of beliefs concerning negative spirits and their relationship with sound, as these perspectives can differ significantly across various traditions and cultures. What might be viewed as a negative spirit in one cultural setting could be interpreted differently in another. Consequently, understandings of sound cleansing and its impact on negative spirits may vary depending on cultural beliefs and customs.

Bells, singing bowls, or chimes are often used in this practice which is slightly different to the methods used in smudging, which involves herbs.

Like any spiritual or energy work, setting clear intentions is crucial. Before beginning, it is essential to establish the purpose of the sound work. This could be to dispel negative energies, create a peaceful environment, or assist lost spirits in finding their way to the light. Intentions serve as the guiding force behind any spiritual practice.

Various instruments can be used to create sound vibrations, each with its unique qualities and effects. Common choices include singing bowls, tuning forks, drums, bells and chimes, The practitioner may choose instruments based on personal preference. Before initiating the sound work, it is essential to create a sacred and safe space. This could involve cleansing the area with sage, lighting candles, or any other ritualistic practices that help establish a conducive environment for spiritual work. The following is a suggested method for doing this kind of cleansing.

- The practitioner begins by centering themselves and attuning to the energy of the space and the individuals involved. This might involve deep breathing, meditation, or other grounding techniques to align with the present moment and connect with higher spiritual energies.

- Using the selected instruments, the practitioner will begin to produce sound vibrations. The sounds can be gentle or intense, depending on the desired effect. The intention behind the sound is what is crucial, as it infuses the vibrations with purpose and meaning.

- As the sound fills the space, the practitioner directs the energy towards dispelling negative energies and guiding lost spirits towards the light. This can be done through visualisation, prayer, or specific intentions communicated through the sound itself.

- Throughout the process, participants should remain attuned to the subtle shifts in energy and sensation within the space. This might involve paying attention to changes in temperature, emotions, or intuitive insights that arise during the cleansing.

- Once the intended work is complete, the practitioner gently brings the sound to a close, allowing the vibrations to dissipate naturally. It is essential to close the energetic space properly, thanking any spiritual guides or entities that may have assisted in the process. Grounding techniques, such as deep breathing or connecting with the earth, help to integrate the experience and return to a balanced state.

Cleansing and setting spirits free, is a profound intention that involves compassion, respect, and a deep understanding of spiritual energies. Your goal is to cleanse any negative energies or attachments and guide lost spirits towards the light.

Approach the process with the reverence it so deserves. Recognise that spirits may be trapped or lingering for assorted reasons and deserve understanding and assistance in finding peace. Set the intention to create a safe and protected space for the cleansing and release process.

It is essential to establish energetic boundaries to ensure that only benevolent energies are allowed in the space. Set the intention to cleanse the space of any negative or stagnant energies that may be holding spirits back. Use sound, visualisation, smudging, or other cleansing techniques to purify the environment.

Finally, direct your intention towards helping lost or trapped spirits find their way to the light. Visualise a pathway of love and light leading them towards their highest good. Offer reassurance and support as they transition to the next phase of their journey. Intend for any attachments or unresolved emotions binding the spirits to be released with love. Encourage forgiveness, healing, and resolution as they move towards freedom. Infuse your intention with love, light, and healing energy. Send waves of compassion and support to both the spirits and any individuals affected by their presence, fostering a sense of peace and closure for all involved.

Conclude the intention with gratitude for the assistance received and a sense of closure for the cleansing and release process. Trust that the intentions set will manifest in alignment with the highest good of all.

Finally, ground yourself and the space, anchoring the intentions into the physical realm. Take a few deep breaths, connect with the earth, and allow yourself to integrate the experience before moving forward.

Once your work is done, regardless of the cleansing rituals used, the owner of a property should try to maintain the positive energy in the home or at the location. This can be done by regularly smudging, with sage or incense, saying prayers or affirmations, and keeping the space clean and harmonious.

Remember that the effectiveness of the cleansing ritual depends not only on the artifacts used, but also on your sincerity, belief, and intention of the people who reside there. If you are uncertain about any aspect of the process, it can be helpful to seek guidance from a spiritual leader or practitioner experienced in these practices.

After completing the cleansing ritual, it is essential to establish protective measures to maintain the purified state of the space. Warding techniques can create barriers against negative energies or entities, ensuring a continued sense of safety and well-being.

WARDING

Welcome, seekers of protection against the unseen. In this section, we delve into the realm of spirits and entities, crafting a shield against the ethereal forces that roam the shadows and knock on the windows. Whether you are a sceptic or a believer, it is wise to be prepared with practical strategies and ancient wisdom, to ward against the paranormal, ensuring tranquillity in the face of the unknown.

When most think about warding against the supernatural, images of ancient rituals, protective symbols, and sacred incantations spring to mind. It is like stepping into a world where the veil between reality and the unseen is thin, where people rely on age-old wisdom, passed down through generations to safeguard themselves against mysterious forces.

Symbols like pentagrams or sigils etched in chalk, bundles of herbs smouldering in the air, and whispered prayers invoking divine protection, all come to mind. There is a sense of reverence mixed with caution, as individuals seek to create barriers between themselves and the unknown, drawing on both faith and folklore to keep the supernatural at bay.

Whereas these images and ideas are in many ways based on truth, they should be resigned to the history books. our updated understanding of the paranormal has shaped the tools and techniques we employ for protection in modern times. However, when we delve into the dichotomy between warding as superstition and warding as spiritual practice, the lines become blurred.

Superstition often invokes images of old wives' tales and irrational fears of devils and witches and other evil supernatural beings. Where rituals are performed out of habit, rather than true belief in their efficacy. Yet, for many, warding holds a deeper, spiritual significance, it that it is a sacred connection to forces beyond the tangible realm. Modern day practitioners, must navigate the complexities of cultural traditions and personal beliefs, examining how superstition and spirituality intersect. Often, we are seeking to understand the profound impact of belief, on the rituals we perform to protect ourselves from the paranormal entities that come to cause harm.

It is the firm opinion of this writer, when completing any kind of cleansing of a home or location, it should then be fully warded. This is to prevent any negative entities or spirits that may have been removed, returning. It also prevents the attraction of any other negative energies, that may wish to call, the now spiritually vacant location, home.

Warding is not a new concept it goes back centuries and permeates through just about every culture and every time.

When we think of warding a house or location, we think of protecting ourselves from a supernatural entity bent on harming the living. The concept of evil supernatural beings' intent on harm, is still very much alive and well. This invoking of protection, is practiced in many places and cultures in today's world.

In Modern day Bali, they have 'Nyepi Day', which is when the Island completely shuts down. People shut their doors and businesses and you are not allowed to venture out, if you do you are likely to get caught by the local watchmen who enforce this isolation. On this day the Balinese people expel the evil spirits and demons, from the Island to create balance between the Gods, the people and nature. The most famous of the evil spirits on the island is Rangda. She is said to be the queen of the Leyaks, (mythological creatures that take the form of a flying head with its entrails spilling out behind it). Rangda is their widow-witch queen.

During this religious holiday, there should be no fire, light or electricity – unless you want to attract the evil spirits that roam freely at this time. There is no work, no travel, and no entertainment. Food is limited and a day of silence ensues, while the ejection and warding of the island takes place. It is a time for self-reflection, meditation, and prayer. But warding is not a new concept.

In the UK, in many of the old ancient stone buildings, you will find colloquially, what are called witches marks. Known as ritual protection marks or apotropaic markings, they are found throughout the UK and in some mainland European buildings. You are most likely to come across them in England, Wales, and Scotland.

The term 'witches mark' is really a misnomer, as witches marks are specific to certain time periods, mainly the Middle Ages, where the fear of witches was at an all-time high. We will refer to them in this book as apotropaic markings, as this is the more accurate description.

The markings are believed to have turned away evil, provided protection to the building and those who lived or worked within them. They are found in houses, old business buildings, old pubs or taverns, Inns, castles and even the Tower of London. There have been markings found in old stables to protect the horses from evil spirits and people influenced by evil, intent on stealing them.

The term Evil could encompass a whole host of entities or even humans, manipulated by evil supernatural influences. This was a very real fear in times when rational thought, was not part of a deeply religious society. The devil was present, and he .and his many supernatural minions, were, without question, out to get you.

Attempts to ward off 'evil' spirits in England, going back hundreds of years, are well known in historic buildings. They can be found carved into wood or stone, burnt into wood and often appear as lines on windowsills and above fireplaces. Cutting off any possible entryway to the building, that the supernatural could use.

80 symbols were discovered in 2015 at the Tower of London's, Queen's House, burnt and carved into the wooden beams. The house was the location where the Lieutenant of the Tower lived and where he interrogated high-profile prisoners, and other 'traitors.' This included the Infamous Guy Fawkes. It was designed to keep the tower and those who loved and worked there, safe from evil.

The prevalent symbols used for warding include interlocking circles, often carved to form a six-petalled daisy flower pattern, concentric circles, and intersecting lines crafting crosses or M's symbolising the Virgin Mary. Additionally, more contemporary religious symbols like crosses and pentagrams, although the latter's association with the occult is a more recent notion, have been historically employed for warding purposes.

In Bath, England, where the Roman Baths are still preserved, there were various stone tablets uncovered with written wards on them. Asking for protection for businesses or family. Additionally, there were curses intended for those perceived to have wronged the writer, which were far from pleasant.

Marks are not the only symbols used for warding against harm or spiritual attack. Some use religious crosses or a medallion of a certain Saint, in order to protect themselves. I know a few people who carry a Saint Christopher, patron saint of travellers in their purse or on their person. It is a common gift at christenings and is believed to protect the wearer from harm, while going about everyday life. My daughter Lillian, was given a Saint Michael and St Christopher medallion for her christening. Saint Michael is the patron saint of protection and strength in battle. Not entirely sure when that will be needing it, but still, it was the intent behind the gift that is relevant for the purposes of this chapter.

When my Italian Mother-in-Law, Bianca Rossi, passed away in late 2023, we found many religious saints' medallions and protective prayer cards, tucked away in her various bags and purses. The idea of a symbolic object used to ward against harm is still a modern one.

In the UK, the infamous, Ancient Ram Inn, located in picturesque Wooten Under Edge, dates to about 1145. The building contains carved warding marks, and they even found a mummified cat and bible walled up behind the chimney. It was common practice in Pagan times to ward off evil spirits. It was believed that cats have a sixth sense and in offering the cat as a sacrifice in the walls or foundation of a building, the cat would go on to protect the home, in its after life. Stroud museum have studied the cat and have said that it was thankfully dead. before its mummification and is roughly 4500 years old.

Warding is often heavily influenced by Pagan rituals that are still in use today. Ironically, the methods often used to ward these days are often associated with witchcraft and the occult. The very thing these historical practitioners were trying to ward against.

I know of some investigators that carry warding bags with them, that has crystals and herbs they believe, have the power to protect, on every investigation. I know of some who have even gone as far as tattooing warding symbols on their bodies. I do not suggest this as an idea for the reader to go and do, but it gives pause to consider, how seriously warding plays a part in paranormal investigation. That is because once you have first-hand experience of the paranormal, especially with more negative spirits and entities, you understand how vulnerable the living can be.

WARDING METHODS

Nowadays, we do not necessarily believe in carving double Vs into our walls and fireplaces. Thankfully, we are more likely to share our homes with pet cats, as opposed to mummifying and encasing them into the foundation of our homes. Yet still warding is, in my view, a necessary and logical step after cleansing a location. Step with me into the realm of modern-day warding, where ancient practices meet contemporary ingenuity to safeguard against the unseen. In this journey, we transcend the realm of superstition and folklore, embracing practical strategies to fortify our defences against the paranormal.

SMUDGING

Imagine this: you stand at the threshold of a home, armed not with swords or shields, but with a humble smudge stick, its fragrant smoke swirling around you like a protective cloak. With each step, you trace the outline of your perimeter, weaving a barrier of cleansing energy that repels negativity and invites harmony. As the sweet aroma fills the air, you feel a sense of empowerment, knowing that you are not just warding off spirits, but also creating a sanctuary of peace and serenity. Here we embark on this ancient ritual with a modern twist, where the simple act of burning herbs becomes a powerful act of protection and renewal. The following is how we ward using smudging.

Firstly, collect your smudge stick (commonly made from sage, cedar, or other cleansing herbs), a lighter or matches, and a fire-safe container like a ceramic bowl or abalone shell, to catch any falling ashes. Before you begin, take a moment to centre yourself and set your intention for the smudging ritual. Use your lighter or matches to gently ignite the tip of the smudge stick. Allow the flame to catch and then gently blow it out, leaving the stick smouldering and emitting smoke.

- Stand at the entrance of the home or the perimeter you wish to ward. Hold the smudge stick firmly in one hand and begin to move clockwise around the space. If possible, start and end at the same point.
- Visualise the cleansing: As you move through the space, visualise the smoke enveloping and cleansing the area. Imagine it dispelling any negativity or stagnant energy, leaving behind a clear and purified atmosphere.
- Pay attention to corners and thresholds: Be sure to focus on corners, doorways, and windows—areas where energy can accumulate or enter.
- If desired, you can recite affirmations, prayers, or incantations that resonate with you as you smudge. These can further amplify your intention and add a spiritual dimension to the ritual.
- Once you've made your way around the perimeter, return to your starting point to complete the circle. Take a moment to express gratitude for the cleansing and protection you've invoked.
- Extinguish the smudge stick: Use the fire-safe container to carefully extinguish the smudge stick by pressing the burning end against the surface until it goes out completely. Make sure it is fully extinguished, before storing it away.

And there you have it. The property is now officially smudged, cleansed, and ready to repel any unwanted spirits. So go ahead, enjoy your newfound sanctuary of positive vibes and fresh energy. And if any lingering spirits dare to test your newly fortified boundaries, well, they better be prepared to face the wrath of your impeccably smudged perimeter!

SALT PURIFICATION AND WARDING

Next, we move to an innocuous kitchen staple, transformed into a mighty shield against things that go bump in the night. That's right, we're diving deep into the mystical powers of salt! From ancient rituals to modern-day superstitions, salt has long been hailed as a potent protector, against the paranormal. Despite its humble origins as a kitchen staple, salt has earned a revered place in folklore and spiritual traditions worldwide, for its purported ability to repel malevolent forces. As we delve into this topic, we'll uncover the rich tapestry of beliefs and rituals that surround salt's role, as a guardian of sacred spaces and sanctuaries. So, with reverence and respect, let us venture forth into the realm where the mundane meets the mystical, seeking to understand the enduring power of this simple, yet profound, symbol of protection.

Superstition around the use of salt has long been prevalent. There is the old belief that throwing salt behind ones back would ward off bad luck. This comes from the belief that the devil, is always standing behind you and throwing salt distracts him from interfering in your life. Salt is commonly used under beds or around doors and windows.

In Jewish tradition, in order to ward off the evil eye, an unfortunate individual only has a few options for safety: Spit three times on your fingertips, then wave them in the air or throw salt. Salt is a fixture in the ancient Temple in Jerusalem; a tradition that continues today, when Jews place salt on their Shabbat (Jewish day of rest) tables and salt is sprinkled over challah (bread) before eating. Salt is preserver, and dipping bread into salt signifies elevating the physical and channelling the spiritual, transforming the transient material world, into something eternal. The Jewish people are also compared to salt: "like salt, the Jewish people never grow stale, but endure forever".

Salt also has traditionally been a protective agent in non-Christian religions, which postulate that its purity, will repel and protect from spirits and evil entities.

It is common in Scotland for family and friends to bring salt to a new house, as a housewarming gift. Sprinkling it about in all the rooms and around the perimeter. It is meant to ward off evil spirits from entering the new home.

In Japan, salt is still used to purify and cleanse their temples, an ancient tradition. A dish of salt can usually be found in a Japanese home, with to ward the house of any negativity. Ancient and traditional Shinto purification rituals, almost always use salt. Some Japanese women during childbirth, will bathe in salt water and use salt to purify the room. This is a practice still used in many parts of Japan today.

Using Salt to ward against wayward spirits and malevolent entities, is possibly the most commonly known method in today's culture. Its use has recently become more widespread, since being popularised in movies and more recently in TV shows like 'Supernatural'. The heroes of the show, Sam and Dean, are usually holed up in some building, which happens to have sacks full of salt laying around, which they hastily put around the doors and windows. This is a good thing, as moments later they are swarmed by ghosts and demons, desperately trying to get in to kill or possesses them. In various spiritualist practices Salt is often used to create a protective circle that a person will stand in, believing that negative energies cannot pass into the circle. I have seen this used in seances and also for those who choose to partake in the Ouija board.

So ingrained is the idea of salt purifying and protecting our homes, it has become mainstream appearing in modern day magazines and books. Better

Homes and Gardens did an article in 2023, which advised dissolving salt in water and spraying it around the home to cleanse the home. They advise doing this on a semi regular basis, to make sure that the energy in the home is not negative. As our journey through belief in salt as a ward draws to a close, we find ourselves standing at the crossroads of tradition and belief, where salt emerges as a timeless symbol of protection against the encroaching shadows of evil.

From the salted thresholds of ancient civilisations to the whispered incantations of modern practitioners, its story is woven into the fabric of human experience. A tale of resilience, faith, and the enduring quest for sanctuary, in a world fraught with unseen dangers. As we look at the method for warding a perimeter with salt, may we carry forward the wisdom of our ancestors, honouring their legacy by embracing the power of salt as a guardian of light, in the ever-present battle against darkness.

To begin you are going to want to collect a sufficient amount of salt. Traditionally, coarse sea salt or rock salt is used, but any type of salt will suffice. Black salt is considered the most powerful against malevolent spirits and entities.

As always, before you begin, take a moment to focus your thoughts and intentions. Decide what you wish to achieve through the warding, whether it is protection, purification, or repelling negative energies.

- Ensure the area you intend to ward is clean and free of clutter. Remove any obstacles that may hinder your movement during the ritual.
- Choose your method: There are several methods for warding with salt. You can create a barrier by sprinkling a line of salt across thresholds, windowsills, or the perimeter of the area you wish to protect. Alternatively, you can place bowls or containers of salt strategically around the space. Another option is using salt water, which Is more appropriate for large locations.
- Sprinkle the salt: If you are creating a barrier, use your fingers or a spoon to sprinkle a line of salt along the desired boundary, it does not need to be continuous. Visualise this line as a barrier that repels negativity and prevents unwanted energies from entering.
- As you work, focus your thoughts on your intention for the warding. Visualise the salt forming a protective shield around the space, creating a sanctuary of safety and peace.
- Pay special attention to key entry points such as doorways, windows, and any areas where energy may flow in or out. Concentrate your efforts on reinforcing these areas with extra layers of continuous salt.

- If it aligns with your beliefs, you may choose to invoke blessings, prayers, or affirmations during the warding process. This can further amplify the protective energy of the salt.
- Once you have completed the warding, take a moment to walk around the perimeter of the area and ensure that all boundaries are securely marked with salt. This is optional but many like to lightly sprinkle salt in the area between the boundary and the building.
- Imagine the space between the building and the boundary is full of positive bright white energy.
- Periodically check the warding and refresh the salt as needed, especially after momentous events or if you sense a decrease in energy levels within the space.

These rituals and practices must be approached with respect, good intentions, and a clear focus on the desired outcome. As with most spiritual barrier work, visualisation and intention is the key. you can adapt and personalise these practices to align with your spiritual beliefs and preferences. remember, whether you are sprinkling it across thresholds or tossing it over your shoulder for good luck, may the power of salt always serve as a beacon of light in the shadowy realms beyond.

Using salt to guide a spirit to the light, involves a different approach compared to traditional warding. Here's a methodology for this purpose:

- Begin by clarifying your intention to assist the spirit in finding peace and transitioning to the light. Approach this process with compassion and empathy. Go through your spiritual protection process.
- Choose a quiet and undisturbed area where you can perform the ritual comfortably. Light candles or burn incense to create a sacred atmosphere conducive to spiritual work.
- Select a bowl or container and fill it with salt. You can use any type of salt for this purpose.
- If it aligns with your beliefs, you may choose to invoke spiritual guides, angels, or divine beings to assist you in guiding the spirit to the light. Offer a prayer or invocation for their presence and guidance.
- Hold the container of salt in your hands and focus your intention on its ability to purify and illuminate. Visualise the salt as a beacon of light that draws the spirit towards it, guiding them to the next phase of their journey.

- Slowly scatter the salt in a path leading from the location where the spirit is present towards a designated exit point or towards a representation of the light (such as a candle or a window).
- As you scatter the salt, speak words of encouragement and guidance to the spirit. Assure them that they are loved and supported and encourage them to follow the path of light towards peace and resolution.
- Maintain a calm and peaceful demeanour throughout the process. Avoid feelings of fear or negativity, as these can hinder the spirit's transition.
- Once you have completed the salt scattering, offer a final prayer or affirmation for the spirit's well-being and safe passage. Thank any spiritual guides or helpers who assisted you during the ritual.
- After the ritual, observe any changes in the energy of the space. You may notice a sense of lightness or peace once the spirit has transitioned.

Depending on the circumstances, you may need to repeat the ritual multiple times, to fully guide the spirit to the light. Trust your intuition and continue the process until you sense a resolution.

What if the thing that needs warding is not a place but a person? Just as spaces can be safeguarded against negative energies and entities through rituals and symbols, individuals can also benefit from similar practices to shield themselves from malevolent forces. Whether it is carrying protective amulets, reciting prayers, or mantras, or performing personal rituals, the goal remains the same: to fortify oneself against spiritual harm and maintain a sense of spiritual well-being amidst the unseen forces that may seek to disrupt it. This is particularly true for anyone who is delving into the paranormal on a regular basis.

WARDING AND SPIRITUAL ATTACHMENT

In the realm of spiritual protection, warding serves as a crucial defence against malevolent entities and energies, both for locations and individuals.

However, in cases where a spiritual attachment has already formed, additional measures may be necessary. Dealing with a spiritual attachment requires a nuanced approach that combines elements of warding, cleansing, and spiritual intervention. This may involve rituals to sever ties with the entity, spiritual cleansing to remove lingering energies, and ongoing practices to strengthen personal boundaries and protection.

By addressing both the external threats through warding and the internal connections of attachment, individuals can reclaim their spiritual sovereignty and restore balance to their lives. Spiritual attachments refer to the belief that entities or energies from the spiritual realm can become connected to individuals or places in the physical world. These attachments are often seen through various cultural and religious lenses and can manifest in diverse ways depending on one's beliefs and experiences.

In many spiritual traditions, it is believed that spirits, souls, or energies can become attached to individuals for a variety of reasons. This attachment might occur due to unresolved issues from a past life, trauma, emotional distress, or even intentionally, through spiritual practices like rituals or ceremonies.

Some common types of spiritual attachments include:

- Entities or Spirits: These are believed to be disembodied beings that can attach themselves to individuals. They might be ghosts, spirits of deceased individuals, or entities from other dimensions.
- Curses or Hexes: In some belief systems, it is thought that negative energies or spells cast by others can attach themselves to individuals, causing harm or disturbances in their lives.
- Energetic Attachments: These are less tangible than entities or curses and may involve the transfer of energetic imprints or patterns from one person to another. This could occur through close relationships, trauma, or shared experiences.
- Psychic Attachments: In psychic beliefs, attachments can occur between individuals through psychic connections, where one person's energy becomes intertwined with another, sometimes leading to emotional or energetic dependencies.

Dealing with spiritual attachments often involves spiritual practices such as energy clearing, rituals, prayers, or seeking the assistance of spiritual healers, shamans, or clergy members, depending on one's belief system. It is essential to approach these matters with care and respect for the beliefs and practices of different cultures and religions. Additionally, seeking professional help from therapists or counsellors can also be beneficial, especially if the attachment is causing significant distress or interference in daily life.

Energetic Attachments and psychic attachments for our intents and purposes, are not relevant, however, they are treated the same as any other attachment, along with traditional forms pf psychological therapy.

In this chapter, we are going to focus our attention on attachments caused by intelligent spirits or entities and those inflicted by another person, which involves a supernatural entity.

SPIRIT ATTACHMENT

If we think of a spirit as energy that has no physical body, then how do they sustain themselves. It takes a lot of energy to interact with the physical world. From what we understand, they take, absorb, or manipulate energy, in the environment in order to sustain their energy. This is why we see the phenomenon of our electrical items being drained on our investigations. Usually there is no harm done to the living, just a very frustrated investigator trying to replace battery packs. But what happens when the dead or a non-human entity, decide that people are the richest source of living energy and attach to that. Feeding of a person's living energy is one example of why a malicious spirit or entity, will attach to a person.

Attachments, it should be noted, can occur for many reasons. It could be due to unfinished business, unresolved emotions, or simply a desire to interact with the physical world. I know a few investigators who have spirits they have interacted with in one location, suddenly appear at another location. Entities may be benevolent, neutral, or malevolent in nature, and their presence can impact an individual's emotional, mental, and physical well-being. Let us look at some of these reason in a little more detail.

- Desire for Interaction: Spirits or entities may attach themselves to a person because they seek interaction with this world. This interaction could stem from a variety of motivations, including a desire for connection, unresolved emotions, or unfinished business from their previous life. As a paranormal investigator, often there will be at least one spirit who tends to pop in at various locations you are at. Just following the investigator around to say hello. These are usually spirits that mean well but are looking for connection or help. This does not lessen the impact on the living person's physical body.

- Resonance and Compatibility: Attachment may occur when there is a resonance or compatibility between the energy signature of the individual and that of the spirit or entity. This resonance can be influenced by factors such as emotional states, past experiences, and spiritual beliefs, creating a conducive environment for attachment to occur. Like energies attract like energies, and if you are around the paranormal enough, this can be a very real threat. Another reason why investigators need to be sound of mind and have good intentions.

- Vulnerability and Openings: Individuals who are experiencing emotional turmoil, trauma, or energetic vulnerabilities may be more susceptible to spirit attachment. These vulnerabilities can create openings in the individual's energy field, allowing spirits or entities to establish a connection.

- Past Life Connections: Some spiritual beliefs suggest that attachments may stem from past life connections or karmic ties between individuals and spirits. These connections may carry over into the present lifetime, leading to interactions and attachments that need to be addressed and resolved.

- Intentional Attachments: In some cases, individuals may intentionally invite spirits or entities into their lives through practices such as mediumship, channelling, ritualistic ceremonies or seeking out and communicating with the paranormal. While these interactions can be voluntary, they also carry potential risks of attachment if not approached with caution, protection, and proper guidance.

- Negative Attachments: Not all attachments are benevolent in nature. Negative entities or spirits may attach themselves to individuals with the intent to cause harm, feed off their energy, or create disturbances in their lives. These attachments often require specialised techniques for removal and protection.

- Transference of Energy: Attachment involves a transference of energy between the individual and the spirit or entity. This exchange of energy can impact the individual's emotional, mental, and physical well-being, influencing their thoughts, emotions, and behaviours.

Understanding the nature of spirit attachments involves recognising the complexities of the spiritual realm and acknowledging the diversity of experiences that individuals may encounter. Cultivating spiritual awareness, maintaining energetic boundaries, and seeking guidance from experienced practitioners can help individuals navigate and address spirit attachments in a balanced and empowered manner.

We have discussed before, how energy tends to attract similar energy. Our emotions play a significant role in determining the type and intensity of the energy we emit. When we experience intense emotions, especially negative ones, our energy output increases. This phenomenon is particularly evident in cases of hauntings, such as poltergeist activity, where heightened fear and anxiety can fuel the intensity of paranormal phenomena. In some cases, entities may intentionally evoke strong emotional responses from individuals to access higher levels of energy, thereby perpetuating and intensifying the haunting.

Negative spirits and entities thrive on emotions like fear, anger, and hatred, often disregarding the harmful effects their energy-draining behaviour has on the affected individual. Visualise an attachment as akin to a parasite feeding off its host, continuously draining energy and causing distress.

Contrary to popular myth, these kinds of attachments are very rare. The most serious attachments are usually defined as needing the transference of energy, between the spirit and the person.

Often these attachments occur to people who have emotional, mental, or other strong emotional issues going on. That is because at times of emotional or mental distress our barriers and boundaries become compromised. People suffering addictions are also prime targets for these kinds of attachments, often by non-human spirits. People who are going through some kinds of upheaval are also more likely to be volatile with their emotions and therefore easy to illicit an emotional response for energy. Negative spirits and entities will be attracted to these kinds of people, who are not at an energetic level to be able to either sustain their energy or fight back.

The second group that are often targets for this kind of issue are sensitives who have not learnt to set their safe boundaries or harness their abilities. This could be an empath who cannot block out the emotions of people or spirits, or a medium who has not learnt to manage their abilities. Paranormal investigators are also a prime target, because we spend so much time interacting with the spirit world.

This is the exact reason at the beginning and the end of an investigation, we make clear that our boundaries are NOT to be crossed and why the emotional wellbeing of your team is essential. The term attachment comes from the fact, that the transferring of energy is through a literal attachment. Spirit attachments can often manifest symptoms that mimic depression, leading individuals to believe they are solely dealing with a psychological issue. The symptom of a parasitic attachment can include the following:

- Lethargy and depression.
- Emotional upset, volatility and feeling overwhelmed and vulnerable.
- Unexplained aches and pains, especially at points of attachment.
- Feeling cold and chilled and the inability to focus or sleep.
- Unexplained illness that seems chronic with no medical explanation.
- General complaint such as stomach aches and headaches.

As with anything in the paranormal field, you should never assume these symptoms are paranormal. Its only when everything else has been ruled out, that you even entertain the notion of a spiritual attachment. This is where jumping the gun and declaring a paranormal events prematurely, can do far more harm than good. Especially when we are dealing with someone who may have emotional or mental difficulties. Think back to the extreme case of Annalise Michel discussed earlier. This is also the reason why having the Catholic church come in and do an actual exorcism is such a long process. They have to rule out any mental health issues.

Firstly, you as an investigator, have to rule out any medical issues – It is a good idea to encourage the client to get a full physical and psychological assessment, to rule out any medical reasons for the symptoms.

If they are being treated by a medical team, then there should be no improvement, despite the best effort of the client and doctors. If this is not the case, then the condition should be medically unexplained. There needs to be caution, because some conditions can take time to improve, such as depression. Sometimes, medications need to be tweaked, in order to be effective. Some are also slow acting and become effective over time.

The biggest indicator and most important question should be, when the symptoms start and have, they been exposed to any kinds of haunting. The other question is had they been involved in any occult type of activity.

Consider the following hypothetical scenario. Louise, a vibrant mother and wife, whose life takes an unexpected turn after moving into a new house. Suddenly, her cheerful demeanour dissipates, replaced by unexplained mood swings and lethargy. Even doctors are baffled by her symptoms, which seem to improve when she's away from the house. Alternatively, picture Louise enjoying an evening with friends, innocently dabbling with a Ouija board or other communication tool. However, they fail to properly close the session, or worse, conduct it in her home, which already exhibits signs of paranormal activity. In such a scenario, Louise's mysterious afflictions might not stem from illness but rather from a malevolent spirit attachment—a haunting reality she's unwittingly become entangled in. this scenario would most likely make most investigators consider attachment and seek a spiritual resolution.

It is not uncommon for many paranormal investigators, over the course of years of investigating, to come home with attachments especially if they have not been keeping up with their protections. Even if they have been keeping up with their protective practices, it can and does happen to experienced investigators. Even more reason to be careful of the locations you visit and have a strong understanding of what is present at a location, before attending.

Consider the following scenario: Alex, a seasoned paranormal investigator, frequently explores haunted locations in search of evidence of the supernatural. During one investigation at an abandoned asylum, Alex encounters a particularly malevolent spirit that seems drawn to their energy. Despite taking precautions and using protective measures, such as grounding techniques and spiritual cleansing rituals, Alex feels an intense connection with the spirit.

After leaving the asylum, Alex begins to experience strange phenomena at home. Objects move on their own, unexplained shadows flicker in the corners of rooms, and Alex is plagued by vivid nightmares. Despite their expertise in dealing with the paranormal, Alex struggles to shake off the oppressive presence that seems to have latched onto them.

As time passes, the disturbances escalate, affecting not only Alex but also his family members. Loved one's report feeling cold spots, hearing disembodied voices, and experiencing feelings of unease whenever they visit Alex's home. It becomes apparent that the malevolent spirit from the asylum has followed Alex home, seeking to continue its torment beyond the confines of the abandoned building.

In this scenario, Alex's knowledge and experience as a paranormal investigator inadvertently attract the attention of a malevolent spirit, leading to a frightening and potentially dangerous attachment that transcends the boundaries of time and space.

In cases where an attachment is suspected, it can be helpful to bring in an energy worker, healer and or a psychic medium who may be able to offer some insight into what is going on.

As of the time of writing we had recently done an investigation on the grounds of the old Sunset Hospital located in Dalkeith in Perth. Known for its high paranormal activity the location did not disappoint. If people are disrespectful, attacks have been known to happen, with one investigator recently being choked by unseen hands. The spirits at this location have been known to follow people home. I received a Class A EVP on that investigation confirming this. When we were telling them they did not have permission to follow us, I received an EVP saying, "we will follow you home". In this case there was the very real chance, as at the quarantine station, something could attach and come home with us. This was not an acceptable scenario for me, by any stretch of the imagination.

As far as investigators go, we should make it clear they are not allowed to follow us home. It is not something that is up for debate. However, one can never be too careful and spirits, much the same as people, often choose to do the opposite of what they are instructed to do.

As an added precaution, the last thing we did before leaving this particular location, was to Sage ourselves, our equipment, and the inside of our cars. This was to make SURE nothing followed us home. Prevention is always the better option, and it is never a bad option to come completely prepared for scenarios such as this.

In contemporary paranormal accounts, there are numerous instances of spirits purportedly following individuals to their homes. These occurrences often involve individuals encountering paranormal phenomena, such as apparitions or unexplained sounds, in a particular location, only to find that the activity persists after they leave. Despite leaving the initial site, individuals report continued experiences of paranormal activity in their own homes, suggesting that the spirits or entities have followed them. These modern cases highlight the unsettling possibility that paranormal encounters can extend beyond specific locations, impacting individuals in their personal spaces.

Here are a few examples of modern scenarios where spirits can allegedly follow people home and cause an attachment.

- The Haunted Object: Someone acquires an antique item or visits a location with a haunted reputation, only to experience paranormal phenomena once they bring the object or energy back to their home. This phenomenon is commonly associated with haunted artifacts or items with attached spirits.

- Visiting a Haunted Location: Individuals visit a reportedly haunted location, such as an abandoned building or cemetery, and encounter paranormal activity. After leaving the site, they continue to experience disturbances, suggesting that a spirit has followed them from the original location.

- Personal Connections: Sometimes, individuals develop personal connections with spirits during paranormal investigations or encounters. These spirits may then choose to follow them home, seeking further interaction or attachment.

- Spiritual Residues: In cases where individuals engage in spiritual practices or rituals, residual energies or entities may linger and follow them back to their homes, leading to ongoing paranormal experiences.

- Electronic Devices: Some individuals report paranormal activity associated with electronic devices, such as phones or computers. In these cases, spirits may allegedly manipulate technology and follow individuals through digital connections.

There are two cases of spirit attachment I have come across in my research. One such case involves a paranormal investigator who experienced a series of unsettling events after investigating a reportedly haunted house. Upon returning home, they began noticing strange occurrences, including unexplained noises, shadowy figures, and feelings of being watched. Despite attempts to cleanse their home and protect themselves spiritually, the disturbances persisted, indicating a possible attachment from the haunted location.

Another documented case involves a group of friends who experimented with a Ouija board during a paranormal investigation. Following the session, one of the individuals reported experiencing frequent nightmares and feelings of unease, even when away from the location. Despite efforts to break the attachment and seek spiritual guidance, the negative energy seemed to linger, affecting their daily life.

While these cases are anecdotal and subjective, they highlight the potential risks associated with paranormal investigations and interactions with supernatural entities. It underscores the importance of caution, respect, and proper spiritual protection when engaging in such activities. Some other cases reported are documented below.

Ed and Lorraine Warren
Renowned paranormal investigators Ed and Lorraine Warren claimed to have encountered numerous cases of spirit attachments during their career. One famous case involved the Amityville Horror, where they alleged to have experienced spiritual oppression and attachments while investigating the infamous house.

Ghost Adventures Crew
The Ghost Adventures crew, led by Zak Bagans, has reported instances of feeling spiritually affected or "possessed" during their investigations. In several episodes, crew members have described feeling sudden changes in mood, physical sensations, or experiencing unexplained behaviour that they attribute to spirit attachments.

The Conjuring House
In the case of the Perron family, whose experiences inspired "The Conjuring" film series, paranormal investigators Ed and Lorraine Warren conducted investigations at their Rhode Island home in the 1970s. Following their involvement, some members of the Perron family claimed to have experienced continued paranormal activity, suggesting that spirits may have followed them home from the haunted house.

In addition to spiritual attachments resulting from paranormal investigations or interactions with negative entities, there are cases where individuals believe they have been targeted by curses or hexes, leading to similar manifestations of negative energy or spiritual disturbances.

CURSES AND HEXES

In various cultures and belief systems, curses, and hexes are thought to be malevolent spells or intentions, cast by individuals with the intent to harm others. These negative energies can attach themselves to individuals, causing disturbances in their lives. Curses and hexes are often believed to be fuelled by strong emotions such as anger, jealousy, or resentment. While the specifics can vary widely depending on cultural context, there are some common elements found in many traditions.

A curse is typically a spoken or written invocation of harm upon someone or something. It is often believed, that the words themselves possess power, and when uttered with intent, they can bring about negative consequences. Curses can range from simple expressions of anger or frustration to elaborate rituals performed with specific intent.

Hexes, on the other hand, are similar to curses but are often thought to involve some form of magic or witchcraft. In many traditions, hexes are seen as a deliberate act of harnessing supernatural forces to bring about harm or misfortune to the target. Like curses, hexes can take many forms, from simple spells to complex rituals involving ingredients, symbols, and incantations.

Throughout history, curses, and hexes have been used for various purposes, including seeking revenge, protecting oneself or loved ones, or simply expressing anger or frustration. However, it is important to note that the effectiveness of curses and hexes is largely a matter of belief. While some people firmly believe in their power, others may see them as nothing more than superstition or psychological phenomena.

In many traditions, it is believed that supernatural beings, such as spirits, demons, or deities, can be invoked or employed to carry out curses or hexes. These entities are thought to possess powers beyond those of humans and can be called upon to enact vengeance, punishment, or other forms of harm upon a target.

Some cultures have specific entities associated with cursing or hexing, such as malevolent spirits or deities of retribution. These beings are often portrayed as agents of justice or balance, punishing those who have wronged others or upset the natural order. In other cases, curses and hexes may be believed to be carried out by restless spirits, or vengeful ghosts seeking revenge from beyond the grave.

In certain belief systems, practitioners of magic or witchcraft may also invoke supernatural entities to aid in casting curses or hexes. These entities could be spirits or deities associated with magic, darkness, or the underworld, and they may be petitioned, or bargained with, in exchange for their assistance.

One of the most famous examples of this, is the belief in the Curse of the Pharaohs, which supposedly, afflicted those who disturbed the tombs of ancient Egyptian rulers. This curse, was said to bring sickness, accidents, or even death upon archaeologists and grave robbers who dared to desecrate the resting places of the pharaohs. After the discovery of the tomb of the Egyptian pharaoh Tutankhamun in 1922 by Howard Carter, rumours of a curse associated with the tomb began to circulate. Several individuals involved in the excavation and study of the tomb, including Carter himself, reportedly suffered from mysterious illnesses, accidents, or untimely deaths. While these incidents could be attributed to coincidence or natural causes, the idea of a curse placed on the tomb to protect it from desecration captured the public's imagination and persists to this day. I have personally visited Tutankhamun's tomb and I did give second thought to entering.

One more modern infamous case involves the murder of Nelson Rehmeyer in 1928 in Pennsylvania, USA. Rehmeyer was killed by three men who believed he had placed a curse on them using witchcraft. The men, John Blymire, John Curry, and Wilbert Hess, sought out Rehmeyer's "spell book" in an attempt to break the curse, leading to Rehmeyer's brutal murder. The case gained widespread attention and contributed to the fear and paranoia surrounding witchcraft in rural America at the time.

In Japanese folklore, there are numerous tales of evil spirits or yokai being summoned to inflict harm on others. For example, the "ubume" is a ghostly figure said to appear to pregnant women and demand their help in caring for her unborn child. If the woman agrees, she may be haunted by the ubume and subjected to torment until she fulfils her promise. Similarly, the "tsukumogami" are inanimate objects that come to life after 100 years, and may seek revenge on their former owners for mistreatment.

François "Papa Doc" Duvalier was the president of Haiti from 1957 to 1971 and was known for his authoritarian rule and use of voodoo symbolism in politics. Duvalier promoted the belief in his supernatural powers as a voodoo priest and used fear tactics, including rumours of curses and supernatural retribution, to maintain control over the population. While the extent of Duvalier's involvement in voodoo practices is debated, his reign was marked by widespread fear and superstition.

In another chilling tale, the infamous Salem witch trials of 1692 saw numerous individuals accused of practicing witchcraft and subsequently subjected to trials and executions. The repercussions of these events extended beyond legal proceedings, with families torn apart, reputations tarnished, and communities haunted by the spectre of alleged witchcraft.

Where as we know many of these cases were just nothing but superstition and fear, let's delve into some intriguing cases where individuals have reported experiencing harm or misfortune, believed to be caused by curses or hexes. These instances, often shrouded in mystery and fear, offer glimpses into the darker realms of the supernatural.

More contemporary cases continue to surface, with individuals reporting inexplicable bouts of bad luck, persistent health issues, or unexplained phenomena attributed to curses or hexes cast by adversaries or practitioners of dark magic. These accounts underscore the enduring belief in supernatural forces capable of inflicting harm from beyond the realm of the natural world.

As we explore these cases further, we'll encounter the intricate interplay between belief systems, cultural practices, and the enduring human fascination with the mysterious and unexplained.

The Case of Charles Peck and Don Decker

One notable case that fits this description is the story of Charles Peck, a railway engineer, and his former manager, Don Decker, who allegedly experienced paranormal activity after Peck's dismissal.

In February 1983, Charles Peck was fired from his job as a railway engineer due to his erratic behaviour. Distraught over losing his job, Peck boarded an Amtrak train to visit family in Michigan. Tragically, the train collided with a freight train in California, resulting in Peck's death along with several others.

After Peck's death, his former manager, Don Decker, reported experiencing strange occurrences. He claimed that water inexplicably began to drip from the ceiling of his apartment, even though there were no leaks or plumbing issues. Decker also reported feeling a presence in the room and experiencing intense emotions of fear and dread.

When paranormal investigators were called to investigate, they concluded that Decker was being haunted by the spirit of Charles Peck, seeking vengeance for his dismissal and untimely death. According to the investigators, the paranormal activity ceased once Decker forgave Peck and expressed remorse for his role in his firing.

The case gained widespread attention and was featured on television programs and in books about the paranormal. Sceptics, however, have questioned the credibility of the claims, suggesting that the reported phenomena may have had natural explanations or could have been fabricated for attention or profit.

Regardless of the veracity of the claims, the story of Charles Peck and Don Decker serves as a cautionary tale about the potential consequences of mistreating others and the enduring power of belief in the supernatural.

The Donner-Houghton Case

In the late 19th century, a man named George Donner reportedly fired a man named Lewis Houghton from his lumber business in Michigan. Following his dismissal, Houghton allegedly placed a curse on Donner, vowing revenge. Soon after, Donner began experiencing strange phenomena, including unexplained noises, objects moving on their own, and sightings of apparitions. Some believed that these occurrences were the result of Houghton's curse.

The Rammelsberg Mine Incident

In 1936, the Rammelsberg Mine in Germany was the site of a mining accident that resulted in the deaths of several workers. Following the accident, the mine manager, Gustav Wenzel, reported experiencing strange phenomena, including sightings of ghostly apparitions and unexplained noises. Wenzel attributed the disturbances to the restless spirits of the deceased miners seeking justice or revenge or a family member of the deceased cursing him.

In a gripping episode of the 2012 documentary series "Cursed," featured in season one, episode four, viewers were introduced to Tiffany, whose decision to terminate a Native American employee from her business unleashed a terrifying ordeal. Subsequently, she found herself besieged by the menacing presence of a large malevolent entity that subjected her to physical assaults and torment. Despite her efforts, Tiffany remained ensnared by the entity, as the original employee declined to lift the curse, and the tribe opted not to intervene.

Similarly, the documentary recounted the unsettling experience of Lawrence, whose ill-fated encounter with a woman bearing a grudge resulted in a Voodoo curse being cast upon him. As a consequence, Lawrence found himself grappling with the presence of a malevolent entity that had become inexplicably attached to him, defying all attempts at removal or dispelling.

Ultimately, whether stemming from spiritual attachments, curses, or hexes, addressing these manifestations often involves a combination of spiritual practices, psychological support, and protective measures to restore harmony and well-being to affected individuals and their environments.

PRACTICE OF REMOVING SPIRIT ATTACHMENTS

Liberating oneself from these otherworldly bonds often necessitates the utilisation of rituals, purification rites, or the expertise of spiritual practitioners, tribal shamans, or religious figures versed in removal methodologies. In my personal experience, when confronting a suspected attachment, I strongly recommend enlisting the aid of a trained energy worker for its removal. The process of detaching from spiritual entities typically entails a multifaceted approach aimed at purging negative energies and entities from one's aura or energetic sphere. Below is a sequential guide you can employ: Should you encounter difficulties in dislodging attachments independently, do not hesitate to seek professional assistance from a spiritual healer, energy practitioner, or therapist specialising in this field. Removing attachments from others necessitates a nuanced approach, requiring utmost respect for their autonomy and consent, coupled with compassionate support and guidance. Here is a generalised procedure you can follow:

- Observation and Assessment: Observe the individual's behaviour, emotions, and energy patterns to determine if they might be experiencing spiritual attachments. Look for signs such as sudden mood swings, unexplained physical sensations, or persistent negative thoughts as well as investigate the source of the attachment.

- Approach the individual with empathy and openness. Express your concerns in a non-judgmental manner and ask if they have noticed any unusual experiences or changes in their life that they'd like to discuss.

- If the individual is receptive, provide information about spiritual attachments and how they can affect one's well-being. Offer resources such as articles, books, or reputable websites where they can learn more about the topic.

- Let the individual know that you are there to support them through the process. Assure them that seeking help is a sign of strength and that they are not alone in dealing with these challenges.

- Respect the individual's autonomy and agency throughout the process. Avoid imposing your beliefs or solutions on them and allow them to make their own choices regarding their spiritual journey.

- Encourage the individual to seek professional help from a qualified healer, energy worker, therapist, or spiritual counsellor Provide recommendations for trusted practitioners if they are unsure where to start.

- Support the individual in incorporating healing practices into their routine, such as meditation, energy clearing rituals, or therapeutic techniques recommended by professionals.

- Offer emotional support and reassurance as the individual navigates the process of removing attachments. Be patient, compassionate, and non-judgmental as they work through any challenges or setbacks.

- Follow up with the individual regularly to see how they are progressing and offer additional support or resources as needed. Check-ins can help reinforce their commitment to healing and provide encouragement along the way.

- Maintain confidentiality and respect the individual's privacy throughout the process. Avoid discussing their situation with others without their explicit consent.

- Encourage the individual to prioritise self-care and empowerment as they work towards removing attachments. Help them identify

315

healthy coping mechanisms and practices that support their overall well-being.

- Respect the individual's boundaries and decisions regarding their spiritual journey. Offer support and guidance without overstepping or pressuring them into actions they're not comfortable with.

Keep in mind that helping others release attachments is a joint effort. Your role involves providing support, guidance, and access to resources while empowering them to manage their own journey towards healing. However, if you're interested in learning the process of attachment removal, let's walk through it together. It is advisable to reach out to a local spiritual healer who can instruct you in this practice. Like any spiritual work, we will begin in a peaceful environment, grounding ourselves and establishing a protective shield. During an attachment cleansing, it is important not to make physical contact with the individual; instead, focus your efforts about 5 to 10 inches away from their body, working with their energy rather than their physical form.

- Perform cleansing rituals to clear negative energies from your aura and space. This could involve smudging with sage, or any other practice that you feel comfortable with.
- Go through the process of drawing white light into your body and into your hands.
- Working 5 to 10 Inches away from the body run your hands over specifically focusing on any parts of the energy field that feels dense or hot.
- Visualise and energetically cut cords attaching the person to the negative energies or entities. Imagine severing these cords with a sharp, glowing sword or ask your spiritual guides for assistance in cutting them.
- Encourage the person to practice forgiveness towards yourself and others involved in the attachment. Release any resentment or negative emotions that may be keeping the attachment in place.
- Set clear boundaries with any negative energies or entities. They should assert their intention to reclaim their space and energy for their own well-being.

Removing spiritual attachments necessitates a deep understanding and comfort with working within the realm of subtle energies. Those embarking on this journey must possess a strong intuition and a comprehensive knowledge of spiritual practices. They traverse unseen dimensions with confidence, utilising tools like visualisation, energy clearing techniques, and communication with spiritual guides or higher entities.

Their proficiency in working with energies allows them to discern and release negative attachments while upholding energetic boundaries and ensuring the safety of all involved. Through their grounded presence and adept application of energy work, they facilitate the process of liberation from spiritual entanglements, restoring equilibrium to the individual's energy field. However, this task isn't suitable for everyone, and often, investigators refer individuals to practitioners specialising in energy work.

Attempting attachment removal without proper training, experience, and ethical guidelines can result in unintended consequences or worsen existing issues. Therefore, it is essential to approach this practice with caution, sensitivity, and respect for the individual's beliefs and boundaries, seeking professional guidance when necessary.

In my experience, addressing underlying issues is crucial before embarking on attachment work. Sometimes, individuals find themselves in such situations through no fault of their own, perhaps due to unfortunate circumstances or the nature of their work, such as paranormal investigations. In these cases, reviewing protection practices is essential to prevent recurrence.

Consider a scenario where a person resides in a haunted house, resolving the haunting takes precedence. Often, during a house cleansing, residents may concurrently undergo attachment removal.

For those dabbling in the occult without proper understanding, addressing these issues is paramount. This involves examining the motives behind their involvement and either discontinuing unsafe practices or seeking guidance to practice safely. Protective measures, such as learning techniques and gaining insight, are imperative in such situations.

In the paranormal realm, some navigate safely, while others encounter significant challenges due to unsafe practices. Addressing attachments involves not only the practical aspect but also exploring and nurturing the emotional and spiritual dimensions. A holistic approach proves more effective than a narrow focus on attachment removal alone.

SPIRITS WHO REFUSE TO LEAVE A PERSON OR PLACE

If a spirit attached to a person or a place refuse to leave, it can be a challenging situation that requires careful handling. Here are some steps to consider: Try to understand why the spirit is unwilling to leave. It could be due to unresolved issues, fear of moving on, or a strong attachment to the person or place.

Attempt to communicate with the spirit through meditation, prayer, or the assistance of a medium. Listen to their concerns and try to offer reassurance or guidance. If the spirit has specific reasons for not wanting to leave, try to negotiate a solution that addresses their concerns while also ensuring the well-being of the affected individual or location.

If communication or negotiation efforts are unsuccessful, seek assistance from experienced spiritual practitioners, mediums, or paranormal investigators who specialise in spirit release or clearings. Perform spiritual cleansing rituals or ceremonies to purify the affected space and create an environment that is less conducive to negative spiritual influences. Clearly assert your boundaries and intentions for the spirit to leave. Enlist the help of spiritual guides, angels, or protective deities to support the removal process if this is part of your belief system.

Implement protective measures such as energy shielding, removing a stubborn spirit attachment may require persistence and patience. Stay committed to the process while maintaining a sense of compassion and empathy towards the spirit.

Once the spirit has left, offer prayers or rituals to facilitate their transition to the next phase of their spiritual journey. Provide closure and gratitude for their cooperation in resolving the situation.

If the situation becomes overwhelming or dangerous, seek assistance from qualified professionals such as priests, shamans, or paranormal experts who can offer specialised skills and support.

KNOWING WHEN TO SEEK SPECIALIST HELP

Knowing when to ask for help is crucial for any paranormal investigator, just like in any other field. Here are some situations where seeking assistance is wise:

Encountering Dangerous Entities
If you come across a particularly malevolent or dangerous entity, it is essential to seek help immediately. This could include demonic entities or spirits that exhibit violent behaviour. Contacting experienced demonologists or spiritual experts can be beneficial.

Dealing with High-Level Paranormal Activity
Some cases might involve complex phenomena that require specialised knowledge or equipment beyond your expertise. Seek assistance from seasoned investigators or paranormal research organisations who have dealt with similar situations.

Protecting Mental Health
Investigating the paranormal can take a toll on mental health, especially when dealing with traumatic experiences or encountering phenomena beyond comprehension. It is essential to have a support system in place, including mental health professionals who understand the unique challenges of paranormal investigation.

Gaining Different Perspectives
Collaboration with other investigators can bring fresh insights and perspectives to a case. Don't hesitate to consult with colleagues or experts in related fields to gain a broader understanding of the phenomena you're investigating.

Technical Challenges
If you encounter technical challenges during investigations, such as equipment malfunctions or data analysis issues, reaching out to specialists in relevant fields like electronics or data science can help resolve the issues effectively.

Ethical Dilemmas
Sometimes, investigations can raise ethical concerns, especially when dealing with vulnerable individuals or sensitive cultural beliefs. Seek guidance from experts in ethics or cultural sensitivity to navigate these situations appropriately.

Legal Matters
In certain cases, paranormal investigations may intersect with legal issues, such as property rights or privacy concerns. Consulting with legal experts can ensure that your investigations comply with relevant laws and regulations.

Remember, asking for help is not a sign of weakness but rather a demonstration of strength, wisdom and above all else responsibility. Collaboration and support from others can enhance the safety, effectiveness, and ethical integrity of your paranormal investigations.

Asking for help in paranormal matters is crucial for investigators who find themselves in over their heads for several reasons: Dealing with the paranormal often requires specialised knowledge in various fields such as psychology, parapsychology, occultism, and even religious studies. Seeking help from experts in these areas can provide insights and guidance that general investigators may lack.

Some paranormal investigations involve potentially dangerous situations, either physically or psychologically. Consulting with experienced individuals who understand the risks and precautions necessary, can help ensure the safety of the investigators involved.

Having additional investigators or experts involved, can provide validation and verification of findings. It helps to ensure that the evidence collected is credible and not influenced by bias or misinterpretation.

Paranormal investigations can sometimes delve into sensitive areas, such as dealing with individuals who believe they are experiencing hauntings or other paranormal phenomena. Seeking guidance on how to approach these situations ethically and with sensitivity is essential.

Collaboration with other investigators or experts can lead to the sharing of resources such as equipment, research materials, and investigative techniques, which can enhance the overall effectiveness of the investigation.

Dealing with the paranormal can be emotionally taxing, especially if investigators encounter disturbing or unexplained phenomena. Having a supportive network of fellow investigators or experts to lean on can help alleviate stress and provide emotional support.

Different experts bring diverse perspectives to the table, which can lead to innovative approaches and new insights into the phenomena being investigated. Collaboration between individuals with varied backgrounds can lead to a more comprehensive understanding of the paranormal.

In summary, asking for help in paranormal matters is essential for investigators because it ensures access to specialised knowledge, promotes safety, validates findings, addresses ethical concerns, facilitates resource sharing, provides emotional support, and fosters cross-disciplinary insights.

12 BEYOND THE VEIL: UNRAVELING THE FINAL MYSTERY

Paranormal investigation, despite its often controversial nature, can offer valuable insights into human beliefs, perceptions, and the mysteries of the universe. Here is an in-depth conclusion on the importance of employing the scientific method, thorough documentation, and conducting ethical research in paranormal investigation:

SCIENTIFIC METHOD

The scientific method forms the foundation of rigorous paranormal investigation. It involves making observations, forming hypotheses, conducting experiments, analysing data, and drawing conclusions. Applying the scientific method to paranormal phenomena, allows investigators to approach their research with scepticism and objectivity, minimising biases, errors and false positives in interpretation.

While paranormal phenomena may challenge our current scientific understanding, adherence to the scientific method enables researchers to systematically explore and potentially uncover new knowledge about the paranormal with credibility.

Thorough documentation is essential in paranormal investigation to ensure the reliability and replicability of findings. This includes recording detailed information about the location, environmental conditions, equipment used, and any observed phenomena. Audio, visual, and written documentation provide a comprehensive record of the investigation process, allowing for thorough analysis and review. Documentation also facilitates peer review and collaboration within the paranormal research community, fostering transparency and accountability.

321

Ethical considerations are paramount to ensure the well-being of both researchers and subjects. Respecting the privacy and autonomy of individuals involved in investigations, including clients, witnesses, and potential spirits, is crucial. Obtaining informed consent and respecting cultural beliefs and sensitivities are essential parts of ethical practices.

Researchers should prioritise the safety and psychological well-being of all participants, including protecting against potential harm from paranormal phenomena or psychological distress resulting from the investigation. Additionally, maintaining integrity and honesty in reporting findings, including acknowledging limitations and uncertainties, is vital for upholding ethical standards in paranormal research.

While the scientific method is a powerful tool for investigating natural phenomena, it encounters several limitations when applied to paranormal research:

Paranormal phenomena often lack falsifiability, a key criterion in scientific inquiry. Falsifiability means that a hypothesis can be proven false, through empirical testing. Many paranormal claims are based on anecdotal evidence or subjective experiences that cannot be conclusively tested or replicated under controlled conditions.

Paranormal phenomena face methodological limitations. Paranormal activity may involve variables that are difficult to control or measure, such as psychic abilities or interactions with non-material entities. Designing experiments to investigate such phenomena in a controlled and replicable manner poses significant challenges.

Human perception is inherently subjective and susceptible to biases. Witnesses' interpretations of paranormal events may be influenced by cultural beliefs, expectations, or cognitive biases like pareidolia (perceiving patterns or significance in random stimuli). This subjectivity complicates the interpretation of evidence and makes it challenging to establish objective criteria for assessing paranormal claims and evidence.

Conducting research on paranormal phenomena raises ethical concerns, particularly regarding the well-being and consent of human participants. Investigating potentially distressing or psychologically unsettling experiences, such as encounters with spirits or hauntings, requires careful consideration of ethical guidelines and safeguards to protect participants from harm.

The scientific community lacks consensus on the existence and nature of paranormal phenomena. While some researchers may approach paranormal claims with an open-minded scepticism, others dismiss such claims outright due to the absence of empirical evidence or theoretical frameworks to support them. This lack of consensus can hinder interdisciplinary collaboration and impede progress in all areas of paranormal research.

Replicating paranormal phenomena in controlled laboratory settings is often challenging. Even when phenomena are observed, replicating them consistently under different conditions or by independent researchers can be difficult. The lack of replicability undermines the reliability and validity of paranormal claims according to scientific standards. It means that we are unable to take away the subjectivity and human perception that goes along with paranormal encounters.

The scientific method is inherently limited to investigating natural phenomena that can be observed, measured, and explained within the framework of natural laws. Paranormal phenomena, by its very definition, transcends or challenges conventional scientific understanding. Spiritual, supernatural, or metaphysical explanations often fall outside the scope of scientific inquiry.

Despite these limitations, some researchers continue to explore paranormal phenomena using scientific methods while acknowledging the inherent challenges and complexities involved. Balancing scepticism with open-mindedness, maintaining methodological rigor, and accepting that it may fall beyond the realm of measurability and fostering interdisciplinary dialogue are essential for advancing understanding in this controversial field.

UNVEILING THE TRUTH: DEBUNKING MYTHS IN PARANORMAL

In the realm of paranormal research, where the unexplained intersect with our understanding of the natural world, misconceptions abound. These misconceptions often stem from sensationalised portrayals in the media, anecdotal accounts that lack truth or reliability, and a lack of scientific understanding.

While paranormal phenomena captivate the imagination and spark curiosity, they also give rise to myths and misconceptions that can obscure the truth. In this section, we delve into some of the most prevalent misconceptions in paranormal research, shedding light on the realities behind ghostly encounters, psychic phenomena, and other inexplicable occurrences. By debunking myths and unravelling misconceptions, the aim to promote critical thinking and foster a better understanding of the complexities inherent in paranormal investigations.

Misconception: Orbs Are Evidence of Ghostly Activity

Orbs, often captured in photographs or videos, are commonly believed to be manifestations of spirits. However, orbs are typically caused by natural phenomena such as dust, moisture, or insects reflecting light in the camera lens. Understanding the optical properties behind orbs can help distinguish them from genuine paranormal activity.

Misconception: Electronic Devices Can Detect Ghosts

While EMF meters and EVP recorders are frequently used in paranormal investigations, their ability to detect ghosts is highly debated. Fluctuations in electromagnetic fields and anomalous sounds may have natural explanations, such as electrical wiring or environmental factors. Critical analysis is necessary to discern genuine paranormal phenomena from environmental noise.

Misconception: Cold Spots Indicate Presence of Spirits

Hot and cold spots, although often present at haunted locations are not always indicative of paranormal activity. Areas where temperatures inexplicably drop, are often interpreted as signs of ghostly presence. However, these fluctuations can be attributed to drafts, air currents, or thermal convection. Investigating environmental factors and conducting temperature measurements can help debunk the myth of cold spots as definitive evidence of the supernatural.

Misconception: EVPs Always Contain Clear Messages from Spirits

Electronic Voice Phenomena (EVPs) are recordings purported to capture spirit voices. However, EVPs often contain ambiguous or indiscernible sounds that can be interpreted subjectively. Pareidolia, the tendency to perceive meaningful patterns in random noise, can lead to false interpretations of EVPs. Scepticism and critical analysis are necessary when evaluating EVP evidence. The majority of EVPs caught are not crystal clear.

Misconception: Ghostly Apparitions Are Always Visually Manifested

While visual apparitions are commonly associated with ghostly encounters, not all paranormal phenomena are visually perceptible. Many experiences involve auditory, olfactory, or tactile sensations that defy conventional explanations. Investigating multiple sensory modalities and considering psychological factors can provide a more comprehensive understanding of paranormal encounters.

Misconception: Haunted Locations Are Inherently Dangerous

Haunted locations are often portrayed as dangerous or malevolent in popular media. However, being harmed by unseen hands is extremely rare. Fear and anxiety associated with haunted places may be attributed to psychological factors rather than supernatural threats. Promoting rational inquiry and dispelling unfounded fears is essential in paranormal investigations. However, this being said, practicing safe encounters with spirits and entities is always a priority. Just because they don't usually harm, does not mean they cant.

<u>Misconception: Paranormal Phenomena Are Always Singularly Explained</u>
Paranormal phenomena are complex and multifaceted, often defying singular explanations. As is evidenced in the case at the gaol with the footsteps and slamming of the cell door. Exploring multiple hypotheses and considering alternative interpretations is essential in paranormal research. Embracing uncertainty and ambiguity can lead to unexpected discoveries and a deeper understanding ghostly encounter.

As you the reader delve into the scientific explanations behind seemingly supernatural occurrences, you undergo a journey of revelation, discovering that many paranormal anomalies have rational, natural causes. This revelation sparks surprise and fascination, as the veil of some paranormal phenomena is lifted to reveal the underlying scientific principles at play.

One of the most intriguing aspects of uncovering these scientific explanations is the way they challenge preconceived notions and debunk common misconceptions. People are often surprised to learn that phenomena like orbs in photographs, cold spots in haunted locations, and anomalous sounds captured on EVP recordings have mundane origins rooted in visual, environmental, psychological and acoustics, rather than otherworldly entities.

Furthermore, delving into the scientific principles underlying these phenomena enables individuals to grasp the intricate relationship between light, sound, temperature, and electromagnetic fields, influencing their perceptions and encounters. My aspiration is that this newfound comprehension empowers you, the reader, to approach your paranormal investigations with a discerning mindset. This involves distinguishing between authentic anomalies and mundane events posing as supernatural occurrences.

Moreover, discovering scientific explanations nurtures a profound appreciation for the intricacy of phenomena that defy natural understanding.

AN INTREPID JOURNEY ONWARDS

As our journey through the mysteries of the paranormal draws to a close, I invite you, to embark on your own adventures in exploring the unknown. Armed with newfound knowledge and insights gleaned from this exploration, you possess the tools necessary to delve deeper into the realms of the paranormal.

But where to begin? Fear not, for I am here to offer practical tips and guidance to help you integrate paranormal investigation into your life, whether as a hobby or a profession. Here are a few suggestions to get you started:

Continuously expand your understanding of paranormal phenomena by reading books, attending workshops, and engaging with experts in the field. Knowledge is your most valuable asset.

Hone your investigative skills by learning techniques for collecting and analysing evidence, conducting interviews, and documenting your findings. Practice critical thinking and scepticism, while remaining open to the possibility of the unexplained.

Connect with like-minded individuals by joining paranormal investigation groups or online forums. Collaborating with others not only provides support and camaraderie but also allows for shared knowledge and experiences that enrich your own investigations. We at Perth Paranormal Investigations Agency can be your first point of call. Get in contact through our website and on our socials.

Familiarise yourself with the latest tools and technology used in paranormal research, such as digital voice recorders, EMF meters, and thermal imaging cameras. Experiment with different equipment to determine what works best for your investigations.

Conduct your investigations with integrity, respect, and ethical awareness. Obtain consent from all parties involved, respect cultural beliefs and sensitivities, and prioritise the well-being of both living and non-living entities encountered during your investigations.

Keep detailed records of your investigations, including notes, photographs, audio recordings, and any other evidence collected. Maintain a journal to document your experiences, observations, and reflections as you delve deeper. We would love to see what you find. Above all, remain curious, open-minded, and receptive to the possibilities that lie beyond the realm of the known. Embrace the thrill of discovery, the joy of exploration, and the wonder of encountering the extraordinary in the everyday.

With these tips and guidance in hand, we encourage you to embark on your own journey of paranormal investigation, venturing into the shadows to seek out the truths that lie hidden in the darkness. May your explorations be filled with wonder, discovery, and enlightenment as you unravel the mysteries of the unknown. Safe travels, intrepid investigators, and may the truth always guide your path.

EXISTENTIALISM AND SPIRITUALITY

Throughout the years of paranormal investigations there have been many opportunities for introspection, moments designed to spark contemplation and stimulate my thoughts about the paranormal. I would encourage you to do the same, as these moments of reflection serve as windows into your own beliefs, guiding you on a journey of self-discovery.

As you navigate the realms of spirits and other mysterious phenomena, pause for a moment, and consider: What do you believe? Are you a sceptic, approaching each claim with a healthy dose of doubt? Or you are a believer, embracing the possibility of the unknown with open arms.

Whatever your stance, these contemplative moments invite you to explore the foundations of your beliefs and the reasons behind them.

As investigators, we tread a fine line between scepticism and belief, navigating the murky waters of perception and interpretation. Each piece of evidence we uncover—whether a mysterious EVP recording or a fleeting shadow in the darkness—adds another layer to the complexity.

But it is not just the phenomena themselves that weigh heavily on the mind; it is the emotional and spiritual implications of our discoveries. What does it mean to encounter the supernatural? How do we reconcile our experiences with our preconceived notions of death? What responsibility do we have to pass on the otherworldly messages captured on our equipment, that we so eagerly sought? These are questions that linger long after the investigation is over, prompting us to confront the depths of our own belief, fear, and morality.

In the midst of uncertainty, however, there is beauty to be found in the complexity of the paranormal. It is a reminder that the world is far more multifaceted than we can ever hope to comprehend—a humbling realisation that inspires us to approach the unknown with reverence and awe.

As you engage with the reflective exercises in this book, I encourage you to embrace the complexity of the paranormal with an open heart and a curious mind. Reflect on your own experiences and beliefs and allow yourself to be guided by the wisdom that lies within. For it is in the exploration of the unknown, we discover not only the secrets of the universe but also the truths that reside within ourselves.

Allow me to share a personal reflection from my own experiences investigating the paranormal field. It is a world that often defies logic and challenges the boundaries of our understanding, both spiritually and mentally. I will never forget the particular investigation, where I witnessed with my own eyes, a full bodied apparition., where every creak of the floorboards and silent footsteps ignited my curiosity, fear, and trepidation. It was the first time I had witnessed a full manifestation.

As I sat and reflected on what I had witnessed, there was a moment of awe, inspiring clarity that this world was not the end. That there is something beyond our capacity to see. Realising that there is more to life than just death, can be a profound and enlightening moment. It is a realisation that transcends the physical and tangible, leading to a deeper understanding of existence itself. Instead of fearing or obsessing over the end, it opens doors to explore the richness of life in all its facets—relationships, experiences, personal growth, and the connections we forge with others. This realisation can inspire a greater appreciation for the present moment, encouraging us to live fully and authentically, embracing every opportunity for joy, learning, and connection.

It is a reminder that while death may be a part of life, it doesn't define it. Instead, it motivates us to seek meaning and purpose, to leave a positive impact on the journey our soul is on.

Reflect. Contemplate. And may your journey of self-discovery be as enlightening as it is profound.

CONFRONTATION OR SHOWDOWN

In writing 'Chasing Shadows' it is my wish that you are not just spectators. That you become active participants in this journey that links us by our very humanity. It is by confronting our innermost fears and with courage and resilience that our real journey begins. I have found that in paranormal investigation, as is the truth in most aspects of a life well lived, that true understanding, often lies beyond the boundary of comfort and familiarity.

Throughout this book, practical strategies have been offered, to empower a person, while navigating the challenges inherent in paranormal investigation. Whether facing the eerie silence of abandoned locations or the spine-chilling presence of unexplained phenomena, you are equipped with the tools needed to maintain composure and confidence, in the face of. uncertainties.

One such strategy involves cultivating a mindset of resilience and mental fortitude. By mastering techniques for managing stress and anxiety, they are better prepared to confront the unknown with clarity and resolve.

Additionally, "Chasing Shadows" hopes to stress the importance of thorough preparation and safety protocols, in mitigating risks during paranormal investigations. From conducting thorough risk assessments to assembling essential equipment and resources. learning and being guided through the process of creating a safe and secure environment for you the reader and your team members. Emergency response procedures and communication strategies are also outlined, ensure the reader can respond effectively to unexpected challenges and emergencies as they arise.

Furthermore, readers are encouraged to cultivate a spirit of collaboration and teamwork, recognising that strength lies in unity. By fostering open communication and mutual support within the community we can draw upon the collective expertise and resources of peers, enhancing safety and effectiveness in the field.

Facing the fear of the paranormal as an investigator requires a multifaceted approach. First and foremost, educating oneself about paranormal phenomena is crucial, as understanding the science and psychology behind these occurrences can demystify them and mitigate fear. Practical experience gained through training and working with experienced investigators also helps desensitise one to the unknown. Setting personal boundaries and seeking support from fellow investigators, can provide reassurance and perspective.

Prioritising self-care, including regular breaks and activities that promote mental well-being, is vital for sustaining resilience in the face of fear. With these strategies in place, investigators can confront the paranormal with greater confidence and professionalism.

UNRAVELING GHOSTLY MYSTERIES AND FINDING CLOSURE

Throughout the book, we have delved into the mysterious realm of ghosts, exploring the tales of apparitions and hauntings that have captivated human imagination for centuries. Now, as our investigations reach their climax, it is time to confront the ghostly presence, which has been the focus of our attention.

As investigators, we have meticulously gathered evidence using various tools and techniques, from EVP (Electronic Voice Phenomenon) recordings to infrared cameras and EMF (Electromagnetic Field) detectors. Our goal has been twofold: to uncover the truth behind the reported haunting and to offer closure to both the living and the departed.

In our final investigation, we present our findings to you, the reader, laying out the evidence we have collected with transparency and objectivity. EVP recordings captured chilling whispers in empty rooms, while video footage revealed unexplained shadows darting across the walls. Eyewitness accounts from credible sources, recounted encounters with a spectral figure that sent shivers down their spines.

But evidence alone is not enough. In the pursuit of truth, we must critically analyse our findings and consider alternative explanations. Could the EVP recordings be attributed to radio interference or natural phenomena? Could the shadows in the video footage be mere tricks of light and shadow? A paranormal Investigator must, with a discerning eye, separate fact from fiction.

If, after thorough analysis, the existence of the Spirit is confirmed, our investigation takes on a new dimension. With compassion and respect for the departed, we must endeavour to offer closure, both for the Spirit and for those affected by its presence. Through spiritual intervention or ritualistic practices, we assist the Spirit in finding peace and resolution, guiding it towards the light and releasing it from our mortal realm.

Alternatively, if our investigation leads us to conclude that the reported haunting has natural or psychological origins, we provide reassurance and support to those experiencing paranormal phenomena. By offering rational explanations and practical solutions, we empower individuals to confront their fears and reclaim their sense of security.

In either scenario, the resolution of our ghostly subplot is not merely a conclusion, but a culmination of our journey. A testament to the power of

329

inquiry, and the enduring quest for understanding.

As our journey through the realms of the paranormal draws to a close, I extend to you, dear reader, a final invitation—one that transcends the boundaries of these pages and ventures into the uncharted territories of your own curiosity.

Throughout our exploration, we have encountered the spectral echoes of history, delved into the mysteries of the unseen, and glimpsed the boundaries of human understanding. Yet, even as we bid farewell to the tales that have unfolded within these chapters, our quest for knowledge and discovery continues. I urge you, then, to carry forth the torch of inquiry with steadfast resolve and an open mind. Embrace the unknown with the same spirit of wonder that has guided you this far.

In the ever-expanding landscape of the paranormal, your voice is both a beacon of insight and a catalyst for change. I invite you to share your own experiences, findings, and hypotheses with the broader, who traverse these uncharted waters. Whether through online forums, local meetups, or personal correspondence, your contributions enrich the collective tapestry of knowledge and inspire others to embark on their own journeys of discovery.

As you navigate the intricate web of the supernatural, remember that scepticism is not the enemy of wonder, but rather it acts as a companion. Question boldly, investigate rigorously, and challenge assumptions with unwavering reason. It is through this synthesis of scepticism and curiosity that we uncover hidden truths that lie beyond the veil of physical Life.

The book concludes with a sense of possibility and wonder, acknowledging that the pursuit of the paranormal is an ongoing journey filled with endless opportunities for discovery. While some mysteries may be solved, there will always be new questions to explore and phenomena to investigate.

Should you find yourself grappling with questions or seeking guidance along your path, know that you are not alone. I extend to you a personal invitation to reach out to me directly, to share your inquiries, reflections, and revelations. Together, we shall navigate the paranormal with courage and compassion, forging new paths and understanding,

As we part ways, remember that the journey is never truly over, for the mysteries of the paranormal are as boundless as the human heart and mind. With each step forward, each question asked, and each discovery made, we inch closer to the elusive truths that lie hidden beneath the surface.

Embrace the unknown. Explore the mysteries. And may your journey be filled with wonder, wisdom, and the eternal pursuit of truth.

With warm regards,

Suzanne Rossi [Author of "Chasing Shadows"]

GLOSSARY

Apophenia: is the tendency to perceive meaningful connections between unrelated things

Apparition-Visual representation of a disembodied entity or spirit. n invisible presence to translucent or barely visible wispy shapes to realistic, lifelike forms.

Clairaudience: The power or faculty of hearing something not present to the ear but regarded as having objective reality.

Clairvoyance:
1. The power or faculty of discerning objects not present to the senses.
2. Ability to perceive matters beyond the range or ordinary perception.

Cold Spot-Cool or cold patches of air. Ghosts draw energy from the air, which leaves the cold spot behind.

Conjure: To summon a devil or spirit by invocation or incantation; to practice magical arts.

Demon (Daemon):
1. An evil spirit; a source or agent of evil, harm, distress or ruin
2. An attendant power or spirit 3: a supernatural being of Greek mythology intermediate between gods and men.

Demoniac:
1. Possessed of influenced by a demon.
2. Of, relating to, or suggestive of a demon: fiendish.

Demonology
1. The study of demons or evil spirits
2. Belief in demons.

Dowsing-Movement of rods or pendulums to communicate with a spirit.

DVP-Direct Voice Phenomenon -audio that is heard live rather than on a recording.

Ectoplasm-Mist associated with paranormal activity.

Elemental spirits refer to the astral gods of former pagan religions or spirits in folklore derived from earth, air, fire, and water.

EMF-Electro-Magnetic Frequency (or Field)- combination of electric and magnetic energy, which is generally experienced in the presence of spirits.

Entity-Intelligent being who may never have been human.

EVP-Electronic Voice Phenomenon -audio that is heard on a recording's playback that was not audible in real time.

Ghost: an apparition of a dead person which is believed to appear or become manifest to the living, typically as a nebulous image.

Ghost lights-Unexplained lights that appear in groupings, usually outdoors.

Haunting -Activities by a spirit or entity at a location or around a person or object.

Levitation: The raising of a body into the air without physical aid.

Lycanthropy: In folklore, the ability of a person to change into animal form. In psychiatry, the delusion

Manifest -Presentation of paranormal activity.

Orb s -Unexplained balls of light.

Paranormal-Experience/activity that is beyond the normal.

Pareidolia – the tendency to perceive a specific, often meaningful image in a random or ambiguous visual pattern.

Phenomenon:
    1. An observable fact or event.

Poltergeist-Paranormal activity that is the result of psychic-kinetic (PK) energy -usually the outflow of pent up emotions.

Portal: A portal, or rift, is doorway that exists between different realms, planes of existence, or universes

Shadow Person/People-One of the more controversial terms in the field. Some say these are human spirits who could not fully manifest. Others say these are non-human entities with malicious intent. (There are many theories for shadow people)

Soul: The immaterial essence, animating principle, or actuating cause of an individual life; the spiritual principle embodied in human beings, all rational and spiritual

Spirit-Interchangeable with Ghost, Former human.

Spiritualism:
   1. The view that spirit is a prime element of reality.
   2. A belief that spirits of the dead communicate with the living usually through a medium; a movement comprising of religious organisation emphasising spiritualism.

Troxler's fading, also called Troxler fading or the Troxler effect, is an optical illusion affecting visual perception. When one fixates on a particular point for even a short period of time, an unchanging stimulus away from the fixation point will fade away and disappear.

Vortex-Central point of spiritual activity or energy.

FURTHER EDUCATION

This book has covered a wide range of topics and touches on many different concepts of the paranormal. As such I encourage my readers to expand their knowledge of the paranormal. These are some resources that the reader may find helpful.

Courses:

paranormalinvestigationsagencies.com
Authors websites offering courses on understanding the paranormal and Investigations, evidence analysis, spiritual protections, and documentation.

ghosttourbookings.com.au
Paranormal 101 online course for beginners

The Australian Institute of Parapsychological Research
www.aiprinc.org
The AIPR offers four courses in parapsychology.

BIBLIOGRAPHY

Adler, S. (n.d.). *Sleep Paralysis: Night-mares, Nocebos, and the Mind-Body Connection.* Rutgers University Press. Retrieved 5 3, 2024, from https://books.google.com/books?id=_t63WJiZb3cC&pg=PA3

Aircraft Accident Report, Eastern Airlines, Inc. L-1011, N310EA, Miami, Florida, December 29, 1972. (n.d.). Retrieved 5 3, 2024, from http://www.ntsb.gov/investigations/AccidentReports/Reports/AAR7314.pdf

Amorth, F. G. (n.d.). *Excerpt from An Exorcist Tells his Story.* Ignatius Insight. Retrieved 4 27, 2024, from http://www.ignatiusinsight.com/features/framorth_excerpt1_aug04.asp

Ancient Roman Ghosts, Spirits and Ghost Stories . (2024, April 30). Retrieved from worldhistory.org: https://www.worldhistory.org

Bai, L., Tian, S., Cheng, Y., Tian, G. Y., Chen, Y., & Chen, K. (2014). Reducing the Effect of Surface Emissivity Variation in Eddy Current Pulsed Thermography. *IEEE Sensors Journal, 14*(4), 1137-1142. Retrieved 4 29, 2024, from https://eprint.ncl.ac.uk/198363

Barbara., W. (n.d.). *Talking to the dead : Kate and Maggie Fox and the rise of spiritualism.* HarperSanFrancisco. Retrieved 5 3, 2024

Barnes, T. D. (1971). *Tertullian: A Historical and Literary Study.* Clarendon Press. Retrieved 4 23, 2024

Belanger, M. (2022). *The Ghost Hunters Survival Guide.* Llewellyn.

Brown, A. (n.d.). *Haunted Tennessee: Ghosts and Strange Phenomena of the Volunteer State.* Stackpole Books. Retrieved 4 26, 2024, from https://books.google.com/books?id=mSLiFwJzOH4C&pg=PA72

Carroll, B. E. (1997). *Spiritualism in Antebellum America. (Religion in North America)*. Bloomington: Indiana University Press. Retrieved 5 3, 2024

Chang, K. (n.d.). *Do Paranormal Phenomena exist?* Retrieved 4 23, 2024, from https://www.nytimes.com/2003/11/11/science/do-paranormal-phenomena-exist.html

Christopher, M. (1970). *ESP, Seers & Psychics: What the Occult Really Is.* Crowell. Retrieved 5 3, 2024

Cohen, D. (1984). *The encyclopedia of ghosts.* Dodd, Mead. Retrieved 5 8, 2024, from https://books.google.com/books?id=5lcMRQryEQMC

Conrad, B. (n.d.). *An Unknown Encounter: A True Account of the San Pedro Haunting.* Dorrance Publishing. Retrieved 4 29, 2024, from https://books.google.com/books?id=Zjw9dQS88jUC&pg=PA128

Covey, H. C. (2007). *The Methamphetamine Crisis: Strategies to Save Addicts, Families, And Communities.* Greenwood Publishing Group. Retrieved 5 3, 2024, from https://books.google.com/books?id=yFGJV5XSNhYC&pg=PA17

DEMONOLOGY - JewishEncyclopedia.com. (n.d.). Retrieved 5 3, 2024, from http://www.jewishencyclopedia.com/articles/5085-demonology

Demons & Demonology. (n.d.). Retrieved 5 3, 2024, from The Gale Group: https://www.jewishvirtuallibrary.org/jsource/Judaism/demons.html

Discernment of Spirits - IgnatianSpirituality.com. (n.d.). Retrieved 5 3, 2024, from http://www.ignatianspirituality.com/making-good-decisions/discernment-of-spirits

Editors, H. (n.d.). *History of Ghost Stories.* Retrieved 4 23, 2024, from A&E Television Networks: https://www.history.com/topics/halloween/historical-ghost-stories

Frater, J. (n.d.). *10 More Mysteries That Remain Unsolved.* Retrieved 4 23, 2024, from Listverse: http://listverse.com/2009/07/03/10-more-mysteries-that-remain-unsolved/

Ghost. (n.d.). Retrieved 4 23, 2024, from http://www.thefreedictionary.com/ghost

Goodspeed's History of Tennessee: The History of Robertson County. (n.d.). The Goodspeed Publishing Co. Retrieved 4 26, 2024, from http://www.tngenweb.org/goodspeed/robertson/history.html

Goodstein, L. (n.d.). *For Catholics, Interest in Exorcism is Revised.* Retrieved 5 3, 2024, from https://www.nytimes.com/2010/11/13/us/13exorcism.html

Group, I. I. (n.d.). *Investigations.* Retrieved 5 3, 2024, from http://www.iigwest.org/investigations/index.html

Haunted Wales. (n.d.). Retrieved 4 24, 2024, from Haunted-britain.com: http://www.haunted-britain.com/Haunted_Wales.htm

Hill, S. (n.d.). *Mothman "reappears" coincidentally close to the 50th anniversary date.* Retrieved 5 3, 2024, from Lithosphere LLC: http://doubtfulnews.com/2016/11/mothman-appears-in-photos-alleged-to-be-from-west-virginia/

Hill, S. (n.d.). *The "Stone Tape Theory" of hauntings: A geological perspective.* Retrieved 4 24, 2024, from http://sharonahill.com/2017/05/11/the-stone-tape-theory-of-hauntings-a-geological-perspective/

Houran, J. (2004). *From Shaman to Scientist: Essays on Humanity's Search for Spirits.* Scarecrow Press. Retrieved 5 3, 2024

Kariyawasam, A. (1995). *Buddhist Ceremonies and Rituals of Sri Lanka.* Buddhist Publication Society. Retrieved 5 3, 2024, from

http://www.accesstoinsight.org/lib/authors/kariyawasam/wheel4
02.html

Klimo, J. (1998). *Channeling: Investigations on Receiving Information from
Paranormal Sources.* North Atlantic Books. Retrieved 4 30, 2024

Lehner, P., Adelman, L., DiStasio, R., Erie, M., Mittel, J., & Olson, S. (2009).
Confirmation Bias in the Analysis of Remote Sensing Data. *IEEE
Transactions on Systems, Man, and Cybernetics, 39*(1), 218-226.
Retrieved 4 29, 2024, from
https://ieeexplore.ieee.org/stamp/stamp.jsp?tp=&arnumber=471
7831

LeRose, C. (n.d.). *The Collapse of the Silver Bridge.* Retrieved 5 3, 2024,
from West Virginia Division of Culture and History:
http://www.wvculture.org/history/wvhs/wvhs1504.html

McCarter, P. K., & Hudson, A. P. (n.d.). *The Bell Witch of Tennessee and
Mississippi: A folk legend.* The Journal of American Forklore.
Retrieved 4 26, 2024

McClure's Magazine. (1922). S.S. McClure, Limited. Retrieved 4 26, 2024,
from
https://books.google.com/books?id=rSAAAAAAYAAJ&pg=PA114

Newell, C. (n.d.). *Wolf Creek – Season 2, Episode 1: 'Journey'.* Retrieved 5
3, 2024, from https://fathersonholygore.com/2017/12/16/wolf-
creek-season-2-episode-1-journey/

Nicholas, M. (1986). *World's Greatest Psychics & Mystics.* Octopus.
Retrieved 4 28, 2024

Nickell, J. (n.d.). *Enfield Poltergeist.* Retrieved 4 26, 2024, from Committee
for the Scientific Investigation of Claims of the Paranormal:
http://www.csicop.org/si/show/enfield_poltergeist

Nickell, J. (n.d.). *Enfield Poltergeist, Investigative Files.* Retrieved 5 3, 2024, from Committee for Skeptical Inquiry: http://www.csicop.org/si/show/enfield_poltergeist

Pobjie, B. (2022). *100 Tales from Australias Most Haunted Places.* Melbourne, Australia: Affirm Press.

Price, C. E. (n.d.). *The Infamous Bell Witch of Tennessee.* The Overmountain Press. Retrieved 4 26, 2024, from https://books.google.com/books?id=plBlDoPkDFMC&pg=PA38

Radford, B. (n.d.). *Investigating Ghosts: The Scientific Search for Spirits.* Rhombus Publishing Company. Retrieved 4 30, 2024

Randi $1,000,000 paranormal challenge. (n.d.). Retrieved 4 23, 2024, from The Skeptic's Dictionary: http://skepdic.com/randi.html

Shadow Beings. (n.d.). Retrieved 5 3, 2024, from http://www.coasttocoastam.com/show/2006/03/27

Shadow People & the "Hat Man". (n.d.). Retrieved 5 3, 2024, from http://www.coasttocoastam.com/show/2008/07/23

Smith, A. a. (2006). *Haunted Birmingham.* Tempus Publishing Limited.

Taylor, T., & Wiseheart, D. (n.d.). *America's Most Haunted: Myrtles Plantation.* Retrieved 4 29, 2024, from Troy Taylor: http://www.prairieghosts.com/myrtles.html

The Ghost of Flight 401. (n.d.). Retrieved 4 27, 2024, from http://www.goodreads.com/book/show/1542032.The_Ghost_of_Flight_401

Tuttle, B. (n.d.). *Queen Mary unveils newly imagined Ghosts and Legends Haunted Experience.* Retrieved 4 23, 2024, from Attractions Magazine: http://attractionsmagazine.com/queen-mary-new-ghosts-legends/

UQ scientist unlocks secret of Min Min lights. (n.d.). Retrieved 5 3, 2024,

from University of Queensland:
http://www.uq.edu.au/news/?article=4265

Victorian Spiritualism. (n.d.). Retrieved 5 3, 2024, from Victorianweb.org:
http://www.victorianweb.org/religion/spirit.html

Warren, E. J. (2012). 'Spiritual Warfare': A Dead Metaphor? *Journal of
Pentecostal Theology, 21*(2), 278-297. Retrieved 5 3, 2024, from
https://brill.com/view/journals/pent/21/2/article-
p278_6.xml?lang=en

Warren, E. J. (2012). *Cleansing the Cosmos: A Biblical Model for
Conceptualizing and Counteracting Evil.* Retrieved 5 3, 2024, from
https://amazon.com/cleansing-cosmos-biblical-conceptualizing-
counteracting/dp/1620324032

William G. Roll. (n.d.). Retrieved 4 27, 2024, from Wikipedia: The Free
Encyclopaedia: http://en.wikipedia.org/wiki/William_G._Roll

Wilson, C. (n.d.). *Poltergeist: A Classic Study in Destructive Hauntings.*
Llewellyn Worldwide. Retrieved 4 27, 2024, from
https://books.google.com/books?id=O68ayjhr3O8C

Winkowski, M. A. (2007). *When Ghosts Speak.* Sydney: Hachette Australia.

Wiseman, R. (n.d.). *Paranormality: Why We see What Isn't There.*
Macmillan. Retrieved 5 3, 2024, from
https://books.google.com/books?id=TO67ZcZ3wUUC

Wiseman, R., & Watt, C. (n.d.). Belief in psychic ability and the
misattribution hypothesis: A qualitative review. *British Journal of
Psychology, 97*(3), 323–38. Retrieved 4 23, 2024, from
http://www.richardwiseman.com/resources/review.pdf

Wiseman, R., Watt, C., Stevens, P., Greening, E., & O'Keeffe, C. (2003). An
investigation into alleged 'hauntings'. *The British Journal of
Psychology, 94*(2). Retrieved 4 23, 2024, from

http://richardwiseman.com/resources/bjp-hauntings.pdf

Withnell, J. G. (1901). *Customs and traditions of the aboriginal natives of North-Western Australia.* Retrieved 5 3, 2024, from http://www.sacred-texts.com/aus/cat/cat.htm

Yanko, D. (n.d.). *Mystery Solved?* Retrieved 4 23, 2024, from http://www.virtualsk.com/current_issue/mystery.html

www.ingramcontent.com/pod-product-compliance
Lightning Source LLC
LaVergne TN
LVHW051252080426
835509LV00020B/2934